The Naphtha Revolution

The untold story of an invention that changed the world.

Graeme Ferguson

©2022, Graeme Ferguson | ISBN: 978-1-988025-90-2 (Hardcover)

All rights reserved. No part of this publication may be reproduced, stored in a retrieval system or transmitted, in any form or by any means, without prior written consent of the publisher.

Library and Archives Canada Cataloguing in Publication data available upon request.

Artistic Director/Designer: Gayle Bonish
Proofreading: Moveable Inc.
Printed in Canada by Friesens.

Publisher: Sarah Scott
Barlow Book Publishing Inc. 96 Elm Avenue, Toronto, ON M4W 1P2 Canada
For more information, visit www.barlowbooks.com

Foreword

I knew and admired Graeme Ferguson for more than fifty years, with memories going back from when he and my father, filmmaker Colin Low, were friends and close collaborators. He was always curious, always exploring, always innovating. I am grateful to both of them for igniting that passion in me. I hope I will instill it in my grandchildren.

Graeme achieved iconic stature in documentary filmmaking and his role in the creation of the IMAX® medium gave us an entirely new way to look at the world. "Have you ever seen an IMAX movie?" he might ask an interviewer. "Well, I am one of its inventors" was his non-boastful response. And as an inventor, he was fascinated by all inventions including the subject of *The Naphtha Revolution*.

A good story is something not heard before and few of you will have heard this one. It begins with Graeme's purchase of a 100-year-old wooden cruiser named *Heather Belle*. Such a boat in the care of most people was just that, a wooden boat, lovingly varnished each year, then often abandoned and left to rot. But great documentary filmmakers are investigators. For Graeme's ever-inquisitive mind, discovering *Heather Belle*'s past was the beginning of meticulous research that would go on for two decades and became this important book, published post-humously. His focused quest led him to shine a beacon on Frank Ofeldt, an unsung but hugely significant inventor, and the history of the naphtha launch.

It's a thought-provoking read from which everyone might take away something different. For me, as we sit perched on the edge of oblivion, having burnt our way through billions of tonnes of fossil fuel – the choices we made, the path we took long ago was, by all scientific accounts, dead wrong.

Heather Belle and her various engines illustrates an alternative possibility. Her naphtha and vapor engines were of modest horsepower and she was able to attain a hull speed of around seven knots. But at a critical moment in the industrial revolution, the likes of *Heather Belle* were brushed aside, a vanished breed replaced by loud diesel- and gas-guzzling plastic monsters. At that key moment in history, we embraced the opposite of maximum efficiency.

We became prisoners of the immense power of fossil fuels dug up beneath our feet and burned as quickly as possible into the air we breathe. As we ponder the way forward, it's never been more important to understand the past and how all this came about.

Graeme eventually settled on a perfect technology to repower his beloved boat. Already equipped with perfect dynamics, *Heather Belle* got an 8 hp electric motor that enables her to move near her hull speed in exquisite silence while carrying a dozen family and friends.

Graeme's book salutes invention and reveals a long-forgotten and fascinating chapter in the story of how modern industrial civilization came about. I am proud to encourage you to read *The Naphtha Revolution*.

Stephen Low
Prolific IMAX filmmaker and Steam Engine Buff

The inventor, Frank W. Ofeldt, whose naphtha launch ignited a revolution.

Contents

Introduction i
Author's Notes ii
Chapter 1. The Naphtha Problem 1
Chapter 2. The Inventor 5
Chapter 3. Everything He Touched Turned to Gold 17
Chapter 4. The Star Gas Machine 25
Chapter 5. Taking the Fifth 31
Chapter 6. The Naphtha Launch 42
Chapter 7. The Steam Regulations 56
Chapter 8. Bostwick's Strategy 62
Chapter 9. Nobel's *Mignon* 77
Chapter 10. Starting Over 91
Chapter 11. The Bostwick Legacy 105
Chapter 12. Competitors 130
Chapter 13. The Presidential Crony 143
Chapter 14. Alco-Vapor 149
Chapter 15. The Height of Fashion 167
Chapter 16. Kapowie! 189
Chapter 17. Combat 195
Chapter 18. Compound Vapor 211
Chapter 19. Ending the Naphtha Glut 231
Chapter 20. Benedict Folds 235
Chapter 21. Speed 241
Chapter 22. Conclusion 248
Chapter 23. Epilogue 249
Acknowledgments 267
Abbreviations 271
Notes 271
Bibliography 288
Picture Credits 292

Introduction

Our lives are shaped by inventions, and we are particularly enchanted by those that enable us to do things that previously seemed impossible. Before the 1880s there were powered conveyances, and there were owner-operated conveyances, but there had never been a powered vehicle that could actually be driven by its owner.

According to *The Rudder*, "Inventor after inventor struggled with this problem, only to add one more blank to the long list of failures. It was not until the idea of using the highly explosive naphtha captured the brain of a genius that a motor was evolved combining in a marked degree the essentials of a perfect power."[1]

It may surprise some readers to learn that the seminal invention of the petroleum age was not the motorcar, but the motorboat. The naphtha launch was not only the first successful personal powercraft, but in fact the world's first owner-operated motor vehicle of any kind. In the 1880s it revolutionized water transportation, just as the automobile would, on land, a generation later. Indeed the invention was so novel, and the patents so unassailable, that for its first decade the naphtha engine enjoyed a complete monopoly, and for several more years continued to prevail over the still-unreliable internal combustion motor.

Frank Ofeldt's charming little vapor launches offered their owners almost effortless freedom of movement, and were such a success that thousands were sold. Among their owners were Alfred Nobel, J.P. Morgan, Emperor Wilhelm II of Germany, and President Grover Cleveland.

Although Ofeldt was cruelly deprived of recognition during his lifetime, it is now time to honor him as one of the great inventors who created the modern world.

Frank Ofeldt's story is not a simple one of a penniless immigrant who makes good in a new land. Unlike Horatio Alger's heroes, Frank was a very real person, a man of hopes and disappointments. A courageous man who experienced both triumphs and betrayals. The story of his life is more than a melodrama; it's a true American saga.

Ofeldt was fortunate to come to America during a golden age for inventors. Edison, Bell, and the Wright Brothers are memorable names among the hundreds of geniuses who created our modern world. And it was also a golden age for brilliant businessmen like Rockefeller, who created monumental combinations of unstoppable power. The time was also unique in that both inventors and businessmen had unprecedented freedom to pursue their dreams. But there was a dark side. Businessmen were also free to exploit inventors, and sometimes to victimize them. Hence, the triumphs and tragedies that Ofeldt experienced.

And hence the near disappearance of his name from the roster of inventors who changed the world. Frank Ofeldt's name did not disappear accidentally; it was intentionally erased by the very businessmen whom he had trusted.

Although Frank Ofeldt was cruelly deprived of recognition during his lifetime, it is now time to honor him as one of the great inventors who created the modern world.

Author's Notes

1: Why celebrate the invention of the motorboat? Wouldn't the world be better off if these stinkpots had never sullied our quiet lakes?

Nearly fifty years ago I gained a useful perspective on this from an indigenous trapper in northern Canada who described seeing his first outboard. That moment changed his life. Many people think that paddling a canoe epitomizes romance; he considered it a waste of energy. After listening to him I realized that if ever an invention was needed, it was the motorboat.

2: It happens that I am old enough to have had some experience with naphtha. In 1945 my family moved to an old farmhouse where there was no electricity, and I studied for my high school exams by the light of a Coleman lamp, fueled by naphtha. That lamp was about as bright as a 60 watt bulb, far superior to a kerosene lamp. A Coleman lamp came with a small hand pump, and every hour or so one gave it a few strokes to maintain pressure. Those naphtha lamps did hiss, a small price to pay for their brilliance. Of course the volatile fuel, unlike kerosene, had to be tightly capped, and stored far away from the wood stove. We kept our fuel can in a shed, and never, ever, filled the lamp inside the house.

3: For the most part I have chosen not to convert prices to present-day dollars. In order to obtain a rough approximation, I suggest that the reader multiply by twenty.

4: The illustrations include a number of drawings from Frank Ofeldt's patents. In order to fully understand the inventions, the reader should refer to the complete patents, which are readily available from the Patent and Resource Center, New York State Library.

5: Although the naphtha launch is occasionally mentioned by nautical historians, its inventor, Frank Ofeldt, has almost disappeared from their pages. And even though Ofeldt's business partner, Jabez Bostwick, was one of the remarkable team who built Standard Oil into a mighty colossus, he too has never found a biographer. Equally surprising, although E.C. Benedict, Ofeldt's second backer, was one of President Grover Cleveland's closest confidants, political historians have underplayed his influence. I can only hope that this book fills in a few of these gaps, and piques the interest of historians.

"Every so often in the progress of mankind some engineer comes along with an invention or machine design for which the world is waiting. A market is broken open, fortunes are made, and the development becomes a milestone in economic history. The invention of the naphtha engine by Frank W. Ofeldt in 1883 was, in its day, as much a benchmark of progress as were, many years later, the Model T Ford, the DC-3 airplane and the Zippo lighter—all superb engineering pegs."

Weston Farmer, *Yachting*, July 1973

Chapter 1

The Naphtha Problem

"Naphtha...is in one respect more dangerous than gunpowder. Gunpowder never explodes unless fire is brought to it. Naphtha, on the other hand, sends out its inflammable vapor and brings the fire from a distance....It is not to be wondered that frightful accidents occur."

Charles Frederick Chandler, Ph.D.[1]

Less than a decade after Edwin Drake struck oil in Pennsylvania, Americans faced a dire consequence – an epidemic of lethal house fires. Most of the victims were women and children. As described in a typical account, "The explosion scattered the burning liquid with which the stove was lighted all over the room. Mrs. Bridget Hughes, who was sitting near the stove when the explosion occurred, had her clothing set on fire, and she was so terribly burned that her life was despaired of."[2] In 1869 the City of New York suffered 98 oil-related fires. A year later the number rose to 157, resulting in at least 21 deaths.[3] Alarmed, the New York Department of Health commissioned Dr. Charles Frederick Chandler, professor of chemistry at Columbia College, to investigate. The Chandler Report placed the blame squarely on naphtha.

The City of New York asked Professor Charles F. Chandler to find the cause of an epidemic of fatal house fires.

1

The Naphthas

In those days the purpose of distilling petroleum was simply to obtain kerosene to burn in lamps. However, there were unwelcome by-products. In a refinery, after the still was fired up, the first fraction to boil off was gasoline (also spelled gasolene). The second was naphtha (pronounced naftha), and the third was benzine. Together these three were called the naphthas, and they were considered next to useless. Only after the refiner got rid of the naphthas did he obtain the product he sought, kerosene.[4] The terminology can be confusing. In Europe, petroleum was called naphtha, and in America, kerosene was often called coal oil or simply oil.[5] In newspaper accounts the terms naphtha, gasoline and benzine were frequently interchanged.

All three naphthas give off explosive vapors. Professor Chandler defined them as "light volatile oils [that] ignite on the approach of a burning match, no matter how cold they may be," and he distinguished them from kerosene, which "can only be ignited when …heated above the ordinary temperature of the air."[6]

As the naphthas would explode if used in kerosene lamps, a new type of burner was designed, which was also used in stoves and heaters. However, after testing these devices Chandler concluded with a stern warning: "These contrivances are all, without exception, highly dangerous.…These stoves have been but recently introduced; when they shall have been more generally adopted we may expect accidents to multiply rapidly. A keg of gunpowder in a building is not as dangerous as one of these stoves."[7]

GRAY'S PATENT.

Vapor lamps were designed to make use of naphtha, gasoline, and benzine, unwanted by-products left over from distilling petroleum. Although professor Chandler was impressed by the elegant design of these lamps, he pointed out that they were extremely dangerous.

STAND LAMP.   HANGING LAMP.

Chapter 1

THE VAPOR STOVE.

D. H. LOWE'S PATENT.

Vapor stoves had also been introduced in the 1860s. Professor Chandler warned, "A keg of gunpowder in a building is not as dangerous as one of these stoves." The Chandler Report concluded with a plea to inventors to find other uses for the naphthas.

Barbarous Traffic

Chandler then turned his attention to an even more sinister threat, the use of the naphthas to adulterate kerosene. In 1870, the United States pumped 6,500,000 barrels of petroleum. No matter how hard they tried, refiners could not get Pennsylvania crude to yield much more than 55 percent kerosene, and they were left with over one million barrels of the naphthas.[8] A little could be employed as solvents, paint thinner, and cleaning fluid, and also to make varnishes, oilcloth and patent leather. However, these products attracted so few buyers that many refiners were happy to give the naphthas away,[9] and some surreptitiously released them into nearby rivers. One Cleveland refiner recounted that there was so much naphtha in the Cuyahoga River that "tugboat men would throw overboard a shovelful of hot coals to start a fire on the water and have some fun."[10]

As a consequence, the naphthas were cheap. While bulk kerosene commanded 20 to 25 cents per gallon, a gallon of naphtha sold for as little as 2½ cents.[11] The temptation was overwhelming. Chandler charged that, "The cupidity of the refiner…leads him to run as much [of the naphthas] as possible into the kerosene, rendering the whole highly dangerous."[12] As a result, in the mid-1870s, five to six thousand deaths a year were caused by lamp explosions due to adulterated kerosene.[13]

How was a housewife to know whether the kerosene she bought at her corner grocery store was safe to use? The simplest test was to see if it could be set on fire. A number of states based their laws on just such a test, and declared it unlawful to sell kerosene that would not extinguish a burning match.[14] Still, plunging a match into kerosene was hardly an experiment that most people would like to try at home, so a more convenient test was adopted. The temperature at which a fuel begins to give off an inflammable vapor is called the flash point, and in 1867 an act of Congress fixed the safe flash point for kerosene at 100 °F, but that law was declared unconstitutional.[15] Then the New York City Board of Health mandated 100 °F for the City. This too was struck down.[16] Chandler's tests found 100 °F too low: "The flashing point should be somewhat higher than the highest temperature the oil ever reaches in the lamps or cans (when) placed in the sun or near a fire," and he recommended 120 °F. In 1869 Chandler tested 636 samples from New York retailers, and found only 21 that met the previous target of 100 °F. Just one, *Pratt's Astral Oil*, met Chandler's own standard, and actually flashed at 125 °F.[17]

When kerosene that flashed at 113 °F was adulterated with ten percent naphtha, its flash point was reduced to 59 °F. Chandler charged that unscrupulous distillers were adulterating naphtha even further, in fact by an average of fifteen percent. In Chandler's judgment, "As long as larger profits can be gained by selling naphtha, benzine, and dangerous kerosene, than by selling safe oil, public opinion cannot…check the barbarous traffic."[18]

A Plea to Inventors

In his conclusion, Professor Chandler made one strong recommendation: "Nothing is more desirable than the discovery of some use to which naphtha can be put, which will make such a demand for it as to raise its value above that of kerosene, that it might be [in] the interest of the refiner to separate as much instead of as little as possible."[19]

With this challenge Professor Chandler identified a worthy goal for an inventor.

Chapter 2

The Inventor

"The introduction of new inventions seemeth to be the very chief of all human actions. The benefits of new inventions may extend to all mankind universally, but the good of political achievements can respect but some particular cantons of men; these latter do not endure above a few ages, the former forever. Inventions make all men happy without either injury or damage to any one single person. Furthermore new inventions are, as it were, new erections and imitations of God's own works."

Francis Bacon, 1620[1]

Innovation

Swedish innovation has long focused on small watercraft. The world now considers Swedes to be peacekeepers, but for centuries they were warriors, and their instrument of conquest, the oar. More than a thousand years ago Swedish Vikings rowed all the way to the Black Sea and the Caspian, and on the way founded the principality of Kiev, which became modern Russia.[2]

The Baltic hides treacherous shallows, and the winds are unreliable, so in the following centuries both Sweden and her enemies continued to rely heavily on oarsmen. In addition to galleys, Sweden depended for coastal defense on *kanonjoller*, very small gunboats – actually rowboats – each carrying a single cannon.[3]

Swedes have long been innovators in applying new technology to shallow-draft boats. Because the Baltic is shallow, Swedish coastal defense depended on small gunboats propelled by oars. Each vessel carried a single fixed gun, facing aft, that was trained by maneuvering the craft. This model is in the *Sjöhistoriska Museum* (Museum of Maritime History), Stockholm.

Naphtha

In Stockholm, a city built on islands, the water taxi was essential. At first the boats were rowed by men, but Sweden's many wars resulted in a shortage of manpower, so in 1818, to meet the needs of the navy, the King declared that henceforth only women would be allowed to ply the trade. From then on all water taxis were rowed by *roddermadamerna* (rowing women).

Around 1830 someone decided to try the paddle wheel, which the women turned by means of a crank *(vev)*, so the boat was known as a *vevslup*.[4] It must have occurred to thoughtful people that the new steam engine might easily power a vevslup, if the machinery could be sufficiently miniaturized. Even better, why not replace the steam engine with something smaller, lighter, and more efficient?

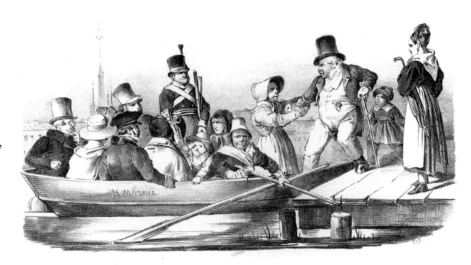

A Stockholm water taxi. Because able-bodied men were subject to conscription, the King ordered that the boats be rowed by women.

At first the water taxis were rowed, but later they were operated by hand cranks. Why not power a water taxi with a small engine? That was a question to challenge the mind of an inventor.

Chapter 2

Frans Åfeldt (later Frank Ofeldt)

The man who would do that was born on May 24, 1836 in Ivetofta (now Bromölla) near Kristianstad, and was christened Jonas Frans Waldemar Åfeldt.[5] The Swedish å is pronounced as ō, so that the English *Ofeldt* sounds very much like the Swedish *Åfeldt*. The name is sometimes spelled Åhfeldt, which emphasizes that the first syllable should be drawn out.[6] We shall call the boy Frans Åfeldt while he lives in Sweden, and Frank Ofeldt after he arrives in America.

In those days it was the duty of the preacher in each parish to examine every church member. Frans achieved an "a" in reading, and "ab" in Christendom, which were very good marks.[7]

From an early age Frans showed a deep interest in mechanics.[8] If he had come from a moneyed family, he might have enrolled in the Technological Institute in Stockholm, but after the death of his father, an army quartermaster, when the boy was eighteen, there was no possibility of that.[9]

No matter. Throughout Europe during the industrial revolution, most technical expertise was acquired on the shop floor. As Joel Mokyr explains, "New hires learned the trade 'on the job' by direct contact with veteran workers, observation, and emulation."[10]

In Sweden there was one city, and only one, where Frans could learn about the most advanced technology, work with a variety of interesting machines, and see for himself the newest inventions. That city was Norrköping, eighty miles southwest of Stockholm, at the mouth of the Motala River.

Frans Åfeldt, born in Sweden, took the name Frank Ofeldt after he emigrated to the United States.

At age eighteen Frans Åfeldt arrived in Norrköping, a busy seaport and manufacturing center.

On July 3, 1854, Frans arrived in Norrköping. Although the railroad had yet to reach the city, there were steamships in the port. The Motala shipyard, Sweden's most advanced, turned out more ships than Stockholm and Göteborg (Gothenberg) combined.

At the time Frans arrived, the shipyard was beginning construction on the paddle wheeler *Svea*. The young man's choice of lodgings, in the *Amsterdam* Quarter near the shipyard,[11] suggests that his first job may have been on the building of *Svea*.

Whether or not Frans ever worked in the shipyard, he received his real education in the city's factories. The swift Motala provides so much cheap power that a number of textile mills had been erected, and Norrköping was known as the Manchester of Sweden.

The steamship *Svea* was under construction in Norrköping when Frans Åfeldt resided in the *Amsterdam* Quarter, near the shipyard.

The Motala River's abundant power drew textile mills to Norrköping, and provided Frans an opportunity to learn about machinery.

Chapter 2

On April 3, 1859 Frans married Augusta Mathilda Söderbäck in nearby Risinge Parish, where she had been born into a family with a background in metallurgy.[12] Augusta's testimonials, both in reading and in Christendom, were "ab" – also very good.[13] After their first son, August Waldemar (always called Walter) was born, the couple moved into the block *The Carbine*.[14] For mail delivery Swedish towns were divided into curiously-named quarters, or blocks.

Then a lucky thing happened. Frans found work as a *jernarbetare* (worker in iron) at *Welander & Kellner*, a company that designed and built machines for the mills.[15] In 1860 the company had 27 employees, few enough that Frans could obtain varied experience on many different machines.[16] More important, Gunnar Welander held a patent on a fulling machine.[17] Now Frans had a real inventor for a mentor.

Abruptly, the young man's hopes were dashed. The American Civil War disrupted textile markets and forced Welander and Kellner to reduce their work force.[18] Frans was laid off, but was soon hired as a *mekanikus* (machine-man) at *Korderoj Fabrik Aktiebolaget*, a company with 36-40 looms.[19] Presumably his duty was to service the plant's corduroy-making machinery.

The Åfeldts' second son, Frans Axel Göthe (Frank) was born on December 13, 1861,[20] and shortly after that the family moved into the promisingly-named *Lyckan* (Happiness) Quarter.[21]

Frans found employment in the workshop of Welander and Kellner, a company that designed and built machinery for the textile mills. One of the company's proprietors, Gunnar Welander (left), had been awarded a patent on a fulling machine, so Frans had an inventor as a mentor. Gustaf Kellner (right).

Old houses in the *Lyckan* (Happiness) Quarter, where the Åfeldt family moved in December 1861, after the birth of their second son. The photo was taken in 1900, when few such houses remained.

Chapter 2

John Ericsson

In the second year of the Civil War, all Sweden was electrified by the news that America had a new hero, the Swedish immigrant, John Ericsson. Born in 1803, Ericsson was a prolific inventor. At age 22 he had conceived the idea of improving on Watt's steam engine, and built a *flame engine*, a form of heat engine, which produced several horsepower. However, Sweden was then an agricultural country, and no place for an inventor. When King Charles John (formerly Napoleon's Marshal Bernadotte) was shown Ericsson's drawings, he advised the young man to go abroad, since his country would never reward him as he deserved.[22]

After some years in England, Ericsson took passage to New York aboard Isambard Brunel's *Great Britain*. He was still convinced that the displacement of the steam engine was essential to industrial progress, and soon designed a practical "caloric" (heat) engine. More than three thousand were built,[23] and some still operate perfectly.

The success of the caloric engine led to an extremely ambitious project, a caloric ship. This was a 260-foot vessel costing half a million dollars. Her machinery was unlike anything ever before attempted. Her four huge cylinders were 14 feet in diameter, and each piston, together with its connecting rod, weighed over fifty tons. The inventor boasted that she was "simply a mechanical marvel, [and her engines] sink the *Great Eastern* machinery into insignificance." One of the ship's admirers declared, "The age of steam is closed, the age of caloric opens. Fulton and Watt belong to the past. Ericsson is the great mechanical genius of the present and future."[24]

In an excess of pride, the inventor permitted the ship to be named *Ericsson*.

The first inventor to become obsessed with replacing James Watt's steam engine was another Swede, John Ericsson. In an attempt to demonstrate that his new heat engine was superior to steam, John Ericsson built the ill-fated caloric ship, *Ericsson*.

We know how the gods reward hubris, but it is startling to learn how quickly they humbled John Ericsson. "At the very moment of success—of brilliant success—fate has dealt me the severest blow I ever received. We yesterday went out on a private preparatory trial of the caloric ship, during which all our anticipations were realized. We attained a speed of from twelve to thirteen turns of our paddle-wheels, equal to full eleven miles an hour, without putting forth anything like our maximum power. All went on magnificently until…our beautiful ship was struck by a terrific tornado on our larboard quarter, careening the hull.…The men…became terrified and ran on deck without closing the ports, and the hold filled so rapidly as to sink the ship in a few minutes.…A more sudden transition from gladness and exultation to disappointment and regret is scarcely on record."[25]

Tornado aside, a heat engine is a formidable nut for any inventor to crack. Donald Cardwell states flatly that the ship's caloric engines were a failure: "Air is a very bad conductor of heat and therefore difficult to heat up; furthermore its expansion is so slight that if reasonable power was to be obtained within a moderate temperature range enormous cylinders had to be used."[26] Even Ericsson's biographer had to agree: "Difficulties innumerable assailed an engine working at a temperature of 444° and constantly subject in all of its parts to the destructive influence of dry heat, burning out its lubricants, loosening its joints, and rapidly destroying its working members by oxidation."[27] Tellingly, no more caloric ships have been attempted.

Monitor

During the Civil War, Ericsson learned that the Confederate Navy was converting the hulk of the *Merrimack* into an ironclad, and wrote to President Lincoln, proposing his own design for a unique warship. The concept was based on Swedish experience with coastal defense, where shallow-draft boats were a necessity. Further, as the inventor explained, "The plan of the *Monitor* was based on the observations of the behavior of timber in our great Swedish lakes. I found that while the raftsman in his elevated cabin experienced very little motion, the seas breaking over his nearly submerged craft, these seas at the same time worked the sailing vessels nearly on their beam ends."[28] Consequently Ericsson's design had very little freeboard, so that the craft offered a stable platform for the two guns, mounted in Ericsson's innovation, a revolving turret.

Fortuitously, Lincoln himself had experience in using shallow-draft boats on the Mississippi and the Great Lakes, and on May 22, 1849 had been issued patent #6469 for *A Device for Buoying Vessels over Shoals*. He was the only President to receive a patent, and had a lifelong love for things mechanical.[29]

The President examined Ericsson's cardboard model and was particularly struck by the rotating turret. He announced his decision with a typical Lincolnian quip, "All I have to say is what the girl said when she stuck her foot into the stocking. It strikes me there's something in it."

Some members of the Naval Board favored Ericsson's idea; others ridiculed it. According to a friend of Ericsson's, "The air (was) thick with croakings that the department was about to father another Ericsson failure." But after Ericsson promised to build the boat for $275,000, and complete it in ninety days, he received the go-ahead.[30]

Throughout his career, a great obstacle to Ericsson's success was his own ungovernable temper. Ericsson's assistant, professor C.W. MacCord, tells us that when a naval authority questioned Ericsson's rudder design, "The hot Scandinavian blood flushed his cheek, his eyes gleamed, his brow darkened; and…the storm broke in all its fury. With the full volume of his tremendous voice, and with a mighty oath, he thundered, 'The Monitor is *mine*, and I say it shall not be done'."[31] On another occasion Ericsson "came into the room in a towering rage…like a lion at bay.…'I have not made any mistake, sir; I do not make mistakes'."[32] Ericsson defended his behavior with the explanation, "You have no right to abuse a man for being angry, since anger is involuntary."[33]

Chapter 2

During the Civil War, John Ericsson sent a proposal to President Lincoln, offering to build a revolutionary new warship. The *Monitor*'s design was based on Swedish naval experience, where shallow-draft craft were essential for coastal defense. Ericsson added his own innovation, a rotating turret. The Battle of Hampton Roads, which pitted the nimble *Monitor* against the ponderous *Virginia* (ex-*Merrimack*), changed naval warfare forever.

After the famous duel between the two ironclads, naval inspector Alban C. Stimers, who had been aboard *Monitor* as an observer, wrote, "Captain Ericsson, I congratulate you upon your great success; thousands here this day bless you."[34]

Ericsson explained what motivated him: "I have not received any remuneration for the Monitor, nor did I patent the invention, as I intended it as a contribution to the glorious cause of the Union.... It was the cannon in the rotary turret at Hampton Roads that tore the fetters from millions of slaves."[35]

Lincoln's administration immediately made plans to order some sixty Monitor-class vessels.[36] And the King of Sweden honored the inventor by naming that country's first monitor after him. Ericsson reciprocated by donating two 15-inch Rodman guns – the most effective ordinance at that time – so that the *John Ericsson* could not be outgunned.[37]

The success of *Monitor* brought John Ericsson great acclaim in the United States and celebrity in his native Sweden. In this commemorative portrait, the hero is garlanded by Swedish and American flags.

John Ericsson must have been an extraordinarily powerful role model for Frans Åfeldt. If the young man pursued a career as an inventor, might not he too achieve fame?

During those years two more sons joined the Åfeldt family, Ernst Gustaf Edmund (Ernest) on November 16, 1863, and Sven Rikard Theodor on September 15, 1865.[38] The Åfeldts continued to change their residences frequently. After *Lyckan* they moved to *Kannan* (The Pot), then *Muskötten* (The Musket), then in 1864 to *Valnöten* (The Chestnut), and after that to *Munken* (The Monk).[39]

Chapter 2

Alfred Nobel

There was another family of restless inventors in Sweden. On September 6, 1864, Frans became aware of the name Nobel when he read a lurid report in the Norrköping newspaper: "Last Saturday…the inhabitants in the capital were taken by surprise by a terrible explosion, so strong that buildings were shaken on their foundations.…A great yellow flame rose into the air, and almost immediately changed to an enormous column of smoke. From the factory building, erected of wood…no more than a few…splinters remained.…The most horrifying aspect of the catastrophe was the sight of mutilated human bodies lying about in the wreckage. Not only had their clothes been blown off but some of the bodies were headless, and flesh had been torn from their bones."[40]

It was Alfed Nobel's experiments with nitroglycerine that led to the explosion, which killed his youngest brother, Emil Oscar, and prompted another brother, Robert, to warn: "Quit as soon as possible the damned career of an inventor, which merely brings disaster in its train."[41] Shortly after the accident Alfred's father, also an inventor, suffered a stroke, but the son, undeterred, proceeded to set up his first nitroglycerine factory.[42] He soon left Sweden, and after his invention of dynamite in 1867, became an international entrepreneur. Although Alfred hated business, he was good at it, and prospered.[43]

America Fever

At this time Frans Åfeldt was beginning to show a new pride in his profession. By the end of 1865 he had started his own business, *Mekanikus Åfeldt*, and had an employee, J.F. Holmqvist.[44] Apparently he was making a good living, for the city archives noted that in 1864 the Åfeldt tax bill of 4.45 was fully paid up.[45] It is obvious that Frans was turning into a confident young man who would march to his own drummer.

So why did he decide to leave Sweden? As we know, John Ericsson had been advised by the King himself to emigrate, and now Alfred Nobel had departed. Although Swedes admired the sciences, there was little financial support for technical innovation, and the more ambitious inventors left in search of something they could not find at home – opportunity.

There was another factor that influenced their decision: the rigid class system. In the words of an early emigrant, "If I should return to Sweden and go into your office I should feel myself obliged to take my cap or hat in hand and bow and scrape and call an ordinary bookkeeper 'Sir' etc., but here in America working men and office employees are on an equal footing." Another wrote: "Here [in America] we have rich men, we have learned men, we have smart men, we have bosses who sometimes treat us like dogs, but *we have no masters*." According to John S. Lindberg, "The result was that the desire to emigrate gripped the individual like an infection. In popular language it was called by the fitting name, America Fever."[46]

If Frans had known how his hero, John Ericsson, felt about America, it might have given him pause. The irascible inventor strongly opposed the emigration of Swedes from their native land. In response to one enquiry he wrote: "Pardon my freedom of expression, but I deem it my duty…to talk plainly, since it appears you are committing a fatal blunder.…I look upon your son's prospects as simply hopeless.…On no account send any youth here. A Swedish engineer has nothing to learn *here*. Confining work, trade fraud, and superficial show are all this country has to offer.…When they have failed in everything they come to me.…If Mr. Jonas has sufficient means to live here for a year without earning anything, together with means to defray expenses of a return passage, after having been effectually cured of his fascination, then by all means send him on, that he may learn to what depth corruption, dishonesty, selfishness and meanness can descend."[47]

But Frans didn't know.

In preparation for his departure, the family moved to the block *Källen* (The Well),[48] probably because the rents were lower there. *Källen* was close to the textile mills, and many people in that quarter did piecework. Perhaps Augusta supported the family in that manner while she waited for Frans to call them to their new home.

Before departing, Frans went to St. Olai Church, where he partook of communion.

Then in 1866, following in the footsteps of John Ericsson, he set out for America.[49]

Before emigrating, Frans Åfeldt took communion in the St. Olai Church. Blessedly he knew nothing of John Ericsson's bitter feelings about the "corruption, dishonesty, selfishness and meanness" that the inventor had encountered in the United States.

Chapter 3

Everything He Touched Turned to Gold

"As an illuminator the oil is without a figure: It is the light of the age. In the opinion of some who have considered the subject, illuminating is its grand office. Those that have not seen it burn, may rest assured its light is no moonshine; but something nearer the clear, strong, brilliant light of day, to which darkness is no party. It tries the eyes of none. For the Christian by means of it to peruse his Bible, is no infliction. It never causes the politician to weep, when he reads at night in his favorite newspaper, the victories of his own party; nor the merchant to shed tears over the price current, showing a turn in trade which puts money into his pocket. In other words, rock oil emits a dainty light; the brightest and yet the cheapest in the world; a light fit for Kings and Royalists, and not unsuitable for Republicans and Democrats. It is a light withal, for ladies who are ladies indeed, and so are neither afraid nor ashamed to sew or read in the evening. An oil man, without any risk of a breach of promise, may warrant them, that by this light, they can thread their needles the first time, and every time they try."

Thomas A. Gale, *Rock Oil in Pennsylvania and Elsewhere*, 1860.[1]

Jabez Bostwick

If Frank Ofeldt was to achieve his dream, he would need a business partner, for his shop-floor education left him ill-equipped to counter the wiles of the business world. The man who would fill that role was as important in ending the hegemony of steam as was Ofeldt himself.

Jabez Bostwick was born in Delhi, Delaware County, New York, on September 30, 1830.[2] According to his *New York Times* obituary, "Bostwick was a self-made man. Like Rockefeller, Flagler, and the other Standard Oil magnates he was a poor boy of humble parentage. …While he was still a boy his father, a farmer, removed to Ohio. The farm life did not suit him and he found employment in a bank at Covington, Ky., just across the river from his father's farm. His early life was a series of struggles, but he always managed to make a way out of them." Like three of the other Standard Oil principals, Jabez was raised a Baptist.[3]

Jabez took an important step by moving to Cleveland to take a job in a commission and hardware firm, which was soon named *Reynolds & Bostwick*. Jabez then returned to Kentucky to take a position as accountant in the bank of J.B. Tilford in Lexington.[4] Allan Nevins tells us that it was in Kentucky that Bostwick acquired the "southern courtesy of manner" that stayed with him throughout his life.[5]

Jabez A. Bostwick, who was to become Frank Ofeldt's backer, was a gifted businessman. During the Civil War he made his first fortune by trading in cotton, and then he turned to oil.

Cotton

The Civil War offered Jabez, like so many other young entrepreneurs, the opportunity to make his fortune.

What should a patriot do: serve his country or seize the opportunity to profit? Judge Thomas Mellon of Pittsburgh advised his son: "I had hoped my boy was going to make a smart, intelligent business man and was not such a goose as to be seduced from duty by the declamations of buncombed speeches. It is only greenhorns who enlist. You can learn nothing in the army.…Here there is no credit attached to going. All now stay if they can and go if they must. Those who are able to pay for substitutes, do so, and no discredit attaches. In time you will come to understand and believe that a man may be a patriot without risking his own life or sacrificing his health. There are plenty of other lives less valuable or others ready to serve for the love of serving."[6]

Jabez chose money-making. Very likely it was Tilford who financed his initial operations, for the banker's son, John B. Tilford Jr., became Bostwick's partner.[7] The enterprise they set up, *Bostwick &Tilford*, went into cotton trading, a business that carried a significant stigma.

During the war it was possible to purchase a bale of cotton in the South for $25 to $50, and sell it in the North for $250.[8] What did an aspiring cotton trader have to do to get in on the action? The answer was easy: friends in high places. In 1861 Congress passed an act permitting some trade in cotton with rebel states, and authorized the Treasury Department to license factors to do the deals. Thurlow Weed, the influential Republican politician, ensured that licenses flowed to traders willing to cut him in.[9]

In addition to the use of licenses, there was a substantial contraband trade. Allan Nevins wrote that, "Steamboats…were being sent out ostensibly on military errands, but really to grab cotton, bearing Army detachments to take it and Army wagons to haul it, while nine dollars in ten went to enrich the illicit partnership of traders and colonels." General Banks wrote to Lincoln that the profits were so gigantic that it was almost impossible to prevent the subornation of subordinate officers, and this prompted Lincoln to complain that the army was diverted from fighting to speculating in cotton. General Washburn testified: "I believe that permitting trade has been of vast assistance to rebel armies. …I know of many disasters of our arms, which, in my judgment, would never have taken place, had not cotton, sugar and trade in general, invited our arms to places where they should not have gone." The Chicago Tribune accused one colonel of returning escaped slaves to their Mississippi masters in exchange for cotton, and Nevins tells us that some officers were anxious to prolong the war until they had their share of the cotton trade.

After three years Bostwick became dissatisfied. Although he was reaping great profits, the Mississippi Valley cotton trade represented only about half of the total, the balance being carried by blockade-runners. One ship, the *Kate*, ran the blockade sixty times, and nearly 400,000 bales of contraband cotton flowed through Boston and New York.[10] Jabez wanted a piece of that action, so midway through the war Bostwick & Tilford transferred its domicile to New York, the center of the trade. Jabez became a member of the Cotton Exchange, and built large cotton docks on Staten Island, where he also lived on a beautiful estate. John Tilford's brother, Wesley Hunt Tilford, after completing two years at Columbia College, joined the firm as a clerk.[11] This was the beginning of a stellar career, which culminated in his serving as treasurer of the Standard Oil Company.

Petroleum

As the war wound down, Jabez looked for other worlds to conquer, and his eyes lit on the petroleum business, where a boom had been under way since 1859.

In our opening chapter we quoted Professor Chandler's strictures about the adulteration of kerosene. As for kerosene itself, Chandler had nothing but praise: "This cheap and beautiful illuminating oil…is an inestimable boon to the world. It adds several hours to the length of the day, and enables the working-classes to devote the long evenings to the improvement of their minds by reading.…It is safe to say that petroleum is one of the great civilizing agents of the nineteenth century."[12]

Kerosene was first isolated by Abraham Gesner, a Canadian surgeon, who distilled it from Trinidad pitch. A consulting chemist, Edward S. Kent, declared, "I am sanguine that your 'Purified Kerosene' is destined to supersede all other oils or burning fluids, as a source of light for artficial illumination." However, according to Williamson and Daum, "Gesner suffered a fate not uncommon among innovators. Having assigned his patents in return for a salary, he profited little from his inventions."[13]

To produce an equivalent amount of light, kerosene cost less than half the cost of gas light, less than a fifth of sperm oil's cost, and less than a tenth the cost of candles.[14] Pennsylvania oil quickly destroyed the whaling industry, leading *The Living Age* to publish an article entitled, "A Good Time Coming for Whales."[15]

If Jabez was to go into the oil business, it was essential to find out where he could extract the maximum profit. His first visit to the oil regions must have given him pause, for it was an industry in chaos.

The place was infested with promoters, just waiting for gullible Easterners. A *New York Times* correspondent, William Wright, observed that it was "almost refreshing to watch how many shrewd, sharp, intelligent Eastern financiers, who feel themselves competent to buy and sell all creation, can themselves be bought and sold and delivered by Petrolian speculators."

John J. McLaurin described them as "capital fellows, true as steel, bright as a dollar and quicker'n greas'd lightnin'.…The schemer with property to sell had 'the very thing he wanted' and would 'let him in on the ground floor'.…He could have it at a bargain-counter sacrifice – one hundred-thousand dollars and half the oil. The engine had given out and the owner was about to order a new one when called home by the sudden death of his mother-in-law. Settling the old lady's estate required his entire attention, therefore he would consent to sell his oil-interests 'dirt-cheap' to a responsible buyer....The visitor...saw real sand on the derrick-floor and everything besmeared with grease. The presence of oil was unmistakable....He did not suspect that barrels of crude and buckets of sand from other wells had been dumped into the hole at night, that the engine had been disabled purposely and that another innocent was soon to cut his wisdom teeth!"[16]

Wright concluded: "The system of swindling... is exquisite, magnificent, stupendous, brilliantly successful....There is reason to believe that one-half of the transactions...are more or less tinctured with fraud and falsehood."[17] If the scams were bad, reality was worse. Journalist Ida M. Tarbell reported that, of the 5,560 wells drilled in the first ten years, 4,374 were dry or unprofitable,[18] and Wright calculated that the average productive life of a good well was only eighteen months.[19] There were other risks, principally fire. The famous initial well, *Drake's Folly,* burned within four months, the first of many oil fires in Pennsylvania.[20] Some drillers posted warnings: "SMOKERS WILL BE SHOT."[21]

Oil prices fluctuated wildly. In 1859 a barrel sold at twenty dollars, but two years later it averaged 52 cents, then rose again to $8.15. According to Tarbell, "Just as the supply seemed to have approached a fixed amount, a wildcat well would come in and knock the bottom out of the market."[22] At one point, the price dropped to ten cents – not worth barrelling.[23] Tarbell, who grew up in the oil regions, tells us that no matter what the risks, the oil men were undeterred: "They loved the game, and every man of them would stake his last dollar on the chance of striking oil."[24]

If oil production was such a crapshoot, what about refining?

Tarbell explained: "The process of distillation also was free to all. The essential apparatus was very simple – a cast-iron still, usually surrounded by brick-work, a copper worm, and two tin- or zinc-lined tanks.... Anybody who could get the apparatus could make oil, and many men did – badly, of course, to begin with, and with an alarming proportion of waste and explosion and fires."[25] A five-barrel-a-day outfit cost a mere $200, and a complete refinery could be set up for $1,500.[26] As a result, some 300 were already in existence by 1863.[27] Because of the rampant overbuilding, most refineries lost money.

Well, what about transportation?

McLaurin described that miserable business: "To haul oil from inland wells to shipping-points required thousands of horses....Travelers in the oil-regions seldom lost sight of these endless trains of wagons bearing their greasy freight....Five to seven barrels – a barrel of oil weighed three-hundred-and-sixty pounds – taxed the strength of the stoutest teams. The mud was practically bottomless. Horses sank to their breasts and wagons far above their axles. Oil dripping from innumerable barrels mixed with the dirt to keep the mass a perpetual paste.... The Oil Creek teamster, rubber-booted to the waist and flannel-shirted to the chin, was a picturesque character. He was skilled in profanity and the savage use of the whip. A week's earnings – ten, twenty and thirty dollars a day – he would spend in revelry on Saturday night....He regulated his charges by the depth and consistency of the mud and the wear and tear of morality and livestock....Many a horse fell into the batter and was left to smother. If one horse died, he bought another....The treatment of the patient creatures – thousands were literally murdered – was frightful and few survived....They were worked until they dropped dead....As a single trip realized more than would buy another the brutal driver scarcely felt the financial loss."[28]

Chapter 3

There were no proper roads to the oil fields. Oil, mixed in with the dirt, produced perpetual paste.

If the first leg of the journey was, at least for the horses, a grim death-march, the next stage was riotously exciting – an exhilarating example of frontier America's can-do spirit, and an extraordinary episode in nautical history.

Boats of all shapes and sizes carried the barrels down Oil Creek to Oil City. Frequently the creek was too low for navigation, so the oil men dammed it back to create a temporary pond, and then twice a week, on Wednesday and Saturday, the water was released to create an artificial flood, called a *pond-freshet*, that briefly raised the water level by two to three feet. Two thousand craft were employed in the trade, and each time the dam was opened, between two hundred and eight hundred boats vied for passage. The smallest, called *Guipers*, held 25 to 50 barrels, and the largest, *French Creekers*, carried up to 1,200.

McLaurin described this 19th century version of an extreme sport: "The boatmen stood by their lines, to cast loose when the current was precisely right. Sound judgment was required. The loaded boat, if let go too soon, ran the risk of grounding in the first shallow-place, to be battered into kindling-wood by those coming after. Such accidents occurred frequently, resulting in a general jam and loss of vessels and cargoes. The scene was more exciting than a three-ringed circus. Property and life were imperiled, boats were ground to fragments, thousand of barrels of oil were spilled and the tangle seemed inextricable. Men, women and children lined the banks of the stream for miles, intently watching the spectacle."[29]

Thousands of barrels of oil were lost due to the chaotic method of shipping petroleum. However, Jabez Bostwick found a way to squeeze money out of oil transportation, and he made a second fortune.

Why not try pipelines? Ida Tarbell recounted the opposition that one inventor and entrepreneur, Samuel Van Syckel, faced when he tried to circumvent the system: "He was greeted with jeers, but went doggedly ahead, laid a two-inch pipe, put in three relay pumps, and turned in his oil. From the start the line was a success, carrying eighty barrels of oil an hour. The day that the Van Syckel pipe-line began to run oil a revolution began in the business. After the Drake well, it is the most important event in the history of the Oil Regions. The teamsters saw its meaning and turned out in fury, dragging the pipe, which was for the most part buried, to the surface, and cutting it so the oil would be lost. It was only by stationing an armed guard that they were held in check."[30]

Chapter 3

A Lucrative Business

Jabez concluded that transportation, anarchical though it was, might be turned into a business. After all, every barrel of oil, somehow or other, had to get from wellhead to customer. Europe was much more heavily populated than the United States, so that was where most of the customers were, and their oil passed through America's seaports. With the decision made, Bostwick & Tilford shifted into the shipping of petroleum.[31]

Much of Bostwick's oil already passed through the Erie Company's terminal at Weehawken, New Jersey. Jabez recognized that the Erie dock, which was almost on his Staten Island doorstep, offered a chokepoint where he could apply a levy on every barrel bound for Europe. All he had to do was persuade the Erie's president, Jay Gould, to turn the terminal over to him. Apparently Gould had no idea of the leverage that the oil terminal offered, for he leased Jabez the facility for a paltry $75,000 a year.[32] Gould was not one to leave money on the table, but in this case Jabez got the better of him.

Wooden barrels were prone to leak, and many had to be repaired before they could be loaded aboard ships. In addition to the actual costs of repairing, Jabez charged about thirty cents a barrel, which included nine cents for handling and nine cents for cooperage, leaving him a profit of twelve cents.[33] This may not sound like much, but in 1870, U.S. production reached 6,500,000 barrels,[34] of which over 60% was exported,[35] mostly through New York. Incredibly, Bostwick soon cornered two-thirds of the New York business.[36]

Weehawken represented only a small part of Bostwick & Tilford's activities. They also bought and sold oil, and a critical part of that business was negotiating the purchase of crude from producers. In the beginning the most powerful men in the oil region were the buyers. Ida Tarbell tells us that "A man with a thousand barrel well on his hands…was in a plight. He had got to sell his oil at once for lack of storage room or let it run on the ground. He had to depend on buyers who came to him."[37] Jabez was a shrewd buyer, and well suited to the role,[38] but, based in New York, he needed a tough-minded man on the spot. Before the war, Jabez had employed a German immigrant, Joseph Seep. Now Seep moved to Titusville to represent the company. Negotiating the price of oil was an adversarial procedure, and Patrick Boyle, editor of *The Derrick*, described Seep's assignment as "one of the most delicate roles that has ever been undertaken by a resident of the oil country."[39] In that same year (1869) Jabez made another astute hire, Daniel O'Day, described by Tarbell as "a man of grit and force and energy."[40] According to Ron Chernow, "O'Day was a profane, two-fisted Irishman who tempered ruthless tactics with wit and charm. He inspired loyalty among subordinates and raw terror among adversaries. On his forehead O'Day bore a scar from an old Oil Creek brawl that was a constant reminder of his bare-knuckled approach to business."[41]

O'Day had previously worked for a transportation company, where he learned the management of railroad cars. To ensure that they would have cars when needed, shippers would seize and hold them, preferring to pay demurrage on empties in order to have them at hand.[42] Producers were also known to hold back cars to manipulate the price of oil.

Naphtha

Daniel O'Day was adept at keeping rail cars out of the hands of Jabez Bostwick's competitors. According to Ron Chernow, he was "a profane two-fisted Irishman who…inspired loyalty among subordinates and raw terror among adversaries."

In 1870, on the outbreak of war between France and Prussia, oil plummeted to $2.60 a barrel.[43] Cannily, Jabez had shorted oil, which led the producers to attempt a bear squeeze. They stored their oil and hung on to the rail cars. On December 6 *The Derrick* reported that the bulls had possession of all the oil cars, and on December 7, "barely three days remain in which to make the deliveries."[44] However, it was extremely dangerous to squeeze a bear like Bostwick. Nevins recounted that at the last moment "Bostwick and some associates, gaining control of the car supply…unexpectedly smashed the corner and turned the tables."[45] On December 9, *The Derrick* announced, "Corner busted."[46] In breaking the corner, Jabez demonstrated to the industry that any man who dared oppose him did so at his peril.

Within three years of acquiring the Weehawken Terminal, Jabez had built a formidable business. Bostwick & Tilford owned a fleet of tugs, barges and lighters in New York harbor. The company also owned a large refinery at Hunter's Point on Long Island, as well as a canning and casing plant. In addition, they were an export marketing agency, probably the largest in the field.[47]

When the time came for Frank Ofeldt to search for a backer, he could hardly have found a more accomplished businessman than Jabez Bostwick. Everything Jabez touched turned to gold.

Chapter 4

The Star Gas Machine

"Invention seemed an American pastime....The greatest sight in Washington, to multitudes of visitors, was not the Capitol but the Patent Office."

Allan Nevins[1]

There is no city like New York for welcoming newcomers. New Yorkers live in a highly competitive world, and to stay ahead they depend on fresh ideas. If you have something new to offer, be it a play, a publication, or an invention, New Yorkers have open ears, and you may well find an investor willing to take a flyer on you. Frans Åfeldt had gone to Norrköping in search of opportunity, and had found it. Frank Ofeldt, as he now called himself, had every reason to believe that New York would be even more rewarding, and he was right.

John Ericsson suffered bitterly from the deviousness of American businessmen. If Ericsson, an American national hero, was so helpless, how could an inexperienced youth like Frank hope to make his way?

Only by luck.

Frederick Law Olmsted

If naked greed is an American trait, so too is selfless idealism. With astounding good fortune, Frank landed his first job with a man whose life was dedicated to the social and aesthetic improvement of his country. That man was Frederick Law Olmsted, described by George Templeton Strong as "an extraordinary fellow, decidedly the most remarkable specimen of human nature with whom I have ever been brought into close relations. Talent and energy most rare; absolute purity and disinterestedness."[2]

Olmsted was an adventurer, having shipped before the mast to China at twenty-one. He then became a journalist for *The New York Times*, and traveled through the Southern states, investigating the economic implications of slavery.[3] His biographer, Laura Wood Roper, tells us that in the course of his journey, "he reached the categorical conclusion that slavery was an economic liability, a moral wrong, and a disastrous handicap to both black and white."[4]

Then Olmsted's career took an unexpected turn. New York City had purchased land for a park, and in 1858, a competition for the design was announced. The site was disgusting, since its bogs received the overflow from pigpens, slaughterhouses, and bone-boiling works, and it stank horribly. Thirty-three candidates vied for the prize, which the city unexpectedly awarded to the inexperienced Olmsted and his partner Calvert Vaux.[5] The result was Central Park, to this day the crown jewel of Manhattan.

During the Civil War, Olmsted's career veered again. The army's medical corps was so woefully unprepared that, of the men who died, two-thirds of the officers and five-sixths of the men succumbed to disease or accident, not enemy fire.[6] In desperation, civilians formed an organization modeled on Florence Nightingale's British Sanitary Commission. (During the Crimean War, Nightingale had so successfully improved hygiene that deaths due to illness, which had been 293 per thousand, dropped to 25 per thousand within eighteen months.)[7] Olmsted was selected as administrator of the U.S. Sanitary Commission, which, according to Nevins, "could be counted one of the minor glories of the war.... It was unquestionably the greatest voluntary organization of benevolent character that America had yet produced."[8]

It is an American compulsion to out-do one's neighbor, so at the end of the war New York's rival, Brooklyn, asked Olmsted and Vaux to design a park that would surpass Central Park. At that time Brooklyn was not a borough, but a separate and proud city. Compared to iniquitous New York, Brooklyn was genteel. New York was notorious for vile tenements, rampant prostitution, and brawling street gangs, while Brooklyn was famed for Henry Ward Beecher, whose sermons drew more than three thousand people to Plymouth Church on a Sunday.[9]

About the time that Olmsted commenced construction of Prospect Park, Frank Ofeldt left Sweden. According to his obituary in *Popular Mechanics*, "At the age of 30 he came to America, the place offering the best advantages for the man who would rise in the world. He had so little knowledge of the English language, however, that he was obliged to accept a position as a laborer in laying out Prospect Park, Brooklyn."[10] His pay was only 16¢ an hour, or $1.60 for a ten-hour day.[11] However, Frank was the beneficiary of Olmsted's attitude to employees. As described by Roper, "Olmsted thought that the way to cultivate responsibility in a man was to lay responsibility on him: a man trusted was, usually, a man whose aroused pride stimulated his best efforts."[12] Accordingly, when Olmsted's foreman discovered that Frank could handle a theodolite, (an instrument used by surveyors), he was promoted.[13]

The idealist and visionary, Frederick Law Olmsted, provided Frank Ofeldt his first job in the United States, on the construction of Brooklyn's Prospect Park.

Chapter 4

Liquid Fuel

No sooner had Pennsylvania oil come on the market than inventors thought of using it to fuel steam engines. In 1860 the *Titusville Gazette* excitedly announced: "A citizen of Pittsburgh of great scientific attainments and great inventive genius, has hit upon an idea which may, if carried out, cause an active demand for all the oil that can be produced. His plan is to construct steamers with the engines so arranged that the boilers may be heated from the burning of oil instead of coal. The calculation is that the weight of the oil would be six-sevenths less than the coal now used. This would vastly increase the carrying capacity of our ocean steamers, as well as create an almost illimitable demand for that which is so much exciting people in the neighborhood of Titusville."[14]

The British Admiralty was interested, but in early experiments at Woolwich Dockyard, soot choked the flues and stifled the draught. In time the Royal Navy obtained somewhat better results, but coal-mining interests successfully opposed the use of petroleum by pointing out that Britain had a worldwide series of coal-bunkering stations, but no chain of oil terminals.[15]

The U.S. Navy also carried out trial runs, which showed great promise, but B.F. Isherwood, Chief of the Navy's Bureau of Steam Engineering, concluded that with coal priced at only $10.00 a ton, the cost of powering a ship with petroleum was eight times higher than with coal.[16] And *Chemical News* reported that in less than 48 hours the pipes and passages became so choked with soot and carbon that the fire went out, and then the fixture had to be taken apart and cleaned. …Moreover, "extraordinary care…must be taken in storing this substance on board ship, in order to guard against accidents of the most frightful character." In conclusion, "there is not the slightest probability… of petroleum ever taking the place of coal as a steam fuel.…It is not likely that any prudent steam navigation company would allow it to be employed in their vessels, even if they could find an engineer to recommend it."[17]

Ofeldt's First Invention

Once Frank Ofeldt became proficient in English, his experience in the textile mills of Norrköping enabled him to find work in a machine shop manufacturing looms,[18] which got him back into the field he loved, machinery.

In American manufacturing, steam engines were indispensible, and Frank turned his attention to the intractable problem of using liquid fuel. It occurred to him that instead of trying to burn petroleum, he would use one of the naphthas, which were plentiful and cheap. Frank needed a place where he could conduct experiments, and he found it across the harbor in Newark, New Jersey.

However, his work was interrupted by devastating news. On August 27, 1870, the Ofeldts' youngest son, Sven Rikard Theodor, died just before his fifth birthday.[19] Frank hurried home, but after an interval he returned to Newark. Mathilda and the boys followed, departing from Göteborg (Gothenberg) on May 16, 1872.[20]

In due course, Frank completed the design of a burner in which he injected steam to assist in vaporising "gasoline or other volatile hydrocarbon."[21] This may seem counterintuitive. Doesn't water extinguish fire? In fact, the use of steam to aid combustion was not new. In the early 1860s, the British inventor, Aydon, used a jet of superheated steam to force fuel oil into the furnace in the form of a cloud of exceedingly fine spray, at the same time converting it into vapor, which burned well. The Russian inventor, Spakovsky, designed a better system, using ordinary steam.[22] Frank may not have heard about these experiments, but he probably knew that in 1870 Whipple & Dickinson of Philadelphia had succeeded in converting fuel oil into a hydrocarbon gas by injecting superheated steam.[23] In Frank's experiments, he found that steam could also be helpful in vaporizing naphtha.

Frank had two uses in mind for this invention. One was "to produce a simple, cheap, and safe steam-boiler for light power, such as required for running a sewing-machine."[24] As the garment industry employed thousands of sewing machines, this could open up a lucrative market, but Frank put the idea aside because the manufacture of illuminating gas was even more interesting.

Before natural gas became widely available, illuminating gas was made from coal, so was also called "coal gas." Gas lighting was a major industry in the United States, with annual revenues of 150 million dollars.[25] Many urban homes had gas jets in every room. Frank's invention would fuel the jets with cheap gasoline. Frank was not the first. In 1865, Charles L. Gilbert, assisted by Hiram Maxim, who later invented the firearm silencer and a machine gun, had designed just such an apparatus, and by 1870 the Gilbert & Barker Manufacturing Company had installed about 600 machines to supply illuminating gas, made from gasoline.[26] In 1869 the Gale-Rand process succeeded in producing a better product, capable of traveling through mains without excessive condensation and loss of illuminating power. By 1872 there were 101 companies manufacturing gas machines.[27] Even where illuminating gas was readily available, gasoline light was able to compete, because gasoline cost less than half the price of coal gas, for an equal amount of light.[28]

Gaslight was expensive and only available in towns, so Frank Ofeldt's first invention was a device, fueled by gasoline (one of the naphthas), to illuminate a household more cheaply. Frank was not the only one to do this, but the novel feature of his invention was the prevention of overflows by the use of a feedback mechanism. This drawing accompanied his first patent.

The problem with devices using the naphthas was their tendency to explode.[29] The early control systems were imprecise or unreliable, and sometimes permitted the fuel to overflow. The novel feature in Frank's invention was a method of automatic regulation (what we would now call a feedback mechanism), which successfully controlled the flow.

The invention was embodied in two patents that were issued three weeks apart in the fall of 1872. According to the preamble of one of these, entitled *Improvement in Oil-Burning Steam-Boilers*, "The invention consists in a combination of devices whereby the amount of fluid fuel admitted to the fireplace of the boiler through an ordinary gas-pipe will be automatically regulated according to the different pressures required and gauged for different purposes, so that the pressure cannot exceed that to which the gauge has been permanently or temporarily adjusted."[30]

Three quarters of a century later, Frank's grandson, August's son, Ernest Frank Ofeldt, described the invention: "In those days gasoline was a by-product in the manufacture of kerosene and was considered worthless by the big oil companies. This posed a challenge to grandfather and soon he began to experiment with this waste product. The first results of his work took the form of a machine for lighting homes with gasoline. So improved was the new lighting over the kerosene lamps then used that Mr. Ofeldt formed the Star Gasoline Machine Company to manufacture the lights."[31]

On June 6, 1873, the *Syracuse Daily Standard* described Frank's gasoline light: "Last evening we had the pleasure of examining a new and apparently practical invention for manufacturing gas for illuminating and heating purposes. The machine is in operation at the dwelling of Robert M. Beecher, No. 283 Grape street, and consists of a reservoir of gasoline capable of holding a barrel of the fluid, the necessary fixtures for conveying the fluid to the gasometer, and a small boiler and tank for heating and working the apparatus for making gas. The gas is made only as it is required, and the apparatus can be got in motion at less than five minutes notice. The gasoline is placed in the ground, where it is impossible that danger should arise from its use, and the whole apparatus is so simple and free from danger that a woman or boy can attend to it. Indeed, it really requires no attention except to supply the tank with water when the indicator shows that a fresh supply is required. The entire dwelling is fitted with ordinary pipe and gas fixtures, and the gas is sent through these fixtures with the most perfect freedom and safety. The light is mellow, white and brilliant, illuminating quite as well, if not better, than the usual...burners of the city gas works. Indeed the beauty, brilliancy and perfection of the light is the theme of admiration of all who have examined the apparatus and observed it work. A large street lamp, suspended over the street entrance, also gives as perfect and bright a light as the best street lamps of the city. Mr. Beecher is confident also that he will be enabled to heat as well as light his parlor by the singular gas after the proper grate has been introduced.

"The entire cost of the apparatus that does all this work so perfectly is less than $200, and gasoline for three months is valued at about $12, which is all the expense for light and heat. The inventor of this 'Star Gas Machine' is Mr. F. W. Ofeldt, and Messrs. Beecher & Worden are General Agents for its introduction in this section. We learn that the machine is not an experiment, as a large hotel with four hundred burners is lighted with this gas at Newark, N. J., and churches and private dwellings in that and other portions of New Jersey....We see no reason why this invention, which is so simple and apparently so perfect, should not come into general use."[32]

One of the first big stores in Newark to use the light was L.S. Plaut and Company's *Bee Hive* on Broad Street.[33]

A year later, *Industrial Interests of Newark, N.J.* carried an account of the progress of *Star Gas*: "Many efforts more or less successful have been made to manufacture illuminating gas at less cost than the usual coal gas. In this direction, as in most others, Newark has fairly succeeded, the inventor being Mr. F. W. Ofeldt, whose Star Gas machine is an acknowledged success. This machine was patented in 1872. The company which is to manufacture it is not yet fully organized, the factory being meanwhile under the direction of F. W. Ofeldt & Co. The main difficulty with previous gas machines has been their tendency to explode; not so, however, with the 'Star,' which has been fully tested by various Boards of fire underwriters, and has their full approval. It occupies but a small space, and is not affected by the weather. The gas produced gives a very brilliant light, its cost being comparatively nominal. The invention is meeting with universal favor. Six workmen are employed in the manufactory, with a weekly payroll of $100. During 1873 the value of the machines made was $10,000, though the production for the present year will be largely increased."[34]

Frank continued to improve his invention, and the changes were embodied in three further patents. The first, which issued in 1875, specified that the reservoir be placed underground, and that preferably it be double-walled, with insulation between the walls, in order to maintain an even temperature uninfluenced by atmospheric changes. The gasometer, which had regulated the gas pressure, was replaced by an aerometer "in which no gas ever enters" and the "air is thoroughly dried and heated before mingling with gasoline for vaporizing it." In addition, "all stuffing-boxes and packings are dispensed with, the oil-level is regulated with the utmost exactness, and the quantity supplied exactly according to the vaporization needed to supply with gas any number of burners used, and a reliable valve is effected, which will not get out of order."[35]

The following patent, which issued in 1876, enabled the machine to get up to speed rapidly if a large number of burners were lighted simultaneously.[36] A year later the fifth patent completed the protection of the gasoline light machine. It finally eliminated the use of steam, and "its necessary accompaniment, the feed-water."[37] In each iteration Frank added more sophisticated feedback mechanisms that made the operation even more automatic and reliable.

Frank assigned his 1875 patent to himself and George W. Hall, and the following two patents to himself and Chandler C. Coats.[38] Presumably these gentlemen had some involvement in the Star Gas Co.

It is hard to know whether Ofeldt's gasoline light was superior to its competitors. Other manufacturers had greater success, but they probably had better access to capital, and more professional promotional skills. Taken as a whole, for some years gasoline light machines provided the largest market for the naphthas, and did help alleviate the naphtha glut.[39] Frank was on the right track.

The Invention Threatened

There is nothing so threatening to an inventor as another inventor. Suddenly Frank faced two. The first was Professor Thaddeus S.C. Lowe, who had served as chief of the army's aeronautical section. As a balloonist, hydrogen interested him, and in 1873 he patented an improved process by which large amounts of it could be generated, usually from petroleum. *Carbureted water gas* was cheaper to make, and had greater illuminating power than coal gas, so it gradually prevailed.[40]

The second inventor was Thomas Edison, a very competitive young man. "I don't care so much about making my fortune," he said, "as I do for getting ahead of the other fellows."[41]

In 1876 he set up a research laboratory in Menlo Park, N.J., not far from Newark, where he perfected a new way of inventing. Instead of working alone, Edison recruited a team of experts, who were able to turn ideas into patentable inventions at a remarkable pace. In an 1878 notebook he set out a new problem for his team: "To effect exact imitation of all done by gas, to replace lighting by gas by lighting by electricity."[42] Before tackling the technical problems, Edison studied the business. Soon few men knew more about the organization of the gaslight industry than he. The team then conducted a multitude of experiments in an astonishingly short time, and by the end of October 1879, had invented the first practical electric light for domestic use.[43]

Although Edison's purpose was to compete with gaslight, not Ofeldt's gasoline light, it was soon apparent that the latter would also suffer. The Star Gas Company was doomed, and soon disappeared from the Newark City Directory. In 1881 Frank's listing changed to "Ofeldt, Frank W. (*Ofeldt Gas Machine*), h. 73 Ferry."[44]

Now that Frank had successfully designed a mechanism that used the naphthas safely, his mind turned to a new invention, the naphtha engine.

Chapter 5

Taking the Fifth

"They are smarter fellows than I am, a good deal; they are very enterprising and smart men; never came in contact with any class of men as smart and able as they are in their business....One man would hardly have been able to do it; it is a combination of men.

Question: *And that is the only way you can account for the enormous monopoly that has thus grown up?*

Answer: *Yes; they are very shrewd men; I don't believe that by any legislative enactment or anything else through any of the states or all of the states, you can keep such men as them down; you can't do it; they will be on top all the time; you see if they are not."*

Question: *"You think they get on top of the railways?"*

Answer: *"Yes; and on top of everybody that comes in contact with them; too smart for me."*

> Testimony of William H. Vanderbilt, President of the New York Central Railroad, when asked about the men of Standard Oil[1]

Naphtha

Standard Oil

In chapter three, we learned how Jabez Bostwick honed his business skills – skills that would be just as important to the introduction of Ofeldt's invention as was Frank's engineering genius. But the success of the naphtha launch also hinged on Bostwick's access to friends in high places, relationships he forged during the next phase of his phenomenal career.

By decisively smashing the men who had tried to corner rail cars, Jabez Bostwick demonstrated conclusively his prowess in business. Not long after that coup, he was approached by the owners of a refining company in Cleveland, who asked whether he would merge his business with theirs. It is easy to see why they wanted Jabez. He was now the strongest oil man in New York, and was as fierce as a pit bull.

But what did they offer in return? It was not their refineries, profitable though they were; it was what the men had in their minds. The scheme they were hatching was breathtaking, a plan to consolidate all the refineries in the United States into one great organization, so powerful that it would eliminate competition once and for all.[2]

John D. Rockefeller in 1872. He was one of the most successful team-builders in business history.

John D. Rockefeller's early colleague, Henry Flagler.

Rockefeller recounted, "We walked to the office together, walked home at luncheon, back again after luncheon, and home again at night. On these walks...we did our thinking, talking, and planning together." It was on those walks that the two men dreamed up a plan to eliminate competition among the oil companies. (John D. Rockefeller, *Random Reminiscences*, p. 13)

Their enterprise, the Standard Oil Company of Ohio, had been incorporated only a year earlier, but it had grown out of a tiny refinery started by Samuel Andrews, a mechanical genius and the first man to distill kerosene in Cleveland. Andrews was not very good at business, so he asked a fellow member of his Baptist congregation, John D. Rockefeller, to be his backer. Because of Andrews' ingenuity, the company was able to outdo its competitors. It distilled more and better kerosene from crude, and did it consistently and more cheaply.[3]

Two other men soon joined the company, John's brother William, and Henry Flagler, a man of fertile imagination. By 1865 the company's two refineries constituted the largest producer of kerosene in the world,[4] and the company took the name *Standard Oil* to reflect the quality of Samuel Andrews' kerosene.

Jabez was a good fit; he was aggressive, absolutely ruthless, and he wasted no pity on losers. He epitomized John D.'s description of the ideal associate: "I wanted able men with me.…I admit I tried to attract only the able men; I have always had as little as possible to do with dull business men."[5] Apparently Jabez felt the same way about Rockefeller. With characteristic decisiveness, he agreed to turn his company over to Standard Oil, and was the first outsider to join what would become the world's most successful company.

Once the merger was agreed to in principle, the mechanism required careful attention. The Standard Oil Company was chartered to do business in Ohio only, and it had no legal right to own shares in other companies. Henry Flagler was not trained as a lawyer, but he drew up most of the early contracts.[6] Relying on English common law, he created a trustee to hold Bostwick's company and administer it on behalf of the Standard.[7] This became the template for subsequent acquisitions, and eventually the model for the Standard Oil Trust.

A new firm, *J. A. Bostwick and Company*, was created. In spite of its name, it was wholly owned by Standard Oil, a development that was kept a secret, even from Bostwick's key employees, Joseph Seep and Daniel O'Day. Henceforth all of Standard's purchases were made in the name of Bostwick, to keep the oil producers from finding out the identity of their real customer.[8]

The South Improvement Company

The railroads competed aggressively for the oil business, and Standard Oil was able to extract large concessions from them, which took the form of substantial drawbacks.[9] In November 1871, in order to head off the threat of an all-out war for the oil trade, Thomas A. Scott, Vice-President of the Pennsylvania Railroad, proposed an alliance between the most powerful railroads and a handful of refiners, one that would dramatically increase the use of drawbacks. Under this proposal, the participants would fix prices and eliminate competition, which they could do by making use of a shell corporation, the *South Improvement Company*.[10]

The terms that Scott proposed were substantially these:

1. Shipments of petroleum products would be allotted, 45 percent to the Pennsylvania, and 27½ percent each to the Erie and the New York Central.
2. The railroads would significantly advance their freight rates, in some cases more than doubling them.
3. The members of the South Improvement Company would be refunded all, or nearly all, of the increased fees. Thus, for members, the net cost would be essentially zero.
4. The increase paid by non-members, estimated to average one dollar a barrel, would also be turned over to the company members.
5. The railroads would report daily to the South Improvement Company complete details of shipments by competitors.[11]

Under this arrangement, Bostwick would not only receive a rebate of $1.06 on every barrel he brought from Titusville to New York, he would also get $1.06 for each barrel shipped by his competitors, who would pay the full rate of $2.56.[12]

Historians of Standard Oil have been aghast at the effrontery. John T. Flynn wrote that "a more deadly arrangement for the destruction of rivals could hardly be invented,"[13] and Allan Nevins called the "savage and destructive drawbacks…utterly indefensible.…The favored refiners were to be given such a crushing advantage over all competitors as to assure the complete ruin of the latter....Of all devices for the extinction of competition, this was the cruellest and most deadly yet conceived by any group of American industrialists."[14] As Ron Chernow said, "This wasn't simply a new competitive threat: It was a death warrant."[15]

The refiners involved in the South Improvement Company assured the railroads that they represented the bulk of the refining business.[16] In fact they did not, but they set out to remedy that.

The first person the Standard Oil men approached was Bostwick's friend, Colonel Oliver Payne.[17] Oliver was the grandson of Nathan Perry, the chief rival of John Jacob Astor in the fur trade, and the leading merchant in Cleveland. Nathan's daughter Mary married Henry B. Payne, a successful lawyer, and her dowry so enhanced Henry's fortune that he became one of the wealthiest of Ohio's business leaders, which provided the springboard for his entry into politics. Their second son, Oliver Hazard Payne (named after a relative, Oliver Hazard Perry, the victor in the Battle of Lake Erie) entered Yale in 1859, but left on the outbreak of war because, unlike many young men who saw the war as the way to build a fortune, he chose to fight. After his father secured him a commission as a lieutenant in an Illinois regiment, Oliver saw much action and was promoted to colonel. He was seriously wounded at Chickamauga, but after a recovery of several months was able to rejoin his regiment. However, the Atlanta campaign so depressed him that he resigned in November 1864.[18]

Oliver's father then gave him $20,000 so that he could enter the oil business,[19] and his refinery became the Standard's strongest competitor in Cleveland.[20] Although Jabez had long shipped Oliver's oil, there was no love lost between Colonel Payne and John D. Rockefeller.[21] W.A. Swanberg wrote that Payne was "a trifle impersonal, seeming always to keep himself in a close rein, felt by some to be toplofty because he came from a mansion on Euclid Avenue in Cleveland and had gone to one of the most prestigious of preparatory schools....He was militarily erect, decisive, and to outsiders so formal and possessed of such seeming hauteur that Henry Flagler...described him as 'kin to God'."[22]

At that time the country's refinery capacity was more than double the crude being pumped,[23] and when Rockefeller met Payne he told the Colonel that the oil business of Cleveland was doomed unless the leading refiners got together. He then offered to purchase Payne's company, but Oliver was skeptical of John D.'s claims about the Standard's efficiency. However, when he was shown the Standard Oil ledgers, the profits astounded him.[24] Rockefeller was so eager to bring Payne aboard that he paid him $400,000 for his refinery, although it was appraised at only $250,000.[25] To demonstrate the Standard's regard for Oliver, and to cement his loyalty, the company named him its treasurer, and he was invited to share a private office with John D. and Flagler.[26] However, according to Ida Tarbell, the clincher was the threat of being left outside the South Improvement Company.[27]

Rockefeller and Flagler now unleashed the blitzkrieg that historians labeled *The Cleveland Massacre*.[28] Tarbell claimed that Rockefeller told the refiners that "there is no chance for anyone outside," and threatened that "it was useless to resist,...they would certainly be crushed if they did not accept his offer."[29] Within three months' time, of the twenty-six Cleveland refineries, at least twenty-one sold out.[30] As each refiner acceded, Rockefeller and Flagler demanded total secrecy. Each party retained its own name and all pretended to be in active competition with each other.[31] With this coup the Standard Oil Company consolidated over one-fifth of the refining capacity of the United States.[32]

Once the South Improvement Company had fully taken shape, its stockholders included Bostwick, Flagler, Payne and the Rockefeller brothers, each with 180 shares, for a total of 900, which gave them 45 percent of the company.[33]

Tarbell tells us, "A little more time and the great scheme would be an accomplished fact," but fate intervened. The Lake Shore Railroad's freight agent had a son on his deathbed. Distracted, he left his office in charge of subordinates, but forgot to tell them that the new schedules on his desk were top-secret. On February 26 the subordinates put them into effect.[34]

In her *History of the Standard Oil Company*, Ida Tarbell described the effect on the men of the oil regions: "Suddenly, at the very heyday of (their) confidence, a big hand reached out from nobody knew where, to steal their conquest and throttle their future."[35] The next day, in John T. Flynn's words, "The streets of all Titusville were black with angry men....(They) talked of violence, of burning refineries, of tapping tanks, lynching the leaders....When the full force and meaning of the proposed drawback was understood, the fury of their anger knew no bounds."[36]

The oil producers convened a meeting of the Titusville Oil Exchange to deal with Bostwick's employees, Daniel O'Day and Joseph Seep. Nevins tells us that "O'Day ... who did not yet know that his employer had joined the combination, denied any connection. Indignant producers surrounded him, yelling, gesticulating, and threatening him with physical violence. They also menaced Seep...who had risen from a sick-bed to go to the meeting on crutches. Facing the infuriated men, both feared for their lives."[37] O'Day was tried, found guilty, and ordered to resign from the Exchange.[38]

The Titusville Herald reported that both men "were advised to leave town unless they wished to be tarred and feathered and ridden out on rails."[39] Their refusal to be intimidated earned Tarbell's praise: "Almost every other employee fled, the principals in the miserable business took care to stay out of the country, but Mr. O'Day and Mr. Seep polished their shillalahs and stood over their property night and day until the war was over."[40]

The Rockefeller brothers and Bostwick also stood firm. On March 23 John D. wrote to his wife, "I haven't any idea of giving up ship." But only five days later the railroads caved in, and soon after that, the Pennsylvania Legislature repealed the South Improvement Company's charter.[41] This forced the men of Standard to change their strategy. They must return to their original plan, and do in the whole country what they had done in Cleveland, consolidate the refiners into one company.[42]

Consolidation

The first two they enlisted were Charles Lockhart and W.G. Warden, the leading refiners in Pittsburgh and Philadelphia, respectively. Both had been participants in the South Improvement Company, so were already convinced of the benefits of combination. After Lockhart and Warden, the men that Standard most wanted were the very ones who had most vigorously opposed the South Improvement Company. It was their determined opposition that proved their spunk – just what the Standard needed.

Charles Pratt had been in the oil and paint business since 1850.[43] *Scientific American* described Pratt's refinery as "one of the largest of its kind in the United States, and [it] does an enormous export business in addition to its large domestic trade, in which the article known as Astral Oil figures largely and is justly esteemed as one of the safest and best kinds of kerosene sold in the American market. This establishment is a model in its way."[44] In 1868 Pratt had brought into his company Henry Huddleston Rogers, the son of a New England sea captain. Thomas Lawson wrote: "This man's every feature bespeaks strength and distinction....His square jaw tells of fighting power, bull-dog, hold-on, never-let-go fighting power."[45] Rogers was also an inventor, who patented an apparatus for separating naphtha fractions from kerosene and for dividing naphtha into its component parts."[46]

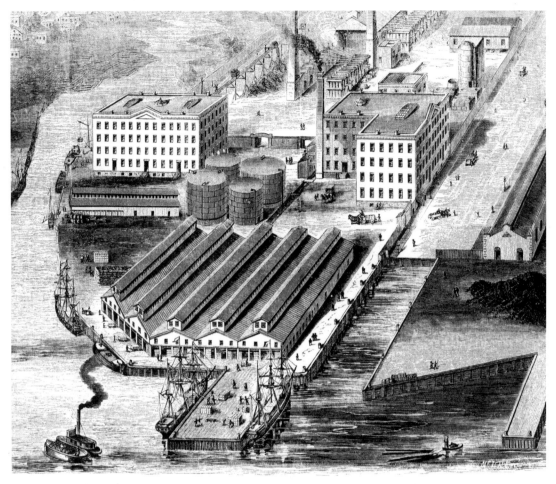

PRATT'S ASTRAL OIL WORKS,
BROOKLYN, E. D.,
OIL HOUSE OF CHARLES PRATT,
Office, 108 Fulton Street.   [Established 1770.]   New York.

In chapter one, we learned that Pratt's Astral Oil was the only kerosene to gain the approval of Professor Chandler. The Standard Oil men were masters at persuading former opponents like Charles Pratt to join them. Soon almost all the industry's leaders were inside the tent.

In October 1874, Lockhart, Warden and Pratt turned over their companies to Standard Oil. As before, the transactions were kept entirely secret.[47]

The next target was the Oil Creek refiners, who had opposed the South Improvement Company the most strenuously of all. Foremost among them was Captain Jacob J. Vandergrift, owner of the Imperial Refinery, the largest in Oil Creek.[48] According to Chernow, "his desertion to Standard Oil was considered treasonous betrayal, and it demoralized local independents."[49]

The final recruit was the most reluctant. John T. Flynn recounted that when the South Improvement scheme was revealed, the producers met at Love's Opera House in Oil City. "A young man arose – small, thin, pale-faced, looking like a young divinity student. He was John D. Archbold. He told in tones full of scorn how he had been approached by the conspirators and sworn to secrecy. He denounced the 'conspiracy' and called on producers and refiners in the regions to 'unite against the common enemy'."[50]

Austin Leigh Moore described the proposition that was put to Archbold: "Join us and we will pay you well in Standard Oil stock for your plant. We will also make you a director of the Standard Oil Company of Ohio. As part of the bargain, you will be expected to purchase, either with cash supplied by the Standard, or with Standard stock, all of the refineries along the creek. All arrangements are to be kept secret to prevent the development of organized opposition to the plan."

Archbold saw that the cause of the independent oil refiner was lost, and he signed on.[51] In September 1875, Standard Oil formed a front organization, the *Acme Oil Company*, to take over local refiners under Archbold's guidance. Within three years he had bought or leased every independent refinery in the oil region.[52]

With the recruitment of Archbold, the Standard Oil men reached their initial goal; they had lured all the able oil men into their tent. In Flynn's words, "All the leadership in the oil industry was in that group – outside there was no leadership. Rockefeller had literally raided the oil business and confiscated all its brains."[53]

The next task was to acquire the lesser independents. As they succumbed, some of their refineries were upgraded, but most were pulled down. Ida Tarbell quotes Rockefeller on the losers: "We want only the big ones, those who have already proved they can do a big business. As for the others, unfortunately they will have to die."[54]

The Standard Oil men later claimed that they had attempted to acquire all their rivals, but as Flynn explained, "Those who would not come in would be crushed."[55] The most effective way of crushing a recalcitrant was by denying him access to transportation. New York was served by two railroads, so Standard Oil set out to gain control of both terminals. The Standard's ownership of Bostwick's company was still a secret, so it was decided that if he operated one terminal and Standard Oil the other, they would appear to be in competition. Accordingly, Jabez gave up his contract with the Erie and purchased the New York Central's 65th St. terminal, and then Standard Oil took over the Erie's terminal. Implausibly, Jabez later denied knowing anything about Standard's contract with the Erie. When asked under oath, "Then you necessarily must have known…in whose hands the Weehawken docks were?" he answered, "No sir; I do not think that I would."[56] Allan Nevins did not believe him, and alleged that Bostwick, familiar with the Weehawken terminal, aided the Standard in knitting it into their system.[57]

To maximize the efficiency of the two New York operations, Jabez Bostwick and William Rockefeller persuaded the city to permit crosstown and underwater pipelines linking both terminals to the Standard Oil refineries at Hunter's Point in Queens.[58]

As the New York Central owned no tank cars, Jabez purchased a substantial number, and eventually owned all the cars that ran on that railroad. When asked whether other parties were permitted to ship oil through his terminal, he later testified:

"Whenever we are not using the cars."
"Does it ever happen that you don't want the cars?"
"Very rarely."[59]

Standard Oil made excellent use of its chokehold on transportation. When the company was attempting to bring Josiah Lombard, an independent New York refiner, to heel, he found constant difficulty in obtaining cars from the Erie because Pratt & Co. had "engrossed its facilities," and the New York Central also discriminated against him.[60] It was not until much later that Lombard discovered that both Bostwick and Pratt were acting for Standard Oil. Ida Tarbell concluded that "there seemed to be no end to the ways of making it hard for men to do business, of discouraging them until they would sell or lease, and always at the psychological moment a purchaser was at their side."[61]

The most egregious feature of the South Improvement scheme had been the drawback on other people's shipments. As soon as Standard Oil was strong enough, Daniel O'Day demanded just such a drawback. The New York Central, the Erie and the Pennsylvania all complied, and paid Standard Oil from 20 to 35 cents on every barrel shipped by the company's competitors.[62]

Exerting Power

By 1876, Standard Oil controlled refining to such an extent that the company could put into effect what it had been organized to do, control prices. In late August, kerosene sold at 21⅜ cents a gallon, but in September the Standard Oil refineries, acting in unison, demanded 26 cents. The exporters refused to pay, and by the end of October New York harbor was full of empty ships. But, observed Tarbell, "Europe had to have its light," and in November the buyers gave in. The Standard kept on pushing, and in December forced the average price up to 29⅜ cents, an advance of nearly 40 percent in four months, vivid proof of the leverage that a business can exert when it has no competitors.[63]

It did not take long for Jabez Bostwick to find an opportunity to impose similar control over the producers. In late 1875, a rich new oil field was discovered at Bradford, northeast of the original oil area. One producer boasted that he could lay out wells "like rows of corn, and every well would be a success." Production in the Bradford field soared, rising from 348,000 barrels in 1876 to 1,346,000 in 1877, and then to 6,180,000 in 1878.[64] Consequently, the price of crude, which had reached $4.23¾ a barrel in December 1876, plummeted to 78¾ cents in September 1878.[65]

Up until then it had been the Standard's practice that if a producer wished to hold out for a better market price the company would store his oil as long as he wished, for a small storage charge.[66] Jabez took advantage of the leverage that the Bradford field gave him, and announced that henceforth he would store only one-fourth of a man's production, and would pay market price or less for the balance.[67] To educate the producer to sell below market, Daniel O'Day let the oil spill on the ground for a few days.[68] Then Jabez introduced a particularly demeaning twist. Up until then the buyer and seller had met freely in the oil exchanges or in their business offices, and transactions had been carried on as among equals. Now the producers were obliged to form in a line before the buyer's office. A hundred or more humiliated men stood hour after hour, waiting to be admitted one by one.[69] As Nevins explained, "To the sturdy individualists of the Regions standing in line was a gross indignity."[70] Typically Bostwick's representative opened negotiations by offering a price twenty percent below market. Then, after a producer had made his counteroffer, he was usually told to come back in ten days to see if Jabez wanted it or not. Even when a price was struck, Jabez stalled on payment.[71]

Bostwick's brutal methods came near to provoking insurrection. Ida Tarbell wrote that, "this long line of men began to talk of revolution,"[72] and Flynn said, "A kind of demoniacal rage greeted this announcement."[73] According to Henry Demarest Lloyd, "processions of masked men marched the streets, and groaned and hooted in front of the newspaper offices and the business places of the combination….One thousand men, wrapped in white sheets, marched by night from Tarport to Bradford, the headquarters in that province of the sole buyer."[74] As Tarbell recalled, "Mysterious things, cross-bones and death-heads, were found plentifully sprinkled on the buildings owned by the Standard interests….It was certain that a species of Kuklux had hold of the Bradford region."[75]

In frustration, the producers turned to the courts. On April 29, 1879, the Grand Jury of Clarion County, Pennsylvania, indicted Bostwick, O'Day, the Rockefeller brothers, Flagler, Lockhart, Vandergrift and others on several charges, including "a conspiracy for the purpose of securing a monopoly of the business of buying and selling crude petroleum, and to prevent others than themselves from buying and selling and making a legitimate profit thereby."[76] However, according to Nevins, "The fact that the producers had committed a tactical error in forcing the indictments for conspiracy was soon clear as noonday."[77]

Chapter 5

In order to keep adversaries in the dark, Standard Oil made all its moves in total secrecy. For many years, oil producers sold their crude to Jabez Bostwick's buyer, Joseph Seep (pictured here), not realizing that J.A. Bostwick and Co. was a front for Standard Oil. The policy of secrecy culminated in Jabez Bostwick's pleading the Fifth Amendment before New York State's investigating committee so that he would not have to divulge the scope of the company's activities.

The Hepburn Inquiry

Six weeks after the indictment, the New York legislature launched its own inquiry, under the chairmanship of a young reform-minded legislator, Alonzo Barton Hepburn.[78] The Hepburn Committee did not have the power to subpoena John D. Rockefeller, a resident of Ohio, nor could it gain access to the books of Standard Oil, legally a "foreign" company, but it did manage to call Archbold, Rogers, and Bostwick.

Because the Acme shares were held by three figurehead trustees, Archbold was able to deny that the Acme Oil Company was in any way connected with Standard Oil. In fact he insisted that he was in active competition with Standard Oil. Charles Pratt and Company was also owned by trustees, but when pressed, Rogers explained that it worked *in harmony* with Standard Oil.[79] Then he made a startling admission: from 90 to 95 percent of the refiners in the country were working in harmony.[80] This was the first public acknowledgement of the extent of the combination's success. Both Archbold and Rogers admitted that Jabez Bostwick was a director of Standard Oil, so the spotlight swung to him. The committee's counsel, Simon Sterne, said that Jabez was "the only witness that we have who is notoriously one of the Standard Oil Company."[81]

Jabez did not appear until he had been summoned three times. Then he arrived without a lawyer, stood by the witness chair, hat in hand, and tried to talk his way out of testifying.[82] He based his argument on a novel premise, which we know today as *pleading the fifth*. "I am placed in a little peculiar position. I am one of the directors of the Standard Oil Company of Cleveland, and as such, have been indicted in the State of Pennsylvania (for conspiracy); and although there is no ground for this indictment, whatever, in my opinion, yet…a number of people who have not been quite as successful in business, and do not keep up their end of the stick, as the saying is; they went before a Grand Jury…and had this indictment brought against us… parties who have freely stated that they expected to get evidence before this Committee, which would be very valuable, before the trial....Now I have no objection to answering very many questions that may come forward (but) they would be construed, perhaps, in the Pennsylvania courts unfavorably, although there is no reason for so doing; therefore, with this indictment on me, I want to ask the Committee to excuse me from answering questions."[83]

Hepburn refused the request, and when Jabez reappeared, he was accompanied by his counsel, John K. Porter.

The witness then answered several questions until asked about freight rates, to which he responded, "I do decline to answer this question on the ground that it may be used in the coming trial there as a link in a chain of evidence, tending to prove that I have conspired in some way or other."[84] Porter defended Jabez by stating that, "it is one of the essential guarantees of American right that no man shall be convicted of crime upon his own evidence unless it be voluntary; that he shall not be compelled to furnish evidence to aid in his own conviction."[85] Hepburn was obliged to concur: "I think, as a matter of law, that the position which the witness has taken here is substantially correct."[86]

Jabez answered several more questions but declined to name the firms connected with Standard Oil or explain whether Rogers' term "harmony" implied that the Standard owned stock in the various firms or vice versa. He eventually refused to answer more than thirty questions, including what firms were operating in harmony with Standard Oil, whether Acme or Charles Pratt & Co. was affiliated with the company or what a Standard Oil share was worth. Jabez did admit that he knew John D. Rockefeller, but refused to say what positions he and John D. held in the company. When asked, "Do you deny that you are connected with the Standard Oil Company?" Jabez replied, "I do not answer the question; I don't say I am not, and I don't say I am."[87]

By pleading the Fifth Amendment, Jabez successfully thwarted Hepburn's aims. In frustration, the chairman exploded: "Are we to go back to the Legislature and say to them that there is such a thing as the Standard Oil Company, that we don't know anything about it, who comprise it, what its business is, but that we know that it controls ninety percent of the shipments of oil, and one hundred percent of the transportation, and yet we can't find out anything from anybody?"[88]

In its report, the Hepburn Committee noted that it was "unable to ascertain the exact relations of these different organizations, owing to the refusal of several members...subpoenaed as witnesses to obey the subpoena, and the refusal of those who did attend to answer our questions." The committee referred to the combination as "this mysterious organization, whose business and transactions are of such a character that its members declined giving a history or description of it, lest their testimony be used to convict them of a crime."[89]

Combination

Henry Rogers had now revealed, and Jabez had not denied, that almost all American refining was in the hands of Standard Oil. The company was, in John T. Flynn's words, "the most complete monopoly that had yet been built in American industry."[90] However, the men of Standard Oil never called their creation a monopoly; it was a *combination*. Rockefeller later wrote: "It is too late to argue about advantages of industrial combinations. They are a necessity....combinations of capital are bound to continue and to grow....The day of individual competition in large affairs is past and gone."[91]

Rockefeller was not alone in questioning the merits of competition. The economist Joseph Schumpeter was particularly vigorous in his criticism: "The large-scale establishment...must be accepted as a necessary evil....Perfect competition is not only impossible but inferior....In the last resort, American agriculture, English coal mining, the English textile industry are costing consumers much more and are affecting *total* output much more injuriously than they would if controlled, each of them, by a dozen good brains."[92]

One reason for Standard Oil's success was the way in which its dozen good brains worked together. Rockefeller was no autocrat.[93] He once said of himself, "I had a bad temper—I think it might be called an ugly temper when too far provoked,"[94] but he overcame this impediment, and became the foremost team builder in the history of American business up to that time, and perhaps since.

The organization was not a dictatorship, but an oligarchy. The company's leaders met five days a week, at eleven a.m. The seating arrangement was fixed, with Charles Pratt, the eldest, at the head of the table.[95] Although the deliberations were secret and unrecorded,[96] Rockefeller has described the process: "We… discussed and argued and hammered away at questions until we came to agree.…It has always been our policy to hear patiently and discuss frankly until the last shred of evidence is on the table, before trying to reach a conclusion and to decide finally upon a course of action. …It was usually a compromise, but one at a time we took these matters up and settled them, never going as fast as the most progressive ones wished, nor quite so carefully as the conservatives desired, but always made the vote unanimous in the end." It was a remarkable team, each member a pronounced individualist. "It is not always the easiest of tasks to induce strong forceful men to agree," said Rockefeller, but there was no alternative.[97] Without such determined men, success would have been impossible.

Standard Oil now owned several companies under individual trusts similar to the one Flagler had crafted for the acquisition of Bostwick's company. This gave such effective protection that in 1880 Rockefeller was able to make a solemn affidavit that, "It is not true… that the Standard Oil Company, directly or indirectly through its officers and agents, owns or controls the works of Warden, Frew & Co., Lockhart, Frew & Co., J.A. Bostwick & Company, C. Pratt & Company, Acme Refining Company," etc. Nevins observed that "Legally this statement was water-tight.…Actually, to call the statement disingenuous would be putting it mildly."[98]

The Trust

However, the time had come for the company to reconsider its legal underpinnings. Standard Oil's practice of co-opting former enemies now paid off. At the time of the South Improvement Company, a brilliant young attorney, Charles C.T. Dodd, had made a fiery speech warning that the scheme was contrary to the law: "Unless we can give the people a remedy for this evil of discriminations in freight, they will sooner or later take the remedy into their own hands."[99] Dodd later became Captain Vandergrift's attorney,[100] and when Standard Oil needed an able corporate counsel, the company lured Dodd with a salary equal to that of the U.S. President.[101]

Dodd came up with an epoch-making scheme, the Standard Oil Trust.[102] Under the agreement, the shares in all the companies that Standard Oil had acquired were turned over to nine trustees, of whom Jabez was one.[103] As Nevins explained, "Legally this corporation did not exist. It had no legal name and no charter. When questioned, Rockefeller, Flagler and Dodd could say – with literal truth – that there was no all-comprehending company."[104] Ida Tarbell described the Trust as "a force powerful as gravitation and as intangible. You could argue its existence from its effects, but you could never prove it. You could no more grasp it than you could an eel."[105]

The trust agreement, signed on January 2, 1882,[106] was kept a profound secret, and it was not until 1888 that the public learned of its existence.[107] Aided by Dodd's invention, Standard Oil grew mightily, and in the eighties, according to Allan Nevins, "was the largest and richest of American industrial organizations – the largest and richest in the world."[108]

Chapter 6

The Naphtha Launch

"The great glory of the Americans is in their wondrous contrivances."
Anthony Trollope[1]

The Disadvantages of Steam

When Frank Ofeldt decided to invent an engine, there was effectively only one kind of engine in the world – the steam engine. For a century steam had ruled. Only John Ericsson with his caloric engine had offered a challenge, but with limited success.

In 1851 Charles Babbage, inventor of the calculating engine (forerunner to the computer) called for a better engine: "One of the inventions most important to a class of highly skilled workmen (engineers) would be a small motive power – ranging perhaps from the force of half a man, to that of two horses, which might commence as well as cease its action at a moment's notice, requires no expense of time for its management and be of moderate price both in original cost and in daily expense. A small steam engine does not fulfill these conditions."[2]

The nautical historian, W.P. Stephens, assessed the problem as it applied to small boats: "The disadvantages of steam increase in a rapid ratio as the size of the hull decreases; the weight of engine, boiler, furnace, tanks, and bunkers is excessive in comparison with the size of the hull, and this weight must, of necessity, be carried amidship, taking up space and in the best part of the boat. The heat of the furnace and boiler makes a small launch uncomfortable in any but the coldest weather, and is particularly trying in the smaller sizes of cabin launches; there are always smoke, coal dust, cinders, ashes, to say nothing of the smell of hot dirt and oil....A long time was required for starting the fire and getting up steam, and the furnace was slow in cooling after a run; then, too, it required the full time and attention of one man on any but the smallest launches to feed and tend the fire and remove the ashes."[3]

The experienced marine engineer, Edward T. Birdsall, added: "They are hot, dirty, liable to disastrous explosions, and expensive to run and keep in repair. One who has never been off for a day's pleasure in a small steam launch cannot imagine the amount of misery that one of these craft is capable of creating. The trip is usually extended beyond the capacity of the supply of fuel, with the result that the boat arrives home minus seats, lockers and floor boards."[4]

"That boiler," remembered the Reverend Malcolm MacDuffie, "though asbestos jacketed and neatly lagged in mahogany, was hotter than love in a haystack. That sturdy, slow-turning engine had a way of flicking oil onto your best girl's starchy dress, even if the canopy deck protected her bonnet from the funnel."[5]

Chapter 6

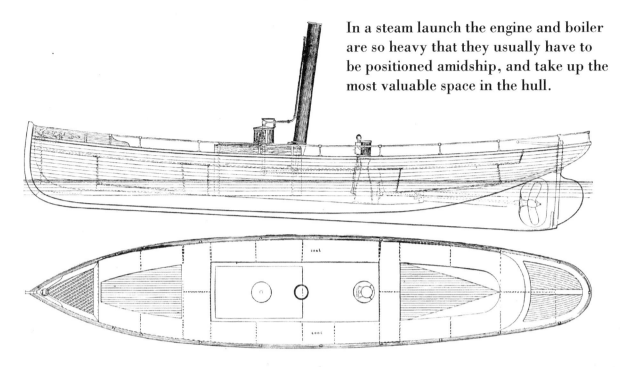

In a steam launch the engine and boiler are so heavy that they usually have to be positioned amidship, and take up the most valuable space in the hull.

The Mind of an Inventor

After the demise of Star Gas in 1881, Frank set up business in Newark as *Ofeldt Gas Machine*. In the patent for his previous invention, he had listed two purposes. Besides the manufacture of illuminating gas, the other purpose was to "provide a simple, cheap, and safe steam-boiler for light power, such as required for running a sewing-machine." Now he would elaborate on that idea, and design not just a boiler, but a completely new engine. His goal was ambitious: to invent a serious competitor to steam power.

In his experiments, Frank was assisted by his three older sons. In 1881, August Waldemar (Walter) was 22, Frans Axel (Frank A.), 20 and Ernst Gustaf (Ernest), 18. George, born in New Jersey in 1874, was only seven. It cannot be doubted that the sons made a significant contribution, for each later became an inventor in his own right. August was awarded six patents. Frank A., whose education ended at age eight before he left Sweden,[6] earned ten. Ernest was awarded no less than thirteen, and George, three.[7] Patenting continued into the next generation, with August's son, Frank W. Ofeldt II, inventing the *Hypressure Jenny*, the first steam cleaner ever made.[8]

Joel Mokyr observes, "The game of invention itself is the solution to a physical or chemical puzzle of some sort, and thus a game between a person and nature."[9] The more violent and unpredictable the force of nature, the greater the inventor's glory. Just as we are in awe of Nobel because of our fear of nitroglycerine, most people remember Frank Ofeldt not for what he did, but for what he dared. In Birdsall's words, "If it had been suggested to the present makers that a good launch motor could be made by using naphtha in the boiler, and giving no other details, they would have considered the proposition on a par with a suggestion to heat a house by burning gunpowder in the stove."[10]

How does an inventor's mind work?

John Hawkesworth wrote: "He who has laid up no materials can produce no combinations, for invention is but the power of arranging ideas selected from the stores of remembrance."[11] Although Frank had never previously designed an engine, he had worked with the naphthas for more than a decade, and had been issued several patents. There was no one in the world better prepared to design the naphtha engine.

Epiphanies

Many inventors, like James Watt, have recounted how, once they have pondered a problem for a considerable time, they have been struck by a flash of inspiration.

In Watt's day, "atmospheric" engines, designed first by Thomas Savery and then by Thomas Newcomen, were pumping out mines. A Newcomen engine was powered, not by the expansion of steam, but by its condensation. These machines were far from satisfactory. One engine could consume as much as thirteen tons of fuel a day, so they were expensive to operate, except in coal mines. There were several Newcomen engines in England, but only one or two in Scotland, and Watt had never seen one.[12] Glasgow University possessed a model of a Newcomen engine, and when Watt had an opportunity to test it, he was perplexed by its poor performance. At least three-quarters of the steam was wasted.[13]

In order to fully understand the properties of steam, he commenced his own careful tests. In the words of William Rosen, "Watt was a demon for measurement," and the effort took two years.[14] Eventually he satisfied himself that two ounces of coal would evaporate a pint of water, and produce 225 gallons of steam,[15] an amount that should perform much more work than a Newcomen engine could deliver. Watt concluded that the prodigious waste was caused by the alternate heating and cooling of the cylinder.[16]

One Sunday afternoon in the spring of 1765, Watt was taking a walk on Glasgow Green, when it occurred to him that the steam could be condensed in a separate vessel, rather than in the cylinder. He later recalled: "I had not walked further than the Golf-house when the whole thing was arranged in my mind."[17] According to Watt's friend, Dr. Joseph Black, "This capital improvement flashed upon his mind at once and filled him with rapture."

Samuel Smiles explained: "There was no accident in the discovery. It was the result of close and continuous study; and the idea of the separate condenser was merely the last step of a long journey – a step which could not have been taken unless the road which led to it had been carefully and thoughtfully traversed."[18]

Your author has a similar story to recount. In 1967 there was a world exposition in Montreal called Expo '67. My brother-in-law Roman Kroitor and I, as well as a number of our friends, made films for some of the pavilions. We pushed the cinema screens beyond their traditional limits, mainly by using multiple projectors, and had spent two years or more learning how to make films for these gigantic screens. The critics called these presentations "expanded cinema," and they became so popular that there were long line-ups outside our pavilions.

One evening, while Roman and I were having a drink at his house in Montreal, a thought occurred to us: "Wouldn't it be better to do this with a single projector?" Our objective was to have a screen ten times the size of a normal movie screen. This would involve a major change in the design of cinemas, but if we could do what we envisioned, it would be possible to put an Expo pavilion in every community.

This would be a new medium, with its own technology. As well as new theaters, we would need a new film format, new cameras, and new projectors. Our idea was to use a film frame of unprecedented size - approximately 2 x 2¾ inches – and we saw at once that we could put such a frame on 70mm film, moving horizontally. We would need a lamphouse three times more powerful than any then in use, and we would also need a novel wide-angle lens. However, our most daunting task would be to find a new projector mechanism that could handle the huge format without ripping film. We concluded all this in about 45 minutes, before dinner. Within a few weeks Roman and I, together with my high school classmate, Robert Kerr, incorporated the company that became IMAX Corporation, and set out to turn our concept into reality.

Serendipitously, an Australian named Ron Jones had just invented the very thing we were looking for: a new film movement called the *Rolling Loop*, and we were able to purchase his patent. As our partner, Robert Kerr, explains, "Ron told me that the whole concept of the Rolling Loop came to him in an inspired revelation one evening as he was driving home from (his workshop in) Archerfield. Since he was in heavy traffic, he was fearful that it would disappear from his mind before he could commit it to paper. On arriving home he began immediately on the mathematical and geometric calculations, worked into the late night and had the basic design before he went to bed. Early next morning he returned to South East Engineering Works (his small engineering company)…and began constructing the prototype. He was able to verify the basic utility of the Rolling Loop before noon. From inspiration to completion in 19 hours. The inspiration was not the result of a stray lightning bolt but was soundly based on Ron's lifelong curiosity, his fascination with all things, but most of all his superb knowledge of mechanics, optics, and electronics and a passion to understand the magic of cinematography."[19]

If Frank Ofeldt experienced a similar Eureka moment, it may have been the realization that in his engine he could use naphtha both as the fuel and the working fluid.

The First Naphtha Engine

On January 10, 1883 Frank filed a patent application entitled *Naphtha-Engine*, which issued on June 12 that year, and described the first, two-cylinder, version of his engine. Two more patents would complete the coverage. In the first patent, Frank began by stating that he had invented "a new and useful Improvement in Naphtha-Engines,"[20] echoing James Watt's modest insistence that he had not invented the steam engine, but merely improved it.

Frank's invention is often described as an engine that boils naphtha, just as a steam engine boils water. That is not what Frank claimed as his invention, and for good reason. Others had already tried to boil alternative fluids, going back at least as far as Watt.[21] In 1791 Robert Street suggested that turpentine could be used, and Michael Faraday observed that liquid carbonic acid possessed amazing elasticity, and he delegated Marc Brunel, Isambard's father, to construct a test mechanism.[22]

Was naphtha vapor really a better working fluid than steam? Donald Cardwell has grave doubts, and tells us that, "By about 1820 virtually all the possibilities of harnessing the expansive force of heat had been exhausted. …Experience and experiment showed that nothing was superior to steam as a working substance."[23] However, others disagree. Frank's selection of naphtha was vindicated by tests conducted under the auspices of *Appletons' Cyclopaedia of Applied Mechanics*. The experimenters concluded that, "the power obtained…was in the ratio of about 5:9 for steam and naphtha – that is, the same quantity of heat was turned into nearly twice as much work by the expansion of vapor as by the expansion of steam under the same conditions." Why was this? The report explained that, "Naphtha only expands to ⅕ the volume of vapor that water yields [but] a given quantity of heat will evaporate nine times as much of this naphtha as of water.…Hence, a given quantity of heat can produce ⁹⁄₅ times the volume of vapor from naphtha…that it would of steam at the ordinary atmospheric pressure."[24] Bill Durham cites another advantage: "As naphtha is nine times as easy to evaporate as water, a boiler of very small heating surface was adequate."[25]

The most notorious feature of the steam engine was its boiler, capable of rupturing catastrophically. To shield his invention from the opprobrium, Frank avoided the term "boiler," instead calling his version a *retort*, or *vapor generator*. In fact Frank's first design was unlike any boiler ever seen. As described in the patent, "The retort or vapor-generator [is] constructed of two heavy metallic plates cast by preference in a circular form, and bolted together face to face.…The inner surface of the lower plate…is grooved either spirally…or in a series of concentric grooves which are made to communicate by transverse channels…and it is covered by the [upper] plate…to form, in effect, a continuous conduit."[26]

Frank concluded that, in his engine, naphtha could serve three functions. Besides burning naphtha to heat the retort, and using it as the working fluid, naphtha could lubricate the engine. In the language of the patent, "A receptacle is…formed beneath the shaft to contain a supply of lubricating oil derived from the naphtha by its condensation, which will serve to lubricate constantly the cranks and bearings of the shaft."[27] Frank would retain that feature, with improvements, in his final 3-cylinder engine, leading Edward T. Birdsall to explain that "The novel feature of this engine, and the one that makes the use of an inflammable working fluid possible, is the draining of leaks from all possible sources into a tight crank case connected with the condenser.[28]

Naphtha

Further tests showed that it was best to use naphtha with a specific gravity between 0.68 and 0.70. "Below the former figure the petroleum does not lubricate satisfactorily, and above 0.70 it does not evaporate sufficiently rapidly."[29] At that time the American petroleum industry seldom rated its products by specific gravity, but instead had adopted the Baumé scale, an unfortunate choice because until 1922 there were two competing versions.[30] According to the version used by the naphtha launch manufacturers, a specific gravity of 0.68 to 0.70 translated into 76°–70° Baumé,[31] and that is why the naphtha catalogs advised, "Use 76° deodorized naptha."[32]

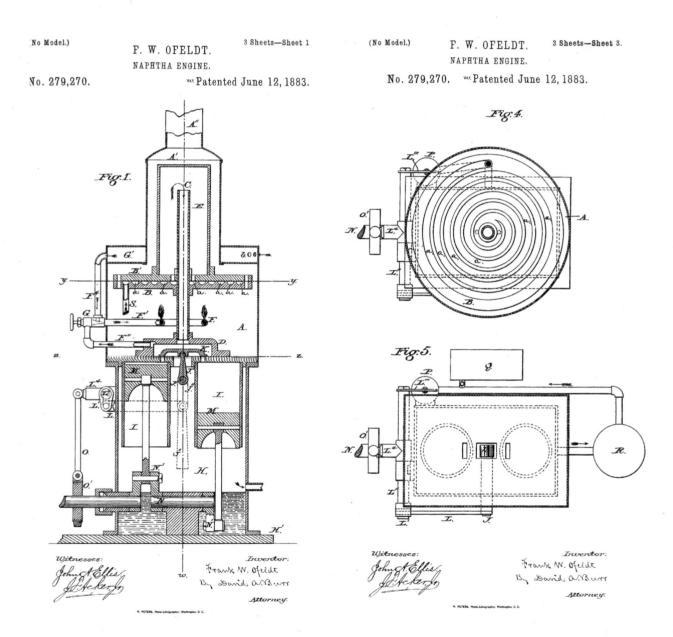

Frank Ofeldt's first design for the naphtha engine. This two-cylinder version featured an unusual spiral-grooved boiler, which he called a retort.

Chapter 6

Frank's patent did not define the engine's purpose, but as Kenneth Durant pointed out, "its manifest destiny [was to] be used for marine propulsion."[33] Weston Farmer explained that "The logical employment…was in a launch because abundant cooling could be had in a keel condenser consisting of a simple length of outboard pipe running along the garboard strake near the keel."[34] Known as an *outboard condenser*, this device had already been adopted in many small American steam yachts.[35]

Frank put his prototype engine in a boat, which he launched on New Jersey's Passaic River in 1883.[36]

Frank and Augusta Ofeldt in the prototype naphtha launch, along with their youngest son George, then nine years old. In designing the naphtha engine, Frank had a great advantage: during his experiments with the Star Gas Machine he had learned how to use the naphthas safely.

Finding a Business Partner

With the patent safely in his pocket, Frank faced a difficult decision, how to exploit his revolutionary invention? We know little about his experience with Star Gas, but that company was probably undercapitalized, and very likely suffered from a lack of marketing expertise. If the same thing happened to the naphtha engine, it would be fatal. This time the marketing must be impeccably executed, and the rollout must be rapid, or the enterprise would surely founder. What Frank needed was a backer with deep pockets and extensive business experience.

Did Frank give the decision sufficient thought? Many inventors do not, and then find themselves tied to unsuitable partners who let them down. There is one famous exception: Matthew Boulton, James Watt's business partner. The two agreed that Boulton would receive two-thirds of the profits from the steam engine. For a considerable time they did not bother to draw up a written contract, but Boulton took no advantage of the unworldly inventor.[37]

The perfection of the steam engine was attended by many failures and disappointments. Watt's biographer,

Samuel Smiles, tells us that, "For years Watt was on the brink of despair. He kept imploring Boulton to relieve him of his troubles; he wished to die and be at rest; he cursed his inventions; indeed, he was the most miserable of men. But Boulton never lost heart. He was hopeful, courageous, and strong—he was Watt's very backbone....He braved and risked everything....He mortgaged his lands to the last farthing; borrowed from his personal friends....During this terrible struggle he was more than once on the brink of insolvency....Watt never could have fought such a series of battles alone. He would have been a thousand times crushed; and, but for Boulton's unswerving courage and resolute determination…it is most probable that he…would have broken his heart over his scheme, and added another to the long list of martyr inventors."

In the end their enterprise was successful, and when the time came to dissolve the partnership, Boulton was characteristically magnanimous. Although the original bargain entitled him to two-thirds of the profits, he divided the proceeds with the inventor fifty-fifty.[38]

If there was one thing that Frank Ofeldt needed, it was his own Matthew Boulton.

It was natural for Frank to turn to the men of Standard Oil, for they were the most successful businessmen in the nation, and they were constantly on the lookout for ways to expand the market for petroleum products, particularly the naphthas. These men must have been watching Frank since the days of Star Gas, and when he came calling with his new invention, they would have taken him seriously.

Might Standard Oil itself be interested? John D. Rockefeller said that the company never went into outside ventures, but in fact it did.[39] Although the relationships were camouflaged, the men of Standard Oil set up, purchased, or encouraged a number of enterprises that aided the Standard in achieving its goals. Ostensibly these enterprises simply operated in harmony with Standard Oil. As an example, the Gilbert & Barker Manufacturing Company was already fabricating gas-making machines before Frank set up Star Gas. Gilbert & Barker not only sold machines, but supplied fuel to its customers, and by 1884 was supplying 75,000 to 100,000 barrels of gasoline annually. It had also branched out into the manufacture of metallic barrels and tanks. That year the Pratt Manufacturing Company, acting for the Standard, purchased a 75 percent interest in Gilbert & Barker, but left the company's management in place.[40]

How did the naphtha engine become Jabez Bostwick's project? Possibly Frank approached him first, or perhaps the Standard assigned Frank to him. We have no idea what logic the company applied in making such decisions. Just as Charles Pratt handled Gilbert & Barker, John Archbold, as we shall see, was given the responsibility of dealing with another inventor, Samuel Van Syckel. Frank and Jabez had one thing in common: Jabez too was an inventor, having patented several safety devices, including the Bostwick Gate.[41]

Jabez now lived in a stately five-floor townhouse at 800 Fifth Avenue overlooking Central Park, in the neighborhood where his Standard Oil colleagues resided.[42] Since 1877 he had made his country home on a 14-acre estate at Mamaroneck, Westchester County. According to *The New York Times*, the site was "one of the most beautiful spots on Long Island Sound," and his large Queen Anne residence was a model of elegance and beauty, with wide verandas offering a splendid view over the sound. Bostwick's stable was a magnificent edifice, three stories in height, 150 feet long, and 100 feet wide. William Rockefeller was a neighbor,[43] and Henry Flagler owned a 40-room mansion nearby.[44]

Yachting had become the rage among men of means,[45] and in 1882 Jabez took delivery of a 125-foot Herreshoff yacht, one of the most impressive craft in the New York Yacht Club's steam fleet of twenty-nine.[46] This provided another reason for Bostwick to be interested in the naphtha launch. Whether or not he yet realized it, Jabez *needed* a motorboat. Like his fellow yachtsmen, when anchored in harbor he had to have himself and his guests rowed back and forth to dock. Some yachts carried steam tenders, but they were heavy and expensive, so were found only on the largest yachts. If Frank Ofeldt's proposed motorboat succeeded, it would be a boon to yachtsmen.

Jabez and Frank soon struck a deal. Jabez agreed to buy Frank's patent and to fund the development of a production version of the engine.

Chapter 6

The Shipman Engine

Before commencing the new enterprise, Jabez must have given careful thought to the possibility of competition. The most likely challenger would be a small steam engine fueled by a liquid, rather than coal. In the early 1880s just such an engine appeared. Developed by A.H. Shipman of Rochester, New York,[47] and manufactured in Boston, the little engine burned kerosene. The manufacturer proclaimed, "No Dirt! No Dust!"[48]

Just as Frank Ofeldt was perfecting the naphtha engine, a potential competitor appeared, the Shipman steam engine.

The Shipman engine was promoted with suitable hyperbole: "One of the most perfect pieces of mechanism on the face of the earth,"[49] and it was described in *The Manufacturer and Builder* as "a practical motor of small power, moderate in cost and maintenance, of such simple construction as to be manageable by any one of ordinary intelligence in any situation, and safe against liability to explosion.…One of its essential features of merit consists in its entirely automatic action, in virtue of which, after steam has once been generated in the boiler, the machine requires no further attention on the part of the operator, beyond the opening and closing of the steam valve in starting and stopping it. The mechanism of the engine regulates the fire, speed and the water supply without outside intervention.… The Shipman engine is built in sizes from 1 up to 22 horse-power, and is adapted to every form of service for which engines of moderate power are required. They are specially serviceable, however, for boats."[50]

Jabez was not deterred. From Standard Oil's point of view, it was useful that the Shipman engine burned kerosene, but much more beneficial that Frank's engine might help reduce the naphtha glut.

Shipman engines burned kerosene, much cleaner than coal, but they could not compete with the naphtha engine, which was positioned aft.

49

The Gas Engine and Power Company

The first press mention of Jabez Bostwick's new enterprise appeared in *Forest and Stream*, December 31, 1885, under the title, "A NEW GAS ENGINE." "The New York Petroleum Gas Engine Co. has erected a two-story factory at Brown Place, mouth of the Kills, Harlem River, adjoining William Kyle's boatshop. They will manufacture engines for steam launches under a patent covering many novelties."[51] Jabez soon changed the name of the company to the *Gas Engine and Power Company*.

Mystery surrounds the ownership of the company. If the real owner was Standard Oil, the ownership would have been camouflaged, with the shares held either by a subsidiary, or by individuals. Frank's descendants knew that at least one of the owners was a Standard Oil man, but they didn't seem to know that it was Jabez Bostwick. Frank W. Ofeldt II said that, "Capital was quickly obtained from people connected with the oil industry (including) Mr. Rockefeller, Flagler etc.,"[52] and Ernest Frank Ofeldt, son of August, claimed that, "Pierre Lorillard and William Rockefeller were prominent shareholders."[53] Perhaps these names were just guesses; unless they can be corroborated it would be wise to discount them.

Bostwick's role was never mentioned in the company's publications. The first press reference we have found was in 1890, and it was only in his obituary that *The New York Times* made public that, "He was the owner of the Gas Engine and Power Company at Morris Dock, on the Harlem, where all the naphtha launches are made."[54] That was seven years after the company's founding, so it tells us little about the original ownership. Whether or not there were other owners, there can be little doubt that the company's purpose was to act in harmony with the Standard, and to advance the sales of naphtha.

Jabez installed his cousin, Clement A. Gould, as President and Manager,[55] and Gould chose *his* nephew, John J. Amory, as his assistant.[56] Frank Ofeldt's title was *Vice-President and Inventor*.[57] As the Bostwick yacht had been built by the Herreshoffs, he was familiar with their team, and lured 25-year-old Charles Lincoln Seabury from that company to be his plant superintendent.[58] L. Francis Herreshoff recalled Seabury's having worked in the boiler shop,[59] and Weston Farmer said that he had been a draftsman.[60] Very likely both were correct, as Seabury would become one of the world's foremost naval architects,[61] and was particularly noted for his innovative boilers. As office manager, Gould chose William J. Parslow,[62] who would later go into partnership with Seabury.

The Revised Naphtha Engine

Frank was now hard at work perfecting his invention, for which he needed a patent application before the first boat could be sold. We know very little about how his mind worked, but it's easy to conclude that, like James Watt, he must have been a methodical inventor, testing each innovation carefully and thoroughly. As many customers testified, all his machines could be trusted for their reliability.

Frank's first design change was to add a third cylinder, "avoiding the effect of the dead point of the stroke....The rotary motion produced is unaffected by the dead points, and continues uniform without the use of a fly-wheel."[63] Frank's grandson, Frank W. Ofeldt II, described the pistons: "A unique feature of the engine was the ball joint 'wrist pin' and this ball joint on the connecting rod allowed the pistons, which were without rings, to align perfectly in the lapped cylinders."[64] *Forest and Stream* reported that "The crankshaft is turned up in one piece, of cast steel, the single valve stem or more properly eccentric, that operates all the valves, is turned from solid stock, so no slipping is possible."[65] Johnston and Kerlin noted that "the great weight of the piston, by calculations 4.92 lbs....is probably twice as heavy as the ordinary piston of this diameter."[66]

Another major change was to the retort. Perhaps the steel plates, even though tightly bolted, leaked vapor, for Frank replaced them with a coiled tube. Although working pressure was 65 to 75 pounds, the coils were tested to 1,000 psi.[67] The company assiduously avoided the word "boiler," and stuck to "retort," but *Scientific American*

Chapter 6

was not fooled, and called it a "coil boiler, for such it is."[68] Frank W. Ofeldt II called it a "flash boiler."[69]

Another useful improvement was the reversing mechanism. "In order to regulate the slide-valves so as to stop and start and reverse the movement of the engine, I have provided…a hand-wheel, by which the gears are manipulated. This consists of a disk with a wooden rim….If it is desired to reverse the engine, it is only necessary to turn the hand-wheel…(or hold it back a little against the motion of the engine)…thereby turning the valve shaft,…and consequently reversing the valves, and thereby the engine."[70] The wooden rim allowed the operator to touch the wheel without getting burned. According to a company catalog, it is "operated without material exertion; in fact, can be reversed with the fore-finger and thumb alone."[71] L. Francis Herreshoff wrote that "A similar arrangement, but called a loose eccentric, had been used on small steam engines for it greatly simplified the reverse mechanism."[72]

For a detailed description of both engines, see Bruce Trudgen's *The Naphtha Launches*.[73]

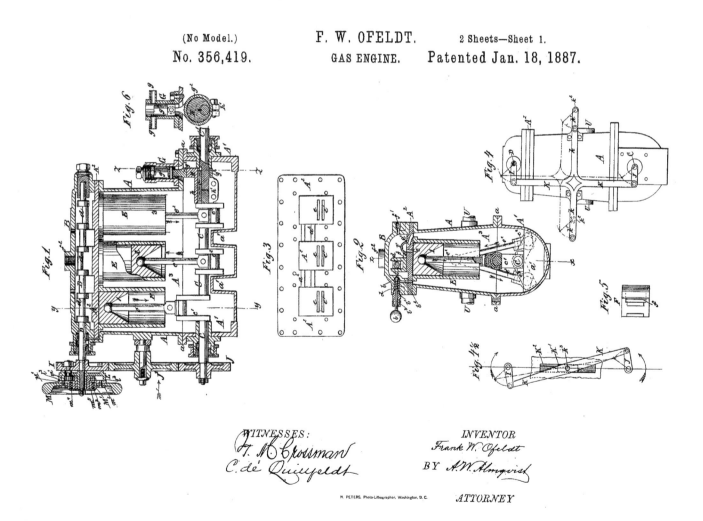

Frank Ofeldt's revised naphtha engine incorporated three cylinders.

Naphtha

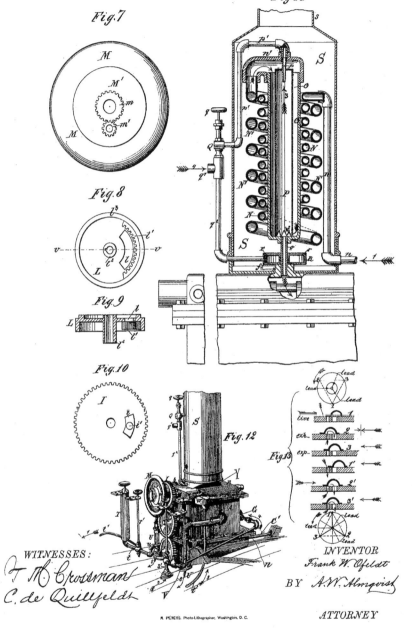

The revised boiler was very different from the earlier one, but Frank still called it a retort. As with steam engines, the naphtha engine could be reversed without the need for a gearbox.

D.W. Fostle points out that, "Since the engine operated at relatively low pressures – about half that of steam – it could be more lightly built."[74] In fact, Frank's naphtha engine was far lighter than its closest competitor, the Shipman.

	Naphtha Engine	Shipman Engine
2 hp	200 lbs	475 lbs
4 hp	310 lbs	806 lbs
6 hp	500 lbs	1,365 lbs
8 hp	600 lbs	1,400 lbs

The difference was even more dramatic in salt water, where the Shipman had to carry its boiler water – 1,500 lbs for a 4-hp engine for a ten-hour run.[75]

An important feature of Frank's engineering was that he made the parts interchangeable.[76]

Perfecting the Naphtha Launch

Once Frank had settled on the improvements to the engine, he set about designing the boat. As the naphtha engine was so much lighter than a steam engine, he decided to move it aft, thereby freeing the entire midship for passengers. According to a company catalog, "The small space taken up by our engine, in the *stern* of the boat, *gives more room*, enabling the boat to seat *twice* as many persons as a boat of the *same* size fitted up with any other engine."[77] *Forest and Stream* also praised the naphtha engine because it produced "no smoke; and the engine being aft the products of combustion and the smell are of no annoyance."[78]

Naphtha is notorious for the ease with which it leaks through joints. Frank lined the engine compartment with tinned-copper[79] (later sheet brass), so *Scientific American* was able to assure its readers that, "if naphtha burns there it does no harm."[80]

Weston Farmer explained that, to balance the craft, "a large supply of naphtha was contained in a vapor-tight tank in the bow of the vessel. This forepeak compartment was bulkheaded off by a vapor-tight and watertight partition extending from keel to deck. To keep the naphtha supply cooler, as it was continually heated and condensed, holes were grommeted through the forepeak planking to circulate water at whatever level it sought."[81] According to *Scientific American*, "water is continually going in and out, washing away any trace of naphtha."[82] Should naphtha be spilled during refueling, or the tank leak, the fuel would escape into the sea.

To avoid passing the fuel feed line through the passenger compartment, Frank placed it outside the hull, and, like the condenser, it ran alongside the garboard. Unless the boat was moving, the condenser was fairly ineffective. Frank's grandson explained how that was dealt with: "One of the things I remember particularly was the instruction to always run the engine backward when the boat was flat to the dock in order to force cold water under the boat to cool the condenser; otherwise the boat would blow up by the gas pressure created in the fuel tank."[83]

Herreshoff critiqued the design: "Naphtha launches were quite nice below the waterline where they were really double enders. Their sterns above water were of the so-called fan tail type and were made so to protect the rudder and propeller....They were not very good sea boats because of the weights at both ends and because they had no flare and little flam at the bow, but their low speed of six or seven miles per hour saved them from being too bad in this respect."[84] Weston Farmer disagreed: "The entire design proved to give good hull trim, with major weights far forward and far aft."[85] As we shall see, many owners who used their boats offshore testified to their seaworthiness, so perhaps Herreshoff was wrong.

During the course of 1885, Frank installed his prototype 3-cylinder naphtha engine in a 21-ft. launch. The 2-hp engine drove a 17" three-blade propeller, producing a speed of 5-7 mph.[86] Wilbur J. Chapman tells us that for at least 75 years that boat was brought out "on festive occasions to lead the parade or flotilla as the 'Father' of all gasoline-powered craft."[87]

The first three-cylinder launch, photographed in 1921 with two Gas Engine and Power Company executives, one of whom was probably John Amory, the president. The prototype launch, described as the "father of all gasoline-powered craft," was brought out on ceremonial occasions and continued in use for 75 years. Although the company's management intended to donate her to the Smithsonian Institution, she appears to have been lost.

Chapter 6

In the prototype launch, the controls faced aft, so it is clear that they were intended to be operated by an engineer or crewman. After the company decided to market the launch as owner-operated, Frank rotated the engine 180 degrees.

In photos of the prototype, one salient feature stands out: the controls are on the back of the engine, facing aft. This indicates that Frank expected the engine to be operated by someone sitting *behind* it, presumably an engineer or other crewman. This was in accord with the original target market, a motor tender for yachts. However, the promoters of the Shipman engine were already trying to open up a new market, owner-operators. To quote their promotional literature: "It requires no expert attendance,"[88] and "you can be your own engineer and fireman."[89]

Why not target the naphtha launch similarly?

Frank rotated the engine 180 degrees, and in all the boats built after the prototype, the controls faced forward. Now one person could easily handle the boat and also operate the engine. As the engine had no throttle, this was particularly important in docking.

Up until that point Clement Gould's market forecast probably totaled a few hundred units. If this boat could be operated without a crew – who knows? – the market might reach into the thousands. There was one glitch. By law it was absolutely forbidden for anyone other than a licensed engineer to operate a steam engine, an impediment that the Shipman promoters conveniently failed to mention.

How could Jabez get around that?

55

Chapter 7

The Steam Regulations

"Ofeldt had another thing going for him. It was the then existing fact that while to operate a steam outfit you had to have a license just to boil water, no license was required to boil naphtha gasoline with a torch under it. Isn't that a daisy?"

Weston Farmer, *Yachting*[1]

Evading the Law

In the early days of steam, boiler explosions were frequent, and often tragic. During an 1871 New York heat wave, George Templeton Strong opened the morning's papers to read the "sickening, heart-rending details of the frightful accident to the Staten Island ferryboat *Westfield*, which blew up at her New York dock yesterday afternoon, crowded with people—men, women, and very many little children....Baby has...been steamed to rags, and also papa or mamma or both; but it is too horrible to write about. Such hideous details I have never read. Not less than sixty are known to have been killed. More than twice as many are badly hurt, mutilated, or parboiled. Cause of all these unspeakable horrors—at which I have only hinted—an ill patched or cheaply cobbled boiler, and the absence of the engineer from his post for fifteen minutes. But 'nobody is to blame'."[2]

That year, in reaction to the public outcry, the government created the Steamboat Inspection Service, and required that steamboats on federal waterways be operated by licensed pilots and licensed engineers.[3] An owner who was sufficiently capable could take out a license as a pilot,[4] but although an engineer's license was fairly elementary, an applicant must have had two years' experience in tending a steam boiler.[5] According to Malcolm MacDuffie, "the old photographs of quite small steam launches show the owner at the wheel and a more or less grimey professional at the throttle. This presence [was] expensive, unwanted and more than a little ridiculous."[6]

A number of otherwise perceptive observers have been mystified by the government's failure to apply the steam regulations to the naphtha launch. L. Francis Herreshoff called it "quite strange,"[7] and D.W. Fostle said that it was "a regulatory absurdity that boiling water required a license but boiling gasolene did not."[8] Malcolm MacDuffie marveled that the government "never turned a hair at the prospect of white-flannelled starched-collared amateurs regulating high pressure gasoline vapor in contact with sizzling hot copper tubing."[9] Bill Durham credited the naphtha launch's bypassing of the steamboat inspection law to Ofeldt's "good fortune"[10] and Weston Farmer thought Ofeldt "lucky."[11]

If you think that the naphtha engine's exemption from the steam regulations was due to luck, I have a bridge in Brooklyn I'd be pleased to sell you. No business person whose competitor employs a lobbyist would ever believe that the drafting of legislation, or its enforcement, happens by accident.

The steam regulations were administered by the Treasury Department, so to obtain an exemption Jabez Bostwick had to appeal to the Secretary of the Treasury.[12]

How would he go about that? Could he argue that the naphtha engine was so much safer than steam that the regulations did not apply? Given the notoriety of naphtha, that argument was a non-starter. Jabez had only one hope: political influence.

Friends in High Places

The history of the steam engine provides an instructive lesson in the efficacy of political influence. When it became clear that James Watt's patent would expire before the engine could turn a profit, Matthew Boulton resolved on a daring course. He would appeal to Parliament for an extension, 25 years instead of the eight remaining. Only a man with friends in high places could hope to push through such a brazen proposal. The bill provoked violent opposition from the Cornish mine-owners, who had the support of many of the most powerful men in the House of Commons, particularly their own member of parliament, Edmund Burke, famed for his oratorical skills. Although Watt quailed at entrusting his fate to politicians, Boulton was unfazed. He had spent a lifetime currying favor in the halls of power, and was confident of success. The debate continued for two and a half months, but in the end Boulton's influential friends prevailed over Burke's eloquence, and parliament extended the patent's life for the period requested.[13]

Could Jabez Bostwick match that?

By now the men of Standard Oil had acquired considerable expertise in the art of influencing politicians. As Henry Rogers explained to Ida Tarbell, "They come in here and ask us to contribute to their campaign funds. And we do it,—that is, as individuals....We put our hands in our pockets and give them some good sums for campaign purposes and then when a bill comes up that is against our interests we go to the manager and say...'We don't like it and we want you to take care of our interests.' That's the way everybody does."[14]

Oliver Payne, as treasurer of Standard Oil, handled donations. After one disappointment he wrote ruefully to Rockefeller, "I wish to say that I have got through with sentiment in politics....We must see hereafter that there is one man in the Legislature from this County that has brains, influence and is *our man*," to which John D. replied, "Do all that is necessary."[15]

To Standard Oil, it had long been a corporate objective to increase the use of the naphthas, so enabling the naphtha launch to evade the steam regulations was a no-brainer. It was a simple matter of political clout.

The Democrats Take Power

Jabez Bostwick was a Republican, as were almost all the other Standard Oil principals.[16] Throughout the history of Standard Oil the White House had been in the hands of the Republican Party, so it was easy to get a hearing in Washington. Now Jabez faced an unexpected impediment. In 1884, for the first time in nearly a quarter century, the Republicans lost a presidential election, and in March 1885 a Democrat was sworn in as President.

The men of Standard Oil were not completely helpless. One among them, the company's treasurer, was a lifelong Democrat. For the next four years, Standard Oil's access to the Administration would have to be through Colonel Oliver Payne and his family.

When Oliver Payne was at Yale, he met William Collins Whitney, son of General James S. Whitney, formerly Collector of the Port of Boston. Although the General's administration was "efficient and satisfactory," he was a leader of the Massachusetts Democratic Party, so Lincoln removed him shortly after his inauguration.[17] Will Whitney never forgot that lesson.

Whitney's biographer, Mark D. Hirsch, recounted that Oliver was "enchanted by Whitney's personality and had spent much time in Will's room." After Oliver returned from the war, they resumed their friendship and Oliver soon concluded that Will was the ideal man for his sister Flora.[18] He introduced them, and in 1869 Will and Flora were married. The celebration was the year's most magnificent social event in Cleveland.[19]

Colonel Oliver Payne, the treasurer of Standard Oil, possessed such seeming hauteur that Henry Flagler described him as "kin to God." Among Standard Oil's principals, Payne may have been the only Democrat, a matter of crucial importance during the Cleveland years.

When William Whitney met Oliver Payne at Yale, Oliver decided that Will was just the man for his sister, Flora. After the marriage, Oliver gave Flora a large block of Standard Oil shares, so from then on, Oliver's partners considered Will to be a member of the Standard Oil family.

In 1875, Whitney, who had been one of the organizers of the fight against Boss Tweed, accepted an appointment as Corporation Counsel of the City of New York,[20] but a year later Mayor Wickham appointed the new Tammany boss, John Kelly, as City Comptroller. Whitney then joined with a number of like-minded Democrats to create a rival organization, the County Democracy, with the objective of taking the city back from Tammany. In 1881, to Kelly's dismay, the upstart organization swept local elections.[21]

A similar struggle was under way in Buffalo. John Milburn described how it brought a young lawyer, Grover Cleveland, into politics: "In 1881 municipal misgovernment and corruption in one form and another were so rampant in Buffalo that a movement was set on foot to elect a strong, able, and fearless mayor, and all eyes turned to Cleveland.... To get his consent was a hard and prolonged task.... There was to him no lure in the prospect of political honors. We gave him no peace, but it was only at the last moment that he surrendered."[22] Grover, not yet 45, was elected mayor by an unprecedented majority.[23] "As gruff as a mastiff,"[24] he immediately became known as the *Veto Mayor*.[25]

In 1882 there was to be a gubernatorial election in New York State, and on the eve of the convention an unlikely new candidate was suggested, the "veto mayor" of Buffalo. The response from state politicians was, "Cleveland? Who the hell is Cleveland?"[26]

Although Grover was a reformer, Will Whitney did not immediately warm to him, and said, "I think there is no more chance of his being nominated for Governor than there is in his being struck by lightning."[27] On the second ballot, out of 317 votes, the mayor stood third, with a paltry 71. At that point Whitney had a change of heart, and swung the County Democracy behind Cleveland, which won him the nomination.[28]

At that time the Chairman of the State Democratic party was Daniel Manning, who, in the words of Henry B. Graff, was "a journalist of considerable talent, during the Civil War he was legislative correspondent of the *Brooklyn Eagle*. Subsequently he worked at the *Albany Argus*…the most influential sheet in the capital."[29] Eventually he became the "shrewd and imperious" owner of the *Argus*, a successful banker, and the political boss of Albany.

Manning and Whitney now found themselves saddled with a candidate who was a complete novice. During the campaign, they kept Grover under cover, and he made no speeches.[30] However, voters felt that it was time for a change, and the result was a landslide. Cleveland, the greenhorn, was elected Governor of New York with a majority of 151,742 over all the other candidates.[31] Nothing like it had ever been seen in an American state.[32]

The new Governor and Daniel Manning "were much together. They had a good deal in common." According to Nevins, Manning was "a man of…great conservatism.…He had a firm grasp of financial principles,…and…kept (his) editorial page filled with sound money doctrine. 'It is folly and knavery to base money on any other than a gold standard,' he declared.…From him Cleveland derived a substantial stock of information, and still more a fixed set of convictions."[33]

Manning and Whitney were alarmed by Cleveland's propensity to antagonize people. "He had little tact, and no diplomacy.…He lost his temper frequently and sometimes unjustly; he could swear violently."[34] "He would fall into moods of stubborn anger and self-assertion, and refuse even reasonable requests with ill grace – with a stubborn jaw, and a heavy fist pounding the table."[35]

A frequent target of Cleveland's wrath was the Tammany wing of his own party. As the 1884 election approached, Grover was mentioned as a possible Presidential candidate, but if he had such ambitions, it was glaringly imprudent to antagonize Boss Kelly. As Nevins explained, "No Democrat could be President without carrying New York State; no Democrat, barring a truly extraordinary conjunction of circumstances, could carry New York against the full enmity of Tammany."[36]

Cleveland showed, in the words of Hirsch, "an almost reckless independence, if not contempt, for Tammany …which unleashed upon him its blazing fury."[37] On the eve of the Democratic convention, Kelly told the press, "I would regard Cleveland's nomination very much in the light of party suicide, and I hope it will not be done. It would kill us.…I will not lift a hand for him."[38]

One man swung the convention. General Edward S. Bragg of Wisconsin, in a speech seconding Cleveland's nomination, turned directly upon the Tammany delegates, saying that the young men of his state loved and respected Cleveland, "not only for himself, for his character, for his integrity and judgment and iron will, but they love him most for the enemies that he has made."[39] Bragg's speech was decisive, and Cleveland won the nomination by a crushing margin.[40]

The Democrats assigned Manning, Whitney, and Boss Gorman of Maryland to manage the campaign.[41] Cautiously, the trio permitted their candidate to make only two set speeches.[42] His opponent, James G. Blaine, a magnetic orator, spoke four hundred times.[43]

Whitney assumed the burden of raising funds.[44] Will himself was a substantial donor, and he raised the campaign's largest contribution from his brother-in-law Oliver, who poured $170,000 into Cleveland's war chest.[45] As it was the policy of Standard Oil to make its political contributions through individuals, there can be no doubt that a significant portion of the Payne money came from the Standard.[46]

The election was a squeaker. After several days of uncertainty Grover was declared the winner, but the tally could hardly have been closer. If a scant 575 New York voters had swung the other way, Blaine would have been President.[47]

The rapidity of Grover's rise was unparalleled in American history.[48] With no previous political experience he had been elected mayor in November 1881, and just three years later was thrust into the Presidency.[49] According to Rexford Tugwell, he was "the most unprepared President who ever succeeded to the office [and] was aghast at his own ignorance."[50]

From the outset Cleveland insisted on having both Manning and Whitney as cabinet members.[51] His first thought was to appoint Whitney as Secretary of the Interior, but the newspapers "raised the specter that Standard Oil would loot public lands."[52] According to the *Springfield Republican*, "There will be serious criticism…on the ground that he represents the Standard Oil Company and corporate monopoly,"[53] and the *Philadelphia Press* called him "Coal Oil Billy."[54]

Grover decided on Daniel Manning as Treasury Secretary. Samuel Tilden, the former Democratic Presidential candidate, also wanted Manning in Treasury because he was a banker and "a man who can command ready access to…the solid men of property and business." But Manning was not in rugged health, and desperately wanted to avoid a cabinet post.[55] William C. Hudson tells us, "He had attained his desires.…He had made a President. He was, by reason of his success, in absolute political control of New York State. He was the most distinguished political leader in the country, probably the most powerful. In arriving at that stage he had reached the summit of his ambition, and he wished to be left in peace to enjoy it."[56] Manning wrote to Tilden, "You must release me. The place has been offered but I have no heart for it. The very thought of it has made me ill for two days. The sacrifice will be too great, and I constantly feel that if I make it, I may as well bid good-bye forever, to comfort and happiness. I am *so* contented now and I will always then be miserable. Telegraph me tomorrow one word 'Released.'" But Tilden was unmoved, and forced Manning to accept.[57]

Cleveland now favored Whitney for the Navy,[58] a post that both Manning and Cleveland harried him to accept. The decision was made by Flora, who had her heart set on Washington, where she could be a luminary in the President's closest circle. When Flora cried, Will gave in.[59]

Whitney was appalled by the state of the Navy.[60] Ericsson's lesson had been forgotten, and most of the vessels had wooden hulls.[61] In Alfred Mahan's estimation, "[We] have not six ships that would be kept at sea in war by any maritime power."[62] Whitney was extraordinarily effective in his new role, and laid the foundation of a new American Navy. Cleveland was highly impressed by Will's acumen, and observed, "Whitney is right more often than any other man I ever met."[63]

Experienced politicians from both parties were firmly commited to the ancient doctrine, "To the victors belong the spoils," so Manning and Whitney were now discomfited to discover that the new President believed that he had been elected to end the reign of Washington's spoilsmen. The President's own supporters were the most offended. It was the first time in a quarter century that a Democrat could go to Washington in search of a job, and, as Matthew Josephson has pointed out, "There were 100,000 deserving Democrats, long-suffering partisans, who might at last be placed in office."[64]

Cleveland's opposition to distributing political plums had no effect on Whitney, who remembered how cold-bloodedly the Republicans had got rid of his father. Now he had the opportunity to even the score. W.A. Swanberg tells us that, as a "firm believer in the political use of patronage, he hired as many Democrats as possible."[65] Whitney also remembered those who had answered his call for campaign funds. Nobody had contributed more generously than his brother-in-law, Oliver Payne. Needless to say, Whitney's door was always open to the men of Standard Oil.

Chapter 7

The Standard's Influence

One of the first to come calling was Henry Flagler, who was then constructing a magnificent hotel in St. Augustine, Florida, the *Ponce de Leon*. Flagler had obtained permission from the city for the use of coquina (a sedimentary rock composed largely of seashells) from nearby Anastasia Island, provided he could obtain approval from the U.S. Government, which owned the quarry. Flagler's biographer, David Leon Chandler, recounts that, "Flagler was a personal friend of the Secretary of the Navy, William Whitney of New York, who secured permission through the Treasury Department for Flagler to use as much of the coquina as he needed."[66]

It was up to Daniel Manning, Secretary of the Treasury, to decide whether the regulations that governed steamboats should be applied to the naphtha launch. The safety of boiling naphtha had nothing to do with his decision. As an experienced political boss Manning was committed to rewarding his party's friends, so his door was always open to Colonel Payne's Standard Oil colleagues.

Hard on Flagler's heels came another Standard Oil insider, Jabez Bostwick, with a request that his new naphtha engine be exempted from the steam regulations. As the regulations were administered by the Treasury Department, just as with Flagler's coquina, the decision was up to Manning. However, Treasury's bureaucrats lacked expertise in marine engineering, so they relied on the Navy for advice. In fact, in some cases the Secretary of the Navy's findings were binding on the Treasury Department.[67] Even if Whitney and Manning had not been political comrades in arms, the Treasury Secretary would undoubtedly have deferred to Whitney's advice on the naphtha engine, for Will was deeply fascinated by new inventions and, unlike most Secretaries of the Navy, enjoyed reading technical books about marine engines.[68]

To Manning, the decision was simply a matter of politics. As co-campaign manager he was acutely aware that the Payne family had made the largest donation to the Democratic cause, so it is inconceivable that he would turn down any reasonable request from one of Colonel Payne's Standard Oil partners.

Daniel Manning's decision left no paper trail, so what proof do we have that he acceded to Bostwick's request? Evidence can be found in the Gas Engine and Power Company's first catalog, published in 1886, where the company announced unequivocally, "No license is required; no engineer needed." Had the statement been erroneous, the Treasury Department could easily have issued a denial, which it never did. Nor did the government lay charges against naphtha boat owners for operating without licensed engineers. Sherlock Holmes would have been satisfied with the evidence. If there was ever a dog that didn't bark, it was the Treasury.[69]

Chapter 8

Bostwick's Strategy

"Ferocity and cunning are of no use to the community except in its hostile dealings with other communities; and they are useful to the individual only because there is so large a proportion of the same traits actively present in the human environment to which he is exposed. Any individual who enters the competitive struggle without the due endowment of these traits is at a disadvantage, somewhat as a hornless steer would find himself at a disadvantage in a drove of horned cattle."

Thorstein Veblen, *The Theory of the Leisure Class*[1]

Introducing the Naphtha Launch

Many new products have faced entrenched opposition; Arkwright's spinning machine provoked riots, and the English landed gentry battled the locomotive for a generation. Other inventions, like the internal combustion engine, encountered such intractable technical difficulties that inventors had to continue tweaking their machines until long after the patents ran out. The naphtha engine suffered from neither defect. It threw no craftsmen out of work, and it was customer-ready even before the patent issued.

For the full seventeen years of the patent's life – well into the twentieth century – the Gas Engine and Power Company luxuriated in the sublime pleasure of monopoly. Frank Ofeldt's superbly-crafted patent was so unassailable that no competitor could get away with building naphtha engines.[2] Moreover, no other small engine was yet viable, so for at least a decade the company dominated the field of motor boating, which at that time meant all personally-operated motor vehicles.

Jabez Bostwick provided the Gas Engine and Power Company with adequate capital. Before the doors opened for business, the factory was turning out both 2 and 4 hp motors, and had on hand hulls of 18, 21, and 25 feet. Launches were ready for demonstration and immediate delivery.[3]

In the spring of 1886, Frank Ofeldt was up against a deadline: before the first engine could leave the shop, he had to finalize the design and file the patent application. That application, filed on June 25, 1886, reveals that Frank was still a Swedish citizen, and that he now resided in New York, not New Jersey. The patent, No. 356,419, entitled *Gas-Engine,* describes an engine adapted "particularly well for use to run the propeller of a launch, boat, or other vessel." The patent was assigned to the Gas Engine and Power Company, and issued on January 18, 1887.[4]

Not a few meritorious inventions have foundered because of bungled introductions. Jabez was no bungler.

Chapter 8

Six months before Frank filed his patent application, the company had initiated its marketing campaign with an announcement in *Forest and Stream*: "The whole thing is so simple that anyone can run it after 10 minutes' explanation. There is no dirt from coal or oil about the machinery. It is extremely light, and occupies only the two ends of the boat, thus leaving the middle body entirely clear for passengers."[5]

In the spring of 1886, the Gas Engine and Power Company issued its first catalog, which contains an interesting omission. Just as in the patent, the company's product was called a *gas engine*, not a naphtha engine. There was indeed an admission that "We expand Naphtha for power and use the same vapor in part for fuel," but no mention of boiling the dreaded fluid.

Naturally the company denigrated its competitors. The steam engine was deemed unsuitable because of its weight, the trouble and inconvenience of using coal, the resultant dirt, dust and ashes, and above all, "the necessity for obtaining a government license and engineer." Secondly, "All engines heretofore constructed to run by the use of oil" (presumably the Shipman engine, and possibly others) "have failed to meet the required demands. They are noisy, dirty, offensive to the smell, and lacking in speed and power."[6]

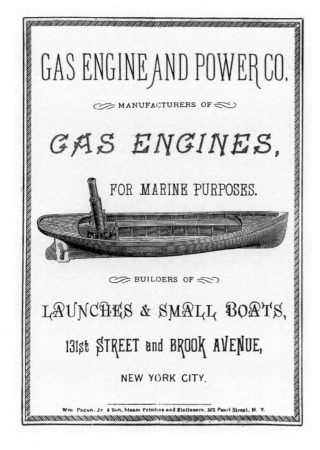

Because of the public's fear of naphtha, the company introduced its new product as a *Gas Engine*, not a naphtha engine.

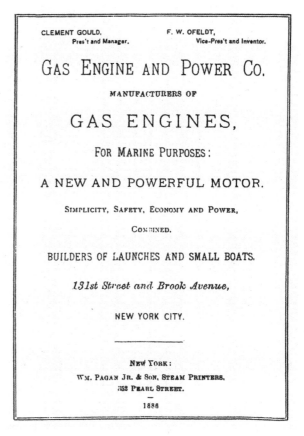

In the first catalog, Frank Ofeldt was listed as *Vice-President and Inventor*.

63

Naphtha

The Power of Celebrity

Jabez Bostwick was a member of the New York Yacht Club, so he naturally looked to his fellow members as potential customers. Jabez devised an effective strategy, based on the well-known phenomenon that celebrities set fashions. He would place a naphtha tender aboard the best-known yacht, in the hope that other yachtsmen would follow the leader.

The nation's most celebrated yacht was easily the schooner *Dauntless*.

During her twenty-year career, *Dauntless* had attracted flamboyant owners, most famously James Gordon Bennett Jr., son of the publisher of the *New York Herald*. In 1867, at age 22, Bennett purchased the yacht, *l'Hirondelle (Swallow)*, which he renamed *Dauntless*. Three years later he pitted her against the America's Cup challenger, *Cambria*, in the first east-to-west trans-atlantic race. The contestants were beset by gales, and *Dauntless* lost two men, swept off her jib boom while furling a sail. Bennett had engaged Captain Samuel S. Samuels, and there is a tale that the skipper, infuriated by his opinionated employer, threatened to put Bennett in irons. "No wonder his nickname was 'Bully'," wrote John Parkinson, historian of the New York Yacht Club. A few months later the club elected young Bennett as its commodore, so *Dauntless* served as the club's flagship during his three-year term.[7]

A later owner was the wealthy playboy, Caldwell H. Colt, whose father Samuel had invented the revolver.

The schooner *Dauntless* was the best-known yacht in America. In this painting by James E. Buttersworth, she is flying the colors of *l'Hirondelle*, as she was named before 1867, when James Gordon Bennett Jr. purchased her.

Chapter 8

Caldwell Colt's quarters aboard *Dauntless* give some idea of the lifestyle of a wealthy playboy during the gilded age.

Caldwell Colt (left) and Samuel S. "Bully" Samuels (right) aboard *Dauntless*.

In the seventeen years since the *Dauntless-Cambria* race, yachtsmen had not challenged the North Atlantic again. Then a businessman, Rufus T. Bush, offered to race his new, "wickedly fast" schooner *Coronet* across the Atlantic for a purse of $10,000.[8] Naturally Colt accepted, but insisted that the race be sailed in March instead of May, and he persuaded the 64-year-old 'Bully' Samuels to come out of retirement to skipper *Dauntless*.[9]

Parkinson described the race: "The press and public were highly excited by this match, thousands lined the shores, and there was a big spectator fleet at the start. …Old *Dauntless* was the favorite." As usual, March was stormy, and both yachts "had to heave to during one fearful gale…and both ran under bare poles in another.…*Dauntless*…was driven hard and leaked badly."[10] Midway through the race, the freshwater tank ruptured and ran dry. For the remainder of the voyage the crew was obliged to slake their thirst from Colt's champagne supply.[11]

Chapter 8

Although she was long in the tooth, and leaked badly, *Dauntless* performed valiantly in her race against *Coronet*.

Dauntless was ten feet shorter than *Coronet*, with less sail area,[12] so it is not surprising that she lost. Still she was America's most celebrated yacht. Every yachtsman knew *Dauntless*, and even before the race Jabez had selected her to receive the first naphtha tender. For the following ten years, every Gas Engine and Power Company catalog proudly featured a picture of that launch.

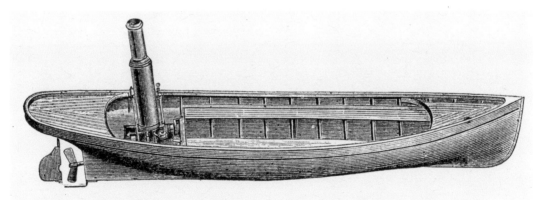

For ten years the Gas Engine and Power Company's catalogs featured a picture of the first naphtha launch the company had delivered.

67

Naphtha

Jabez Bostwick and Clement Gould set themselves the initial goal of selling a naphtha launch to every American yachtsman, and they very nearly succeeded. By the end of the second season, *Forest and Stream* reported that "Nearly all the schooners and steam yachts may be seen with the small brass stack which indicates the naphtha launch, in the stern of at least one of their light boats, while many sloops of moderate size carry one, or have one as an attendant when in port."[13] Among the first owners, besides Jabez Bostwick, were J.P. Morgan, (*Corsair*), as well as Jacob Lorillard, (*Daring*), and Pierre Lorillard, (*Reva*).[14]

Yacht owners supplied fulsome testimonials:

"I can only speak in praise of the engine. It is a powerful motor and an ingenious invention, and is, to my mind, the 'only' engine suitable for 'this' purpose. Its simplicity (for any one of ordinary intelligence can run it), its cleanliness and economy, are points in themselves that recommend it in the highest sense. I am sure no yachtsman who has ever had an opportunity to see the working of your engine could wish to be without one. There is absolutely nothing in connection with it but that contributes to one's pleasure and comfort. A chief point, also, is in its lightness, admitting of such easy handling, for it is no more trouble to hoist or lower the boat from the davits than my six-oared gig; and then there is no delay in getting under way. The launch is always ready, and in three minutes from the time she is in the water the pressure is up and she is ready for use."

W.H. Starbuck[15]

"I have built more than thirty launches for my own use, trying various motive powers, but have seen nothing to compare with your little naphtha engine for lightness, compactness, convenience and safety, and gladly recommend them to my friends as preferable to anything ever produced for the purpose."[16]

Jacob Lorillard[15]

Jabez Bostwick's strategy was a resounding success. Other yachtsmen followed the example of Caldwell Colt and within two years most American yachts carried naphtha tenders.

Chapter 8

In 1887 the company's second catalog no longer coyly described the new product as a gas engine, but boldly proclaimed it the *Naphtha Engine*, However, with this admission, the company had to deal with the obvious question, "Is it safe?" Rather than answering in detail, the words "they ARE SAFE" simply appeared in very large print.

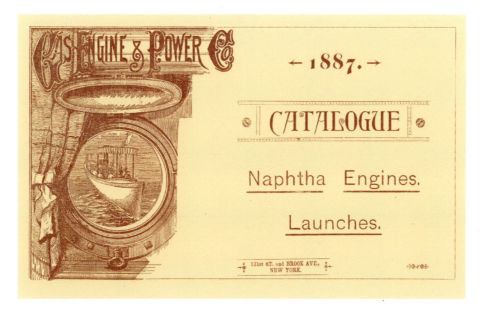

On the cover of its second catalog, the Gas Engine and Power Company called their engine by its real name, the Naphtha Engine.

In the second catalog the Gas Engine and Power Company made an attempt to assure its customers about safety, but the question would not go away.

69

Naphtha

In the second year of production the company offered more capacious boats including 35 and 40 footers of up to eight horsepower, the latter carrying 40 persons. Prices were quoted, both for complete boats and for engines alone.

Launches with Engines Complete

16-18 ft. 2 hp	Depending on Finish	$600-$800
20-21 ft. 2 hp	Yacht Tender Lap-strake	$850-$950
25-30 ft. 4 hp	Depending on Finish	$900-$1500
35-40 ft. 8 hp		$1800-$3500

Prices of Engines

2-Horsepower	4-Horsepower	8-Horsepower
$500	$650	$1000

The company explained, "We do not care to furnish Engines without the boats at present, unless the hulls are sent to our works for that purpose, or that we send a competent man with the motor to set it up properly. Owing to the fact that they are so entirely different from all others, it would be impossible for anyone to set them up in a manner satisfactory to the purchaser or ourselves."[17]

The second catalog contained a few clarifications:

1. Start-up time: "One to two minutes in warm weather; but in cold weather much longer."
2. "Nothing is used that comes in contact with sea-water, but brass and copper, and so, no galvanic action can occur to one metal to the detriment of the other."
3. The whistle is powered by the air pump, not by naphtha vapor.
4. "Use 76° deodorized naphtha (no other), which can be bought in any city, or ordered from us direct."[18]
5. "Use only alcohol in the lamp."
6. Speed is regulated by the injector valve, which supplies fuel to the burner.[19]

A Child Can Operate It

Once the Gas Engine and Power Company had cracked its initial market – yacht tenders – it turned to a second target, the general public. Up until that time, engines had seldom been operated by amateurs, but the company's catalog stated that, "a child of 12 years can run our engine with ease and safety."[20] Customers were now putting that to the test. In the words of Kenneth Durant, "Whereas steamboats could be run only by licensed engineers, anyone could run a naphtha launch – the amateur owner, his children, the camp caretaker and the chore boy."[21]

One attractive characteristic was the ease of starting. Malcolm MacDuffie, who had cranked a number of gasoline engines in his time, wrote that, "it was self-starting, a feature that was lost with the coming of internal combustion for years to come."[22]

Captain Chrystie McConnell (U.S. Coast Guard) learned how to operate a naphtha launch in 1898 when she was six. At age 75, she recalled the starting procedure:

"Picture yourself facing the engine, trying to get under way. Before you is a bulkhead, with its after side and the whole engine compartment lined with sheet brass, soldered at the seams to prevent any leakage from getting into the bilges. Mounted on this bulkhead are two pumps and two valves.

"You should have ready a fusee, or some wind-proof matches. Give a stroke on the pump to *your left*. If the whistle toots, turn the adjacent valve so that it doesn't toot. The pump will now pump vapor-filled air, from above the fuel in the supply-tank, to the burner – after several strokes, that is. Then stick the lighted fusee through the small hole near the pressure-gauge connection to the boiler. Keep trying until the burner ignites.

"After five minutes or so of this exercise, transfer your attention to the naphtha (gasoline) pump on *your right*. Keep the fire going this way until the gauge shows 50 pounds or so. Then give what appears to be a flywheel a slight turn, and the engine will start. (This hand wheel is really the reverse gear).

"Now that the engine is going, shut off the supply valve to the naphtha pump, because, from now on, the engine-driven pump will supply fuel.

"Look into the open butterfly valve on the brass pipe in front of the boiler, and you will see a jet of steamlike naphtha vapor on its way to the burner. This burner is, in principle, a Bunsen burner; the butterfly valve

Chapter 8

regulates the air mixture to give the clean, blue flame."[23] Although there is no throttle on this engine, it is possible to control the speed to some extent by manipulation of the fuel valve on top of the brass mixture pipe."[24]

According to *A Story of the Naphtha Launch*, "When a landing is to be made, close the injector, with a single turn of the hand, close the naphtha valve, tie up the ship to the landing place – and go ashore."[25]

It wasn't quite that simple. Bruce Trudgen explains how a skipper, lacking a throttle, managed the task:

"Once up and running, a naphtha engine could be slowed or reversed, but to stop it, you had to shut it down. With no clutch, the propeller turned whenever the engine ran. This posed a problem when docking. Timing was everything. You slowed the engine by partially closing the injector valve before reaching the dock. Next, you slapped the spinning wooden wheel to reverse the engine. Then, to stop the engine you closed the injector valve at just the right moment as the boat came to a stop. With a little luck, the boat would be resting quietly at its intended spot. A naphtha launch could be held in position by repeatedly reversing the engine rotation, but once you stopped the engine, you couldn't restart it quickly."[26]

If one needed to make an abrupt stop, a naphtha launch could be brought to a halt in less than five yards.[27] Chrystie McConnell described one occasion when this backfired:

"My affluent grandfather, who lived at Erie, Pennsylvania, had a 40-foot naphtha launch. My two brothers were some 21 years older than I, and the oldest, now dead nearly 60 years, was an engineer and so ran the launch engine. Grandfather had a boathouse with a nice padded slip that just fitted the boat. My brother had found out that, if he threw the control wheel into reverse, just as the bow reached the entrance to the boathouse, the launch would stop in her own length.

"One time, my brothers had a party of young friends along, and I, being only six years old, was left on shore. My engineer brother tried to make one of his 'cowboy stops' and was left staring at the control wheel in his hands. The pin holding it to the shaft had come out while the engine was still at ahead. My other brother, who told me of the crash and the pileup of people and cocktail glasses, always maintained that the statue of William Penn on the green nearby was moved several feet south of its charted position."[28]

Now that there were a number of owner-operators, the company printed their testimonials. Some, like C. Deavs, had previous experience with steamboats:

"I did not think when I first saw the Engine, that they were as powerful as a steam engine; but since running mine for one summer, I must say it surprises me, the power and steadiness there is in such a small Engine. They are easily handled; can start out in two or three minutes after lighting the gas, and in two or three minutes can regulate the valve, to the pressure I want, and then I have no more to do but to steer my boat, as the engine will run all day at the pressure set at."

C. Deavs

"If I could not get another, would not sell it for five times its cost."

Com. C.H. Osgood

"We used the one we bought of you last June almost daily during the summer, in all sorts of weather, and never found Lake Champlain so rough but what we felt perfectly safe in her. She runs very smart for a two-horse power engine; has never cost a cent for repairs, and her engine is so simple that Mrs. Witherbee became an expert after the trial trip, and has acted as engineer almost constantly since, and has never had a particle of trouble in managing her."[29]

W.C. Witherbee

Frank Ofeldt's Naphtha Engine was so easy to use that an amateur could easily master it.

Chapter 8

An advertisement from *Harper's New Monthly Magazine*, May 1887. At first the company had targeted the owners of yachts, but within a year switched to owner-operators, using the tag line, "Every Man His Own Engineer!"

In 1887 *Forest and Stream* published a report on the company's expansion under the heading, "A New American Industry – The Naphtha Launch":

"It is less than two years since the first engines were built as an experiment by what is now the Gas Engine and Power Co., the enterprise being commenced on a small scale, the first boats being built for the company by outside builders. Though inferior in many details to the present boats, these experimental craft were successful from the first, and in the summer of 1886 the concern secured a site on the Kills, at the junction with the Harlem River, and not far from Port Morris, where a boat shop and factory were built, and the construction of the hulls as well as engines begun. The demand grew so rapidly in the first season that the shops were enlarged, but even with the present extensive facilities the company have been unable to keep up with their orders this season....The company has lately bought ground further up the Harlem River, near Morris Dock, where the new buildings, covering between three and four acres, will be ready by next summer."

Inventors and Businessmen

One passage in the *Forest and Stream* article must have been particularly gratifying to Frank Ofeldt, as well as to Jabez Bostwick and Clement Gould: "The success which the naphtha launch has attained in a very short time must be taken as very strong proof of the inherent excellence of the machine itself, as well as of the skill and ability of the leaders and directors of the enterprise."[30]

Seen from outside, the Gas Engine and Power Company appeared to be an example of outstanding teamwork, but in reality there were tensions.

Businessmen and inventors see the world very differently. As James Watt explained, "The man of ingenuity in order to succeed…must seclude himself from Society, he must devote the whole powers of his mind to that one object, he must persevere in spite of the many fruitless experiments he makes, and he must apply money to the expenses of these experiments, which strict Prudence would dedicate to other purposes. By seclusion from the world he becomes ignorant of its manners, and unable to grapple with the more artful tradesman, who has applied the powers of *his* mind, not to the improvement of the commodity he deals in, but to the means of buying cheap and selling dear, or to the still less laudable purpose of oppressing such ingenious workmen as their ill fate may have thrown into his power." Watt's conclusion was that an inventor should "be considered an Infant, who cannot guard his own rights."[31]

An 1867 Congressional report styled technologists as "confiding and thriftless,…mere children in the rude conflicts which they are called on to endure with the stalwart fraud and cunning of the world."[32]

But what if the child was obstreperous?

In *David and Goliath*, Malcolm Gladwell points out that, "Innovators need to be *dis*agreeable. By disagreeable, I don't mean obnoxious or unpleasant.…They are people willing to take *social* risks – to do things that others might disapprove of. That is not easy. Society frowns on disagreeableness.…Yet a radical and transformative thought goes nowhere without the willingness to challenge convention.…As the playwright George Bernard Shaw once put it: 'The reasonable man adapts himself to the world: the unreasonable one persists in trying to adapt the world to himself. Therefore all progress depends on the unreasonable man.'"[33]

Some inventors may be unreasonable, but others can be cantankerous curmudgeons. When Commodore William N. Jeffers, Chief of the Naval Bureau of Ordnance, first went to see John Ericsson, he asked William C. Church, editor of the *Army and Navy Journal*, "to accompany him somewhat in the character of a body-guard."[34] Church, in his biography of Ericsson, explained: "Naturally amiable and generous, Ericsson was, at the same time, a man of ungovernable temper. Like the Scandinavian hero, Odin, 'he looked so fair and noble when he sat with his friends that every mind was delighted, but when he was in a heat then he looked fierce to his foes.' He was controlled by a strong sense of justice, but he did not readily brook opposition, and he had his experiences of the 'Berserk fury,' such as compelled the Norse warriors of old to bite their shields, and to wrestle with the stones and trees, lest they slay their friends in their rage. 'There was no king who would not give them what they wanted rather than suffer their overbearing;' and they were few who cared to encounter John Ericsson when the Berserk fury was on him."[35]

There is no evidence that Frank Ofeldt shared Ericsson's temperament, but he certainly was entitled to be self-confident on technical matters, and doubtless stood his ground. It is very likely that he and Jabez had disagreements, and not impossible that they had fierce disputes.

Jabez Bostwick had also become gun-shy from his experience with Samuel Andrews, the technical genius who had given Standard Oil its initial advantage. In the face of the company's rapid expansion, Andrews began to fear that his partners were becoming reckless,[36] and the mounting risk kept him in a state of nervous terror.[37] When Andrews finally asked to be bought out, his partners were more than pleased to be rid of him. In the judgment of John D. Rockefeller, "I never felt the need of scientific knowledge, have never felt it. A young man who wants to succeed in business does not require chemistry or physics. He can always hire scientists."[38]

Chapter 8

There was another inventor who threatened to disrupt Standard Oil's routine, the man who had previously pioneered pipelines, Samuel Van Syckel. His sad story was recounted by Henry Demarest Lloyd:

Petroleum had always been distilled in batches. Between batches, as Van Syckel explained, "We had to draw the fires and wait perhaps ten hours—the best part of a day—for the still to cool off, so that the men could go in with iron chisels to chop it all loose and clean it out....The still would be idle for a day and a half, and then the same process would have to be gone through with again with every charge....My greatest idea came to me, of making oil by a continuous process, so that I could feed in petroleum at one end and have kerosene running out at the other in a continuous stream."[39]

In 1876, as soon as Van Syckel started to build his new refinery, John Archbold turned up, and demanded that the inventor desist from attempting to compete with Standard Oil.[40] "He then said that I could make no money if I did refine oil. He also said if I did I could not ship it. He said he would say to me confidentially that they had made such arrangements with the railroads in reference to...getting cars—he knew I could make no money if I did make oil."

Samuel Van Syckel, who had previously pioneered the pipeline, invented a method of distilling oil continuously, rather than in batches.

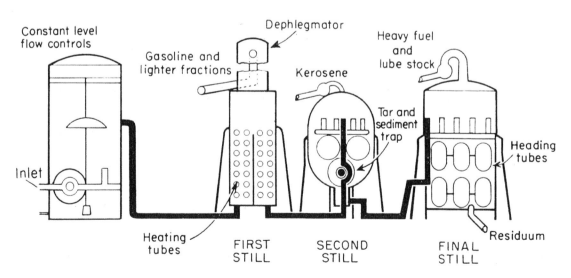

Van Syckel's invention performed as he had intended, but Standard Oil thwarted its introduction.

Van Syckel refused to quit, so the two struck a deal, according to which the Acme Oil Company, representing Standard Oil, would pay him a salary of $125 a month, and – if the process worked – $100,000 for the rights.

Within three years Van Syckel obtained four patents, but then Archbold told him that, "they had had a meeting of all their wise-heads, and they had called in chemists, and they all unanimously agreed that oil could not be made by a continuous process."

The inventor persevered. With the assistance of a German backer, Van Syckel built a continuous refinery, which ran for twenty days without stopping. According to the testimony of dealers in oil, his product was superior to Standard's. "It did not gum the lamp-wicks, and did not smell."

Then one of Standard Oil's companies bought out Van Syckel's backer and demolished the refinery, so Van Syckel sued. The Standard admitted having made the contract, but argued that Van Syckel had sustained no damages. According to Lloyd, "They took the ground that his possessing a creative mind was the cause of Van Syckel's ruin, not their betrayal of him. 'Mr. Van Syckel,' they argued to the court, 'is an instance of what it means to get out a patent, and deal in patents—in nine cases out of ten. He was an inventive man. He has got out a good many patents. No question they were meritorious patents. And what is the result? Poverty, a broken heart, an enfeebled intellect, and a struggle now for the means of subsistence by this lawsuit.'"

Although the jury decided against Standard Oil, the judge – in a telling demonstration of the low esteem then accorded to inventors – instructed the jurors to fix the damages at a mere six cents, and the jury complied![41]

The Dream Shattered

In Van Syckel's case the men of Standard never did want the invention to succeed. The naphtha launch was quite different. They very much wanted it to succeed, but they had no stomach for dealing with another inventor.

When these men were building the Standard Oil Company, they had bought up every independent refinery they could lay their hands on, while ridding themselves of the entrepreneurs who had created those enterprises. In the minds of his partners, Jabez was the ideal man to separate an inventor from his invention. John McLaurin, who knew Jabez, wrote that, "He was strict almost to sternness in his dealings, preferring justice to sentiment in business."[42] In other words, Jabez was pitiless, and would have no qualms about getting rid of Ofeldt once the inventor had surrendered control of the invention.

When did Jabez decide to dispose of Frank? Did he arrive at that decision because the two had a disagreement, or had he simply strung Frank along until the patent was approved? Probably the latter. The Standard men were masters at cloaking their real intentions; that was exactly how they had built their empire.

Jabez Bostwick's grand strategy is now clear. The first step was to persuade yachtsmen to use naphtha rather than steam to power their tenders. The second was to open up a market for motorboating among the general populace. And the third step was to eliminate the inventor.

By putting his faith in Jabez, Frank had made a tragic mistake. To the trusting immigrant, Bostwick's callous betrayal must have been nothing less than the shattering of the dream that brought him to America.

In Jabez Bostwick's world, the fate of an inventor was of no more concern than the fate of a horse in the Oil Regions. Both were expendable. As Matthew Josephson explained, it was the destiny of inventors to be "used and flung aside by men of ruse and audacity."[43] If Frank Ofeldt was offended, that was merely collateral damage.

Once Frank's patent issued on January 18, 1887, the Gas Engine and Power Company had no further need for his services. His departure was abrupt. When the company's second catalog went to press early that spring, Clement Gould was still President and Manager but Frank Ofeldt's name was gone. Instead there was a new Vice President and Superintendent, Charles L. Seabury, formerly the plant superintendent.[44]

The Gas Engine and Power Company never again mentioned the name of Frank Ofeldt. Even though the company's success depended on Frank's invention, Jabez made sure that the inventor himself received no recognition.

Chapter 9

Nobel's *Mignon*

"On the lake at Zürich he had his small elegant launch of his own design, the first one in the world to be made entirely of aluminium. In the early 1890s we find the sixty-year-old man at the surrounding watering places with various guests on board, dressed in light, but not yachting clothes. On one of these trips a photograph was taken, the only one known to exist of a contentedly smiling Alfred Nobel on holiday."

Erik Bergengren, *Alfred Nobel*[1]

The Nobels

It may come as a surprise that Alfred Nobel, as famous for his business success as for his inventions, was treated just as badly in the United States as was Frank Ofeldt. According to Erik Bergengren, Alfred's initial attempt to sell nitroglycerine in America was "frantically opposed" by the gunpowder manufacturer Henry DuPont. Alfred then assigned his nitroglycerine patents to a company that, "increasingly in the hands of unscrupulous jobbers, turned out to be a swindling firm." His patent rights were threatened, and he had to engage in a "stubborn and uncompromising battle for justice and progress, fought among crafty sharks of finance, adventurers, swindlers and their unscrupulous lawyers." Although he owned over ten percent of the three million dollar enterprise, the Americans outwitted him at every turn. In 1885 he finally gave up, and received only $20,000.

Alfred's conclusion: "I found life in America anything but agreeable. The exaggerated chase after money… spoils much of the pleasure of meeting people and destroys a sense of honour in favour of imagined needs."[2]

Alfred and his brothers had been brought up in St. Petersburg, and Ludwig still lived there, manufacturing gun carriages, rapid-fire cannon, artillery shells, and rifles by the hundreds of thousands. Robert Tolf tells us that Ludwig was an enlightened employer. He refused to employ child labor, and reduced the workday from the usual twelve or fourteen hours to ten and a half hours. He also instituted the first profit-sharing plan in Russia, and perhaps the world. Needing walnut for rifle stocks, Ludwig sent his older brother Robert to Baku, to see if any was available in the marketplace, and he gave Robert 25,000 rubles to buy the walnut.[3]

Since antiquity "eternal pillars of fire" had burned in the neighborhood of Baku, Azerbaijan, and from at least the seventh century Parsees, the fire-worshipping followers of Zoroaster, had performed their devotions in temples there.[4] In the vicinity of Baku it was easy to scoop petroleum from hand-dug pits, and for centuries it had been traded throughout the region. The Greeks called it naphtha; in Assyrian it was naptu; in Persian, naptik; in Hebrew, nepht or naft; and in Arabic, neft.[5]

At the time Robert Nobel arrived in Baku, 415 hand-dug pits were producing 22,000 tons of petroleum a year. The first drilled wells had just been brought in, and Robert immediately became smitten with oil fever.[6] Twenty-three small refineries were in operation,[7] and Robert impulsively bought one, using the walnut money. Robert was an accomplished chemist and soon became the most competent refiner in Baku. His product was so good that it could compete in quality with American kerosene, and in 1876 Ludwig came to Baku and joined him.

Ludwig Nobel, Alfred's brother, created an oil company in Russia that became a rival to Standard Oil.

Like Alfred, Ludwig was a successful inventor. He had already invented a process for hermetically sealing the hubs of axles to protect them from sand and dirt. Called the *Nobel Wheel*, it could withstand Russian roads, and was famed throughout the country.[8]

As we have seen, in 1868 the U.S. Navy rejected petroleum as fuel for steamships, but America possessed abundant coal. Russia had to import its coal from England, and in many parts of the empire firewood was scarce. Small wonder that the Russians were the first to use fuel oil in both steamships and locomotives.[9]

Now, faced with the industry's practice of shipping oil in barrels – often leaky and expensive, Ludwig conceived the idea of the oil tanker, but found no support for the scheme.[10] According to Charles Marvin, "Wiseacres in Russia asserted, that as the gifted Americans had never deemed it feasible to bring oil to Europe in cistern-steamers, it was sheer folly for anyone to attempt it in the Caspian region."[11] In fact it was the American practice to ship oil only on sailing vessels, for fear that coal-burners might start a fire at sea.[12]

As we have seen with Ericsson and Van Syckel, it is common for inventors to face rejection. The computer pioneer, Howard Aiken, commented on the difficulty that inventors have in persuading people to open their minds to a new idea: "Don't worry about people stealing an idea. If it's original, you will have to ram it down their throats."[13]

Ludwig was undeterred. Together with Sven Almqvist, Director of the Motala Shipyard, he designed the world's first oil tanker, *Zoroaster*, which was launched in 1878 in Norrköping. Ludwig rejected the advice of associates that he patent the oil tanker, on the ground that he should not restrict the dissemination of ideas that could benefit the entire industry.

Zoroaster paid for itself in its first season.[14]

Alfred was now an investor, and in 1879 the company was incorporated as *Naftaproduktionsaktiebolaget Bröderna Nobel* (Nobel Brothers' Petroleum Production Company).[15] Like Samuel Andrews, Robert was becoming alarmed at Ludwig's feverish expansionism, so his brothers bought him out, and he retired to Sweden. The development that precipitated the rupture was Ludwig's plan for continuous distillation. This was just at the time that the Standard Oil men were assuring Von Syckel that the idea was impossible, and Robert Nobel was of the same opinion. However, in 1882 Ludwig's continuous distillation process succeeded, many years before Standard Oil would adopt it, and the invention made Nobel the largest refiner in Russia.[16] In 1883 the Nobel refinery was able to turn out 220,000 gallons of kerosene daily.[17]

Chapter 9

The Baku oil field produced a prodigious amount of crude. Just as in the United States, the naphthas were despised by-products.

The output from Baku was almost beyond belief. In 1881 the Nobels hit their first *fountain*, as gushers were called in Russia. For six straight months the derrick crew drew four thousand tons a day.[18] Two years later the Nobels had over forty wells, of which fourteen were fountains.[19]

Continuous refining, which Standard Oil claimed to be impossible, was perfected by Ludwig Nobel, and this invention made the Nobel Company the largest refiner in Russia.

Two hundred refineries were clumped just north of Baku in an area called the *Black Town* (Tchorni Gorod). In 1883 Charles Marvin wrote that, "A more noisome town than the Black Town it would be difficult to find. …The buildings are black and greasy, the walls are black and greasy; the roads between consist of jutting rocks and drifting sand, interspersed with huge pools of oil-refuse, and forming a vast morass of mud and oil in wet weather. Inside the greasy entrances to the refineries gangs of natives may be seen at work, half naked; their bodies and their ragged clothes saturated with oil. Not a tree, not a shrub, not a flower or a blade of grass, not a single object to raise or refine a man is to be found in this wretched hole.…There is one very notable exception. This is the refinery of the Nobel brothers. The two hundred other refineries are buried in smoke; the atmosphere above Nobels' place is not polluted by a single whiff. The squalor of the 200 is appalling – Nobels' establishment is kept as clean and bright, considering the nature of the business, as any English barracks."

In 1883 kerosene sold for a penny a gallon in Baku, but it was next to impossible to sell the naphthas at any price. According to Marvin, "At one native manufactory I saw as much as 17 per cent of the light oil running away like water to the Caspian, the firm having no means of utilizing it.…Of the lighter oils a deal is either barbarously allowed to run to waste or is used to adulterate good kerosene.…Nearly all the small firms, while distilling perhaps an excellent oil originally, largely adulterate it with the lighter product." However, the larger firms, including the Nobels, refused to do so.[20]

The rate of growth was hectic. Tolf says that "Ludwig was building and buying like a man possessed." *Zoroaster* was such a success that he ordered several more tankers. By 1883 he had 1,500 tank cars, and soon he had 1,500 barges, including one of the largest in the world, more than five hundred feet long with four rudders and a capacity of nine thousand tons of oil.[21] He also built several large storage facilities, one of which held 18 million gallons of kerosene.[22] By 1883 the Nobel refinery was distilling half of all the illuminating oil produced in Russia.[23]

Alfred was the only board member with the capital to help finance the expansion, but the unending demands severely tried his patience.[24] Bergengren tells us, "The harried inventor was well aware of his hereditary fiery temperament.…When he is indignant and 'the Nobel blood surges up, there is no lack of my own explosiveness, I get so angry that the sparks fly – but it lasts for only half an hour'."[25] During the latter half of the 1880s, he was subject to moods of extreme depression,[26] and described himself as "a worthless instrument of melancholy, alone in the world and with thoughts more gloomy than anyone can imagine."[27]

Alfred's guilt was aggravated by his own role in the frenetic arms race then under way in Europe. About this time, Ludwig died, and some newspaper men, confusing Ludwig with Alfred, published obituaries on the latter. According to Bergengren, Alfred "thus had the unusual and dubious pleasure of himself reading the world's opinion of and judgment on his person and life's work."[28] The newspapers assigned him most of the blame for the arms race, and described him as a "merchant of death."[29] As a result, his innate melancholy deepened and he became a desperately lonely man.

Alfred Nobel's gloom was lightened by his discovery that boating brought him pleasure.

Chapter 9

In spite of his despair, Alfred's curiosity led him to a new interest. During the 1889 World Exposition in Paris, he learned about a revolutionary development in the production of aluminum. The element aluminum (spelled and pronounced *aluminium* in much of the world) was only discovered in 1824. At first it was so valuable that, while Emperor Napoleon and his consort and their most honored guests dined off precious aluminum plates, the others at the table had to put up with simple gold plates. A breakthrough came in 1886 when the Frenchman P.L.T. Héroult and the American, C.M. Hall – in the very same week – invented the electrolytic production method, and the first large-scale production was started in 1888 in Neuhausen, Switzerland, powered by waterfalls on the Rhine. Alfred Nobel, intrigued by the World Exposition exhibit, immediately began to correspond with Héroult, and the two became good friends. Nobel then bought a substantial number of shares in the Neuhausen firm, *Aluminium Industrie A.G.*, and became active in several other aluminum companies.[30]

Escher Wyss

Nobel hired a consulting engineer, Erich Messmer, who was also the representative in France for a Swiss firm, *Escher Wyss & Co*.[31] The two men made a number of trips to Neuhausen and Zurich, and in the latter city Messmer introduced Nobel to something that was to him a completely new phenomenon, the pleasure boat.[32]

Escher Wyss had already built some hundreds of steamboats and marine engines, as well as thousands of pumps, turbines and paper-making machines.[33] The company obtained a license from the Gas Engine and Power Company, and in 1888 began building naphtha launches.[34]

The Swiss boat-builder, Escher Wyss, secured a license from the Gas Engine and Power Company, and launched its first naphtha boat, *Sarcelle*, in 1888.

81

The *Nouvelle Gazette* of Zurich described the marvelous invention:

"A new type of boat has been attracting the attention of people walking along our docks for several weeks, and more especially those interested in nautical sports. We want to tell you about the elegant little boat, equipped with a very unobtrusive engine, which runs as though pushed by invisible hands, sometimes going like an arrow, sometimes doing vertiginous circles around bridge pilings, and which executes the most graceful elegant movements...

"According to the information we were given, it was an American engineer to whom we owe this surprising invention, no doubt designed to play a big role, both from a practical point of view, as well as in the sporting world. The license to the patent has been acquired by Escher Wyss & Co., which has already sold several of these vessels."[35]

In another article the same newspaper reported that the Escher Wyss mechanical construction shops had made an improvement that had eluded the Americans, "a mechanism allowing a steady flame to be maintained for as long as one wants to stop."[36]

The Escher Wyss literature spelled out the advantages of naphtha over steam, comments that have particular validity because the company had built many steamboats:

"In boats and ordinary small pleasure craft the interiors of the boilers soon become coated with scale deposits such that after 200 hours of operation they must be thoroughly cleaned. There is no limit on the length of time a naphtha boiler can be in service because naphtha leaves no solid deposits. From this it follows that the naphtha engine operates independently of the kind of water in which it operates.

"Any leak that might develop in a naphtha boiler is immediately obvious since the naphtha vapor burns like illuminating gas. One can therefore repair such defects as soon as they become obvious. In steam boilers such fissures or problem areas become covered with scale and can only be located with difficulty."

The company listed the attributes required for a good launch engine, including that, "Its construction should be as simple as possible, whilst being solid, so that the first handyman or mechanic to arrive can take it apart and put it back together easily....Its construction should also be such that after being out of service and without maintenance for a long time, it can if necessary be put back in operation without special preparations."

The Gas Engine and Power Company specified the use of Baumé 76° naphtha, but Escher Wyss permitted a wider range: naphtha or benzine or néoline with a specific gravity of 0.680 to 0.700 (76°-70° Baumé).

These 2, 4, and 6-hp engines, built by Escher Wyss & Co., look much like the American ones, but the Swiss company added an innovation that allowed the engines to idle.

Under the direction of Chief Engineer, J.W. Reitz, the company began exploring alternative boat designs. Most revolutionary was the world's first aluminum boat.[37]

Again, the newspapers were impressed. An American correspondent, writing under the pen name *Old Hand*, reported on a recent trip to Switzerland: "I witnessed a sight which was of itself sufficient to pay me for my journey. It was nothing less than the launching of the first boat ever built of aluminium....This boat is not a large affair. It resembles in appearance and size the small naphtha-launches, and, in fact, its motive power is an engine of this kind, which has an improved device whereby the flame can be maintained while the boat is not in motion....It is only on near approach and close examination that a person would notice that the boat was not painted gray, but was made of a white, shining metal. Inside everything has this silver-white color, for even the seats, gunwales, and hand-rails are made of this beautiful and untarnishable metal." The launch weighed 970 pounds, whereas "one of equal size built of wood and iron would weigh from 1,400 to 1,700 pounds. The plates forming the shell of the launch are only half as thick as the iron plates used on other launches....The castings of the engine, the rudder, and even the tiller ropes are made of the same metal....The speed developed was also greater than in other boats of the same class."[38]

Naphta-Launch No. I «Zephir» aus reinem Aluminium.
Modell für 8 Personen. Maschine von 2 Pferdekräften. 5,50 m. lang, 1,50 m. breit, 0,68 m. Bordhöhe, 0,50 m. Tiefgang. Gewicht des complet ausgerüsteten Bootes 440 Kilogramm. Geschwindigkeit 5–6 Knoten per Stunde.

The naphtha launch, *Zephir*, the first boat to be built of aluminum.

The *Nouvelle Gazette de Zurich* described *Zephir*'s first voyage down the Rhine: "Today at noon, a boat arrived flying the flag of Switzerland, built by Escher Wyss & Cie., at Zurich, and destined for the Electrical Exposition at Frankfurt on Main. This little boat, equipped with a removable wickerwork cabin, left the upper bridge on the Rhine at Basel at 9 a.m. the day before yesterday. In a little less than 6 hours it ran the distance of 127 km to Kehl, which corresponds to a speed of 21 km/hr. The little boat is not only fitted out for great comfort, but it also passed in complete safety through the numerous deep valleys, under all the bridges and along the rapids of the upper Rhine. At the border it was cheered by the population, and from Spire to Mannheim further down the Rhine the big steamboats of the Rhine saluted this minuscule boat with cannon shots. After a little side excursion to Rudesheim, it will arrive at Frankfurt tomorrow, where the head of Escher Wyss & Cie. who, with his family, has made the trip here from Basel on the little vapor-boat, and with the collaboration of Engineer J. W. Reitz, will look after marketing the aluminum boat, the first one to be built using this metal of the future."[39]

Alfred Nobel was convinced. He must have his own aluminum launch. However, he did not immediately place an order with Escher Wyss. First he analyzed two other means of propulsion: electricity and the internal combustion engine.

Electric Boats

Inventors had been building electric boats since at least 1838,[40] but it was the Austrian, Anthony Reckenzaun, who produced the first commercial product. His 26-ft. iron-hulled *Electricity*, powered by two Siemens motors, carried twelve passengers.[41] Reckenzaun then joined with the experienced nautical designer, Alfred Yarrow, to build a 40-ft. galvanized steel electric launch capable of carrying forty passengers.[42] Again Siemens supplied the motor,[43] and the launch made numerous trips on the Danube.[44]

In 1883, Alfred Yarrow designed a 40-ft. galvanized steel launch, with an electric propulsion system designed by Anthony Reckenzaun, and using a Siemens motor. The launch, which was capable of carrying 40 passengers, was shown at the Vienna Exhibition of 1883, and made several trips on the Danube.

Chapter 9

To demonstrate the capability of electric power, Mr. Reckenzaun crossed the English Channel and back in his 37-ft. launch *Volta* on a single battery charge. The boat was so quiet that one of the party reached out his hands and captured a sleeping gannet afloat on the waves.[45] By 1890, Moritz Immisch was operating a fleet of twelve electric boats on the Thames. There was one land charging station, with plans for three more, and there were a number of floating charging stations. Business was good.[46]

Siemens & Halske offered to build an electric launch for Nobel powered by 80 batteries, with a capacity of 30 persons, the price to include a steam-driven generator.[47] As Alfred contemplated using the boat in Switzerland and Italy, and also in Sweden, the need for charging stations must have been a serious deterrent.

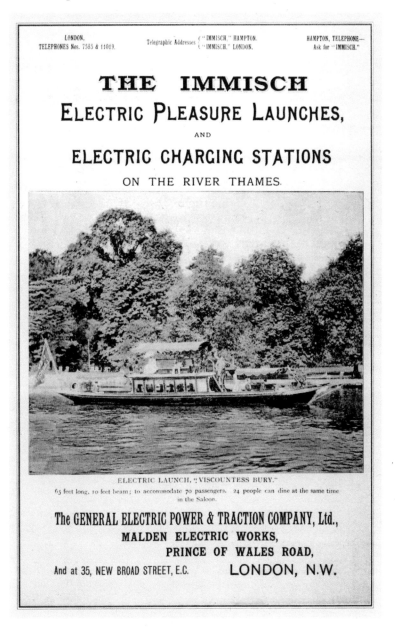

By 1890, a fleet of electric boats was operating successfully on the Thames.

Internal Combustion

Alfred's second alternative was internal combustion. By 1876, Nikolaus Otto, with Gottlieb Daimler and Wilhelm Maybach, had developed a fully practical "explosive engine,"[48] but the engine was fueled by gas supplied by the city's lighting system. Then in 1885 Otto developed a practical vaporizer that allowed the use of liquid fuel. In October 1886, Daimler was granted a patent for a motorboat. Because of the prevalent fear of gasoline, he and Maybach would put the engine into a lapstrake launch at 2:30 a.m., and camouflage it with a few wires and insulators, hoping to make people believe that the boat was electrically powered. A local newspaper reported that it "appears to be propelled by some unseen power up and downstream with great speed, causing astonishment on the part of bystanders."[49]

In the autumn of 1891, Alfred Nobel went to Berlin where he was given a test ride on the river Spree in a Daimler launch. He then requested a proposal for a launch suitable for use on the Italian coast.[50] Apparently he expressed some doubts about the engine, for two days later Frederick P. Simms wrote, regretting that no decision had yet been made, and assuring him that, "We are now in a position to give you the assurance and guarantee that the petrol we are using, with the specific gravity of 0,680-0.70, burns almost totally, and that particularly with our system the engine remains very clean. There can be no talk of carbon, soot or smell." Mr. Simms also provided names of satisfied customers, including Prince Bismark. He closed with the hope that the comparison between naphtha and the petrol-powered boat would tilt in the latter's favor. Alfred was not persuaded, and three days later he informed Simms that he had chosen the naphtha engine.[51]

Mignon

Alfred then entered into a correspondence with the manager of Escher Wyss, Gustave Naville,[52] on the specifications for his boat, which was to be powered by Escher Wyss' standard 6-hp engine. Although the engine may have been from stock, Alfred's yacht *Mignon* was anything but. Alfred himself designed her,[53] with the assistance of his 25-year-old nephew Ludwig, Robert's second son.[54]

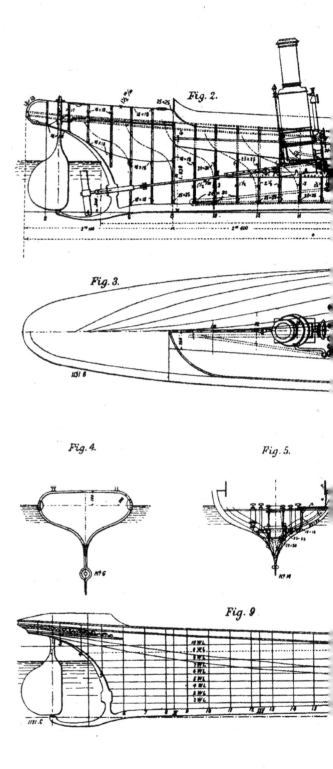

Chapter 9

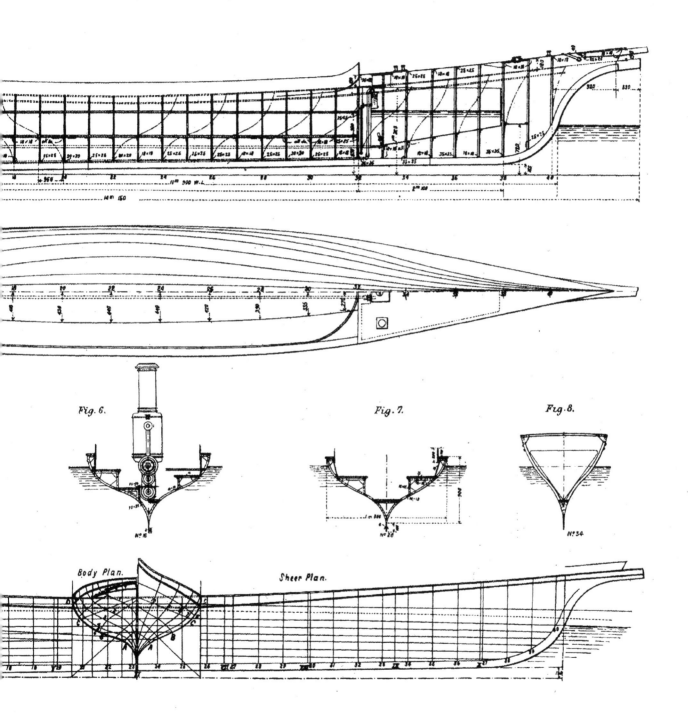

With the assistance of his nephew, Alfred Nobel designed his own naphtha launch.

Naphtha

Mignon, the largest aluminum craft yet constructed, was described in the 1897 Escher Wyss catalog as "a pleasure yacht, whose wickerwork deckhouse has been taken off in the illustration. Operating only on vapor, the boat has easily done 7 knots, or 8 knots with sails. Thirty to thirty-five people can be accommodated on board. Watertight partitions separate the boat into four compartments; also, several lockers filled with cork render it unsinkable. The boat is elegant in appearance, very comfortable and stable."

Chapter 9

Mignon's trial trip, on June 1, 1892, led to an article in the British publication, *Engineering*: "This is the first vessel of her size which has been built of aluminium. Her principal dimensions are: Length between perpendiculars, 43 ft., breadth moulded, 6 ft., depth moulded, 2 ft. 11 in., draught in fresh water, 2 ft. 2 in. On account of air-tight compartments with which she is constructed, she is rendered unsinkable, while she has a very large range of stability. She has a cut-water stem ornamented with a beautiful figure-head, and an elliptical stern; she is constructed on exceedingly fine lines, carries two pole masts, and is rigged as a fore-and-aft schooner.…At the fore end of the vessel is situated a portable willow cabin 8 ft. in length, weighing only 86 lb., and extending the whole width of the vessel; the roof is ornamented with blue silk, relieved with gold. Situated at the fore end of the vessel is a nickel silver binnacle fitted with a double liquid needle compass. The shell of the ship is innocent of all paint and composition, and is allowed to retain its natural silver colour.…The whole of the machinery is constructed of aluminium (including the propeller) with the exception of the cranks and shafting.…The standing rigging is of aluminium wire, set up with screws of the same metal.…The keel, stem, and sternposts are of forged aluminium, 7 in. x 1 in.…15,000 aluminium rivets hold the ship together. She is fully equipped, having a balanced rudder and quadrant of aluminium, bollards and fairleads of the same material, aluminium awning stanchions which support a pink-coloured sunshade extending the whole length of the yacht, aluminium flagpoles surmounted with silken flags."[55]

In September 1892, Alfred took some of Zurich's notables on a memorable ride. A newspaper correspondent wrote: "Soon after setting out it commenced to rain and there was a violent wind. This circumstance could not help being somewhat disagreeable for the participants, only a few of whom could take refuge in the wicker cabin of the "Mignon," nevertheless it was an occasion for the boat to demonstrate what it could do. It went through the crests of the waves with the greatest of ease, thanks to the characteristic slender shapes which the lightness of aluminium had made possible. The boat sliced through the waves without being lifted by them. The boat glided so silently on the agitated surface of the lake that it was able to get quite close to a flock of wild ducks before they took off. With the rain getting even heavier, the run was shortened.… Mr. Nobel offered a collation in the halls of the "Sonne" and it was a graceful way for the company to console itself for the turn taken by the excursion as a result of the change in the weather. A series of speeches praised the lovable amphitrion, the new metal and its future, Swiss industry and the freedom in which it was born, technical progress, etc."[56]

Alfred Nobel was extremely proud that he could skipper his own yacht.

The Peace Prize

A few weeks earlier, an old acquaintance, Bertha von Suttner, had reappeared. Alfred had once been enchanted by her, but she had married another, and was now a leader in the peace movement.[57] Alfred agreed with Bertha on the urgency of her campaign, but rejected her belief in general disarmament: "Good wishes alone will not ensure peace. The same can be said about banquets and long speeches. One must be able to give favourably disposed governments an acceptable plan. To demand disarmament is really only to make oneself ridiculous without doing anyone any good." In the year following *Mignon*'s launching, Bertha invited Alfred to attend the peace conference in Bern, which he did – incognito.[58]

Alfred thereupon invited Bertha and her husband for a ride in his beloved boat. During the outing, Alfred pointed out some large villas owned by wealthy silk merchants, to which Bertha commented that dynamite factories were even more profitable but definitely not as innocent,[59] to which Alfred retorted, "My factories may well put an end to war before your congresses. For in the day that two armies are capable of destroying each other in a second, all civilized nations will surely recoil before a war and dismiss their troops."[60]

After the boat ride, the two engaged in an exchange of letters, and, according to Alfred's biographer, Erik Bergengren, Bertha "influenced Nobel's attitude to the peace question [and] the formulation of his testamentary provisions regarding the peace prize." In January 1893, five months after the *Mignon* outing, Alfred first described what would become the Nobel Peace Prize: "I should like to leave part of my fortune to a fund for the creation of prizes to be awarded every five years (let us say six times, for if within thirty years one has not succeeded in reforming society such as it is today, we shall inevitably relapse into barbarism) to the man or woman who has contributed in the most effective way to the realization of peace in Europe."[61]

The Nobel prizes are often thought to have been financed from explosives. In fact, a significant portion of Alfred's estate came from petroleum. His largest single investment, amounting to nearly one quarter of his wealth, was in the Nobel Brothers' Oil Company.[62]

In late 1895, Alfred arranged for *Mignon* to be shipped from Zurich to Stockholm, where she lay at the Finnboda slip. It is believed that he intended to give her to the Lutheran school for Scandinavian children, founded by his brothers at Astrakhan in the Volga Delta, but after Alfred's death in the following year there was a titanic struggle over his will, and poor *Mignon* was forgotten.[63]

An outing with Bertha von Suttner in his naphtha launch influenced Alfred Nobel to offer the Nobel Peace Prize.

Chapter 10

Starting Over

"In business…Americans of the nineteenth century found the Great Game. They played it with zest and gusto, they enjoyed it even when it was perilous, and they took its ups and downs with equanimity. As Herbert Spencer said in 1882, for Americans it was the modern equivalent of war. If it was hard-hitting and ruthless, so is war; and even when the blows were hardest, it remained a game. 'Business in America,' wrote Brooks, 'is not merely more engaging than elsewhere, it is even perhaps the most engaging activity in American life'."

Allan Nevins[1]

Now that we have seen how heartlessly Jabez Bostwick treated Frank Ofeldt, we can understand why John Ericsson and Alfred Nobel were so embittered by their experience in America. It was true that, for an inventor, America was a land of unlimited opportunity. But it was equally true that, in the Great Game, American businessmen had almost unlimited freedom to victimize inventors.

If Frank was to survive in the business jungle, he had only one weapon, his fertile imagination.

Ofeldt's New Engine

Frank returned to his machine shop in Newark, and within a few months – on June 9, 1887 – applied for a new patent, which issued on December 4, 1888 as No. 393,850, *Hydrocarbon Furnace for Steam Boilers*, in essence a naphtha-fueled steam boiler. Frank wanted to retain the quick start-up of the naphtha engine, but no longer had the advantage of naphtha as a working fluid, so he concentrated on maximizing the transfer of heat within the boiler. He accomplished this by using ¼" tubes, coiled very tightly.

Frank called his invention the *Improved Naphtha Launch*, a name so similar to the Gas Engine and Power Company's product that it was bound to cause confusion. *Outing* referred to it as the *Ofeldt Improved System*, and in later years Frank and his sons called it the *Ofeldt Improved Steam System*,[2] but in Frank's obituary,

Naphtha

Popular Mechanics referred to it as the *Ofeldt Naphtha Steam System*.[3] We shall call it the *Ofeldt Improved System*, in the hope of avoiding misunderstandings.

Frank licensed the invention to the Hohenstein Manufacturing Company of New Jersey, and he also served as that company's mechanical engineer.[4]

Like Jabez Bostwick, Hohenstein's sales agent, Ellis R. Meeker, sought as his first customer a high-profile yachtsman, and found one in Elbridge Gerry, Commodore of the New York Yacht Club.[5] Gerry's grandfather had signed the Declaration of Independence, was Vice-President under James Madison, and also Governor of Massachusetts, but is best remembered as the originator of the practice of gerrymandering. Grandson Elbridge inherited a fortune and owned a huge mansion on Fifth Avenue where he entertained lavishly. His luxurious steam yacht *Electra*, the New York Yacht Club's flagship,[6] may have been the first yacht to be equipped with electric lighting, as well as an ice-making machine that also provided rudimentary air-conditioning.[7] *The New York Times* marveled that Gerry fed his guests on beef that cost a dollar a pound,[8] and *The Rudder* reported acidly, "Commodore Elbridge T. Gerry will command the New York Yacht Club for another term. This will doubtless prove glorious news to the horde of Bohemian newspapermen who infest the *Electra* and feed on the simple and frugal fare prepared by the $5,000 a year *chef* of the flagship."[9]

Electra already carried a naphtha tender, but in September 1888 *Outing* reported that "Commodore Gerry, of the New York Yacht Club, has changed the Naphtha System in his launch *Electra* and put in the Ofeldt Improved System, using Naphtha Gas for fuel only. This work was done by the Hohenstein Manufacturing Company."[10] The story was premature. At that very moment the Hohenstein Company failed,[11] and Frank was forced to find another way to complete *Electra*'s launch.

Commodore Elbridge Gerry's *Electra* with the Ofeldt Improved tender in her davits.

Chapter 10

Naphtha

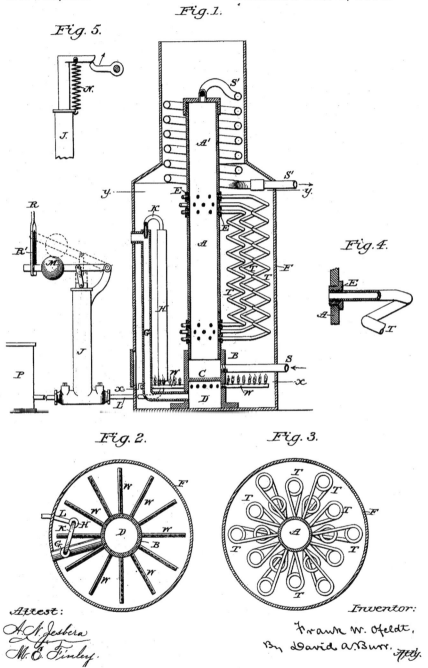

The *Ofeldt Improved System* was a steam engine fueled by naphtha, but the tightly-wound boiler pipes were only 1/4" in diameter. This provided such a large heating surface that the engine's start-up time was similar to that of the naphtha engine.

Earlier that year Frank had moved back to Brooklyn, where he set up a new company, *F. W. Ofeldt and Sons,* at the foot of 55th street.[12] Three sons joined their father's firm, Frank A., Ernest, and George.[13] The eldest, August (Walter), already had an established business in Nyack. Frank A. had recently returned from the West, where he had been a steamboat engineer on the Columbia and Snake Rivers.[14]

Ofeldt joined forces with the well-known Brooklyn boat builder, Samuel A. Ayres, and together they delivered Commodore Gerry's launch in April 1889. The *Brooklyn Eagle* reported, "One of the handsomest boats that ever floated is the 27 foot launch Ayres has just completed for Commodore Gerry's Electra. It is a model of symmetry and lightness, and the motive power is one of the new coil boiler naphtha engines. The launch is very roomy. The engine occupies scarcely any space. The interior and exterior are finished as finely as a costly piece of furniture."[15]

A month later the *Eagle* published an account of Frank's mistreatment by Jabez Bostwick. The writer was mistaken in reporting that Frank had failed to patent the original naphtha engine, but clearly understood that Frank had been treated badly:

"Ayres has just laid the keel and ribs of another fifty foot steam launch for the Rev. Mr. Aspinwall, formerly of Bay Ridge, now of Washington. She will be fitted with one of Ofeldt's naphtha engines and is intended to be a beauty. By the way, Ofeldt is reaping the reward due to genius and honesty. A poor man on the Harlem River, he was the inventor of the old naphtha launch. Not being protected by patent his invention was pirated; he received scarcely any benefit from the product of his brain and skill. He at once started to improve on the idea and invented the present naphtha launch, which is simply a marvel of speed, beauty, economy of fuel and engine space, and can be under way in a couple of minutes from the time the fire is started. An *Eagle* reporter who had heard its praises frequently chanted and who received them with a good deal of mental reservation was fairly astonished last evening at Bay Ridge. He was standing by when the engineer pumped up the naphtha and applied the match, at the same time his companion shoved the launch from the float and, while yet in motion from the impetus given, the screw began to revolve, and before he could recover from his surprise the launch and its occupants were out of the basin and half way to Gowanus....No steam yacht, in fact, any other yacht is now complete without one, and Ofeldt & Ayres are unable to supply the demand. It is needless to say that the inventor has patented this invention."[16]

The Gas Engine and Power Company attempted to distance the naphtha launch from Frank's new boat:

"There is but one Naphtha Launch built, the distinctive feature of which is the use of naphtha for *both fuel and power*, and we can do the boat-loving public no better service than to caution against confounding these boats with the so-called "Improved Naphtha Launches," making steam by burning wood, coal, petroleum or naphtha. The unprecedented success of our launches has been the incentive to unscrupulous competitors who produce and advertise a pretended improvement, and sell a craft no more akin to the NAPHTHA LAUNCH than any other steam craft, unless it be alone the use of naphtha for fuel."[17]

Frank's business was a success. Three years after he left the Gas Engine and Power Company, the *Eagle* reported that, "Ofeldt's naphtha steam yacht building establishment at Bay Ridge is one of the busiest boat centers this Spring on the bay shore. Scarcely a day goes by that a vessel is not launched, and many have been sent away, while others are in course of construction for foreign shipment." The article went on to list several Ofeldt launches, from 25 to 50 feet, including three for South and Central America.[18]

In May 1890, the *Eagle* described the trial run of the 48-ft., 18-hp *Crescent*, piloted by one of Frank's sons, with the members of the Board of Managers of the Crescent Athletic Club aboard: "Of course, the boys had to toot the whistle frequently, just to get it in working order, and nearly everything, from a mud scow to an ocean steamer, was saluted with equal energy....The trial was in every way satisfactory, and the members are greatly pleased with the new craft."[19]

Another of Frank's customers was the Coast Guard, which purchased two 25' boats, *Bouquet* and *Bluebell*. *Bouquet* had a copper-sheathed oak hull, and tended a string of experimental electrically-lighted buoys in New York Bay. *Bluebell* was built for the Lighthouse Service, and assigned to the Tender *Clover*. When the Coast Guard sold her in 1910, she still had her Ofeldt engine.[20]

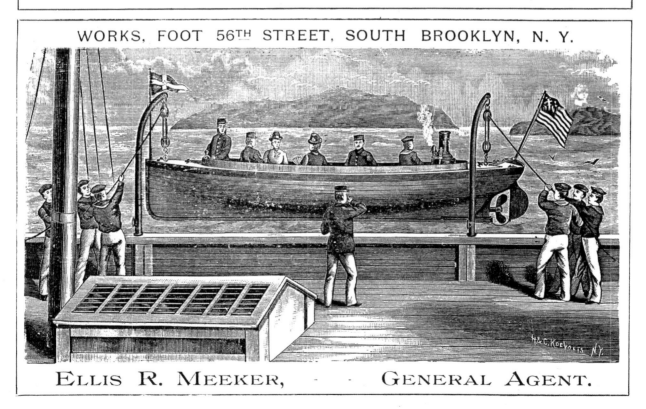

The name Frank Ofeldt chose for his new invention was bound to cause confusion.

What was Frank's private opinion of the Ofeldt Improved engine? Did he have doubts about its significance? After all, his naphtha engine had been a major leap in technology, whereas his new invention was merely an incremental improvement on Watt's engine. He must have felt that he could do better, or perhaps he was driven on by the sheer pleasure of inventing.

Moreover, if Frank's next invention was to compete with the naphtha launch, it would require significant investment, something that Frank's little company could never provide. To counter the Gas Engine and Power Company's head start, Frank would have to find a business partner with Bostwick's strengths, but with one crucial difference; he must be a man that Frank could trust. Once again, what Frank needed was a Matthew Boulton. But Boulton was a product of the eighteenth century, an age of paternalism. In that era, it had been Boulton's *duty* to take care of James Watt, not to dupe him. Now, in the time of the Great Game, were there still any Matthew Boultons?

In spite of the odds, Frank had his eye on a possible candidate, one of his own customers. Let us take a close look at that man's career, and form our own conclusion about Frank's choice.

E.C. Benedict

Born in Westchester County in 1834,[21] Elias Cornelius Benedict never called himself by either of his Christian names; he was always E.C. The boy's father, the Reverend Henry Benedict, married the daughter of a Norwalk sea captain. The memory of his maternal grandfather must have persisted, for E.C. spent much of his life at sea. He later told a writer for *The Rudder*, "Nature intended me for the skipper of some ship, but destiny made me a poor curbstone broker."[22]

In 1849, at age 15, the boy left school to seek his fortune on Wall Street, where his brother Henry was already a member of the New York Stock and Exchange Board, as the New York Stock Exchange was then called. At age 28, the precocious Henry was elected the Exchange's Vice-President.[23] On Wall Street E.C. joined the banking house of Corning & Co,[24] but he had been in New York for only a few years when Wall Street was struck by the worst collapse up to that time, the Panic of 1857, which caused many brokers to fail.[25]

One might expect such a debacle to weigh most heavily on the young and inexperienced, but the opposite happened. According to Henry Clews, a stockbroker of E.C.'s generation, "This crisis sounded the death knell of old fogyism in the 'street.'....Much of the old conservative element had fallen in the general upheaval, to rise no more. This element was eliminated, and its place supplied by better material, and with young blood."[26] Robert Sobel described the consequence: "It marked the advent of a new, less polite period of American finance....The 'rules of the game,' often broached but never disavowed by the former generation, were now completely disregarded. The panic of 1857 proved to be the watershed for the most exciting, lawless, and unscrupulous period in American finance."[27] E.C. saw his opportunity. Although he was only 23, he offered to take over the business of his employer, and he and his brother formed *Benedict and Company*.[28]

Like Jabez Bostwick, E.C. founded his fortune during the Civil War, and the commodity that he specialized in – gold – was just as reprehensible as cotton.

The price of gold reflected the fortunes of war. Gold bulls gambled that the North would lose, which would render greenbacks worthless, and with the Union's early disasters the price of gold did indeed shoot up, so the bulls profited mightily.[29]

The gold trade was conducted in murky smoke-filled quarters. James K. Medbury described the scene as "a den of wild beasts....The gloom or the gladness over success or defeat of the national flag mingled with individual passions. Men leaped upon chairs, waved their hands, or clenched their fists; shrieked, shouted; the bulls whistled 'Dixie', and the bears sung 'John Brown;' the crowd swayed feverishly from door to door, and, as the fury mounted to white heat, and the tide of gold fluctuated up and down in rapid sequence, brokers seemed animated with the impulses of demons, hand-to-hand combats took place, and bystanders, peering though the smoke and dust, could liken the wild turmoil only to the revels of maniacs."

Many people considered gold speculators to be traitors, and Francis Bicknell Carpenter recounted that the mention of gold prices occasioned "the strongest expression I ever heard fall from the lips of Mr. Lincoln. Knotting his face in the intensity of his feeling, he said, 'Curtin, what do you think of those fellows in Wall Street, who are gambling in gold at such a time as this?' 'They are a set of sharks,' returned Curtin. 'For my part,' continued the President, bringing his clinched hand down upon the table, 'I wish every one of them had his *devilish* head shot off!'"[30]

It was clear that the time had come for reform. The more responsible dealers came together, and established a new Gold Board. It was imperative that they choose officers who would command respect, so as president they elected E.C.'s brother, Henry M. Benedict.[31]

Gold Room transactions could amount to a hundred million dollars a day, and messengers delivered the gold regularly between ten and two, in bags clearly marked with the value of their contents. Although an extra police force was on duty, thefts were frequent. Obviously, there had to be a safer way. Why not let accountants transfer the funds? During 1866 the Benedict brothers organized the Gold Exchange Bank to act as a clearing-house, with Henry as president.[32] To avoid any conflict of interest Henry then ceased trading in gold,[33] but E.C. continued to manage the brothers' brokerage house.

The Gold Room followed the practice of the New York Stock Exchange in that verbal agreements were scrupulously honored. Matthew Hale Smith described how it worked: "The exactness with which business is transacted is marvelous. Millions pass, not only without error, but without the slightest irregularity.... There are no witnesses to these contracts. The transaction is between man and man alone. Yet no mistakes are made – no misunderstandings. Millions change hands daily in these scenes of confusion. No man backs down from his bargain....A person would be instantly expelled by the Board should he do so."[34]

The system depended solely on the honor of gentlemen, and therein lay the fatal flaw. What if someone came along who chose to play by his own rules, not the rules of gentlemen? For such a man, as Kenneth D. Ackerman put it, "The Gold Exchange was a sitting duck."[35]

There was such a man. At age 33, Jason (Jay) Gould was already president of the Erie Railway Company, but he had grander ambitions. He now formulated what Sobel called "the most audacious plot in American financial history; he would corner the nation's gold supply."[36] "Of all financial operations," explained Henry Adams, "cornering gold is the most brilliant and the most dangerous, and possibly the very hazard and splendor of the attempt were the reasons of its fascination to Mr. Jay Gould's fancy."[37]

Just about everybody on Wall Street thought that there was so much gold in circulation that it could never be cornered. Furthermore, the federal government possessed a considerable hoard, so it could easily break a gold corner.[38] "It was therefore essential," explained Adams, "that Mr. Gould should control the government itself, whether by fair means or foul, by persuasion or by purchase."[39]

How could Gould possibly persuade President Ulysses Grant? If there was one thing General Grant abhorred, it was speculating in gold. During the war, newspapers had called the gold traders "General Lee's left wing,"[40] and Grant probably still considered the practice akin to treason. Gould had to come up with a cover story that would appeal to Grant's patriotism, for the General knew nothing about economics.

Gould formulated what he called the "crop theory," according to which, in order to help western farmers move their crops, the government should not force down the price of gold.[41]

That summer Gould mounted a clever campaign. According to Clews, "The President was carefully shadowed after this by the detectives of the clique, and great care was taken to throw men across his path who were fluent talkers on the great financial problems of the day, the absolute necessity of stimulating the export trade and raising the premium upon gold for that patriotic purpose. In this way, President Grant began to think that the opinion of almost everybody he talked with on this subject was on the same side, and must, therefore, be correct."[42]

Chapter 10

"RUINED."—Drawn by C. G. Bush.

Harper's Weekly recorded the anguish that investors experienced on Black Friday, when Jay Gould cornered the gold market and provoked a severe stock market crash. In order to carry out his scheme, Gould also had to wreck the Benedict brothers' Gold Exchange Bank.

By early September the President had swallowed the crop theory, and expressed to Treasury Secretary Boutwell his strong opinion that, because it was so important to help western farmers move their crops, the government should not force down the price of gold.[43]

"In ten short weeks," marveled Ackerman, "Jay Gould …had done the unthinkable: [he] had maneuvered 'Unconditional Surrender' Grant into a 180-degree retreat."

Gould had another asset, Boss Tweed, who controlled a number of New York's judges. Gould had already installed Tweed as a director of the Erie railroad, so he could call upon Tammany judges whenever he needed them.

On Thursday, Sept. 23, 1869, Gould and his associates held calls exceeding $100 million – more than six times the amount of gold available in New York.[44] The next morning, in Stedman's words, "The Furies seemed to have broken loose. Men rushed around the little enclosure shrieking their bids or offers like barbarians running amuck. Curses and protestations burst from their lips. The jargon of speculation was interlarded with the raving of disordered minds. While the premium advanced, more than one man seemed for the time to have gone insane.…The groans that rose from the mob of onlookers at the outer rail added to the tumult as the price mounted steadily higher.…To the great body of men in the Gold Room it meant disaster, or even ruin."[45]

As Black Friday ended, Henry Benedict finally grasped the enormity of Gould's plan. That evening nine of the ring's brokers refused to submit their accounts, or submitted inadequate ones.[46] As a result $500 million in transactions could not be cleared.[47]

Up to this point, all Gould's moves had been preparatory. Now he fired the coup de grâce – his weapon, Boss Tweed's judges. Using as his excuse the bank's inability to settle accounts, he proceeded to wrest the bank from Henry's hands. Judge Albert Cardozo gave no notice, hearing, or chance for rebuttal, but simply placed the bank in receivership, and as receiver he chose the law partner of New York's Tammany Mayor.[48]

Eventually the receiver returned the shell of the Gold Exchange Bank to its owners, and it limped along for a time, with E.C. Benedict as its final president.[49]

What lessons did E.C. learn from this debacle?

First, there was nothing more important to Wall Street than its relationship with the White House. Gould's success rested entirely on his ability to manipulate President Grant. It was clear to E.C. that Wall Street, to get its way, must co-opt a President, not bamboozle him. In due course the handling of a President would be E.C.'s job, and he would do it much more deftly.

Second, he now understood the real rules of the Great Game, which he went on to play with notable success. He continued his career as a stockbroker, but made the bulk of his fortune in illuminating gas.

The Yachtsman

On Wall Street the pressure of business burned out many a hard-driving man. In E.C.'s words, "I took up yachting…because I had reached such a state that my physician said that I would have to do something of that kind to save my life."[50] In 1887, at age 53, he purchased an ocean-going yacht, the 138 ft. *Utowana*, built in 1883 for the stockbroker, Washington Connor. Benedict changed her name to *Oneida*, and purchased a tender from Frank Ofeldt, powered by one of Frank's new engines. Although E.C. had little nautical experience, he quickly metamorphosed into an enthusiastic seaman. He made such constant use of his yacht that in thirty years she had traveled 231,000 miles.[51]

Chapter 10

After E.C. Benedict recovered from the Black Friday debacle, he pursued a very successful career on Wall Street, and then took up yachting.

The first of Benedict's two yachts, both named *Oneida*.

Jennie Flagler

That was a time when the Standard Oil men were buying summer homes outside New York. John D. Rockefeller and John Archbold headed up the Hudson, while Jabez Bostwick and Henry Flagler chose the Connecticut shoreline. Henry Flagler's estate, *Satan's Toe*, was near Greenwich, where E.C. Benedict already lived, so the two were almost neighbors. In the fall of 1887, Henry's daughter, Jennie, married E.C.'s son, Frederick. Jennie's courtship with young Benedict was noted in the newspapers as being "as exquisite as any of the tales of fiction," but the marriage was ill-starred. Flagler's biographer, David Leon Chandler, recounts the sad story: "On February 9, 1889, the Benedicts' first child, a daughter named Margery, was born. Complications set in, however, and the child died within hours. Jennie's condition also worsened, and her doctor recommended that she be taken to Florida for rest and recuperation. Her father-in-law, a well-known yachtsman, offered his finest schooner, the *Oneida,* for the trip. Her doctors felt that the luxurious care she would receive on the yacht would be less strenuous, and the ocean air more healthful, than the trip by rail, even if made in Henry Flagler's private car."[52] Jennie was accompanied by a physician, but she developed a high fever and entered a coma. Henry Flagler was waiting at quayside, but when *Oneida* came into port, her colors were at half-mast.[53]

Grover Cleveland

During the summer of 1890, E.C. Benedict's daughter Helen visited the family of the editor of *The Century Magazine*, Richard Watson Gilder, who had a summer home at Marion, Massachusetts. At the end of Helen's stay, E.C. arrived in *Oneida* and went ashore in his Ofeldt launch to pick her up. He later recalled, "Toward the middle of the evening two strangers entered, one rather short, but the other a very powerfully built figure, and dressed in a manner somewhat in contrast to the rather summery garments of the others present. The suit had evidently seen much wear, and he wore a dark outing shirt. A soft, nondescript hat was crushed in his hand and his whole aspect denoted to my practiced eye the natural born fisherman. A moment later I was shaking hands with Grover Cleveland."[54]

After a day of fishing, Grover Cleveland, right, chats with L. Clarke Davis, editor of the *Philadelphia Public Ledger*. It was Cleveland's love of fishing that led to his lifelong friendship with E.C. Benedict.

Chapter 10

E.C. and Cleveland soon discovered that both were sons of Presbyterian ministers, "and found, to our delight, that we had both suffered in about the same measure from the severity of the Calvinistic Puritanical atmosphere which had surrounded our boyish days. …There was the Saturday night gloom over the approaching Sabbath which we were expected to enjoy but didn't.…We envied our unfettered associates who could whittle or whistle or take a swim, or fish on Sundays, or even go barefooted without incurring divine displeasure."[55]

Grover was now ex-President, and in the spring of 1891 bought a summer home near Marion, which he called *Gray Gables*. The fishing was excellent in Buzzard's Bay, and *Oneida* could moor offshore.

Herbert J. Satterlee described the Cleveland-Benedict fishing expeditions: "They were intimate friends. The President often cruised on *Oneida* for two or three days. On these occasions, he fished for cod over the side, trolled for bluefish from a small sailboat; or they both went off in a launch and anchored over some ledge where they caught 'the run of the tide' in pollock, perch, cod, and flounders, or whatever fish might be in that neighborhood, and then returned to their cribbage. The games lasted far into the night, as I know from many personal experiences."[56]

Grover soon became fond of *Oneida* and, according to her guest book, was welcomed aboard 57 times.[57] Benedict was called *Commodore* by his friends, so out of deference he addressed Cleveland as *Admiral*.

When he was in office, Grover had invested in a small way, but avoided speculation, asserting that, "a man is apt to know too much in my position that might affect matters in the least speculative."[58] Now that he was free to invest, he turned to Benedict for advice. According to E.C., "He sent me what little money he had been able to save up with the request that I do with it as I would with my own."[59]

E.C. explained how he and Grover came to live in adjacent houses. "I had just bought a place on 51st Street and when I found I could get him for a neighbor I added the next house, No. 12, to mine and offered it to him for a home. The rent was a good deal less than he was paying, and as an added inducement I promised to cut a door to connect the two houses. This proved a great convenience to Mr. Cleveland, for whenever callers appeared whom he could not see he simply walked into my house and the servant could truthfully say Mr. Cleveland was not at home."[60] There was another attraction; E.C. had installed a stock ticker at home, and Grover was fascinated to watch the progress of his investments.[61]

This raises a pertinent question: How did E.C. Benedict influence Cleveland's thinking?

Grover was a lifelong conservative, but during his first term he had come to the conclusion that the interests of the American people were threatened by the growing power of big business. His parting message to Congress was so radical that it could have been written by Eugene Debs, socialist presidential candidate:

"The fortunes realized by our manufacturers…are largely built upon undue exactions from the masses of our people. The gulf between employers and the employed is constantly widening, and classes are rapidly forming, one comprising the very rich and powerful, while in another are found the toiling poor. As we view the achievements of aggregated capital, we discover the existence of trusts, combinations, and monopolies, while the citizen is struggling far in the rear or is trampled to death beneath an iron heel. Corporations, which should be the carefully restrained creatures of the law and the servants of the people, are fast becoming the people's masters."[62]

E.C.'s views were the polar opposite. The only concern he is known to have expressed for the toiling poor was the fear that they might join unions, which he hated with a passion.[63]

After leaving office, Cleveland had joined the law firm of Francis Lynde Stetson, whose clients included J.P. Morgan. As we shall see, when Grover returned to the Presidency, he was a man transformed. Under the influence of Stetson and Benedict, he had totally absorbed Wall Street's values, and during his second term neither farmers nor labor would have a sympathetic ear in the White House.

Defeat of the Ofeldt Improved Launch

Up until 1891, Frank Ofeldt's business had been doing well, but that year it suffered a setback. Since introducing the Ofeldt Improved engine, the company had insisted that it was superior to the naphtha engine. Now Jabez Bostwick put that claim to the test.

In its 1892 catalog, the Gas Engine and Power Company announced the result: "Not long since we had an opportunity to test the relative merits of one of our Launches compared with a supposed 'World Beater,' and the illustration…shows result of race, which was between an Ofeldt Naphtha Steam Launch and a Naphtha Launch.…The power in both boats claimed by builders to be same—10 hp.…The photographs were taken shortly after the start, and just before the finish, distance run being somewhat less than two miles. It is hardly necessary to add that the leading boat is the Naphtha Launch."[64]

In a head-to-head race, a naphtha launch (with white hull), decisively defeated an Ofeldt Improved launch, but Frank was undeterred.

The result was decisive, and sales of Ofeldt Improved launches dropped off. However, Frank was undeterred. He had decided to take a chance on E.C. Benedict, and in 1892 moved back to New Jersey, where he opened a workshop at 240 Communipaw Avenue, Jersey City. Apparently he left his sons to run the Brooklyn yard. Frank called his New Jersey business the *Ofeldt Naphtha Steam Launch Works*,[65] as if he were still building his Ofeldt Improved steam engine, but he wasn't.

Frank's output was prolific; between January 1893 and April 1894 he applied for no less than four patents, which included a launch that would be so much safer than the naphtha launch that, in Frank's opinion, it would terminate the reign of naphtha. We can assume that E.C. Benedict underwrote the experiments, for Frank assigned all four patents to a company set up by E.C. to manufacture the new launch.

Chapter 11

The Bostwick Legacy

"Few meritorious inventions have been so novel, and have been brought to perfection in such a short time as the naphtha launch."

Edward T. Birdsall, *The Rudder*[1]

The Man of God

On the last evening of his life, Jabez Bostwick and his wife, Nellie, were joined for dinner by two neighbors, one of whom was Clement Gould, Bostwick's cousin and president of the Gas Engine and Power Company.

Jabez Bostwick was described by *The New York Times* as "a restless man, always entering into new ventures." In 1886, shortly after founding the Gas Engine and Power Company, he had been elected president of the New York and New England Railroad Company[2] and in the following year resigned his position as a Standard Oil Trustee. His interests were in safe hands, watched over by his protégé Wesley Hunt Tilford who, although only 37, was immediately elevated to the vacant trusteeship.[3] If Tilford's rapid rise seems surprising, it should be understood that the Standard Oil men perceived the ownership of their company as being vested, not in individuals, but in families.[4] As the Bostwicks and Tilfords had been allied for over 30 years, Jabez undoubtedly regarded Wesley as almost next of kin, and a reliable custodian of the family's interest.

Jabez Bostwick. The phenomenal success of the naphtha launch was just as attributable to Bostwick's brilliant business skill as to Frank Ofeldt's inventive genius.

105

The Standard Oil Company did not announce Bostwick's resignation, so for several years the press thought that Jabez was still accountable for the Standard's actions. In 1892 the *Herald* denounced a "gigantic robbery" which would "give the trust full and exclusive control of two miles of waterfront" on what the newspaper called *Bostwick's East River*.[5]

After six years Jabez tired of railroading and again looked for new fields to conquer. He was still a member of the Cotton Exchange, and now bought a seat on the New York Stock Exchange.[6]

Ironically for an oilman, Jabez was nearly killed by a gasoline explosion in his own home. While bending over a fuel tank to mend a leak, he incautiously lit a match, and was burned severely on his hands and face. *The New York Times* noted that Jabez "always afterward had a dread of fire,…a peculiar coincidence with the sad manner of Mr. Bostwick's death."[7]

On the evening of August 16, 1892, after Nellie retired, the men went to the billiard room where they played until 10:30. About an hour after the guests departed, a fire broke out next door and then spread to the Bostwick stable. The coachman and groom saved Bostwick's eight horses and began pulling out the twelve carriages. Nearing 62, Jabez was no longer enjoying robust health. His physician had prescribed quietness and rest, but he had difficulty complying. According to *The New York Times*, Nellie endeavored to dissuade Jabez from playing an active part in fighting the fire, reminding him of his condition, but he paid no heed. He quickly took command, issuing directions, and pulling at the vehicles.

In the course of his work he took hold of the front axle of a large dray in order to guide it. The coachman, not knowing that Jabez was there, pushed with his full strength. "As the dray came out of the stable Mr. Bostwick attempted to guide it down the path, but the whiffletree flew out of his hand and he was thrown with violence against the outer wall of the stable, the wheels pinning him tight." Clement Gould returned from his house to find Jabez groaning with pain. "The flames from the burning stable lighted up the dying man's features; the little group that surrounded him, and the trees, shrubs, and bushes were all illuminated by the dancing light, making a weird scene. Every one now appreciated that he was dying." A physician was summoned, but to no avail. Just at midnight Jabez died.[8]

The widow and children inherited twelve million dollars.[9] As the assets consisted largely of Standard Oil shares, the estate continued to appreciate, and in 1920 Nellie was worth $30 million (some $600 million today).[10]

Among the attendees at Bostwick's funeral were William Rockefeller, Henry Flagler, John Archbold and H.H. Rogers, all Standard Oil trustees. Dr. Armitage, Bostwick's former pastor, delivered an eloquent eulogy, dwelling especially on his "stanch, unchangeable character as a friend and his simple, lovable disposition under all circumstances."[11]

As we know, this was not the whole truth about Jabez Bostwick.

There can be no doubt that he was a devout Christian. As a young man he had sold Bibles door to door,[12] and he was now a trustee of the Fifth Avenue Baptist Church, as were both the Rockefeller brothers.[13] Jabez never missed Sunday service, and he also attended the weekly prayer meetings. He donated generously, not only to Baptist churches and colleges,[14] but to those of other denominations as well.[15]

How are we to reconcile Jabez Bostwick, the man of God, with the strict businessman who treated Frank Ofeldt so unfeelingly?

Most of the Standard Oil men were brought up in Calvinist families, and religion shaped their lives. Both Henry Flagler and John Archbold were sons of preachers, but it was Jabez Bostwick, Charles Pratt, and John D. Rockefeller who were the most conspicuously pious. To find an explanation for Jabez Bostwick's behavior we need to examine his – and his colleagues' – deeply-held religious views.

Ron Chernow, who has been given unprecedented access to Rockefeller's records, tells us that, "John D. regarded God as an ally, a sort of honorary shareholder of Standard Oil," and he quotes Rockefeller's statements that, "The Standard was an angel of mercy, reaching down from the sky, and saying 'Get into the ark,'" and that Standard Oil was "the Moses who delivered them [the refiners] from their folly." Rockefeller and his partners viewed themselves as "missionaries of light" who "tried to treat weaker competitors with compassion, [but] there were limits to their tolerance since they could not 'stop the car of salvation in their great enterprise'."[16]

An earlier historian of Standard Oil, John T. Flynn, had the advantage of being brought up in Victorian times, so well understood the powerful influence of the Old Testament. Flynn asserted that the Standard Oil men, steeped in the ethics of the Old Testament, never doubted that their achievement justified the cost. "Was not Jehovah himself ruthless in pursuing his righteous plans? Did not the Lord turn a river into blood and cover the land with frogs? Did not Moses turn the dust into lice and fleas, and cover men and beasts with boils? Did he shrink from these necessary stratagems because weak men suffered?"[17]

If the reader doubts Flynn's theory, a simpler explanation can be found in the writings of R.H. Tawney, who pointed out that, to a Puritan, "conscientious discharge of the duties of business is among the loftiest of religious and moral virtues....Success in business is in itself almost a sign of spiritual grace, for it is proof that a man has labored faithfully in his vocation, and that 'God has blessed his trade'."[18]

Business was Jabez Bostwick's calling. If people like Frank Ofeldt got hurt along the way, Jabez was untroubled, for his wealth provided clear evidence that he had fulfilled the divine will.

Be that as it may, it is time for us to measure Jabez Bostwick's achievement in masterminding the introduction of the naphtha launch. It is useful to compare him to Matthew Boulton. It was said of Boulton that, "Had Mr. Watt searched all Europe, he could not have found another person so fitted to bring his invention before the public in a manner worthy of its merit and importance."[19]

Much the same could be said of Jabez. His successes in cotton and petroleum were no accident. He always moved quickly and decisively, and gave his opponents no quarter. Now he had an additional advantage, Frank Ofeldt's watertight patents. Those patents gave the Gas Engine and Power Company, and its licensee, Escher Wyss, an effective monopoly for several years, something that Jabez had never enjoyed before. Accordingly, Jabez developed a strategy for introducing the naphtha launch to the public that was nothing less than brilliant.

Let us examine what the Gas Engine and Power Company was able to achieve during the years when Jabez guided it.

It had not all been easygoing, and at times had required nimble footwork. Not surprisingly, the first challenge came from the fertile mind of the English inventor, Alfred Yarrow.

The First Challenger: Alfred Yarrow

The prolific nautical designer, Alfred Yarrow, mounted a challenge to the Gas Engine and Power Company's monopoly.

In the course of his career, Yarrow had designed a successful steam carriage, numerous novel steamboats, and, as we have seen, one of the first viable electric boats. In 1888, two years after the introduction of the naphtha launch, he announced a new invention, the *petroleum spirit vapor launch*.[20] His claim: "For pleasure boats it far excels anything that has been brought before the public in convenience. It possesses all the advantages of electricity while the fuel used can be bought at any oil shop."[21] Pictures of Yarrow's *Zephyr* show a boat very similar to the naphtha launch.

The reader will easily guess how Bostwick dealt with Yarrow. The Standard Oil men had long mastered the art of co-opting their most dangerous adversaries, so Jabez did exactly what he and his colleagues had done to Rogers and Archbold; he turned the talented Englishman into an ally. Alfred Yarrow built no more naphtha launches, and in exchange the Gas Engine and Power Company made him its British agent. Yarrow was well-connected, and within two years sold more than twenty launches to customers that included the Duke of Marlborough, the Sultan of Turkey, Prince Eyetwertynski and the Government of Japan. Equally important, Bostwick was now able to draw on Yarrow's extensive experience with steam engines. In January 1892, the company announced that it would now build yachts of fifty feet and upward, powered by steam: "In selecting the motive power for our Steam Yachts we have been largely aided by the well-known firm of English yacht builders, Messrs. Yarrow & Co."[22]

Alfred Yarrow's *Petroleum Spirit Vapor Launch* threatened to be a competitor, but Jabez Bostwick parried the threat, and turned Yarrow into an ally.

Charles L. Seabury

Another challenge came from within the company. It appears that Jabez continued to have troubles in getting his team to work together harmoniously. Charles Seabury had replaced Frank Ofeldt as vice-president, but Seabury left after two years, together with William J. Parslow, Clement Gould's office manager, to found *Charles L. Seabury & Company* in Nyack, New York. That company soon became famous for its steam yachts, engines, and boilers.

Curiously, Seabury – like Ofeldt – chose to offer a product calculated to confuse Bostwick's customers. He called it the *naphtha steam launch*, and drew the following testimonial from a satisfied customer:

> "I am very much pleased with the naphtha steam launch which you built for me, and I cannot say too much in praise of it....The machinery developed so much power for the small space occupied in the stern of the launch, I decided to give you the order, and from my experience during the six months (from May to November) using the boat almost daily, I believe yours to be the best liquid fuel launch in the market, and consider it absolutely safe....The engine and boiler have been a wonder to everyone who saw it in operation last season....Can obtain 200 lbs. pressure in five minutes, and hold it steady right along with valve wide open."[23]

Chapter 11

After Charles Seabury left the Gas Engine and Power Company, he – like Frank Ofeldt – built a steam launch fueled by naphtha (left foreground) to compete with the naphtha launch.

At least one other builder, H.V. Partelow & Co. of Boston, sold naphtha-fueled steam launches[24] so it was imperative that Bostwick distinguish his product from the competition. As early as 1889, the Gas and Engine and Power Company began describing its launch as *The Only Naphtha Launch.*

In an effort to ward off competitors like Ofeldt and Seabury, the Gas Engine and Power Company began calling its product *The Only Naphtha Launch.*

109

Fear of Naphtha

The most difficult obstacle to the engine's acceptance was the notoriety of the fuel itself, but by 1890 the press was beginning to give the naphtha launch the benefit of the doubt. The following passage appeared in the *Columbus Daily Enquirer*:

"Few inventions have been met with deeper prejudice against them and with quicker acceptance at the same time. At first everybody was afraid that they would explode, for naphtha in its various uses has been on record as a terrible destroyer in cases of misapplication or improper treatment. The method, however, by which naphtha is made to serve as a fuel precludes any possibility of explosion. That, at least, is what the inventor and the manufacturers say, and experience thus far has confirmed their statement."[25]

Still it is only human to fear the worst, as demonstrated by the *Brooklyn Eagle*'s efforts to untangle what really happened to the naphtha launch *Ethel*. In its initial version, headed "Down To Death," the *Eagle* recounted a curious story about a group of fishermen who passed a large red and black striped buoy off Coney Island. "The captain noticed something very peculiar about the buoy and said to us, 'It is very strange to see anything on top of a buoy so far off shore.' We thought nothing of this and sailed along for about twenty minutes when Mr. Bremmer happened to look in that direction, and as he did so he put the spy glass to his eyes and said: 'Why, there is a man on the buoy waving for help.'" The man turned out to be Captain Louden White, the only survivor of the *Ethel*. The newspaper also reported, "The launch came ashore on the beach at Far Rockaway this afternoon. The bottom was blown out of her."

After Captain White regained enough strength, he told the story: "We were going along at a good rate of speed, although the waves were running high, when all of a sudden the steering gear of the launch became unmanageable and I had no control of the boat. We ran ashore on the shoals at Long Beach and in less than ten seconds a large wave was sweeping toward the launch, when I heard a terrific explosion and the next instant was struggling in the water."

Suspicion naturally fell on *Ethel*'s naphtha engine, so the *Eagle* sought out an expert, William A. Powell, superintendent of boiler inspection, who said "I have not made a particular study of the naphtha boilers, but what I have seen of them leads me to believe that they are far more dangerous than the steam boilers, for the reason, particularly, that they are usually in the hands of inexperienced people. Naphtha boilers should be under inspection, as steam boilers are, and it will take only a few such accidents as that of yesterday to convince the public of the fact. The history of the steam boilers was the same. Ignorant people were allowed to jeopardize life until the fatalities were so frequent that the use of steam was put under legal restraint."[26]

Two days later a neighbor of one of the victims called the newspaper to refute the original story. "White has made himself very much disliked by the people of the village by his conflicting statements and there is some talk of drilling him out of town. He it was who made the statement that the boat blew up. This gave Mrs. Caemmerer the impression that her husband had been blown to atoms and made her feel bad, as she wanted to recover the body.... The story that White had been badly burned is untrue. He is as sound as a dollar.... The boat is also uninjured and looks as good as before it went on its fateful trip. We went to Far Rockaway yesterday and examined her. Only her rudder is a little bent and the smokestack has been broken off.... We rigged up a mast and brought her to East Rockaway. Her machinery worked all right and nothing seemed the matter with her."[27]

The Gas Engine and Power Company recommended that intending purchasers not rely on hearsay evidence, and under the heading, "Are They Safe?" used the *Ethel* story as an illustration:

"The newspaper accounts of the wrecking of the launch 'Ethel' at Long Beach were described by headlines as 'A Yacht Blown Up at Sea,' 'The Explosion of a Naphtha Launch,' etc., yet the launch was picked up afloat the following day, with hull in perfect condition and machinery intact. The facts finally brought out by investigation were that, by an error in judgment, the party attempted to cross a bar where there was too little water, the boat struck and damaged her steering gear, and thus becoming unmanageable was swamped in the breakers. There has never been an explosion of tank, boiler, engine, or any part of the mechanism of a Naphtha Launch. In two or three instances fires have occurred, due solely to careless handling of naphtha....

"Would-be competitors, jealous of our success, have not hesitated to circulate all manner of malicious reports, in order to prevent parties, if possible, from buying our boats, and to attract attention to their own productions.

"Do not be misled by stories coming from prejudiced sources, but ask for positive proof from principals or participants. We defy anyone to prove a single accident where an explosion of any part of the machinery of one of our boats has occurred, or where anyone was injured by fire from such a cause. Not infrequently we have letters from parties who say they have heard of certain terrible accidents, but whenever asked for names they decline to give them. Slander thus protected is hard to reach.

"To demonstrate, if possible, more forcibly our confidence in the absolute safety of the system, we offer $500 to the person who can explode boiler or machinery of our Launch. We furnish, without charge, Launch for the test, requiring a deposit of $100 from the party making experiment, to be forfeited to us in case of failure."[28]

Cautionary Notes

In order to educate its customers in the safe handling of naphtha, the company included a set of *Cautionary Notes* with each boat. Here are excerpts from the 1890 version:

"WHAT NOT TO DO:
- Don't neglect stuffing boxes.
- Don't shoot through your tank.
- Don't fill tank when Engine is running.
- Don't light match to look into Naphtha tank.
- Don't allow bilge water to remain about Engine.
- Don't unscrew top of tank when there is fire under retort.
- Don't use any but 76° Deodorized Naphtha, or Stove Gasoline.[29]
- Don't leave open any barrel or other receptacle containing naphtha.
- Don't have light, or fire of any kind, about when filling tank, or when trap-screw is off the tank.
- Don't fill tank when Launch is in a closed boathouse, and afterwards start the fire there, unless you are sure that no gas has accumulated.

"Everyone using (Naphtha) should thoroughly understand that, when exposed to the air, it evaporates rapidly, and forms a gas which, if confined, explodes, when ignited, with terrific force; also when it is thrown or spilled on water, it will float on the surface, and burn there if ignited by a flame. Therefore, there should never be a fire or flame near where Naphtha is being handled, or even when any tank, barrel or other receptacle containing Naphtha is uncovered. A current of air passing over an open vessel containing this fluid, may carry along sufficient gas to ignite, and following back, set it on fire. Naphtha, or gasoline, is now utilized for many different purposes, but in no instance so safely and successfully as in connection with the Naphtha Launch. The only instance where an accident has happened, was solely due to gross carelessness in the handling of the Naphtha.

"It is important to often examine the stuffing-boxes on crank shaft, front and back (which are at bottom of engine); and keep set up in good shape, for if neglected, Naphtha will leak out and take fire; which is unnecessary and often alarms timid persons, though the engine pit is entirely lined with sheet brass, as a protection to those who neglect to do this work as instructed.

"*These instructions appear to be invariably not followed; and, as a consequence, inexperienced people are sometimes alarmed.*

"Knowing as we do, however, the intelligence of the owners of Naphtha Launches, our Launches, and the people who ride in them, are far safer in their hands than those who intrust their lives to pilots and engineers, who, at the best, are but of ordinary intellect.... There has been but one accident, in four years, with over 450 launches built by us."[30]

The Opposition Builds

At that time launches were fueled from cans or barrels, and occasional spillages were inevitable. One of the first fires occurred while the launch was still in its boathouse. On August 5, 1889, the *Oswego Palladium* carried an article headed: "A BUFFALO HOLOCAUST, Fatal Explosion on Board a Naphtha Launch, FOUR PEOPLE WERE CREMATED:

"While the yacht *Cedar Ridge*...was being gotten in readiness for a trip down the river, and just as the engineer had started the fire, two explosions occurred on board in rapid succession. The yacht at once took fire and burned to the water's edge." The owner's young son, on the yacht's deck, "fell back into the fire and was burned to a crisp in full view of the horrified spectators."[31]

This explosion, and another similar one, caused *The New York Times* to question why the government had not applied the steam regulations to naphtha launches:

"Persons who seek pleasure on the water in the Summer months will not fail to note a second fatal explosion on a "naphtha launch." These little boats are so numerously used, and are so widely advertised as perfectly safe and not subject to the requirements of the law regulating steam engines, that much anxiety will be caused. For the public's reassurance it may be noted that neither the *Leo* nor the *Cedar Ridge* appears to have killed its passengers by the explosion of naphtha in the boiler. In both cases the fatal naphtha appears to have been that used as fuel. In the *Leo's* hold, it is expressly stated, forty gallons of the inflammable stuff was carried.[32] The distinction is worth noting, for, to some people, anything is a naphtha launch which uses naphtha at all, whereas the only naphtha launches fairly entitled to that name are those in which naphtha is used expansively, like steam....

"It is not intended to express any opinion here as to the comparative safety of the system of using naphtha vapor instead of water vapor in the boiler. But it is very obvious that if the law regulating steam engines does not include naphtha engines there is a very possible source of danger in the use of naphtha engines by inexperienced persons, and possibly under dangerous conditions of pressure or deterioration of apparatus, which the law regulating the use of steam would disclose or prevent. The matter is worth attention, for naphtha launches are used, and permitted to be used, by many who would not dream of thus trifling with steam."[33]

Three weeks later the company sought support from naphtha launch owners. One reply came from Rufus B. Bullock, ex-Governor of Georgia:

"After three seasons' use and observation of your power in a launch which we own, and our children use, I can say positively that bringing Naphtha Launches under same restrictions governing steam, is entirely unnecessary as a safeguard to human life, and would be a wholly unnecessary interference with individual rights and comfort."[34]

However, Congressional reaction was swift. Two bills were introduced in early 1890, aimed at bringing naphtha launches under the steam regulations. The Gas Engine and Power Company denounced "the folly of such legislation...as being uncalled for, unnecessary and unjust." When both bills were beaten back in committee, the company exulted that, "This settles definitely the question of Inspection and License with the Naphtha Launches."[35]

So much for Congress, but what about the administration? With Manning and Whitney gone, and *The New York Times* on the warpath, might Treasury buckle?

Chapter 11

Charles Foster

Benjamin Harrison's first Treasury Secretary died in office, and Harrison nominated Charles Foster to replace him. Foster had a warm spot in his heart for Standard Oil. He and Henry Flagler had shared a rowdy adolescence along with Dan Harkness, Flagler's cousin. According to Flagler's biographer, one weekend "the Three Musketeers…had a few too many at the new Tremont Hotel, and the boys were asked to leave after running across tables and breaking dishes. They paid for the breakage and returned two weeks later for more of the same. The table running became sort of a regular thing."[36]

Treasury Secretary Charles Foster had close ties to the Standard Oil Company, so – like Daniel Manning – he chose not to impose the steam regulations on the naphtha launch.

Charles Foster served in the House of Representatives for four terms and then was elected Governor of Ohio, serving two terms. Ron Chernow tells us that during Foster's political career he was "a recipient of Standard Oil campaign largesse." In 1884 Foster went into the natural gas business, and two years later secretly merged with his supposed rival, owned by Standard Oil.[37] According to John T. Flynn, "These two companies applied to the city authorities of Toledo for franchises to supply gas. The people thought this an excellent thing – two companies competing for their trade. They granted the franchises. Then they discovered that both companies belonged to the oil Octopus and that they had been hoodwinked. Great was their chagrin at the deception."[38]

The flagrancy of Foster's nomination to the Treasury raised a storm of protest.

"It isn't pleasant," the *New York World* wrote, "to have a Secretary of the Treasury who holds intimate relations with the Oil Trust."[39] *The New York Times* reported that Foster had been defeated in Ohio as a candidate for Congress in 1890 entirely due to his connection with the oil combination, and "He could not be chosen to the Toledo Council from any ward today, so bitter is the feeling against him."[40] However, the *New York Press* noted that President Harrison did not regard Foster's connection with Standard Oil as serious enough to have any weight, and the appointment went ahead.[41] Needless to say, during Foster's term as Treasury Secretary, there was no change in the steam regulations.

Naphtha

Thomas Fleming Day

Besides fending off questions about safety, the naphtha launch faced an aesthetic challenge. No matter what its merits, it was a motorboat, and every true sailor despised engines. One potential opponent was the "hard-bitten deep-water sailor," Thomas Fleming Day, who launched a new publication, *The Rudder*, in 1890.[42] L. Francis Herreshoff wrote that the naphtha launch was "just the sort of apparatus that he would dislike."[43] If Herreshoff was right, it seems odd that Day's new publication, *The Rudder*, featured a picture of a naphtha launch on its masthead.

In the third issue, Day clarified his position: "The black-blight that invades and destroys the racing spirit in yacht clubs is the steam yacht. What quality of blood runs in the veins of a man who will willingly exchange the exciting and exhilarating pastime of sailing for the monotonous privilege of being driven around in a kettle? With obligations to the late Lord St. Vincent, we remark, that a yachtsman who descends to running a steam yacht is d----d for the sport!

"But since this lubberly individual exists in numbers, it is necessary for us to cater to the perverted taste, though against inclination; therefore we have inserted in this issue an article on the 'Naphtha Launch.'"[44]

The article, signed I.I.A., was fulsome in its praise: "A few years ago the only power-driven boats to be had were steam launches, using coal or wood for fuel. These launches cost a small fortune to build, and an income to keep. The running of them upon navigable waterways was hampered by government restrictions, the owner being obliged either to qualify as an engineer, or keep a licensed man aboard at a season's expense almost equaling the original outlay.

"With the rapid expansion of aquatic sport, a demand arose for something simpler and safer than the steam power—a power derived from a fluid easy of procuration, cheap, and capable of automatic control. Inventor after inventor struggled with this problem, only to add one more blank to the list of failures. It was not until the idea of using the highly expansive naphtha captured the brain of a genius that a motor was evolved combining in a marked degree the essentials of a perfect power. The fact that one fluid contained within itself not only the power of expansion, but the capability of producing that expansion by heat generated from the combustion of its own gas, was a gigantic stride in the direction of simplicity.

"Naphtha, the residuum of an article of enormous domestic consumption, is easily and cheaply procured, and, though highly inflammable, is not necessarily dangerous. All solids or fluids capable of producing power by expansion are more or less dangerous to careless people. The idiot who hunts gas leaks with a candle, warms nitroglycerine in the stove oven, or inspects the interior of a naphtha tank with a match, is a social eccentricity whose only excuse for existing is the object lesson he furnishes now and then to the rising generation."[45]

The Rudder's masthead featured a naphtha launch.

Chapter 11

Although Thomas Fleming Day hated engines, he reluctantly bowed to the "perverted taste" of some of his "lubberly" readers, and published an article about the naphtha launch. Surprisingly, the writer extolled Frank Ofeldt as a "genius" for inventing a "perfect power."

115

The Company's Growth

The Gas Engine and Power Company's success was abetted by the country's prosperity. The boom, which had begun in 1879, was providing more and more Americans with discretionary income. In consequence, year after year, the company ramped up production, and in 1889 announced that "there are four acres of buildings and docks, costing over $300,000,"[46] and by 1892 the company was able to boast that nearly a thousand naphtha launches were in use.[47] Customers were urged to visit the works, which were only "seventeen minutes from the Grand Central Station by the New York Central Railway."[48]

BOAT SHOP.

In 1892, at the time of Jabez Bostwick's death, the plant was humming.

Chapter 11

Craftsmen

Machine Shop.

The framing shop with three 53' boats, in 1892 the largest naphtha launches built.

By 1892 the Gas Engine and Power Company was offering a wider range of engines. The three largest – 10, 12, and 16-hp – were rectangular in configuration, because their boiler tubes were iron pipes, with threaded joints.[49] According to Bruce Trudgen, the large engines were fitted with two burners.[50]

The range of naphtha engines, from 1 to 16-hp. The larger engines had a rectangular configuration.

Chapter 11

Show Room, Winter, 1891-1892.

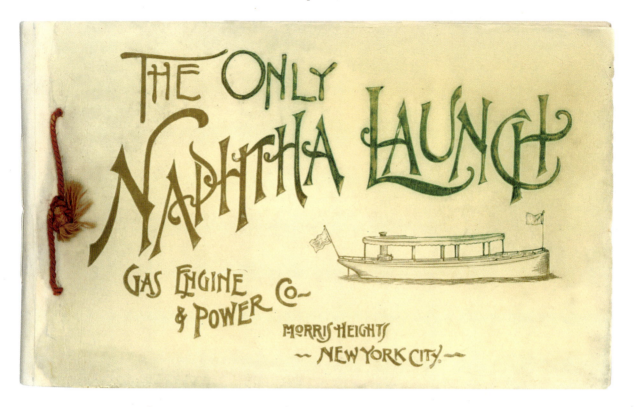

The 1892 catalog illustrated the range of the Gas Engine and Power Company's products at the end of Jabez Bostwick's regime.

Chapter 11

A deluxe version of the 21-ft. open naphtha launch with 2-hp motor. The price at $850 included mahogany finish, coaming around the cockpit, lockers under the seats, a steering wheel, and brass railings.

A 30-ft., 6-hp launch with a glass enclosure forward, and a standing roof aft.

Naphtha

A 35-ft. cabin cruising launch, with woodwork of polished mahogany, sliding windows, and lockers with lids that opened to form bunks for sleeping.

Chapter 11

The Gas Engine and Power Company described this 42-ft. boat as a yacht, not a launch. The rectangular configuration of the 12-hp motor is clearly visible.

At 53 ft., with a 16-hp motor, *Nellie* was the largest naphtha-powered craft the company built in 1892. She had a separate pilothouse with a brass binnacle and bell pulls for signaling the engineer, a galley with oil stove and refrigerator, and a toilet room with a Bishop's patent water closet and a folding washbowl. The windows featured damask draperies, and the floors were of linoleum, except in the main cabin, which had a Wilton carpet. A removable canvas curtain enclosed the engine compartment.

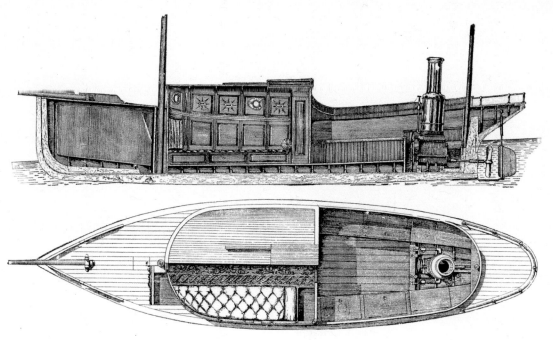

Sailboats had always been helpless when becalmed, so the naphtha engine provided a much-needed source of auxiliary power. *Etcetera* was built by the Gas Engine and Power Company in 1889 for L.Q. Jones of Hartford, Connecticut.

Chapter 11

THE "RACER" UNDER FULL SPEED.
PHOTOGRAPH TAKEN JULY 4, 1891, AT NAPHTHA LAUNCH RACE, AMERICAN YACHT CLUB, MILTON POINT, NEW YORK.
THE FASTEST BOAT OF HER SIZE IN THE WORLD.

The *Racer*, very narrow and light, was powered by a 6-hp naphtha engine. In 1892 she was the fastest boat for her size in the world, and was "always kept in readiness for a friendly trial of speed, with anything of the same inches afloat." (Gas Engine and Power Company 1894 catalog, p. 39)

Some naphtha launches were designed as workboats, including a sturdy model used for dredging oysters.

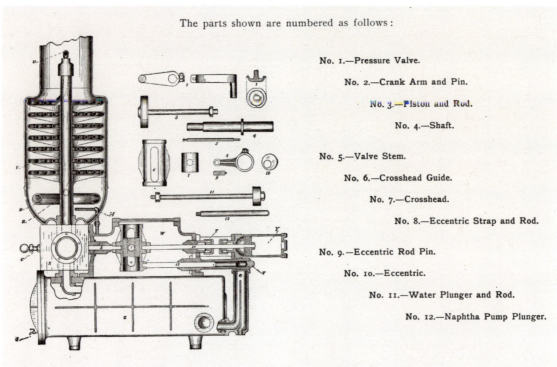

The parts shown are numbered as follows:

No. 1.—Pressure Valve.
No. 2.—Crank Arm and Pin.
No. 3.—Piston and Rod.
No. 4.—Shaft.
No. 5.—Valve Stem.
No. 6.—Crosshead Guide.
No. 7.—Crosshead.
No. 8.—Eccentric Strap and Rod.
No. 9.—Eccentric Rod Pin.
No. 10.—Eccentric.
No. 11.—Water Plunger and Rod.
No. 12.—Naphtha Pump Plunger.

To augment the nautical market, the company introduced a 2-hp stationary pumping engine with a capacity of 1,000 gallons per hour, at a price of $300.

Chapter 11

The Joy of Boating

Let us sum up Frank Ofeldt's relationship with Jabez Bostwick by observing that without Ofeldt there never would have been a naphtha launch, but without Bostwick, Frank's invention would very likely have gone nowhere. If Jabez had not been able to appeal to his friends in high places, the naphtha launch would have been a mere footnote in the history of technology. And without his business skills and marketing savvy, the revolution in personal transportation would have been deferred until the twentieth century. It was Frank Ofeldt who engineered a motorboat that was reliable and easy to operate. But Bostwick's achievement, by making motorboats widely available and affordable, was to establish that boating could be enjoyed, not only by yachtsmen, but by the general public.

In 1889 the *Brooklyn Eagle* noted how the naphtha launch had changed the lives of Americans:

"The cleverness and ingenuity of the Yankee mind has made possible, and thereby put within reach of half of the New Yorkers who go away for the Summer a pleasure which used to be considered the prerogative only of the very rich. The value and uses of the naphtha launch are beyond praise, and this Summer, for the first time, the average Summer resident is beginning to catch on to the possibilities of pleasure these little craft contain for his Summer sojourn.…These little boats are as easy to run as a sewing machine and very nearly as comfortable as one's own drawing room.…The people who have been using them tell me they never knew before all the beauties of the neighborhood in which they have lived for years, but that this Summer they have been exploring all the creeks, bays and waters of every sort within thirty miles of their homes and have a thousand interesting adventures and discoveries to put down to the credit of their little boats."[51]

As naphtha launches became more widely available, they offered a change in life style. Owners began to use their naphtha launches just to go for a ride, much as they would use their cars, a decade or so later.

The naphtha launch made power boating a pleasure.

127

The naphtha launch was the first motor-powered conveyance that could be operated by its owner, and it preceded the motorcar by more than a decade. Here we see the Durant family out for a ride in their naphtha launch, *Mugwump*, on Forked Lake in the Adirondacks. The young man nearest us is Kenneth Durant, whose book, *The Naphtha Launch*, provided some of our firsthand information. In the photo's caption he apologized for the position of the American flag, which normally flew at the stern.

Chapter 11

Granville Henchele and companions enjoy an outing in his naphtha launch on Lake Erie.

The naphtha launch introduced a multitude of people to the simple pleasure of messing about in boats. As the wise Water Rat observed, "Nice? It's the *only* thing....Believe me, my young friend, there is *nothing* – absolutely nothing – half so much worth doing as simply messing about in boats." (Kenneth Grahame: *The Wind in the Willows*, p. 7)

Chapter 12

Competitors

> *"AN INVENTION THAT CANNOT BE IMITATED: The wonderful success attained in the manufacture and use of Naphtha Launches has aroused inventive energy to find, if possible, a substitute....Each successive competitor has come in with a burst of vainglorious or specious puffery and each in turn has disappeared amid a storm of ignominious failure, after taking in meanwhile many a dollar and leaving disappointed many an indignant pleasure seeker. ...Now all this could have been avoided at the outset by the purchase of an article — our Launch — demonstrated by practical use and work to be right. ...Although we have carefully and without prejudice investigated all recent inventions, with the idea that possibly there might be something worth our while to acquire, we have found nothing deserving the name and rank of competitor for our celebrated and well tried Naphtha Motor."*
>
> Gas Engine and Power Company 1894 catalog, *The Only Naphtha Launch*[1]

Steam Fights Back

In spite of the company's assurances, in the 1890s the naphtha launch finally did begin to experience serious competition. The first challenge came from builders of steamboats who tried moving their own engines aft. In 1891 *The Rudder* explained that "The advent of the pipe or sectional boiler made it possible to materially reduce …the great weight and cumbersome appearance of the steam generators, and also their liability to disastrous explosions in unskilled hands."[2] The article was accompanied by a picture of a 17-ft., 1-hp yacht tender built by Clay & Torbensen of Camden, N.J., that weighed only 500 lbs. The engine was positioned well aft.

This was a steam launch, not a naphtha launch. Built by Clay & Torbensen, the 1-hp engine was so light that, like the naphtha engine, it could be placed aft.

Chapter 12

The Columbian Exposition

There were other, more serious competitors. One of them was brought to the fore by Frederick Law Olmstead, Frank Ofeldt's first American employer, who became a key figure in the design of the 1893 World's Columbian Exposition in Chicago. In the words of his biographer, Laura Wood Roper, the site Olmsted selected, was "to the eye of common sense…quite unsuitable,"[3] and others described the location as "remote and repulsive,…one square mile of desolation, mostly treeless.…It was ugly, a landscape of last resort." As with Central Park, Olmsted loved a site so appalling that no one but he would attempt to beautify it.

Olmstead transformed the wasteland into a Venice-like chain of picturesque lagoons, and ensured that all the important buildings could be approached by both land and water. He was particularly interested in the boats that would ply the lagoons. "Their use for transportation [is] incidental; their main purpose decorative, to enhance the grace and gaiety of the scene."[4] He was distressed when a tugboat manufacturer presented a proposal to supply steam launches, on the grounds that steam was the most economical way to move the greatest number of passengers.[5] Olmsted loathed "abominable steamboats, graceless, noisy, and as out of place in the lagoons as a cow in a flower garden." To him, "Boats, birds, shores, waterways, were all design elements contributing to a coherent scenic effect; and the boats, to be appropriate in the landscape, should be small, nimble, light, quiet, and low."[6] He wrote to Daniel Burnham, chairman of the consulting board: "You perfectly well know that the main object to be accomplished [is] poetic.…Put in the waters unbecoming boats and the effect would be utterly disgusting."[7]

Olmsted heard about the fleet of electric boats operating on the Thames, and after visiting England to inspect them, recommended electric boats for the Exposition.[8] At that time there were fewer than a half dozen electric boats in the United States, so Olmsted's proposal met with a good deal of skepticism. To settle the question, the Fair's managers held a competition.[9]

The Gas Engine and Power Company elected not to enter a naphtha launch, but two steam launches competed, one of which used an "Ofeldt non-explosive boiler." According to the *Chicago Tribune*, the steam launch builders were well aware of Olmsted's antipathy, and "constructed their boats to burn hard coal, which gives out no smoke, and by equipping them with keel condensers did away with the appearance of steam, so that there is neither smoke, steam, nor puffing." However, the Electric Launch and Navigation Company's *Electra* won handily, and that company was awarded the contract.[10]

Before the Exposition, the Gas Engine and Power Company had dismissed electric power as unsuitable for small boats,[11] but now Clement Gould was forced to take note. As an experiment, the company joined with A. Glose & Son to build a very different electric boat, powered by primary batteries. Unlike the Exposition's launches, whose batteries required a charging station, primary batteries can be charged simply by replenishing the chemicals. The Gas Engine and Power Company's boat, named *Electric*, got 12 hours on a charge, and a tank in the bow carried enough extra solution for three more charges, but it took a man 1½ hours to change out the chemicals.[12]

Primary batteries could wait. Clement Gould was keenly aware of the competitive threat from rechargeable electric boats, and moved quickly. Just as Bostwick had done with Alfred Yarrow, he co-opted the opposition. The two companies combined their operations at the Gas Engine and Power Company's works at Morris Heights,[13] and the naphtha builder now expressed an enthusiasm typical of the newly-converted: "No electrical feature of the World's Columbian Exposition scored so instant a success as did the *Electric Launches*,…the grace and beauty of their design, and the charm of their quick and restful motion, elicited universal surprise and admiration. Hitherto regarded as somewhat experimental, electricity, as a motive power for pleasure boats, was demonstrated not only to be an ideal power, but a commercially successful one as well."[14]

An electric launch at the 1893 World's Columbian Exposition in Chicago. The electric boats were selected after Frederick Law Olmsted campaigned vigorously against "abominable steamboats" because he feared that they would destroy the scenic effect he had labored so hard to achieve. During the course of the Exposition, over one million people rode in the 55 electric launches. (Martin & Sachs, *Electrical Boats and Navigation*, p. viii). Clement Gould wasted no time in bringing the electric launch into the Gas Engine and Power Company's fold.

Chapter 12

Although there were no naphtha launches on the Exposition's lagoons, they were on exhibit in the Transportation Building, and the accompanying handout announced that in seven years the company had sold over one thousand naphtha launches.

That year the annual catalog boasted of the company's role in satisfying "the taste of the American public for nautical and aquatic pursuits, [and] the enthusiasm with which it seizes on any means that will help to satisfy that craving. No matter how great the innovation may be, if it is meritorious it 'goes' and it stays….The Naphtha Launch…is still a new thing, but never before did a novelty in methods of recreation and travel become so quickly standard and popular.

"But for its appearance, the larger part of our coast line, our noble rivers, our lakes and inland seas, would have been virtually unknown. To-day, however, the Naphtha Launch has given everybody the opportunity to see these nearby beauties and remote scenes at the most moderate cost and at the maximum of safety, ease, comfort and pleasure. It is as ubiquitous on water as the bicycle is on land. It is also no exaggeration to say that American Naphtha Launches are already, at this early date, better known all over the world than the American street cars and American sewing machines."

Some excerpts from the new testimonials:

"We have run our launch now for four summers and hardly know how we could get along without it. The engine has never been out of order."

"I ran her more than 2000 miles last summer."

"More genuine pleasure and satisfaction than anything I ever possessed."

"My youngest boy, eleven years old, is Captain, Engineer and Pilot."[15]

"She behaved splendidly in the face of a heavy sea and stiff wind. In fact, is far ahead of my expectations."

"I think they are as much ahead of steam, for a small boat, as steam is ahead of the old-fashioned stage coach."[16]

William Steinway

For the Gas Engine and Power Company, the Columbian Exposition turned into a battleground. Not only was the naphtha launch vigorously challenged by its electric rival, an even more determined attack was mounted by the internal combustion engine. As we know, Alfred Nobel had turned down the Daimler proposal in 1891. By then William Steinway, the piano mogul, had acquired the American rights, and in that year he began selling boats and engines.[17] In March 1893, *The Rudder, Sail and Paddle* (the new, and temporary, name for *The Rudder*) reported, "The Daimler Motor Co….are coming very rapidly to the front with their line of launch machinery. Their factory at Steinway, L.I. is a model establishment of the kind and at the present writing is running full on orders for yachts and launches complete, as well as for the outfits for boats of other build."[18]

Once again Clement Gould attempted to co-opt an opponent. He and Steinway met, but apparently Clement discovered that Steinway's sales were faltering, so he backed off. What went wrong? D.W. Fostle suggests that the Panic of 1893 (see our next chapter) dampened demand, but neither the panic, nor the depression that followed, had any significant effect on the ever-increasing sales of naphtha launches. More likely, the Daimler engine was simply overpriced. In 1892, in the euphoria of the boom, Steinway charged $1,225 for a 4-hp engine,[19] while an equivalent naphtha engine sold for just $650.[20] Perhaps his success in the lucrative piano market impaired Steinway's ability to understand the art of pricing.

Steinway's engine also faced prejudice from yachtsmen. In 1895 the Larchmont Yacht Club haughtily refused to permit a Daimler launch to compete in its naphtha launch races.[21]

Steinway became discouraged, and wrote that "I have serious apprehensions as to monetary outlook and curse the Daimler Motor Company for its draining me of money and resolve to stop it." Steinway was an able businessman, but when he died in March 1896, the appraiser declared his $181,100 investment in the stock of the Daimler Company to be worthless.[22]

Chapter 12

Steinway mounted a serious challenge to the naphtha launch, but he in turn faced vigorous competition from rival builders of internal combustion engines.

The Monitor Engine

One cause of Steinway's difficulties was that competition was wide open among the manufacturers of internal combustion engines. In the United States, by 1896, three hundred companies were fighting for a share.[23] One of these, the Monitor Vapor Engine and Power Company of Grand Rapids, produced an engine that was much cheaper than Steinway's,[24] and that also challenged the naphtha engine by its unusual design. In a blatant effort to deceive the public, the Monitor engine sported a brass funnel just like the one on the naphtha engine, but this one was a fake.[25] Not only was this oddity a remarkable tribute to the success of the naphtha launch, it proved that flim-flam could be profitable, for the Monitor Company was able to sell a number of these ridiculous launches.

The Monitor internal combustion engine was camouflaged with a fake brass funnel, to make it look like a naphtha engine.

FOUR HORSE POWER MONITOR ENGINE.

135

Naphtha

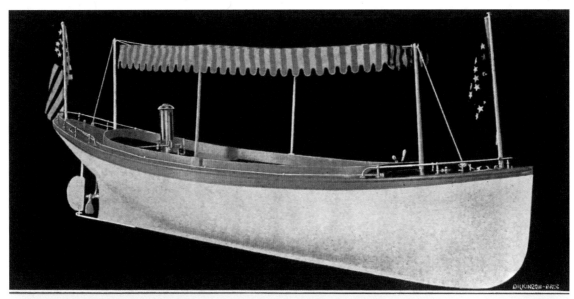

20 x 5 Launch, with Two Horse Power Monitor Engine.

The deceptive appearance of the Monitor launch proves how completely the naphtha launch had captured the public's esteem.

The masquerade was such a success that the company introduced a two-cylinder engine, and added a second false smokestack. In an age when the power of a steamship was indicated by the number of its smokestacks, such subterfuge was not unusual. The White Star Line's *Titanic* and her sister ships each had a dummy funnel in order to match the four-funnel Cunarders.

6 HORSE POWER DOUBLE MONITOR ENGINE.

136

Chapter 12

An Attack on the Naphtha Engine

Although the Gas Engine and Power Company must have scoffed at the Monitor engine's ludicrous appearance, the company had to take note of the Monitor catalog's criticism of naphtha engines. Some excerpts:

"We claim absolute safety in boats using the Monitor Engine for power, for there is no free burning fire, no vapor of gasoline, naphtha or water under pressure, no storage of pressure in boiler or retort.

There are no condensing pipes under the boat liable to damage.

- No roaring noise from a fire, for there is no fire.
- No matches to light in the wind.
- No gasoline pump to clog and give trouble.
- No time lost in getting under way, as the engine develops full power at once.
- No pressure to raise before starting.
- Speed governed by the throttle, from very slow to full speed."[26]

Escher Wyss Responds

It was not the Gas Engine and Power Company, but Escher Wyss, who mounted the most comprehensive counter-attack on the internal combustion engine:

"To start an explosive engine, it must first be cranked by hand, which above all is tiring. Further, this operation requires a degree of experience and precautions to avoid the shocks that may occur as a result of premature explosions. It may also happen that the explosions do not occur at the right time,…the motor sometimes giving a powerful kick in case of premature ignition of the explosive mixture.

"The internal combustion engine can only operate on its own in one direction and to be able to reverse direction one must make use of complicated auxiliary mechanisms.…The heavy flywheels which internal combustion engines must have, as well as the gear boxes and even adjustable propeller blades, are mechanisms that are…big and heavy and often occupy as much space as the engine itself.…Because of their complications [they] require almost continual repairs while giving relatively unreliable performance, failure often occurring at the time of landing, when it becomes very dangerous because of the risk of hitting the pier at the moment of docking. When going into reverse, from full ahead to astern, to come to a quick stop in case of an obstacle, or an unforeseen encounter, the internal combustion engine often fails to turn, which can cause very unpredictable results.

"In winter and cold weather, internal combustion engines are more difficult to operate than in ordinary temperatures. The petrol is difficult to vaporize, and the ignition system may fail entirely in mid-journey. Below 0° C, benzine does not vaporise easily and must be heated beforehand and kept warm."[27]

Naphtha vs Internal Combustion

In one respect the internal combustion engine had a very real advantage. It was much more fuel-efficient than the naphtha engine. A 4-hp naphtha launch cost fifteen cents an hour to run,[28] while fuel for a 4-hp Monitor came to only about four cents.[29] The Gas Engine and Power Company dismissed the difference as inconsequential: "The question of a few cents per hour in operating a launch which has cost a thousand or more, and which is used but a few months each year cuts but a small figure. Our engines *will run* and *will last* and *do use* some Naphtha. The Naphtha savers are economical because they don't run. A rowboat or wheelbarrow have the same qualifications."[30]

The company pointed out that, "When one has a train to catch or appointments to keep, it is pleasant to know that when you jump on board your boat she takes the bit in her mouth and starts right off."[31] The company was right; it was the internal combustion engine's unreliability that gave the naphtha engine such a competitive advantage.

Nowadays few people remember how ornery those early gasoline engines could be. For a firsthand account, we again turn to Edward Birdsall, newly-hired as

The Rudder's editor for power boating.[32] As the reader will recall, Birdsall had been outspoken in describing the miseries suffered by the owners of steam engines. Now he used his acid tongue to enumerate the tortures that the internal combustion engine could inflict.

Birdsall's description is so apt that it is worth quoting at length:

"All the makers [of internal combustion engines] will say that the coil and battery described in this article are entirely too large for the work, but after *rowing* a launch a few miles on account of a weak spark failing to ignite the charge, one's opinion is apt to change. There is nothing that gives one such a feeling of utter helplessness as to be a few miles from home in a launch that will not work, and the writer has yet to meet the owner of a gas-engine launch who has not had this experience.

"One of the most exasperating tricks of these engines is the liability – while apparently going along exactly according to all thermodynamic chemical and mechanical principles – to suddenly give a few preliminary chokes and then stop. This usually occurs when you are in a hurry to get somewhere and have gotten a mile or so away from home and off shore. In a few moments the launch loses headway and begins to drift backwards with the tide, while the wind comes up and makes just enough swell to make your particular size of boat roll in the trough like a log. Taking out the instruction book, if by some miraculous chance it is aboard, you find it says that when the engine stops it is either because there is a weak or no spark; or, the burner is out under the hot tube; or there is dirt in the pump valves; or, there is an obstruction in the spray jet; or, the gasoline is used up; or, the mixture is too rich; or, the mixture is too lean; or, too much or too little oil is being fed; or, the cylinder is hot because sea weeds have clogged up the circulating pump; or, a piece of paper has blown into the air valve; or, the insulation on the igniter where it passes into the cylinder has burned out; or, one of the wires has broken from the constant vibration; or, the battery has given out; or, the propeller has become fouled with rope or sea weed and has thus overloaded the engine; or, your thrust bearing is dry and hot, or several other things – varying in true cussedness – according to the make of the engine.

"After having found out what *may* be the trouble it becomes necessary to find out what actually *is* the matter. Before doing this, however, *anchor* – unless you have left it home or are off soundings for your cable – for while the treatment is simple, the diagnosis is liable to be long and heated.

"The writer has found that the most frequent causes of stoppage are – but why repeat the above list? At this point you will suddenly notice that the waters as far as you can see are devoid of craft of any sort; this, while a little startling at first, only adds to your determination to find the cause of the trouble and you set to work, gradually shedding your clothes as the good work proceeds. You hope to strike the trouble on the first trial, but from the writer's experience the only person who could do this would not require a launch for his transportation, as he would use his wings; you try the spark and find it gives a blinding flash, you try the naphtha pump and squirt naphtha over everything, then you put the crank on the shaft and turn until you are red in the face, and your companions – if you are so fortunate as to have any – fearing apoplexy implore you to desist. Everything is investigated and found to be in good condition, and at intervals – depending in length upon the time it takes you to recover your breath – you turn the flywheel several thousand times, notwithstanding the fact that the instruction books and everybody who knows anything about it tell you that it is perfectly useless to give more than *two* turns. Finally having exhausted the list of possible causes you sit down and make remarks that the editor would not print, even if I should write them; and after a while – as a matter more of habit than in any hope that it will accomplish anything – you give the crank a couple of turns and off she starts just as if nothing had been the matter. The run home is occupied in cooling off, putting court plaster on your skinned knuckles (the crank always turns too close to the bottom), and hoping that the Recording Angel could not write fast enough to get it down as fast as you said it.

"The next few trips are made in fear and trembling. Any unusual noise in the engine makes your heart jump, and you give every valve and handle in sight a turn as a precautionary measure. However, after making several trips without any trouble developing you gain confidence in the engine and your ability to run it; but don't be misled, it is simply waiting to get you off shore again."[33]

Chapter 12

Superb Engineering

In contrast, the success of the naphtha engine rested largely on its reliability, an enduring testament to the skill of Frank Ofeldt. Although we think of him as an inventor, we should honor him equally as an engineer.

John Ericsson once wrote to a friend: "Allow me to remind you that I am an engineer and designer rather than an inventor....Edison, in his ignorance, discovers or invents; Ericsson, acquainted with physical laws, constructs."[34]

In fact, Ericsson was both an inventor and an engineer, and so was Ofeldt. There can be no doubt that the reliability of the naphtha engine was solely due to Frank's meticulous engineering.

One consequence was that, sixteen years after the engine's introduction, the company was able to boast that, "All our engines built in 1886, the initial year of our experience, are still running apparently in as good shape as ever."[35]

A Pleasure to Operate

Naphtha engines were so trustworthy that even amateurs *enjoyed* operating them. As Richard M. Mitchell observed, "Before the naphtha launch, heat engines were operated by men from the lower classes. Upper-class men might command machines, but they did not touch them. The naphtha launch builders saw that this antique social narrowness went against human nature, and they at last made it respectable for the well-to-do to operate mechanically powered machines (for amusement only, of course)."[36]

In its 1894 catalog, the company expanded on the idea: "Any person of ordinary intelligence – whether having any knowledge of machinery or not – can run our Engine with ease and safety. Any man of a little leisure and means, who wishes for the chance to run a neat little bit of machinery for himself – and it is a passion strong in most of us – will find the Naphtha Launch the very thing his fancy has painted."[37]

Were Naphtha Engines Quiet?

The curse of motorboats is their noise, so for a pleasant family outing it was good to have a quiet engine. Compared to the early internal combustion engines, the naphtha engine was peaceful indeed. John W. Lincoln remembered that, "the most exciting feature ...was the total silence of its motions,"[38] and Weston Farmer wrote that, "There was no noise except a gear rattle at first."[39] However, after a ride in *Frieda* in 1959, W. J. Chapman reported that, "The burner gives a low hum – not above conversation level, however."[40]

Kenneth Durant, in *The Naphtha Launch*, took issue. His family had cottaged on a quiet Adirondack lake and he recalled that, "The sound was the steady note of a blowtorch, deeper toned....It was not quiet. In the Camp Cedars guest book a visitor described it as a 'sullen roar.' Neighbors did not like the noise, though the home camp welcomed the herald of morning mail from the carry or the return of fishermen at nightfall. The naphtha engine could not pretend to the privacy of Rushton's electric.

Voices had to be raised above the roar of the retort." Durant also reported another exasperating feature – the amount of brass. "An arduous job was to keep shiny bright the brass jacket and stack which carried away the fumes of burning naphtha and gave distinction to the launch. The 'samovar,' a Russian visitor called it. Metal polish was applied with cotton waste and a shammy and a vast amount of 'elbow grease.' The display of gleaming brass became a recognizable status symbol."[41]

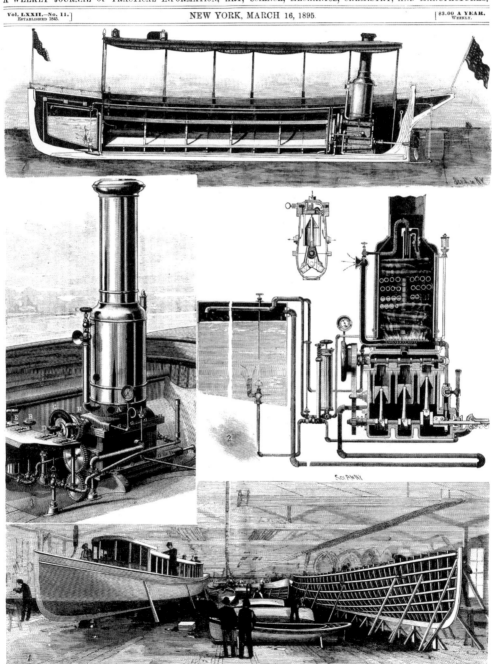

1. Longitudinal section of launch. 2. Cross section of boiler and engine. 3. Perspective view of the engine. 4. General view of the building shop.

THE MANUFACTURE OF NAPHTHA LAUNCHES BY THE GAS ENGINE AND POWER COMPANY

Chapter 12

2,000 Sold

In 1894 Clement Gould died, and the presidency of the company passed to his nephew, John J. Amory, who had been secretary-treasurer.[42] In the following year, the company was able to announce that its works were the largest of their kind in the world, with an output of one launch daily, and that total sales exceeded 2,000.[43]

In 1895 *Scientific American* extolled the naphtha launch: "No type of power-propelled boat has acquired such popularity in so short a space of time as has the naphtha launch. The proprietors of the establishment where these boats are manufactured…term it 'the only naphtha launch,' and with very good reason, as hitherto it has been without real competitor.

"These little boats have won for themselves an astonishing record. They seem to be as absolutely secure from accident as any kind of power-driven craft can be. Every possible precaution is adopted in their construction to render accident impossible.…The company's tests have been most exhaustive, but nothing proves the safety of the boats as the record which they have made since the foundation of the company."[44]

Further Threats

Besides the efforts of competitors to bite into naphtha sales, there remained the possibility of government intervention. Under the heading IMPORTANT! the Gas Engine and Power Company brought its customers up to date on the threat of legislation: "The matter was again agitated in 1894, resulting as before, the legislation proposed being considered as wholly uncalled for, unnecessary and unjust, the extreme simplicity of the motor, its ease of management, showing the absurdity of such restrictions.…The crucial test of years of experience has demonstrated the safety of the system and the folly of such legislation." The company noted that, "It is a common occurrence to see notices of accidents to steam, sail and row boats, but rarely any accounts of mishaps to Naphtha Launches, and these, when investigated, have proved to be wholly without foundation, or grossly exaggerated."[45]

A year later a new legislative threat appeared, this time in Albany. *The New York Times* responded scornfully: "A somewhat absurd measure about naphtha launches pends in the Legislature. It requires anybody who operates a naphtha launch or an electric launch to take out a license as an engineer. Now, everybody knows that the main uses of the launch are to serve as a tender to a yacht or as an adjunct to a country place. The man who runs the launch is commonly a humble sailorman, at $15 a month, who could not pass an engineer's examination, or any other, except perhaps in composing a Mathew Walker.[46] Sometimes he is a gardener, or a man of all work, who could not pass an examination in anything. If any owner of launches proposed to carry passengers for hire, it might plausibly be required of him to take out licenses for the men who run his launches. But when he intrusts to the launches only the lives of his family and his guests, the exaction is absurd. What could possibly have put it into the head of Assemblyman Gleason to introduce this ridiculous measure? There is no money in it. There is no popularity in it. There is nothing in it."[47]

The members of yacht clubs took fright. The Seawanhaka Corinthian Yacht Club, which had recently purchased the 30-ft. naphtha launch *Corinthian*, appointed a special committee to oppose the bill,[48] and the Larchmont Yacht Club sent a committee of two to Albany to see what could be done to stop the legislation. In gratitude the Gas Engine and Power Company presented to the club an exquisite model of a 42-ft. cruising launch.[49]

In 1895, the Gas Engine and Power Company presented this model of a 42' naphtha cruising launch to the Larchmont Yacht Club, N.Y., in gratitude for the club's lobbying against legislation that threatened to restrict the use of naphtha launches.

For the moment, the Gas Engine and Power Company was outpacing its opponents, but there was another competitor preparing an attack, and it was none other than Frank Ofeldt. This time, he would be armed with the financial strength, and political influence, of E.C. Benedict.

Chapter 13

The Presidential Crony

"A sick President was a tragedy for the American people in any circumstances. When they were beset by depression that amounted to disaster...it would be almost the final calamity if the President should be lost to his duties....To have known that he was incapacitated was unthinkable. It must be prevented."

Rexford Tugwell, *Grover Cleveland*[1]

Benedict's Elevation

There is an omission in the U.S. Constitution. No matter how diligently you search, you will find no description of the duties of the Presidential Crony, one of the most important offices an American can hold. Think of Harry Hopkins, Sherman Adams, and "Bebe" Rebozo.

The elevation of Frank's new business partner to this exalted position was demonstrated on the day that Grover Cleveland, after four years out of office, returned to the Presidency. E.C. Benedict was the President's special guest, and later wrote: "When Mr. Cleveland returned to the White House from the inaugural ceremonies of his second term, President Harrison was still the host of the White House. A few moments before his departure he poured out three glasses of rye, one for Mr. Cleveland, one for himself and one for me. It was an historic drink....I was witnessing an outgoing President of the United States drinking to the health and prosperity of the incoming one."[2]

Cleveland trusted few men, and seldom sought advice from his cabinet as a whole. On all important questions the President consulted only his chosen advisers.[3] There were six of these. Two were members of his previous cabinet: William Whitney and Charles Fairchild (who had become Treasury Secretary after Daniel Manning suffered a stroke while in office). Two were members of his present cabinet: Daniel Lamont, Cleveland's former private secretary and now Secretary of War, and Richard Olney, the Attorney General. Another was Grover's former law partner, Francis Lynde Stetson, and the sixth was E.C. Benedict.[4] Thus E.C. had vaulted into a position where he wielded more influence than all but two members of the cabinet.

143

The Crash

Shortly after Grover returned to the presidency in 1893, a thunderbolt hit Wall Street. The most actively traded company on the New York Stock Exchange went belly-up. This was the manufacturer of binder twine, the National Cordage Company, and its failure precipitated the immediate demise of six Wall Street firms.[5]

Week after week, the bankruptcies snowballed. In June, twenty-five national banks succumbed, at that time the largest one-month total ever recorded, but that number was to be eclipsed in July, with the demise of no less that seventy-eight.[6]

The boom, which had gone on for fourteen years, had finally come to an end, and although Wall Street was accustomed to the business cycle, this time there was an additional cause, *invention*. Ever since the Civil War, prices had been falling, a by-product of successful innovation. James Grant points out that, "productivity-enhancing devices had reduced the cost of commodities and manufactured goods....Twice as much production with one-half the payroll was nothing out of the ordinary."[7] This made life easier for consumers, but deflation was painful for farmers. Corn, which had brought 75 cents a bushel in 1869, fell to 28 cents in 1889, and wheat fell from $1.45 a bushel to 69 cents.[8] Farmers had opened up the West by borrowing heavily, but interest rates on those loans were now as high as twelve to fifteen percent.[9]

What farmers wanted was a healthy dose of inflation, but bankers wanted debts repaid in currency whose value was not debased. To bankers and businessmen, adherence to the gold standard was an article of faith. But the farmers and their new allies, western silver miners, believed that the unlimited coinage of silver would be their salvation, for it would lead to higher prices. However, the real issue was deeper, a struggle between the business interests of the East and the agrarian interests of the West over who would control the economy.[10] Before Cleveland's second presidency, the agrarian interests had always prevailed. Now it was E.C.'s role to try to reverse that by keeping the President sympathetic to the views of business.

In 1895, under western pressure, Congress had passed the Silver-Purchase Act, requiring the Secretary of the Treasury to buy four and a half million ounces of silver a month. The law proved disastrous; one hundred and fifty million in gold fled the country, and the monetary system became badly distorted.[11] By the time Treasury Secretary Charles Foster left office, there were only one hundred million dollars remaining in the gold reserve, barely above the statutory limit. The financial historian, Alexander Noyes, declared, "Probably no financial administration in our history has entered office under such disheartening conditions."[12] In his first weeks back in office, Cleveland found himself deluged with requests that he immediately call a special session of Congress to repeal the Silver-Purchase Act. The business community was unanimous, and was bolstered by a drumbeat of editorials.[13]

A Medical Emergency

On the morning of May 5, the day following the bankruptcy of National Cordage, Grover noticed what he thought was a canker sore on the roof of his mouth. At first he gave it little attention.[14] However, after six weeks of increasing discomfort, the President called in the White House physician who, with the aid of a pathologist, concluded that there was strong indication of malignancy. The President's own physician, Dr. Joseph D. Bryant, quickly came to Washington, confirmed the diagnosis, and gave the President the unwelcome news: "Were it in my mouth I would have it removed at once."[15]

Grover wanted to defer the surgery until a special session of Congress could repeal the Silver-Purchase Act, but Dr. Bryant said that he could not assume the responsibility for any delay, if the growth progressed as it usually did in such cases.[16] Matthew Algeo points out that there was a "very real possibility that Cleveland would suffer the same fate as General Grant. If the tumor had grown too large to remove, the President, like the General, would meet a most unpleasant demise, slowly suffocating."[17]

Given the country's financial crisis, the situation

was explosive. Rexford Tugwell explains: "The discovery was so untimely as to be very nearly disastrous. The dependence of the American people on their President is something they do not fully realize, ever, until something happens to weaken his authority....A sick President was a tragedy for the American people in any circumstances. When they were beset by depression that amounted to disaster, and when something needed to be done that might set the conditions for recovery, it would be almost the final calamity if the President should be lost to his duties. It would be bad enough even if the people merely suspected that he might be absent – that he was not there in the White House carrying on sturdily day after day in their interest, using such wisdom as he had and exerting his will to coerce reluctant cooperators. To have known that he was incapacitated was unthinkable. It must be prevented."[18]

Just at the moment when President Cleveland was wrestling with the country's financial crisis, his doctor informed him that he had a tumor in his mouth, and that it must be operated on immediately.

Grover insisted that the public be kept in the dark. According to Algeo, "He had witnessed firsthand the ghoulish hoopla surrounding Ulysses Grant's illness, and he had no intention of becoming the object of such a spectacle." The best hospitals were in New York, Baltimore and Washington, but Grover was never alone in those cities. He had no Camp David, and even at Gray Gables there were always reporters keeping watch.[19] If only he had a presidential yacht. But he *did,* or something just as good, a Presidential Crony who was a yachtsman. Grover quickly decided that the only place for an operation was at sea, aboard E.C. Benedict's yacht.

Oneida was a terrible choice. If anything went awry, there would be no way for the doctors to summon expert assistance, or life-saving equipment. MacMahon and Curry, in *Medical Cover-ups in the White House,* condemned the doctors for performing "a procedure that at the time, and in view of their patient's physical condition, was perilous. Carrying it out in a makeshift, floating operating room, they subordinated standards of medical practice to political ends."[20]

Grover was not at all sure that he would survive the operation.[21] Although Dr. Bryant had performed only two such operations himself, he had published a paper on the history of 250 cases in which he reported that one of every seven patients died.[22] Bryant enlisted Dr. William Williams Keen, the nation's most celebrated surgeon, to participate,[23] and he explained to Keen's assistant that Dr. Keen could "assume responsibility, in part, in the event of a fatality."[24] On June 30, one week after Dr. Bryant told Cleveland that he dare not wait, Grover left for New York. Two hours later, the Cabinet and the press were both surprised to learn that the President had issued a call that day for an extra session of Congress, only the eleventh in the nation's history.[25]

To maintain privacy, *Oneida* was anchored well out in the East River,[26] and by the time her Ofeldt tender brought Grover aboard, the launch had already made a number of unobtrusive trips from different piers to fetch the doctors and their assistants.[27]

The next morning, *Oneida's* saloon was disinfected,[28] and a straight-back chair was lashed to the interior mast.[29] The only source of illumination would be an electric light bulb connected to a portable battery.[30]

Dr. Keen later explained his greatest fear: "Our anxiety related not so much to the operation itself as to the anesthetic and its possible dangers. These might easily arise in connection with the respiration, the heart, or the function of the kidneys, etc., dangers which are met with not infrequently as a result of administering an anesthetic, especially in a man of Mr. Cleveland's age and physical condition. The patient was 56 years of age, very corpulent, with a short thick neck, just the build and age for a possible apoplexy – an incident which had actually occurred to one of my own patients."[31]

After the doctors removed part of Grover's jaw, they discovered that the tumor extended into the sinus cavity. Dr. Keen wanted to remove the entire left upper jaw, together with the sinus and floor of the bony eye socket. But this would have left the president with a sagging eye and double vision. The team decided not to go further, and Dr. Keen went along, perhaps thinking the case hopeless.[32]

The operation took place on July 1, and four days later *Oneida's* launch ferried the President home to Gray Gables. Members of the press were inquisitive, and there was even a rumor that the president had cancer. E.C. Benedict told *The World* that the story was "all rot."…The President had merely had a tooth extracted and a piece of the jawbone came away. Asked about reports that the procedure had incapacitated the president for more than a day, Benedict huffed, "All bosh! We played cribbage every day, and the President never missed a meal."[33]

That's what cronies are for. [34]

The operation was a complete success. Although Grover lived fifteen more years, the cancer never returned.[35] But had it really been worth risking the President's life to keep it secret? That depended on the outcome of the special Congressional session.

The Cleveland Depression

The debate on rescinding the Silver Purchase Act opened in stifling August heat, but filibustering kept the issue undecided until late October. One session lasted thirty-eight hours, and a speech by a senator from Nevada filled a hundred pages of the *Congressional Record*.[36] After some weeks a number of Democratic senators convinced themselves that Cleveland would compromise,[37] but they did not understand the man. At a Cabinet meeting on October 23, "he smote the table with his fist and declared that he would not yield an inch." It was clear that "His Obstinacy," as William Allen White dubbed him, would continue the fight, if it took all winter.[38]

President Cleveland survived the operation, and turned his attention to the impasse that was splitting the country. Even at the risk of destroying the Democratic Party, he sided with the Wall Street bankers. And once Grover Cleveland had made up his mind, he was immovable.

Chapter 13

Eventually, in the face of the President's determination, some of the silverites caved, and the bill was repealed.[39] Cleveland's victory was a turning point in American history. Business finally succeeded in wresting control of the economy away from the farmers. Wall Street's emissary, Elias Cornelius Benedict, had accomplished his mission. The defeat of William Jennings Bryan in the following election would confirm the victory of business, and make it permanent.

What the victory did not do was end the depression. In the words of Henry Adams, the crisis turned into a "financial storm,…the most deep-seated and far-reaching in the history of the country,"[40] and many called it the *Cleveland depression*.[41] By the end of 1893, 642 banks and 15,242 businesses had declared bankruptcy."[42] According to Tugwell, "the country had reached the very nadir of exhaustion and despair."[43]

Gold continued to flee the country, and Carl Hovey tells us that "President Cleveland and the Treasury officials…engaged in a continuous struggle, both to keep the Treasury from running completely out of gold and to prevent the public from finding out the actual state of affairs. These insiders were convinced that if the situation became generally known, the blackest kind of panic would follow."[44]

J.P. Morgan concluded that the situation was dire, and at the last moment he was able to persuade Cleveland to agree to a bailout, under which the House of Morgan and the Rothschilds provided the government with 3.5 million ounces of gold in exchange for $65 million worth of bonds.

However, the terms were extremely harsh, and Matthew Josephson called them, "worthy of a loan for a banana republic."[45] Gustavus Myers described the clamor that ensued: "From every public quarter came the severest denunciations of Cleveland, on one hand, and Morgan on the other. Even partisan newspapers… condemned the bargain as scandalous, and declared that the government had been shamelessly buncoed.[46] Nevins tells us that, "by hundreds of thousands, hard-handed Americans believed that Cleveland and Carlisle [the Treasury Secretary] had sold the credit of the republic to the Morgans and Rothschilds, and had pocketed a share of the price.[47] There were also allegations that four insiders were allowed to buy the bonds at the same preferred rate as the banks, and those four included Benedict and Stetson.[48]

Secret Rendezvous

Morgan was successful; the gold outflow stopped, and the Treasury reserve was again intact. This led to a real recovery of trade in the following months. However, Morgan had promised Cleveland that the syndicate would prevent the outflow of gold for about six months, but in July an importer who was not a syndicate member sent one million dollars in gold tender abroad.[49] This caused uneasiness in the White House.

Cleveland's private military aide (and Morgan's future son-in-law), Herbert J. Satterlee, explained that "The President wanted to see Mr. Morgan. However, he did not want the idea to get abroad that there was to be a conference. If Mr. Morgan should be sent for, it would look as if the Treasury was in bad trouble again."[50] The only way Cleveland could now meet with Morgan was to do it in secret. That was easy, as Morgan had his own yacht and Cleveland was free to use *Oneida*.

Morgan's yacht was his second *Corsair*, 39 feet longer than her predecessor, and 241½ feet overall.[51] Like the first *Corsair*, she carried a naphtha tender.[52] Frederick Lewis Allen recounted that Morgan "spent most of his leisure time aboard the great yacht. She would lie at anchor in the North River and he would pile guests into a little naphtha launch to go out and dine aboard her; usually he slept there."[53]

Corsair and *Oneida* anchored in an out-of-the-way bay at Gardiners Island, near the tip of Long Island. According to Satterlee, "That evening Mr. Morgan stayed long on the deck of *Oneida*.…At the end of the conference the President's uneasiness…was quieted."[54]

The subterfuge succeeded, and the press never learned of the meeting.

Naphtha

When the nation's financial crisis became dire, J.P. Morgan stepped in and arranged a loan that saved the government from defaulting. However, the press suspected that Cleveland and Morgan had colluded, and that the country had been cheated. After that, if the two were to meet, they had to do so in secret. In 1895, in order to carry out a clandestine meeting, Morgan's second *Corsair*, pictured here with her naphtha tender, rendezvoused with E.C. Benedict's *Oneida*.

The country's troubles continued to mount, and the President's gloom deepened. E.C. sought a way to buck up his low spirits. Grover was always happiest in a fishing boat, and his friend Gilder said that was what kept him alive: "I have heard him say that while on the water he could cast his public cares aside, but they would come crushing down upon him the moment he put his foot on dry land."[55]

It was perfectly clear that what the Admiral needed was a new boat, and that brings us back to Frank Ofeldt.

Chapter 14

Alco-Vapor

"The great objection to the employment of naphtha lies in the fact that while it has excellent properties for being quickly vaporized under pressure, it is very objectionable to have in a launch, because being highly inflammable it is liable to ready ignition, and if from any cause it should become ignited it burns with an intense heat."

Frank Ofeldt, patent: *Apparatus for Operating Vapor-Launches*

Ofeldt Recants

For twenty years Frank Ofeldt had dedicated his life to finding uses for the naphthas. He had invented the Star Gas machine, the naphtha launch, and the Ofeldt naphtha steam engine. His name was, and ever would be, tied to naphtha. It now occurred to him that another substance might serve as the working fluid in an engine, and his attention turned to alcohol.

He was not the first. Ninety-five years previously – in 1797 – the Reverend Dr. Edmund Cartwright, famous for his invention of the power loom, proposed an engine that boiled alcohol. Cartwright reasoned that because alcohol turned to a vapor at a lower temperature than water, there would be a smaller consumption of fuel.[1] Frank concurred. Alcohol's low boiling point gave it an advantage, not only over water, but also over naphtha. His next engine would use alcohol as its working fluid.

Frank had also, belatedly, come to recognize the danger posed by the handling of naphtha. In an astonishing recantation, Frank turned his back on twenty-five years of effort, and renounced everything that he had previously championed.

Frank's new invention was embodied in two patents, one of which described the alco-vapor launch, and the other, its engine. In the preamble to the former, Frank mercilessly attacked his earlier invention:

"The great objection to the employment of naphtha lies in the fact that while it has excellent properties for being quickly vaporized under pressure, it is very objectionable to have in a launch, because being highly inflammable it is liable to ready ignition, and if from any cause it should become ignited it burns with an intense heat. If it should escape upon the water it does not mix with the water and would burn upon the surface, so as to endanger the lives of the occupants of the vessel.

"Another and more important defect in the use of naphtha from a commercial standpoint is that naphtha after being expanded and condensed a few times loses its property of ready expansion and in a great measure is useless for further use. In any event it is not economical to use it for more than about six or eight complete vaporizations. In practice it seems to lose in time its property of becoming a vapor under the temperature of the generator, and for this reason and owing to the lack of a sufficient naphtha supply or the liability of not being able to secure fresh naphtha it becomes difficult to take long cruises in the launch.

"The object of my invention is to overcome all of the defects due to the employment of naphtha—that is to say, I eliminate the tendency to fire, I reduce the temperature required for maintaining a given pressure in operating the engines, and I do not require changing or replacing the vaporizable liquid.

"In carrying out my invention I provide the launch at the forward end with two tanks, one of small size and containing alcohol, and the other of large size and containing a hydrocarbon oil, such as head-light oil, which is fire-proof. The alcohol-tank is preferably at the bottom, so as to be adjacent to the cool surface of the keel and be protected also against the rays of the sun as its contents are more volatile than that of the oil-tank....

"The headlight-oil will not burn if fire is suddenly applied to it. It will not ignite if it escapes upon the water or into the boat. It is not as volatile as naphtha and therefore has less liability to generate explosive gases. The alcohol is volatile at a lower temperature than naphtha and generates a higher pressure for the same heat. It is possible to more quickly raise the necessary pressure to operate the engine, and the pressure medium is practically inexhaustible. In practice five gallons of alcohol will suffice a twenty-five foot launch for a whole year, and even then the only loss is due to leakage. Owing to the fact that alcohol vaporizes at a lower temperature, it is evident that a given supply of oil burned in the vapor-burner will propel the launch to a greater distance than when naphtha is used both as the pressure agent and the fuel."[2]

Chapter 14

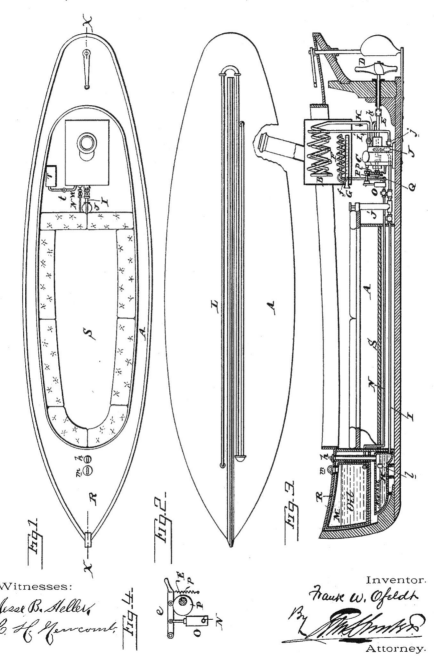

The drawing that accompanied Frank Ofeldt's 1895 alco-vapor patent. In the patent's preamble, Frank denounced his own previous invention, the naphtha launch, because its fuel, being highly inflammable, was "very objectionable to have in a launch." He also warned that if naphtha escaped into the water, it might endanger the lives of the occupants of the vessel.

The patent specified that the "engine may be of any suitable construction,"[3] but the companion patent, *Vapor-Engine,* described Frank's preferred engine. In this patent's preamble, Frank stated that his invention was "a vapor engine which shall be of compact construction and effectual in the performance of its functions." The liquid to be vaporized was "preferably alcohol," heated by the "combustion of oil" (presumably kerosene).[4] Frank's illustrations show a three-cylinder radial engine, with a configuration similar to that of the existing *Brotherhood* engine.[5]

Frank was still gun-shy after his experience with Jabez Bostwick. Although he assigned the patents to E.C.'s new enterprise, the *Marine Vapor Engine Company,* he took care not to become an employee.

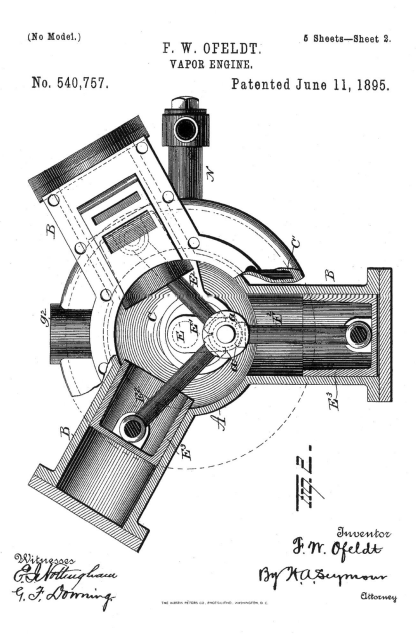

Frank Ofeldt's alco-vapor engine. Frank assigned the alco-vapor patents to E.C. Benedict's Marine Vapor Engine Company.

Chapter 14

Charles Wright's Contribution

As soon as the second patent was filed on April 20, 1894 the company began delivering alco-vapor launches,[6] but their engines incorporated a significant change. Frank's patent had included a reversing mechanism, but not a throttle.[7] An engineer, Charles W. Wright, came up with an ingenious improvement that combined both controls, a single lever which, in the company's words, "has five functions, viz: causes the engine to run back, go ahead, expand the vapor to any degree, reduce the speed irrespective of the pressure, and throttle off vapor altogether, thereby stopping the engine, with no possibility of it starting itself, the last three features being lacking in the naphtha engine."[8] In present-day motorboats, such a control lever is the norm, but W.J. Chapman described its effect on contemporaries: "One lever gave both speed control and reverse – very ingenious."[9]

The company also offered to "furnish an auxiliary lever in the bow at a slight additional cost that will enable the helmsman to manoeuvre his engine, should he wish to do so, in less time than a signal could be given. This arrangement would admit of the skipper having the entire launch under his control, while occupying the most advantageous position. Price, $25.00."[10]

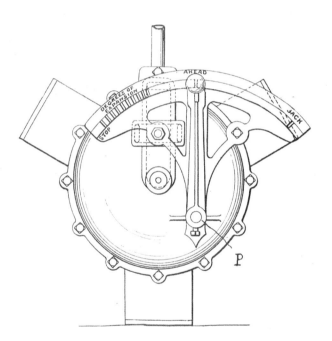

Charles Wright improved on Ofeldt's design, with a single lever that combined a throttle and a gearshift. This device was a forerunner of the control handle used in modern motorboats.

The Rudder was delighted by the forward control lever: "One novel feature made possible by this method of controlling the engine, which the manufacturers claim is new, is the connecting of the [engine's] lever with a similar lever in the bow, by a chain, which enables the helmsman to have the launch under perfect control, making it unnecessary to go to the stern to maneuver the engine when making a landing, which, judging from the many approving comments, is highly appreciated." (*The Rudder*, December 1895, p. 306, "The Alco Vapor Engine")

153

The company also changed the design of the boiler. Frank's patent drawings had shown a cylindrical boiler containing coiled tubes, but the production model was completely different. Since at least 1892, the Gas Engine and Power Company had used rectangular boilers for its three largest naphtha engines, and the tubes were straight rather than coiled. Now the Marine Vapor Engine Company adopted a similar boiler configuration, with threaded steel tubes.

As in the naphtha launch, the engine compartment was separated from the passengers by a bulkhead, "thereby insuring the occupants immunity from oil and heat. This feature enables the ladies to wear any costume that best suits their taste without fear of getting their clothing soiled." Although the patent drawing showed the fuel tank in the forepeak, that was not always the case. "Our fuel is *absolutely* safe, and we are enabled to place our tanks amidship, thus avoiding the ever-varying dead weight carried at the bow of other launches."[11]

How did Frank respond to Wright's contribution? Did he see it as a helpful improvement, or was he offended at Wright's horning in on *his* invention? Although Wright made a very valuable contribution, it was Frank Ofeldt who conceived the naphtha launch, as his two patents prove. He later described himself as the inventor of the "Alco-Vapor Launch system," so there can be no doubt that he considered the invention to be his.[12]

However, the company's catalogs listed Charles Wright as the sole inventor of the Alco-Vapor engine: "The new *Wright* engine, with which all our launches are now equipped (patents of which are controlled exclusively by this Company) makes it possible for even a novice to use the vapor as expansively as steam is used in the well-known four-valve Corliss engine."[13]

For E.C. Benedict to deny Frank Ofeldt authorship of his own invention was grimly reminiscent of Bostwick's behavior.

Why did Benedict treat Frank so badly? Was the inventor impossible to deal with? Or did E.C., like Jabez, consider inventors to be expendable? One thing is clear: the immigrant's story was turning into a true American tragedy.

Charles Wright assigned his patents to the Marine Vapor Engine Company and then made the same mistake that Frank had made with Jabez Bostwick. He became an employee, and was given the title, *Secretary and Treasurer*.[14]

Chapter 14

7 H.-P.
Retort and Engine

View of Retort
With Jacket Removed

The alco-vapor engine combined features from both Frank Ofeldt's and Charles Wright's designs. Although E.C. Benedict's company gave sole credit to Wright, Frank claimed that the invention was his.

Naphtha

E.C. Benedict's yacht, *Oneida*, with her alco-vapor tender, *Oneida II*, in the aft davits.

Chapter 14

President Cleveland's Alco-Vapor Launch

Like Bostwick, Benedict needed a prestigious customer to attract the public's attention, and who better than the President of the United States? Cleveland already had a fishing boat named after his first daughter, so he made a cautious reply to E.C.'s offer: "I have no doubt the launch will often fit my case, but I want, so far as is consistent, to be true to *Ruth* and therefore do not intend to see her superseded. The launch I must regard as a sort of extravagance for me, so I hope you will not allow her cost to be increased on account of any embellishment, ornamentation, or extra fitting."[15] Grover named the new launch after his second daughter, Esther.

Grover Cleveland named his first fishing boat for his first daughter, Ruth (right) and his alco-vapor launch after Ruth's sister, Esther.

President Cleveland's new launch made the nautical world aware of the alco-vapor engine.

The Rudder described *Esther* as "Thirty feet over all; six feet seven inches beam; thirty-three and one-half inches depth. The extreme draft is two feet. The engine is seven horse-power, and is capable of driving the boat at a continuous speed of nine statute miles. For the protection of the crew from rain and sea-fly the launch is fitted with a hood, which can be extended aft so as to cover nearly the whole cockpit. The launch is said to be a very able sea boat, she having had a thorough trial in the not by any means very smooth waters of Buzzard's Bay. The interior of the boat is finished in ash and quartered oak, giving her an exceedingly serviceable and clean look."[16]

Chapter 14

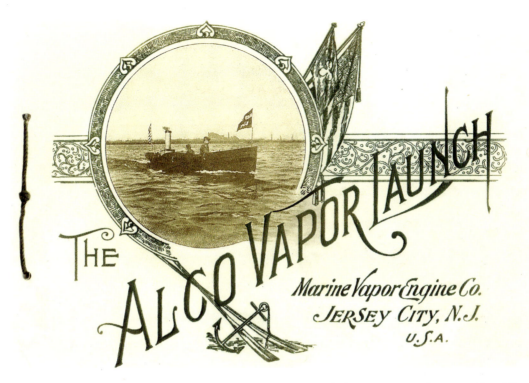

The 1896 catalog. Later the company hyphenated the name, making it Alco-Vapor.

Marketing Alco-Vapor

About March 1896, The Marine Vapor Engine Company issued its first catalog. The thrust of the sales pitch was that alco-vapor was "a system of propulsion that would not only be free from the dangers necessarily attending the use of gasoline or naphtha, but should not have the unpleasant vibration of the (explosion in the cylinder) gas engine." The company explained the difference from the naphtha launch in some detail:

"As we use alcohol expansively for power, it may be asked, wherein does it differ and in what respect is it better than the use of naphtha? In answer to the first query, we will state that alcohol has the peculiar property of expanding a greater number of times and at a lower temperature than naphtha. John W. Nystrom, Civil Engineer, a recognized authority, gives the boiling point of naphtha at 320° Fahr., water at 212° Fahr., and alcohol at 173° Fahr. So it will appear quite obvious that should we begin to create pressure at 173°, by the time we increased the temperature to the boiling point of water we have fifteen pounds, and before we reach the boiling point of naphtha we have a pressure of one hundred pounds. In fact, owing to the low boiling point of alcohol, it is not necessary in starting the Alco engine to laboriously work the liquid out of the cylinders by turning the engine by hand as in the case of the naphtha, for immediately we have 25 lbs. pressure—our engine starts without aid, and owing to the small amount of heat required one can fearlessly place their hand upon the casing of the engine when running at 100 lbs. pressure. But our intelligent critic may say, admitting all the advantages you claim, is not alcohol dangerous? Our answer is, *No*; for, unlike naphtha, it combines with water in all proportions, and should any be allowed to escape, the fact that there is always a small quantity of water in the bilge eliminates any likelihood of fire. This could be demonstrated by the simple experiment of taking a spoonful of alcohol, igniting it and then pouring it into a glass of water, the flame will be immediately extinguished, while it is a well-known fact that naphtha burns more intensely upon the surface of the water than elsewhere.

"As we carry but one-tenth as much alcohol as is usually carried of naphtha by naphtha or gasoline launches, and use the same over and over with but little attention during the entire season, the convenience and safety of our system will be readily seen and appreciated."

The company's claims included the following:

"It is lighter than any other known Launch of the same Horse-Power.

Greater speed per pound weight of Engine than any other known Launch.

Weight of Motive Power so small that the Launch will not Sink, even though filled with water to the level of the Combing. (A feature sadly lacking in the electric launch, with its immense weight of batteries, weighing, in the case of a 30-foot launch, 3000 pounds and over.)

No gears to rattle.

No damper to regulate.

No glands subject to pressure to leak and cause a flame.

No babbit metal to melt and stop the engine.

No dangerous fuel.

No expensive three-way crank to break.

Fuel can be procured any place in the civilized world."[17]

Since 1892, the Gas Engine and Power Company had offered $500 to anyone who could explode their boiler or machinery. The Marine Vapor Engine Company now doubled the offer to $1,000.[18]

In 1897 the company turned its guns on the internal combustion engine: "The Alco-Vapor launches are all equipped with a motor that derives its power from the vaporization of alcohol in a retort or boiler. The vapor then expends its force on the pistons (not with a violent shock, such as in the explosive engines, but with a constant pressure to the end of the stroke of the piston. Hence the absence of vibration in the Alco Motor)." As a consequence the engine required "No heavy fly wheel."[19]

The company's catalogs also carried the assurances: "No government inspection" and "No licensed engineer or pilot."[20] How could the company, not having Standard Oil behind it, be so sure? Again it was a matter of having friends in high places. The decision was up to John G. Carlisle, Secretary of the Treasury. The Carlisles, who were close personal friends of Grover and Frances Cleveland,[21] summered near Gray Gables, and in September 1895, Carlisle came to visit the First Family, whereupon Grover came out in his new alco-vapor launch to fetch Carlisle and his wife.[22] It is inconceivable that Carlisle's Treasury Department would have placed restrictions on the President's use of his own launch.

E.C. was a good friend of Colonel Lamont, the Secretary of War, so it is not surprising that the War Department ordered two alco-vapor launches. The Army assigned one of these 20-hp extra-heavy craft to Fortress Monroe in Hampton, Virginia, and the other to be used in New York Harbor.

Chapter 14

Alco-Vapor Launch Builders

In May 1896, *The Rudder* listed fourteen alco-vapor launches in production, and noted that "The Marine Vapor Engine Company is enjoying the most prosperous season of their existence. Every stock in their boat shop is occupied, and they have contracted with outside builders to furnish them with hulls." The article also listed several alco-vapor launches being built by Messrs. Lawley & Son of South Boston.[23]

Another such builder, John Stuart & Co. of Wollaston, Massachusetts, supplied *The Rudder* with elegant drawings of a 26-ft. alco-vapor cabin launch that the company had designed and built.[24]

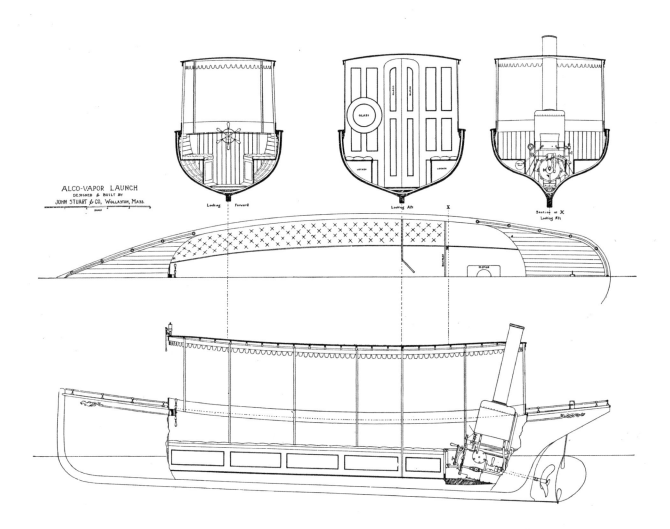

A 26-ft. alco-vapor launch designed and built by John Stuart & Co.

The Marine Vapor Engine Company, like the Gas Engine and Power Company, offered auxiliary engines for sailboats, and in fact advertised, "Auxiliary power a specialty."[25]

Another target was yachtsmen. The 1896 catalog explained: "Should many steam yacht owners be asked why they do not use a naphtha or gasoline tender, they would in all probability state that they do not care to carry such a dangerous fluid as naphtha or gasoline in the hold of their yacht, as also the difficulty of procuring same while cruising in foreign waters. Both of these disadvantages are entirely obviated in our system. The small quantity (five gallons) of alcohol carried in our tender is never handled, and but one gallon of fresh alcohol added per month, if then, while the 150° test kerosene we use is not only safe to carry, but can be easily procured in any foreign port. Wood alcohol at one dollar per gallon will answer as well as the more costly variety."[26]

The marketing campaign had considerable success. According to L. Francis Herreshoff, "Alco-Vapor launches quickly took the place of the naphtha launches on the up-to-date yachts. Certainly their smell was much more pleasant."[27] The 1897 catalog named twelve yachts that carried alco-vapor tenders.[28] At least two of these, *Puzzle* and *Starling*, had previously appeared on naphtha lists.[29]

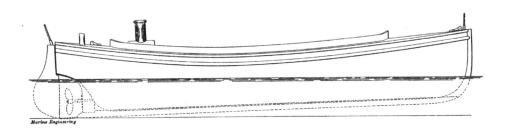

The steamship *Paris* carried two alco-vapor boats used for taking passengers ashore in the Caribbean.

During a voyage up the Amazon, E.C. Benedict made good use of his alco-vapor launch.

OFF TO VISIT THE GOVERNOR
(Silk hats and 127° in the sun)

How did the price of alco-vapor boats compare with naphtha? The Gas Engine and Power Company stated that, "There are plenty of cheap Launches with cheap power to be had; but our prices are as low as is consistent with first-class labor and material, and we believe intelligent buyers always recognize the fact that *the best is the cheapest in the end*."[30] If his competitor declined to compete on price, E. C. would do just that. In 1896, 18-ft., 2-hp naphtha launches, finished in ash and oak, cost from $650 to $700, so E. C. priced a similar alco-vapor launch at $600. A 25-ft., 4-hp naphtha launch cost from $950 to $1,050, so E. C. offered a 5-hp model of the same length at $900. A 30-ft., 6-hp naphtha, in ash and oak cost $1,450, so E.C. priced a 30-ft., 7-hp alco-vapor at $1,350. Both companies also sold engines separately. A 2-hp naphtha engine cost $500, while an alco-vapor engine came in at $400; for 12-hp the prices were $1,500 and $1,250, respectively.[31]

Chrystie McConnell recalled her family's alco-vapor launch, which apparently lacked the forward control lever: "After my father's naphtha launch, we had a somewhat similar affair, an alco-vapor, which boiled alcohol over a kerosene fire. It took some time to get up steam but, like the steam engine, it could be regulated to any speed from full ahead to barely turning over. This craft had its engine and passenger sections separated by a bulkhead and a glass door, and at the wheel were two bell pulls, for a gong or a jingle in the engine compartment. My father could never get the signals straight in his mind, and our landings often sounded like a recital at the Bok Singing Tower, with slight overtones of the ballad concerning the *Victoria-Camperdown* disaster."[32]

The company published testimonials from satisfied customers:

"*Your system is the soundest for this class of craft. I ran the boat about remote islands on the Maine coast, where it would be almost impracticable to obtain naphtha with certainty. What is more important still is the feeling of security from explosion or serious accident on account of dangerous fuel.*"

"*By far the best engine in the market.... One of the finest features of the engine is being able to operate it either from the bow or stern.*"

"*I have used her in all weathers, in the rivers, in the bays, and on the ocean, and found her a staunch, shifty, able craft. She has made the round trip from Annapolis to Ocean City, N.J., and weathered Cape May, going and coming in the teeth of a gale. She behaved beautifully in the 'riff-raffs' of the Delaware Bay and Atlantic Ocean. She has seen rough weather in the Chesapeake Bay, and is as strong to-day as the day I bought her.*"

"*I, who know nothing whatever about machinery, have been unable to get the boat out of order.*"[33]

President Cleveland's Experience

Of course the company published only favorable testimonials, but there is another source of information: Grover Cleveland's letters to E.C. Benedict. These offer a rare glimpse into the actual experience of an alco-vapor owner.

Grover's first concern was whether he needed a man to operate *Esther*. "Must I have a man to run it, and if so can I get a man on very reasonable terms to do that and perhaps make himself useful in other ways besides? If you can will you put me in the way of securing such a man?"[34]

E.C. replied, "The motor people diligently searched for some one to run it, and found a gentleman in reduced circumstances, by the name of Elliott, quite familiar with engines. He can take this one apart and put it together, and understands its working perfectly. He is willing to do anything to make himself useful about your place, and he impresses me favorably; but he knows that his tenure of occupation is entirely at your disposal. I think he would be satisfied with say $35. or $40. per month, and such plain board as he could get in your neighborhood. That is what I have to pay."[35]

But the President replied with a new plan: "I understand the engineer at the White House would like to spend his vacation at Gray Gables....He is a nice fellow, I believe, and as there is nothing for him to do here I am inclined to take him up with me. At any rate, I think you had better tell Mr. Elliott that I have made other arrangements."[37]

Four weeks later Grover thanked E.C. for sending ten barrels of oil, and reported that, "My launch is improving every day and I take lots of comfort with it. I think my engineer is getting a good hold of it."[37]

In the following year troubles arose. Cleveland, again ex-President, wrote: "I am having the devil's own time with my launch. I have had but one satisfactory time with her since I came and that was the day after I arrived when Brad [the Gray Gables handyman] ran her. I get so cursed mad every time I go out that I almost swear I'll never go in her again. I think I would lay her up if I had not loaned by catboat to Olney for the summer. It needs something done to it that the boy they sent up don't know enough to do. He says himself that an expert ought to overhaul it and that he has written to the company to that effect. He had only been in the shop three weeks, is evidently afraid to take the machine apart, and I am *afraid* don't know much about running the boat. It goes pretty well after it starts, but it's enough to make a man jump overboard to see this young man start it. I think he is a nice fellow and perhaps could get along if he had a little instruction about this particular boat. I am very certain that no one would buy any such a boat if all he knew about them was derived from the action of mine."[38]

The aggravation continued. In September Grover wrote, "I hope your engineer will have a chance to look over my launch before we put her up for the winter. I am afraid she has not been treated very well."[39]

That winter, Grover wrote to E.C. about alco-vapor's prospects: "I received a copy of the circular you sent me in regard to launches. I was looking it through in a listless sort of way, when I saw a picture of a boat that looked familiar; and upon further examination discovered to my great gratification that the motive power most approved by the important builders represented by the pamphlet was alco-vapor. I believe this thing will 'go' some of these days and be profitable."

Based on his previous experiences, Grover did not want any more inexperienced boys, nor did he want another engineer. "If I can afford to keep my launch, I must make early arrangements to secure someone to run the engine. I want some such a man as one of your sailors, that knows or can learn at the shop of the Company before the 1st of June, how to manage the machine and take care of it, and who besides will be able and *willing* to do any kind of work about my place as in any way related to fishing. I do *not* want any more such boys as I have had. Can you, through some of your men, put me in the way of the person I need? If I have one who claims to be in any degree an engineer, he will not be willing to do the other things I want of him. So I have made up my mind that I can be best suited by an active intelligent sailor, with wit enough to run and care for the launch, and not too nice or too lazy to do anything else I desire him to do."[40]

Esther's troubles must have abated, for in the spring of 1899, Grover sold *Ruth* for $500.[41] However, that summer the aggravation returned: "Something seems to ail the alcohol apparatus in my launch. It don't appear to feed right and hold up the pressure as it ought. Billy pumps and yanks at it in a manner that irritates me to the point of uncomfortable [indecipherable]. I think the fault is largely with him in some way."[42]

In the same letter Grover thanked E.C. for sending ten barrels of kerosene. *Esther*'s 7-hp engine consumed 3½ gallons per hour,[43] so the shipment provided Grover with some 120 hours of cruising.

In 1900 *Esther* was five years old, so her components suffered from normal wear and tear. In September Grover wrote, "As you anticipated, the condenser pipe in my launch is leaking again. I have telegraphed the company to send at once a new section of pipe which we can put in to last through the season. I don't want to leave the launch here next winter and think I will want her thoroughly overhauled."[44]

Grover had difficulty in getting the company to bill him, so he wrote to E.C.: "I do not think it is just the thing to have my intention to pay the launch bill thwarted. I don't know what to do about it now except to express my grateful appreciation of your kindness in treating me to such a fine going boat."[45]

Grover was not interested in speed, but other alco-vapor owners were particularly proud of the performance of their launches.

"She goes like the wind. I can outrun any naphtha boat of like dimensions that I come across."

"The twenty-one foot boat I got from you last year has given me entire satisfaction, and although she was not intended for speed, I have been more than able to hold my own with her against any twenty-five foot naphthas that I have met."

From the owner of a 20 ft. boat: "I am not troubled save by 28-foot 6 horse-power naphthas, though 21-foot 2 hp are out of the game. Should you make as great an advance next season as you have this last, you would have about perfection."[46]

Naphtha

Alco-Vapor Wins

In the Larchmont 1900 race, two alco-vapor launches defeated the naphthas.

On July 18, 1899, the Larchmont Yacht Club held separate naphtha and alco-vapor races. In the 21-foot and under category, the winning alco-vapor launch beat the fastest naphtha time by a minute and a half.[47] That year, on an eight-mile run in the Lake George cup races, an alco-vapor launch finished fifteen minutes ahead of her next competitor. A year later, according to the company, "The 'Alco-Vapor' launches, in the races of yacht tenders at the Larchmont Yacht Club on Long Island Sound, season of 1900, were easy winners and outdistanced all contestants in a most astonishing manner."[48] The manufacturer, in its next catalog, included a photograph of the alco-vapor winners.

When Frank Ofeldt began experimenting with naphtha, it was a substance that oil men despised and the public feared. Frank's naphtha engine reversed the opprobrium, but then Frank disavowed the fuel he had made respectable. Now alco-vapor launches were consistently and decisively defeating naphtha launches, but Frank was denied credit for either craft.

We may see Frank Ofeldt as a tragic figure, but that is not how he saw himself. He had already patented his next invention, and had not the slightest doubt that it would surpass all his previous ones.[49]

Chapter 15

The Height of Fashion

"In order to gain and to hold the esteem of men it is not sufficient merely to possess wealth or power. The wealth or power must be put in evidence, for esteem is awarded only on evidence. And not only does the evidence of wealth serve to impress one's importance on others and to keep their sense of his importance alive and alert, but it is of scarcely less use in building up and preserving one's self-complacency."

Thorstein Veblen, *The Theory of the Leisure Class*[1]

Majestic Yachts

According to Erik Hofman, "The steam yacht was the most striking personal possession ever produced by man. It pronounced achievement. It publicized the millionaire as no other possession did.... The steam yacht, particularly in the United States, was there for everybody to see and envy, naturally at a distance. Anchored off New York City, moving on the Hudson River or on Long Island Sound, in full view of thousands, it served as a goal for the ambitious."[2]

When she was constructed for William A. Slater by the Bath Iron Works, 1893-1894, *Eleanor*, at 232 feet, was the largest steam yacht yet built in the United States. According to *The New York Times*, she was "especially designed to meet the requirements of her owner in a two years' cruise around the world, and, as the home of his family for that time, is to be furnished with regal magnificence. A gallery of $60,000 worth of oil paintings will be among the attractions of the beautiful craft.... She is fitted with water-tight bulkheads, and will carry seven boats, including a steam launch and a naphtha launch, and will be armed with two rapid-fire rifles, which can put a pound shot through a solid inch of steel, and can both be fired ahead or astern, or to either side."[3]

William A. Slater's *Eleanor*, seen here with her naphtha tender, proves the validity of Thorstein Veblen's assertion that in order to impress one's importance on others, one's wealth must be put on display. Conspicuous consumption came to be a feature of what Mark Twain called *The Gilded Age*.

Chapter 15

Naphtha

Colonel Oliver Payne had been slow to take up yachting, but he tried it out by chartering *Eleanor*, and he was so pleased that he asked the same builder to construct a much larger yacht, the 302-ft. *Aphrodite*. He also placed an order for two naphtha tenders, built of mahogany. A writer for *The Rudder* noted that the sides of those launches shone like a piano top, and they were so beautiful that he would like to steal them.[4]

Aphrodite was constructed by the Bath Iron Works for Colonel Oliver Payne, the former treasurer of Standard Oil. Seventy feet longer than *Eleanor*, she was now the largest steam yacht built in America, and effectively advertised Colonel Payne's eminence. One of *Aphrodite*'s two naphtha tenders lies alongside.

Chapter 15

Frederick W. Vanderbilt's *Conqueror* at first carried one steam tender and one naphtha, but Fred so much preferred the latter that he replaced the steam tender with a 27-ft., 6-hp naphtha. (*The New York Times*, March 8, 1896, "Bits of Yachting News.")

An Idiosyncratic Designer

As we know, Alfred Nobel exercised his creative passion by designing *Mignon*. He was not alone. When Alfred Van Santvoord, proprietor of the Albany Day Line, decided that he needed a yacht, he designed her himself. At a time when almost all yachts were steel-hulled, *Clermont* was made of wood, and she was powered by a walking beam engine which drove paddle wheels, just like the speedy boats that had made him rich.

When Alfred Van Santvoord, proprietor of the Albany Day Line, decided that he needed a private yacht, he designed her himself. Unlike other luxury yachts, *Clermont*, seen here with her naphtha tender, had a wooden hull and a walking beam engine.

Chapter 15

Clermont on her way to a new anchorage. Van Santvoord explained: "It has the advantage of being able to change its location as often as we may desire. Some people make the mistake of buying a country home, which they soon tire of and then are unable to sell. We are able to enjoy all the comforts of a home on the yacht." (*The New York Times*, July 2, 1899)

By 1892, 79 leading yachts had naphtha tenders (Gas Engine and Power Company 1892 catalog, pp. 18, 20). *Seabord* noted "their almost complete displacement of the steam-launch for communication between large yachts (sail and steam) and the shore, their immediate readiness making them in every way preferable." (May 24, 1894, p. 611, "Naphtha Launches for Pleasure or Profit")

In *A Story of the Naphtha Launch*, J. Chamberlain explained that, "With a speed of eight miles an hour she skips over the white caps, without an effort....Thus the Naphtha Launch is a necessity of the fleet....The habitué of the fashionable club or the assembly room need have no fear as to costume, when he entertains his friends in his Naphtha Launch. The kid gloves he wears need not be soiled."[5]

Chapter 15

Naphtha Races

From the beginning, yachtsmen took pleasure in racing their tenders against each other. On July 16, 1886, just weeks after the company opened its doors for business, Clement Gould organized the first naphtha launch race. One competitor was *Orienta*'s Launch, owned by Jabez Bostwick, another was *Lagonda*'s Launch, owned by J. C. Hoagland, and the winner was *Tillie*'s Launch.[6]

For the 1888 race Clement Gould offered a handsome prize, a miniature naphtha launch of silver, its interior a receptacle for cigars and the smokestack for matches.[7] *The New York Times* described the event: "The American Yacht Club once more opened its hospitable arms yesterday, and welcomed to its home waters all sizes and kinds of naphtha launches,…and 13 of the saucy little craft appeared at the starting line. …The rush of the little racers to cross the line was so sudden and impetuous that the Regatta committee… had very lively work to take the time as they came puffing and whizzing by."[8] According to the *Brooklyn Eagle,* "Clement Gould's *Adroit* crossed last, with the owner at the helm, to see fair play."[9]

Other clubs also conducted naphtha races. In an 1891 race held by the Cherry-Diamond Yacht Club, John J. Amory, secretary and treasurer of the Gas Engine and Power Company, entered his 22-ft., 6-hp launch, *Republic*. It came in second, but the winner *Maspeth* had a 10-hp engine. While attending the same race, Clement Gould's *Adroit* beat the steam launch *Pharos*, much to the surprise of the latter's owner.[10]

A naphtha launch race at the Larchmont Yacht Club

Status Symbols

The Gas Engine and Power Company was so proud of its prestigious customers that the 1892 catalog listed more than 750 by name. Among the owners were several of Jabez Bostwick's Standard Oil partners, including Henry Flagler, whose yacht *Alicia* carried a naphtha tender. Flagler must have been pleased, for a later catalog stated that he was the owner of six naphtha launches.[11] Other Standard Oil men included J.J. Vandergrift, who had a 40-ft. cruising launch,[12] and John Archbold, who owned the 38-ft. naphtha cabin launch *Vixen*, as well as a steam yacht of the same name.[13] William Rockefeller stated in a testimonial that his naphtha launch "is very staunch, and the machinery works to perfection. We are much pleased with her."[14]

W.P. Stephens wrote that a naphtha launch "could be found moored at the pier of every waterside estate."[15] Like the steam yacht, the naphtha launch became a status symbol, and the *Brooklyn Eagle* pronounced that "No home near the water's edge was complete without one." A naphtha launch can "make the man in a dinghy feel like thirty cents."[16]

A naphtha launch at a waterside estate near Detroit.

Mr. and Mrs. H.B. Ogden prepare to board their 36-ft. cabin launch in Brooklyn. Like the steam yacht, a naphtha launch provided evidence of its owner's social standing.

Chapter 15

Many cabin launches were decorated like their owners' parlors.

Interior View of
42-foot Cabin Launch

There was very little that was nautical about the interior of this 50-ft. naphtha yacht.

Interior View of
50-foot Cabin Yacht

177

The Futurist

If the naphtha launch was now a status symbol, the Gas Engine and Power Company's electric launches offered even greater evidence of their owners' eminence. As Weston Farmer explained, "If the rich man at the lake wanted full safety and exquisite elegance from 1893 to about 1910, he bought an electric launch – the acme of grace, initial cost, and Rolls Royce quality....I can still see the typical electric launch boathouse: all gingerbread Byzantine carpentry, elegantly installed in a private basin into and under the roof of which the boat was nurseried when not in use, and over which was a fashionable "gazebo" – the *in* term for a screened lolling place where pallid ladies swapped gossip and swatted mosquitoes with their fans of an evening."[17]

John Jacob Astor IV was one of the wealthiest men in the world, but he was also an inventor. One of his patents was for a bicycle brake, and he won a prize at the Chicago World's Fair for his pneumatic walkway. However, the patent office rejected his idea for pumping warm, moist air from the earth's surface into the atmosphere to make rain.[18]

In 1894 Astor wrote a science fiction novel, *A Journey in Other Worlds*, set in the year 2000, when electricity would be used for "almost every conceivable purpose" including the powering of 300 mph magnetic railways, ships whose electric motors were powered by the wind and the tides, "marine spiders" that walked across the seas at a mile a minute, electric phaetons (automobiles) whose batteries could be recharged in almost every town or village from Hudson's Bay to Patagonia, and airplanes whose batteries had been so perfected that eight ounces of battery yielded one horse power for six hours. "However enjoyable the manly sport of yachting is on water, how vastly more interesting and fascinating it is for a man to have a yacht in which he can fly to Europe in one day, and with which the exploration of tropical Africa or the regions about the poles is mere child's play, while giving him so magnificent a bird's-eye view."[19]

John Jacob Astor IV was fascinated by electricity, and for several years backed Nikola Tesla's experiments.

Chapter 15

In 1894 John Jacob Astor published a science fiction novel, *A Journey in Other Worlds*, set in the year 2000. In it he predicted that people would travel to other planets, and electricity would power almost everything on Earth.

Astor was so entranced by the electric launches at the Chicago Exposition that he ordered one for himself, *Corcyra*, which he put into commission that same year. The Navy then ordered a similar launch as a Captain's gig for the cruiser *New York*. Grand Duke Alexander of Russia, while being entertained by Mr. Astor at Rhinebeck-on-the-Hudson, was much pleased with Astor's launch, and shortly afterwards had an opportunity to inspect the Navy's electric gig. The craft so captured his fancy that, at the request of Grover Cleveland's Secretary of State, the Navy Department directed the Gas Engine and Power Company to deliver that launch to him and to begin the construction of a duplicate for the U.S. cruiser.[20]

According to William C. Swanson, "Back in St. Petersburg, the Grand Duke's cousin, Czar Nicholas II, liked the launch so much that in 1897 he ordered a 37-foot Elco launch as tender for his royal yacht, *Pole Star*. The gig had an oak hull sheathed in brass, mahogany decks, velvet carpets, and two wicker chairs upholstered with Russian leather cushions."[21]

Grand Duke Alexander's electric launch was modeled on Astor's *Corcyra*. It so appealed to his cousin, Czar Nicholas II, that the Czar had to have one of his own, and ordered a 37-ft. electric tender from the Gas Engine and Power Company.

Chapter 15

A year after *Corcyra*'s launching, Astor ordered a cabin launch named *Progresso*, the largest electric boat yet built in America,[22] but he was obsessed with pushing the envelope of boat design, and soon decided to construct an electric yacht that would represent the ultimate in technology and also the epitome of elegance. To create a vessel that matched his vision, Astor turned to Charles D. Mosher, who had designed the electric launches for Chicago's Columbian Exposition, and whose steam yacht *Feiseen*, with a 600-hp Mosher patent quadruple expansion engine, had set a new world speed record in August 1893.[23] Mosher came up with a concept that would suit a futurist like Astor – a yacht propelled by both electricity and the wind.

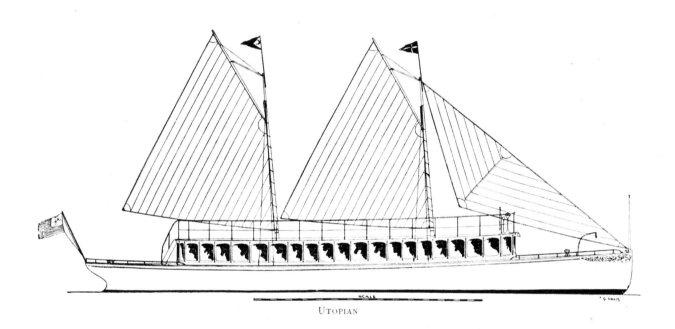

UTOPIAN

Astor, one of the world's wealthiest men, decided to build the ultimate cabin launch, so he turned to Charles D. Mosher, who had designed the electric boats for Chicago's Columbian Exposition. Mosher's futuristic design for *Utopian* combined features of a two-masted schooner and an electric yacht.

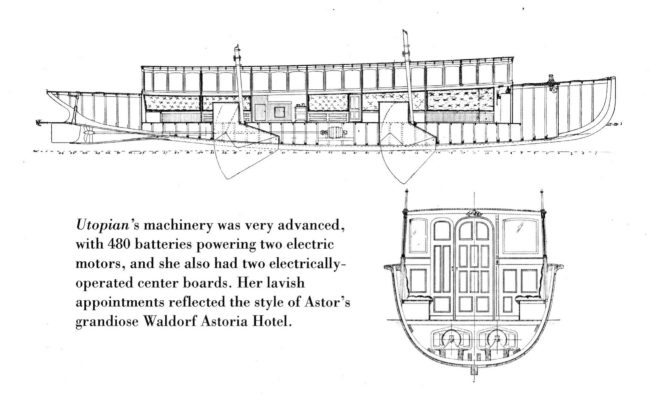

Utopian's machinery was very advanced, with 480 batteries powering two electric motors, and she also had two electrically-operated center boards. Her lavish appointments reflected the style of Astor's grandiose Waldorf Astoria Hotel.

Up until then the Gas Engine and Power Company had built Astor's electric boats, but the company had no patent protection on electric propulsion, so Mosher chose a different builder, Samuel Ayres, who had once constructed boats for Frank Ofeldt, and was now based in Nyack.

In October 1896, *The Rudder* described the launching of the aptly-named *Utopian*, "the largest and most handsomely appointed electric auxiliary yacht in the world.

"The dimensions are as follows: 72 feet over all, 12 feet beam, and 4 feet draught. The boat is fitted with twin screws. They are run by two electric motors of at least 25-horse power. These, with the shafting and propellers, were in the yacht when she was launched, but the 480 cells that are to supply the electricity will be put in over at Rhinecliff, where Mr. Astor has his electric light plant, and where the batteries can be charged, it is said, for a twelve-hour continuous run. The cells as well as the motors are placed entirely below the floor so as to leave the boat entirely unobstructed.

"The hull is of a peculiar form, having a channel way for each of the propellers so as to enable them to work in solid water. There will also be two Tobin bronze center-boards, which may be raised or lowered by electric winches from the promenade deck. The boat is also to be fitted with electric capstans; also a large air chamber connected with the air pumps to supply air for blowing the whistles, which will consist of an elaborate set of chimes.

"The saloon, 18 feet long, [extends] the entire width of the boat. It is fitted on either side with seats arranged to fold out and form wide berths. They will be beautifully upholstered with brocatel velvet, and fitted with drawers under same, and finished with elaborate gold trimmings. It is also to be fitted with a large folding table. When the leaves are down this table will occupy a space of 4 feet across, and it will form the trunk for the center-board, at the forward end of which is the mast.

"The boat will be rigged as a two-masted schooner, and is provided with hinged masts, steel-wire rigging, and sails by Hemmenway & Son, which are intended to be used as an auxiliary power."[24]

Prior to 1896, Astor had ordered a new electric boat each year, but *Utopian* fulfilled his dreams. He was so delighted with her that he took her to Newport every summer for at least six years.[25]

Chapter 15

Naphtha Yachts

For long trips it was the custom of wealthy Americans to travel in private railroad cars. The larger naphtha launches matched Pullmans in their amenities, so some owners began to embark on extensive voyages. The *Brooklyn Eagle* announced that, "Thomas Edison Jr., and William Edison, sons of the noted inventor, with several invited guests, will sail from Baltimore next Wednesday in a 60-foot naphtha launch for a trip to the Edison winter home in Florida. They will take the inland water route from Norfolk by way of the North Carolina sounds and canals, but a part of the voyage in the little craft will be on the ocean. Stops will be made at various points for gunning and fishing and some fine sport is expected."[26]

A year later S.C. Clayton's *Regina* made one of the longest cruises on record. Again, the *Brooklyn Eagle* described the odyssey: "The yacht left Philadelphia last Christmas and proceeded down the coast to Florida, where the winter months were passed. Then it journeyed back to New York and came to the islands, via the Hudson River, Erie and Oswego canals and Lake Ontario. It is now bound down the St. Lawrence and up the Saguenay River, whence it will return to Chicago through the Great Lakes. From Chicago the boat will be canaled to the Mississippi and will winter in Florida. The little craft is only sixty feet long and carries a sixteen-horse power naphtha engine."[27]

Regina slept six, plus two crewmembers. She had a very large saloon, with divans and a dining table, and also a galley with a refrigerator compartment, and a dressing room and toilet. Her owner, S.C. Clayton, made a trip in her that extended over most of eighteen months.

Naphtha

Chapter 15

The Gas Engine and Power Company was finding clients with a taste for bigger boats. In the 1894 catalog, the company announced, "The demand for larger launches, more particularly where increased speed or light draught is required, has led to an experiment of putting in two motors."[28] Both *The New York Times* and *The Rudder* defined twin-engine naphthas as yachts, not launches, and by early 1896 seven or eight had been constructed.[29]

Twin-engine naphtha craft were classified by the company as yachts, not launches. *Griffon*, with 12-hp motors, was owned by Dr. E.P. Hicks, Burlington, Vermont.

Frank L. Camp's impressive 67-ft. twin-screw naphtha yacht, *Victor Roy*.

Clermont had a naphtha tender, which so pleased Alfred Van Santvoord that he decided to try his hand at designing a naphtha yacht. On January 26, 1896, *The New York Times* reported that the Gas Engine and Power Company was building him a twin-screw naphtha yacht at a cost of $12,000.[30] In February *The Rudder* wrote that, at 76 feet, the craft was "notable as the largest boat ever built to be propelled by naphtha power." The new yacht will be "equipped with two twelve H.P. motors, operating twin screws (and) her naphtha capacity is sufficient for a continuous run of five hundred miles, but she will also have an auxiliary sail rig, designed for practical use, if required.... Quite contrary to the prevailing custom, the pilot house is also placed well aft."

As the owner planned an extended cruise in Florida, she was of shallow draft, and "The windows throughout will be fitted with shutters and fine brass screens to prevent the intrusion of the myriads of small and obnoxious insects which infest that section of the country.... The two large staterooms will be equipped with all the conveniences afforded by the most modern large yachts... in fact, the available space is equal to that of a steam yacht fifty percent larger, and can be used to better advantage as it is not disintegrated.... The interior finish will be in white wood, and the upholstery of the most expensive and elegant materials."

The author, possibly Charles G. Davis, who drew the accompanying illustration, noted that, "in this new craft the builders have taken quite a stride as to size, which would tend to strengthen the predictions often made that steam power for the propulsion of large craft will soon be superseded by naphtha or electrical power."[31]

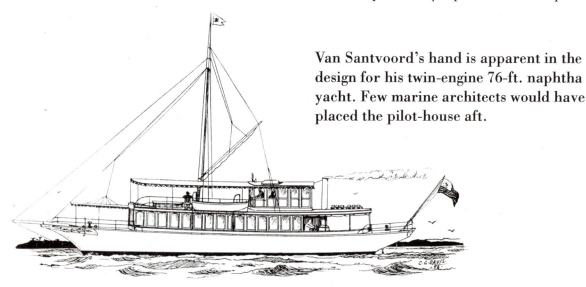

Van Santvoord's hand is apparent in the design for his twin-engine 76-ft. naphtha yacht. Few marine architects would have placed the pilot-house aft.

186

Chapter 15

A Conflagration

Another man who chose to be his own marine architect was the Brooklyn sugar refiner, J. Adolph Mollenhauer, "well known as a Corinthian navigator" (an amateur who skippers his own boat). The Gas Engine and Power Company built the 76-ft. twin-screw *Thelma* for him at a cost of $11,500.[32]

In the spring of 1896, Mr. Mollenhauer was elected fleet captain of the Penataquit-Corinthian Yacht Club of Bay Shore, L.I.[33] Soon after that, the club conducted a race for steam and naphtha launches owned by members, the prize "a very valuable silver cup."[34] Mollenhauer entered his brand new *Thelma*, and Frank L. Camp entered *Victor Roy*. The race was very exciting and *Thelma* won.

A week later *Thelma's* luck turned. The *Brooklyn Eagle* carried the horrifying tale, under the heading, "MAY RAISE THE THELMA."

"Mr. Adolf Mollenhauer, who arrived here with his wife after their rescue from their burning yacht, the Thelma, yesterday off Matinnecock point, left for Northport today to see if it would be possible to raise the sunken yacht, or recover any of the valuable silverware and other property on board."

On the second morning of a two week cruise, the Mollenhauers had just finished breakfast, when, in Mrs. Mollenhauer's words, "I went on deck, and almost as soon as I reached the deck I saw an immense tongue of flame shoot up through the door of the engine room to the deck. In an instant it seemed as if there were flames everywhere and all around me. I called my husband and he and the crew saw that nothing could be done to save the yacht and we would be lucky if we got away with our lives, for the naphtha was blazing furiously. There were several hundred gallons in the tank. A signal of distress was made by blowing the whistle continuously, but after that it was impossible to enter the engine room or cabin because of the heat. Fortunately for us a tugboat that was towing a barge up the sound saw us, and came to our rescue. The last I saw of the Thelma was a great heap of flames, with the two tall masts just toppling over. I do not think there was any loud explosion; the naphtha just seemed to make everything blaze with tremendous heat. We were all frightened and nervous of course, but had to keep cool."

The *Eagle* concluded with the statement: "Mrs. Mollenhauer says she does not want to see a yacht again for a year, at least, after the fright of yesterday."[35]

Mr. Mollenhauer, anxious that no blame should fall on the company, wrote to the Gas Engine and Power Company, with a copy to the *Eagle*:

"Gentlemen – As a matter of justice to you, being the builders of my twin screw naphtha yacht *Thelma*, which was burned last Tuesday, I wish to state that the yacht or its machinery was in no way to blame for the accident. It was entirely owing to carelessness on the part of the engineer in charge removing the injector valve from one engine while the other engine was running, the escaping naphtha hereby igniting. My confidence in the safety of your naphtha boats is such that I shall place an order with you at an early date for another boat. Regretting this unfortunate affair, believe me, yours very truly, J. Adolph Mollenhauer."[36]

Thelma's design so pleased other yachtsmen that the Gas Engine and Power Company built two sister ships, one of which was *Corinthia*, described as "one of the largest vessels propelled by naphtha power, the length over all being seventy-six feet, beam eleven feet, eight inches, and draught about three feet, six inches. She was designed primarily for day service…and has a large deck space over main cabin, enclosed by bulwark, and protected by awnings. There are comfortable accommodations for four people below for sleeping, made by dividing the one large compartment into sections by portierres. A dressing room, toilet and galley, with refrigerator, dish lockers, glass racks and pantry, occupy the space between the saloon and engine compartment. The crew have the use of the forecastle, in which may be placed three or four berths."[37]

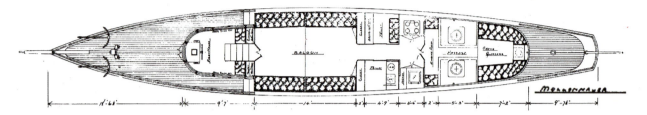

PROFILE AND DECK PLAN OF 76-FOOT TWIN SCREW NAPHTHA YACHT,
Two of which were built in 1896, one for Mr. J. A. Mollenhauer, Brooklyn, N. Y., and the other for Mr. C. Everett Clark, Boston, Mass.

The twin-engine naphtha yacht, *Thelma*, was designed by her owner, J. Adolph Mollenhauer.

76-FOOT TWIN-SCREW NAPHTHA YACHT. TWO 12 H.-P. MOTORS.
MR. WILLIAM BANIGAN, PROVIDENCE, R. I.

Thelma's design so pleased other yachtsmen that the Gas Engine and Power Company built two sister ships, one of which was *Corinthia*, proudly described by the company as "one of the largest vessels propelled by naphtha power."

Chapter 16

Kapowie!

"No early writer on the subject of these boats could restrain himself from a bit of verbal clowning. I don't think it was justified, because they were very safe boats if the operators had any sense. I remember one such passage that, if memory serves correctly, stated:

'To get underway and raise steam, open the naphtha valve into the flame pan and toss in a match and go about your busi –

KAPOWIE!

– no calamity!

Go about your business. It will burn off and you will be underway to heaven or the devil in a few moments'."

Weston Farmer, *Yachting*[1]

Naphtha

Nautical historians marvel that their forebears dared to use such a dangerous contraption as the naphtha engine. In 1995, Gordon Millar wrote that "it seems inconceivable in today's world of risk avoidance that anyone would venture on the water in a naphtha-powered launch,"[2] and Richard Mitchell concurred: "Today one's imagination recoils at the thought of lighting a fire under a vessel filled with gasoline."[3] The story that naphtha engines blew up has persisted for more than a century. Was there truth to it, or was it just a legend?

In 1904, naphtha explosions were such accepted lore that the popular songwriter Glen MacDonough celebrated them in *The Song of the Naphtha Launch.*[4]

THE SONG OF THE NAPHTHA LAUNCH.

I.

You talk about your raging main
And your barks so trim and stanch,
But they don't compare, I do declare,
With the rakish Naphtha Launch.
The perils of the briny deep
Are wondrous grave, they say,
But they fail to mix
With the troublesome tricks
A Naphtha Launch can play.

II.

It's fine to rise on a lofty wave
Or to slide on a briny bank;
But it thrills you more to rise and soar
With a bursting naphtha tank!
Your friends may try to call you down,
But you look at them askance;
And you gayly fly till you land by and by
In the arms of an ambulance!

III.

It's fine, of course, to sail away
On a steamer, bark, or brig;
But it's simply great to go up straight
On a busted thing-a-majig!
A Naphtha Launch is a curious bird
When once it starts to jump!
Then it's up to you and the rest of the crew
To look out for an awful bump.

IV.

A friend of mine who owed a launch
That he thought was just the kind,
Invited me to sail the sea,
But I, with thanks, declined.
That day the naphtha all ran out.
My friend did angry seem.
He thought he knew;
So, unknown to the crew,
He used some kerosene.

Refrain.

With a yeave-heave-ho! my hearties!
We'll plough the sea, my boys!
We'll also plough through a lazy scow
On the larboard watch ahoy!
With a yeave-heave-ho! my hearties!
Yeave-heave-ho! my men!
When the boiler bursts, "it's many a day
Till Jack comes home again."

GLEN MACDONOUGH.

Misrepresentations

The public's fear was reinforced by newspaper accounts like the one that appeared in *The New York Times* on July 24, 1900. The headline read, "NAPHTHA LAUNCH BLOWS UP IN SOUND: Two Occupants Killed Instantly; One Seriously Injured," and it was followed by a lurid account of the explosion:

"A more tragic ending to a day's sport than that of the Larchmont Yacht Club's regatta yesterday afternoon, yachtsmen along the Sound never hope to see. Just thirty seconds after the last racing boat had crossed the finish line, off Larchmont Harbor, a terrific explosion two miles or so down the Sound rent the air and shook the fleet of pleasure craft that had drifted into anchor off the clubhouse. An instant later a sheet of flame leaped high from the water off Premium Point, New Rochelle.

"The naphtha launch Sasco, having on board Mr. and Mrs. Alfred E. Crow and their fourteen-year-old son Harold, of New Rochelle, had exploded while

Chapter 16

bearing them home at the end of an afternoon spent in watching the regatta. Fifteen minutes later the mutilated bodies of Mrs. Crow and the boy were taken out of the water. Mr. Crow, clinging to a cushion, with a broken leg, and more dead than alive, was rescued at the same time....His recovery is doubtful."

Clinton Crow, a member of the victims' family, said that, earlier in the day, "the naphtha tank began to leak, and his father had seemingly stopped the ooze with a soft plug. The young man's theory is that, despite this plug, the naphtha leaked out into the bottom of the boat and that in some manner this took fire and caused the tanks to blow up. He says the launch had never given any trouble before and the leak early in the day was thought to be a trivial thing."

Only toward the end of the account did the *Times* reveal that the engine was not naphtha, but internal combustion: "The *Lasco* (sic) was a thirty-foot boat, driven by an Empire motor, which was worked by the explosion of the naphtha by electric sparks."[5]

It was the headline that did the damage. Readers of the *Times* would long remember the deadly explosion of a naphtha launch.

Such mistakes were common. Three years earlier the manufacturer had protested to the editor of the *Times*. "As a matter of justice to our naphtha launch, we beg to advise that the so-called naphtha launch (Rambler) accident at Bath Beach yesterday, reported in this morning's papers, was a "wing" motor boat, and we believe that a correction should be made, and boat and motor designated by its proper name, otherwise we are the sufferers. We ask this correction from the fact that numerous accidents of all classes of launches heretofore have been erroneously reported as naphtha launches, which, upon investigation, are found to be boats equipped with explosive engines of different types, and the public and yachting world in general are not aware of the error, and we are unfortunately obliged to suffer the consequent damage from such reports."[6]

It is hard to blame the journalists. That was a time when the terms gasoline and naphtha were often used interchangeably, and technically both were naphthas.

Most boat builders took care to explain to the public which type of engine they used, but the New York Yacht, Launch and Engine Co., the manufacturer of *Wing* boats, was guilty of intentional deception. Earlier that year the company had published an advertisement, promoting the *Wing*'s internal combustion engine with the heading, "Safety, Speed, and Economy, The Fastest Naphtha Launch." Is it any wonder that the *Times* was misled?

In a blatant misrepresentation, this boat builder identified the *Wing*'s internal combustion engine as a naphtha engine. When a *Wing* motorboat suffered an accident, *The New York Times* blamed the boat's naphtha engine – hardly surprising, given the manufacturer's misleading advertisements.

Naphtha

Handling Naphtha

Apart from misrepresentation, there was a real problem. Even if the naphtha engine was safe, naphtha itself was not. On April 20, 1895, an article appeared in the *Brooklyn Eagle* under the heading, "EXPLOSION ON NAPHTHA LAUNCH." The story led off: "There was a terrific explosion at 10:45 o'clock this morning at the dock of the Gas Engine and Power Company, at Morris dock, in the Twenty-third ward, New York. The explosion was heard for about two miles." Again the headline was misleading. Subsequent reports clarified that although the accident happened at the naphtha boat works, the explosion actually took place aboard the steam yacht *Reva*, where two sailors were using the fluid for cleaning purposes. The mate was reported to have been blown as high as the masthead, while a deckhand was hurled overboard. *The New York Times* reported that "the upper works and cabins of the Reva for a distance of sixty feet from the stern, were blown in fragments, sent 200 feet in the air, and scattered all around.…The maintopmast had been broken and splintered as if it had been struck by lightning, and the bridge had been entirely carried away."[7]

Handling naphtha requires great care. *The New York Times* reported that, as the naphtha launch *Dorothy* was being refueled at the Standard Oil works at the foot of East 125th St., "in some way the naphtha flowing into the twenty-gallon tank was not shut off when the tank was full, and flowed over in a considerable stream into the bottom of the boat. Just as one [crewman] was going forward to the valve to shut off the supply, this loose naphtha was exploded by the heat of the motor …and in an instant the boat was wrapped in flames. Four men were on board, and as the blazing fluid flew in all directions much of it fell upon them and three of them were burned, Theodore Dunham, the engineer of the launch, so badly that he is likely to die. He was in the cockpit with the engine at the time of the explosion and was blazing from head to foot as he leaped up the short ladder and threw himself into the river. Joseph Collis, a seventeen-year-old prisoner, deckhand on the Randall's Island steamer Refuge, which was just making the dock, leaped after the writhing man and after a desperate struggle brought him to the pier.…Capt. Grace of the Refuge said he would make an effort to secure Collis's liberty as a reward for his heroism."[8]

In a naphtha launch, the fuel tank was in the forepeak, bulkheaded off from the rest of the boat. Below the waterline, holes in the hull allowed seawater to flow in and out of that compartment, so that if the fuel tank leaked, the naphtha simply ran out through the holes. This was not foolproof. Naphtha does not disperse in water, but rises to the surface. The *Brooklyn Eagle* recounted an unfortunate misadventure: "While Dr. E. A. Evans of Brooklyn and his daughter were preparing for a lake trip at their summer home at Guilford Lake, last evening, a match was thrown from a naphtha launch into the water, setting fire to a large quantity of naphtha that had leaked from the reservoir. The launch was surrounded by a sheet of flame and with the boathouse was totally destroyed. Dr. Evans and his daughter were fearfully burned about the face and hands, but will probably recover."[9]

With more and more cabin launches coming into use, there was also a problem caused by the use of naphtha in enclosed spaces. *The New York Times* described the destruction of the *Boggabor*, a 35-ft. naphtha launch: "About 7:30 o'clock McDonald decided to go below to get something to eat. He lighted a lantern and climbed into the cabin. He put the lantern on the floor and started to rummage through the icebox. Mr. Elliott, senior, who had been lying down, saw the lantern at that moment and sprang to his feet. 'Take that light out of here, I smell gasoline, there's a leak somewhere,' he shouted. McDonald, thoroughly frightened, dropped the lid of the ice chest and seized the lantern. He had not gone two feet before there was an explosion. The elder Elliott, Herbert, and McDonald were near the door of the cabin at the time and they were lifted bodily from their feet, hurled through the air and landed into the water several feet from the boat. Young Elliott was not so lucky. He was sitting in the forward part of the cabin, close to the tank of naphtha, and got the full force of the explosion. He was blown clear through the roof of the cabin and landed unconscious fifteen feet away in the water."[10]

Tellingly, in 1899, the company dropped the sentence that had appeared in the 1896 catalog, "We defy any one to prove a single accident where an explosion of any part of the machinery of one of our boats has occurred, or where anyone was injured by fire from such a cause."[11] Perhaps the company was worried that readers might interpret "any part of the machinery" to include the fuel tank. The company also revised its previous challenge, which had offered "$500 to the person who can explode boiler or machinery of our Launch."[12] The new wording was more cautious: "We make a standing offer of $500 to any person who will explode, or suggest a plan for exploding the engine or any part of the power plant, under any conditions which might obtain from proper usage."[13]

Blaze-Ups

The Herreshoffs were familiar with naphtha launches. Nathaniel G. can be seen standing in *Shearwater* alongside his brother, John Brown Herreshoff (with white cane). Nat's son, L. Francis, wrote that most naphtha launches blazed up occasionally, but because the engine compartments were copper-sheathed, "these blaze-ups were rather laughed at."

Most people who had actual experience with naphtha launches sided with the company. One person with considerable credibility was L. Francis Herreshoff: "Certainly as we look at the naphtha launch today it seems a most infernal machine. Strange to say, however, these launches had few explosions or fatal accidents 'though most of them blazed up occasionally. Many were copper-sheathed in the engine compartment so these blaze-ups were rather laughed at or thought to be part of the game. I have seen these blaze-ups at night when they certainly were alarming to the uninitiated."[14]

Kenneth Durant explained one cause of the fires: "In starting a cold engine, the operator had to use judgment and not be impatient. If the naphtha in the coils was not sufficiently heated when the needle valve was opened, it came through in liquid form instead of spray. If not checked, this might overflow the pan under the burner and take fire and at worst might spill into the brass-lined engine pit.... They could be avoided by not opening the injector valve prematurely and by closing it promptly if the fuel was not atomizing. The condition of the jet could be seen clearly through the damper at the front of the injector, which might account for the blaze-ups at night when the stream could not be seen. A trained ear learned to distinguish between silent flow of cold liquid and the hiss of atomized fuel."[15]

A second cause of fires was the packing glands at each end of the crankshaft and the valve shaft. When a flame appeared at one of these glands, it reminded the operator to tighten the packing.[16] From personal experience, Weston Farmer was able to assure his readers that the naphtha engine was "perfectly safe as long as all seals were tight."[17]

If the boater forgot to tighten the seals, there was a recourse. In a 1905 issue of *Motor Launch* magazine, W. P. Hartford advised, "If the boat catches fire, keep cool, smother or let the fire burn out, then dash water on whatever is burning, if you get excited, jump overboard."[18]

But what if you couldn't swim? Chrystie McConnell described just such a dilemma: "Back in those days, lard came in tin pails, and every boat had on board one or two empty lard pails as utility buckets. One afternoon, my mother, my father, his niece, and I were out for a ride when the stack started to spout six-foot flames and black smoke. While Dad poured water by the lard pailful down the stack, Mother and I were wondering, 'What next?' It was only about half a mile to shore, and the two of us could swim like otters, but Dad and his niece were another story. Both of them had been brought up on inland farms, and although they were technically able to swim, they were far from being in our class. (Back in those interesting days, life preservers and fire extinguishers were not required on pleasure craft and, besides, no one ever thought of them.) Well, Dad finally got his Vesuvius under control, and we got back to the dock safely."[19]

British Caution

The British were skeptical, and for many years imposed legal restrictions on the use of the naphthas.[20] An 1891 letter in *Industries* cautioned boaters: "In the *Field* of the 18th ult. there appeared a notice of an explosion on board a "naphtha launch" at Henley, in which reference is made to a similar explosion of which accounts have been received from America, and also to another explosion of the same kind at Cowes. In the notice, readers of the *Field* – i.e., principally yachtsmen – are advised to have nothing to do with these boats, and the editor congratulates himself on having originally opposed their introduction into this country."[21]

Americans, who now had considerable experience with naphtha launches, were blasé. *The Horseless Age* pointed out that the alternatives were more accident-prone: "If any additional government inspection of small boats is needed, it is needed for sailboats, which are certainly the most dangerous of all small craft, particularly in inexperienced hands. Every Summer squall in New York Bay bears witness to the truth of this statement."[22]

Time to Compromise

It was time to compromise. In 1896 the Gas Engine and Power Company decided to support legislation that would apply only to "vessels of above fifteen tons burden, carrying freight or passengers for hire, propelled by gas, fluid, naphtha, or electric motors." The company stated that, this bill "undoubtedly accomplishes all that is necessary in the way of legislation, and probably would stop further agitation."[23]

In 1901 a congressman, General Charles H. Grosvenor, introduced an amendment, extending the restriction to commercial vessels of any size. Launch owners feared that the bill might be further amended to apply to private users, to which General Grosvenor issued a tart response: "The bill does not pretend to debar any private user of a launch, however propelled, being of less than fifteen tons, from choosing any way he may prefer to blow himself and his family to perdition."[24]

In 1977 the nautical historian, John Gardner, reviewed the record of the naphtha launch, and reported that, "Their safety record was unexcelled, and in fact, perfect so far as is known, for there is no record of any serious accident resulting from an explosion of a naphtha launch."[25] Gardner oversimplified, for there were certainly explosions related to leaking fuel in both naphtha and internal combustion launches. As to the naphtha engine itself, he may well have been right.

Chapter 17

Combat

"The attacking force was not a regular torpedo boat, but was only a small naphtha launch in command of a young naval officer, who had with him three jackies. The launch mounted a small machine gun and carried three torpedoes."

Wayne County Review[1]

Consolidated

After William Whitney reversed the U.S. Navy's decline, Americans found a new pride in its strength. Significantly, the Gas Engine and Power Company's 1893 catalog opened with a patriotic statement, "It is true that our new navy is now the fifth in the world for size and importance, and every one interested to see the maritime supremacy of the United States established once again rejoices in the rapidity with which we are re-assuming the position which belongs to this country."[2]

It would not be long before the Gas Engine and Power Company entered into the construction of armed vessels. This initiative was the result of a momentous change in the company itself. In 1896 the company's catalog went to press in the late spring, but before the pages were bound, a copy of a recent *New York Times* article was inserted. The article contained an important announcement:

"The Gas Engine & Power Company, whose specialty, the Naphtha Launch, has gained such worldwide popularity, and Charles L. Seabury & Co., whose unprecedented success in the production of high-class Steam Yachts has put them far in advance of all competitors, have just united forces, and will at once commence the erection of new buildings and other extensive additions to their already large plant at Morris Heights, including several sets of ship's ways, and probably a sectional dry dock. When the plant is completed it will represent not only the largest of the kind in the world, but the most complete....In point of fact, it is the intention to establish an up-to-date Yacht Emporium....The new company will...complete boats from keel to truck, even to the furnishings and supplies. The yachtsman who places his order in the fall can take his customary winter trip aboard, and returning in the spring have his new yacht meet him down the bay, fully equipped, manned and provisioned for the summer cruise."[3]

Why did Seabury choose this moment to return? If we are correct in our assumption that he had departed due to a conflict with Jabez Bostwick or Clement Gould, the timing makes sense. Gould was now two years dead, and Jabez four, and apparently there was no bad blood between Seabury and John Amory, the new president. Upon the merger, Seabury was named vice-president, and C.P. Harmon moved down to second vice-president. W.J. Parslow, who had left at the same time as Seabury, also returned, and became third vice-president.[4]

The company's officers and products, following the return of Charles L. Seabury in 1896.

For nearly a quarter century after the merger, the owners of the *Gas Engine & Power Company and Charles L. Seabury & Company, Consolidated* stuck doggedly to that cumbersome name. Only in 1919 would they surrender, in favor of *Consolidated Shipbuilding Corporation*.[5] For convenience, we shall call the company *Consolidated*, even though prematurely.

The company's works in Morris Heights.

Chapter 17

The General Machine Shop.

The Naphtha Engine Room. On the left can be seen several rectangular boilers, and on the right, tubes for both the cylindrical and the rectangular boilers.

Naphtha

Late in 1898 a writer from *The Rudder* visited the plant, which then employed six or seven hundred workmen, and reported that, "We needed no guide to direct us to the works, for the ground from the railroad to the Harlem River, covering an area of twelve acres was covered by several large, low white buildings, with cornices, window and door sashes, painted red.... Large signs called attention to steam yachts, naphtha launches and sail yachts, but we noticed the words naphtha launches were spelled with much larger type than the others, and on the peak of the roof was affixed a full-size complete launch, with her naphtha pipe showing, although, I suppose there was no power for her....Having been to these works before in the winter time, when every one of the buildings were stored so full of launches you had to crawl under or climb over them to get through the building, I was now struck by the emptiness that was apparent. In the long showroom where about two hundred new launches were formerly on display, complete and ready for sale, there only remained four twenty-five footers, and the condition was explained by the fact that the present season had been a very prosperous one, they having sold nearly two hundred boats, bringing the total number of naphtha launches they have turned out up to about three thousand."[6]

The Fastest Ship in the Navy

In 1896 *The New York Times*, in addition to announcing the consolidation with Seabury, predicted that, "ere long the building of torpedo boats will be a feature" of the company's production.[7] The *Times* was prescient, or maybe was tipped off. Within a year Consolidated signed a contract with the U.S. Navy for the design, construction, and powering of *Bailey*, one of the world's first torpedo-boat destroyers.[8] Without the talents of Charles Seabury, such an undertaking would have been unthinkable.

Bailey was armed with four 6-pounder rapid-fire guns, and two torpedo discharge tubes for Whitehead torpedoes. Much of her hull was taken up by four Seabury-designed triple expansion engines, each capable of developing 1,400 horsepower. Each Seabury boiler had its own funnel, and each was equipped with two furnaces. Because *Bailey* carried no protective armor, she displaced only 265 tons when in commission, and the Navy intended her survival in battle to depend entirely on her remarkable speed. "The principal duty of the new craft will be to drive off and annihilate with gun fire the torpedo boat torments of the battleships and cruisers."[9]

During construction, *The Rudder* described "the immense steel frame of the destroyer Bailey with her steel shell encased in a cage of trestle work that enables the workmen to get at her, and also prevents anyone from taking pictures of her....Looking under this long racing shell, with a bow like a knife and a stern as flat and square as a skiff, one wonders how plates an eighth of an inch thick, even if they are of steel, can stand the enormous strains that will be put upon them when this craft is being driven thirty-five miles an hour, as called for by the Government."[10]

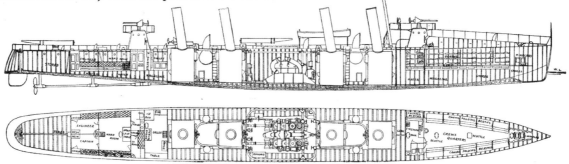

With Seabury's expertise in building steam engines, the company was well-positioned to bid on naval craft. The Torpedo Boat Destroyer *Bailey* was the first warship built by Consolidated.

Chapter 17

For several years, at speeds of over 35 miles per hour, *Bailey* was the fastest ship in the U.S. Navy. This advertisement appeared in 1901.

Bailey was not completed in time for the Spanish-American War. However, that conflict inadvertently benefited Consolidated, and other boat builders. Early in the war a number of yachtsmen had sold or donated their yachts to the government. The war was brief, and at its conclusion the yachtsmen needed replacements. Within three months, the *Brooklyn Eagle* reported that there were "no less than twenty magnificent yachts" under construction.[11] Almost all were larger and faster than the vessels they replaced.[12] Most of the owners also ordered new naphtha tenders. In the spring of 1900, the *Brooklyn Eagle* listed seventeen, and also named the owners of 45 other naphtha launches under construction.[13]

The victory over Spain whetted the nation's passion for naval eminence. As hoped, *Bailey* became the fastest ship in the United States Navy, and held that honor for several years. Based on the success of *Bailey*, Consolidated continued building naval vessels, including the destroyer *Stewart*, the torpedo boat *Wilkes*, and the gunboats *Dubuque* and *Paducah*.[14]

The launching of the Torpedo Boat *Wilkes* at Consolidated's yard on the Harlem River.

199

Escher Wyss

In addition to naval vessels, Consolidated continued to build almost one naphtha launch a day. Escher Wyss, on the other hand, was not even constructing one boat per month, and by 1896 had delivered only 132.[15] However, many of that company's products were built to order, so, as with *Mignon*, they reflected their owners' idiosyncrasies.

The 1896 Escher Wyss catalog cover.

Chapter 17

The Escher Wyss Naphtha Boat Harbor in Zurich.

One customer, C.W. Staehelin, had owned boats from both companies, and wrote to Escher Wyss: *"Following the experiments carried out in America over twenty years with small pleasure-boats with all kinds of possible and impossible engines, I become more and more convinced that your naphtha engine is the only one that always operates with complete safety under all conditions. On the rivers and lagoons of Florida where navigation is very difficult and where all parts of a boat are tested down to the last nail, the boat which I had there never refused service at critical moments such as going through rapids or coral reefs, and I was often able to get out of muddy places where a steam-boat of the same size would have been stuck....I believe that the boats delivered by you and the firm in New York are not only the best, but really the only true pleasure-boats, and would greatly please yachtsmen who are still struggling with steam or internal-combustion engines."*

Paul Kupelwieser complimented the company on the seaworthiness of his boat during two crossings of the stormy Bay of Quarnero: *"The boat can be considered as offering complete safety even in heavy seas. Thus when in a bad storm other heavy boats are washed over by the crests of the waves, the lightweight naphtha boat is lifted up by them and glides over the wave while retaining about the same draft, which makes it easier for regular and continuous operation of the engine. Operation of the boat is not impaired and it only encountered air-borne water spray carried by the wind. It is true that this spray is enough to wet everything on board the boat, but the quantity of water that gets in is relatively small and can easily be got rid of so that it is completely without effect on the safety of the boat. As a consequence I feel much safer in your naphtha boat than in boats of other types of construction, even though they are bigger and may look stronger."*

Viscount Georges Vilain XIV reported that his launch was *"ideal for someone who likes hunting along the river because of the speed with which it can be put into operation and its very easy maneuverability. The outings are even more pleasant because there is no need for the presence of a mechanic."*[16]

A Future King

After the success of Alfred Nobel's *Mignon*, Escher Wyss sought other customers for aluminum boats, but, given the high cost of the metal, only those with very deep pockets were eligible. One such was Wilhelm, Prince of Wied, brother of Queen Marie of Romania, and owner of enormous estates along the Rhine and in Silesia. In 1892 Escher Wyss supplied the Prince with an aluminum rowing skiff, which he kept anchored at his winter residence in Santa Margherita, Italy. He was delighted that after more than a year in seawater the aluminum was unchanged, and the boat totally watertight.

Prince Wilhelm of Wied, later King of Albania, ordered the naphtha yawl, *Aluminia*, from Escher Wyss, and helped build her himself.

The Prince also purchased a naphtha launch, though not of aluminum. After a year's experience, he wrote to the company expressing his pleasure: "The most interesting experience I have had with this boat was while keeping up with a powerful port tug about 13 metres long, in very heavy seas following a storm which lasted all night, we went 3½ leagues looking for a shipwrecked fisherman. During this run I was always able to maintain the same speed as the little tug, and the engine ran without trouble and maintained its quiet and regular operation, whether the waves were coming into the boat over the bow or the stern."

In January 1894, the Prince ordered a third boat that would combine the merits of the first two, a coastal-yawl to be named *Aluminia*. "I am persuaded that with this yawl I will have a boat that will be better at sea than any other of similar size and where the hull, as well as the interior construction will be in aluminum, these parts will always have the same value. In fact, except in case of accident, the boat can not leak, nor can it be attacked by sea-water; in addition I believe that it will have an engine that will never let me down, even in storms."

The company's design chief, Naval Engineer Wilhelm Reitz, supervised the construction, which took a year. The press was fascinated: "The Prince has been living in Zurich for a long time and has shown himself to be a very expert technician not only for his collaboration in preparing the plans, but also during the actual construction itself, working on bolting it together as well as with hammer and file."

Aluminia was designed for long cruises along the Italian and Greek coasts. It was the Prince's intention to use the naphtha motor only during flat calms, but the fuel tank, located in the stern (the forepeak contained a sail locker) held enough naphtha to operate at full power for 50 hours or 600 kilometers. Three tanks held drinking water for eight days. The cabin doors were fitted with rubber gaskets to make them absolutely waterproof, "so that the cabin behaves as an air-tank or flotation device, and it thus becomes impossible for the boat to sink to the bottom."

Just as with *Mignon*, everything possible was made of aluminum, even the two-bladed propeller, which

Chapter 17

could be aligned with the keel when operating under sail. One exception was the interior of the cabin, a "jewel-box" paneled inside with precious woods. The salon could be converted into a bedroom for four to five people, with cabin lighting provided both by electricity and a long-life magnesium lamp equipped with a clockwork mechanism. The *Nouvelle Gazette de Zurich* reported that, "Overall, the boat gives the impression of a small arsenal; there are four cannons on the deck and the interior of the cabin is fitted with rifles." On delivery the naphtha engine drove the 12-meter long boat at 12½ km/hr, two more than agreed upon in the contract.[17]

The Prince of Wied did not have a felicitous career as a ruler. In 1913, the Great Powers, in an attempt to keep peace in the Balkans, created Albania, and appointed Wilhelm of Wied as its first King, although he knew nothing of the country. Unwisely, Wilhelm chose "the sinister and beguiling Essad Pasha Toptani," the most hated man in the new nation, as his defense minister. This enraged the King's new subjects and, as historian Margaret MacMillan tells us, "Wilhelm lasted six months before he fled back to Germany, leaving five separate regimes each of which claimed to be the government of Albania."[18]

Aluminia was equipped with a small arsenal, including four cannons and a number of rifles.

The Emperor

In those years Europe was increasingly fractured by the rivalries that would culminate in the Great War. A principal protagonist was the German Emperor Wilhelm II, called Willy by his British kinfolk, and Kaiser Wilhelm by Americans.[19] The Emperor's grandmother, Queen Victoria, said that Willy was a "hot-headed, conceited, and wrong-headed young man, devoid of all feeling."[20] The Prince of Wales owned a fast racing yacht, *Britannia*, and Willy decided that he must outdo his uncle. He set his eyes on *Thistle*, the America's Cup challenger in 1887. In spite of her loss to *Volunteer*, she had a successful career in Britain, and in 1891 the Emperor purchased her from her Scottish owners for 90,000 gold marks,[21] and immediately ordered a naphtha tender from the Gas Engine and Power Company.[22]

Wilhelm renamed his new yacht *Meteor*, and for four years raced her against *Britannia* at Cowes Week, and every year his uncle defeated him. Robert Massie explains that, "Cowes brought out the worst in William. The Kaiser never let the Prince of Wales – or those around him – forget that the older man was only heir to a throne, whereas he himself was a crowned sovereign."[23] Bertie (as the Prince of Wales was known) referred to his nephew as "the most brilliant failure in history."[24] In response Wilhelm called his uncle "a Satan."[25] Can we be surprised that this all ended badly?

As a consolation, Wilhelm acquired a steam yacht that outstripped all others, *Hohenzollern*, 383 feet long. She had been laid down as a naval vessel, but at her launching in 1893, as John Rousmaniere explains, the Kaiser "surprised everybody by announcing that she was now his royal yacht." Wilhelm was particularly pleased to show off *Hohenzollern* at Cowes Week in 1894 in front of his grandmother, whose *Victoria and Albert II* was 83 feet shorter.[26]

Rudder, Sail and Paddle praised the yacht's unusual attributes: "The Hohenzollern has a ram, and is armed with eight quick-firing Krupp guns. The emperor's cabins are…lighted by electricity, which is all over the ship, and furnished with telephones.…There is a family salon in blue and silver; a council room, a workroom for the emperor, and a sumptuous boudoir for the empress, whose sleeping cabin has a nickel bedstead hung with gray satin. There are endless cabins and bathrooms, both for royalties and members of their suites, and numerous salons. The whole residential part of the yacht is simply a marvel of magnificence, comfort and luxury, in all respects worthy of Monte Cristo."[27]

Escher Wyss fairly burst with pride in announcing on the first page of its 1896 catalog that "We were particularly favored to receive the order for a 6 horsepower naphtha cutter as the tender for the new yacht "Hohenzollern" for His Majesty the Emperor of Germany, and we believe that in this instance it was selected as being *the best* of its type."[28]

The German Emperor, Wilhelm II, owned two naphtha tenders, one built by the Gas Engine and Power Company, the other by Escher Wyss & Cie.

Chapter 17

Hohenzollern was laid down as a naval vessel, but Emperor Wilhelm commandeered her to serve as his royal yacht.

The Escher Wyss company was very proud that their naphtha launch was selected as a tender for the Royal Yacht *Hohenzollern*.

Gunboats

In the era of colonial expansion, the most potent warship was not the dreadnought, but the gunboat. In *The Tools of Empire*, Daniel R. Headrick tells us, "Few inventions of the nineteenth century were more important in the history of imperialism....The gunboat had become not just the instrument, but the very symbol of Western power along the coasts and up the navigable rivers of Asia." When a British gunboat flotilla advanced up the Yangtze River, "the court at Peking realized its precarious situation and a few days later sent a mission to Nanking to sign a peace treaty. Steam had carried British naval might into the very heart of China and led to the defeat of the Celestial Empire."[29]

If steam-powered gunboats were so effective, why not try naphtha? In 1894 the Zurich *Indicateur Journalier* described the launching of Escher Wyss' first naphtha gunboat: "Last Friday a large boat of this type, easily capable of carrying 40 men, left the construction shop at Neumuhle. Transported overland to Kaufhaus, it was there launched in the Limmat in the midst of large crowds on the shores. This boat, no doubt intended by its type of construction for armed coastal service and equipped with rapid-fire cannons, is a very well-done construction, made with elegant shapes and appears to run in excellent form; it was seen to respond with the greatest of ease to the rudder."[30]

The newspaper did not reveal the name of the purchaser, but in the following year the company delivered another naphtha gunboat, *Wilhelmina, Koningin der Nederlanden*, to the Dutch government. Again we turn to the Zurich *Indicateur Journalier* for a description:

"In the port of Schipfe there is now an aluminium gunboat destined for Lake Toba on the Island of Sumatra. This lake is located completely inland on heights surrounded by virgin forests, without any kind of road, so that it had never been possible to bring in a steamboat. Escher Wyss & Cie. received an order from the Dutch Government for a boat, capable of being separated into compartments, none of which could exceed 2½ quintals[31] including the packing necessary for their transport over the mountain. This boat will carry 28 soldiers and equipment, and the foredeck will have a rapid-fire Hotchkiss 3.8 cannon in order to inspire respect amongst the savage people of the mountain. Once the boat has arrived at its destination the cannon won't have long to rest, since the Atchinois continue to give the colonial army a hard time. The shape of the boat is very elegant and observing it under way one can appreciate its extraordinary maneuverability. The engine and the compartment for naphtha storage are specially protected by steel armor-plating. Construction of this boat can only add another jewel to the reputation of Escher Wyss & Cie."[32]

Wilhelmina arrived on Lake Toba, the largest lake in the Dutch East Indies, in 1897. Evidently she was a success, for she was still in service eighteen years later.[33]

Chapter 17

Escher Wyss received an order from the Dutch Government for a naphtha gunboat, built in sections, to be carried up to Lake Toba in the interior of Sumatra.

Wilhelmina, Koningin der Nederlanden, assembled. She was armed with a rapid-fire cannon, and the engine and naphtha fuel tank were protected by 5/16 inch armor plating. She could carry 28 fully-equipped soldiers for 25 hours at full speed.

Troop Carriers

Escher Wyss also built a number of troop carriers for the Russian Military. The specific mission of these boats was to transport teams of pontoon bridge builders.[34] That may seem of little significance, but pontoon bridges have long been vital for the movement of armies across the wide rivers of Russia. Historian Paul Kennedy tells us that, in order to advance on the Eastern Front in 1944, the Red Army would require 68 pontoon bridge battalions.[35]

The Russian authorities specified steel-hulled boats capable of carrying 20 fully-equipped soldiers and fuel for 30 hours, at a speed of 6½ knots (12 km per hour). As these boats were to be used in shallow rivers, the draft was not to exceed 0.370 m (12½ inches). Escher Wyss did not build naphtha engines more powerful than 8 hp, so the company chose to use twin 6-hp engines.

Engineer Reitz explained his novel solution to the shallow draft requirement: "Ordinary twin propellers suited for this draft would naturally not have been able to efficiently transmit the 12 horsepower required. Neither could one use paddle wheels because the machinery would have been much too heavy and the wheels too cumbersome and too exposed to damage during maneuvers and combat. To obtain the desired speed and taking into account the shallow draft the only option was to use a new propulsion system, and the helicoidal turbine system was selected. This system, despite its relatively small diameter, has the effect of projecting the water backwards with a strong push, but without whipping it up and producing white foam. The longitudinal section shows how the helixes are relatively large in diameter, which was made possible by the provision of tunnels at the back of the boats. When started up the helices blow the air out of these tunnels; the water is drawn in at the entry and goes out at the rear at the same height (rather like a siphon)." During acceptance tests, the draft was only .35 meters, 2 cm less than required, while the average speed was 14 km/hr, 2 km faster than had been guaranteed.[36]

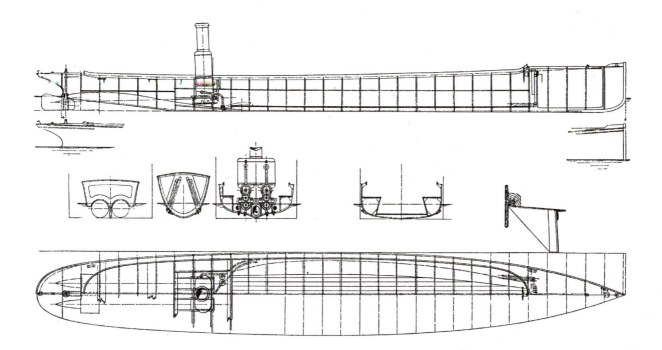

The Russian military asked Escher Wyss to design troop carriers capable of carrying twenty fully-equipped soldiers at 6½ knots, and with a draft not to exceed 12½ inches.

Chapter 17

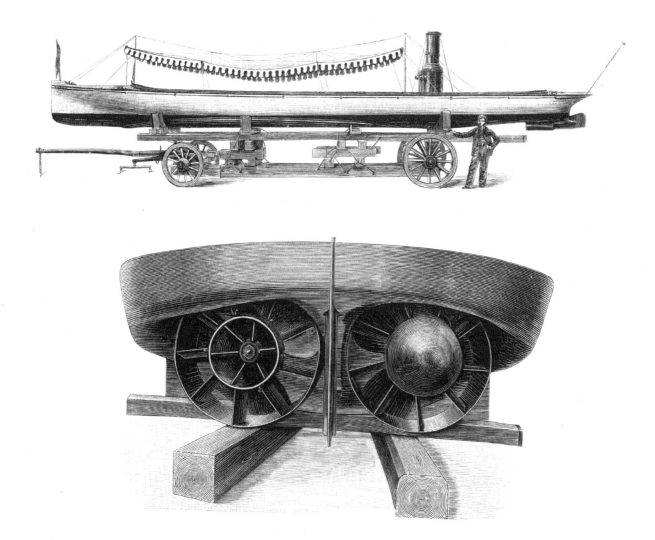

Escher Wyss solved the shallow draft problem by using a Helicoidal Turbine Propeller System, driven by twin 6-hp naphtha engines which shared one funnel.

A Naval Success

It would be an exaggeration to claim that naphtha launches played a significant role in combat, but we have found one account. During the war between Russia and Japan, the Russians fitted out one or more naphtha launches as motor torpedo boats. The press carried a remarkable story of one encounter:

"The Russian fleet scored its first distinct naval success May 10 by the torpedoing and crippling, though not the sinking, of an armored Japanese cruiser in Tallenwan Bay. The attacking force was not a regular torpedo boat, but was only a small naphtha launch in command of a young naval officer, who had with him three jackies. The launch mounted a small machine gun and carried three torpedoes.

"When darkness fell the launch crept out of Port Arthur with no lights aboard and no glow from the engines to betray her presence. It was late when the launch gained the outer line of the Japanese squadron. She slipped through the torpedo boat pickets and selecting the nearest warship, a big armored cruiser, stole toward her and succeeded in exploding against her side a single torpedo. A deafening roar followed the explosion which echoed far in-shore. Immediately flames enveloped the cruiser, which evidently was badly crippled.

"The crew of the cruiser was seen to be fighting the fire, which they at last succeeded in extinguishing. A sister ship took the damaged vessel in tow and disappeared to the southeast.

"The launch escaped the hot fire directed against her by the Japanese ships, but being unable to return to Port Arthur or to get into Dalny she was beached not far from Dalny."[37]

It would be fair to say that this miniscule Russian craft was a direct descendant of the *kanonjoller* (cannon dinghies) that defended Sweden against Russian warships a century earlier.

Chapter 18

Compound Vapor

"It is the last production of the ingenious mind of Frank W. Ofeldt"
F.W. Ofeldt and Sons, 1903 catalog

The Vapor Launch Works

Between January 18, 1893 and April 20, 1894 – just over fifteen months – Frank Ofeldt applied for four patents, and he assigned all four to the Marine Vapor Engine Company. As we know, two of those patents were for the alco-vapor launch and its engine, but two were for totally different inventions, a steam whistle and a compound engine. Perhaps E.C. Benedict had originally intended to exploit the latter, but thought better of it. It seems likely that he and Frank struck a deal, under which Frank relinquished his interest in the alco-vapor invention in exchange for the rights to the compound engine. Whatever the arrangement, Frank returned to Brooklyn, where F.W. Ofeldt & Sons became the sole manufacturer of the Improved Compound Vapor Motor.[1]

For some time Frank had needed a name that would encompass all his inventions. He chose *Vapor Launch*, and painted a sign in large letters on the side of his boat shop: "F.W. OFELDT & SONS, VAPOR LAUNCH WORKS."

The F.W. Ofeldt & Sons shipyard in Brooklyn, 1896

Frank Ofeldt chose *Vapor Launch Works* to show that he was responsible for several inventions, including the Naphtha Launch, the Ofeldt Improved System, the Alco-Vapor Launch, and the Improved Compound Vapor Motor.

Cover of the F.W. Ofeldt & Sons catalog, 1903.

Chapter 18

His Finest Invention

The opening page of the company's catalog extolled Frank's achievements: "Introducing this engine we will say that it is the last production of the ingenious mind of Frank W. Ofeldt, former inventor of the original Naphtha Launch, the Ofeldt improved steam system,[2] and the Alco-Vapor Launch system. This new motor embodies many of the advantages of his previous inventions with additional ones and is by far the most compact, complete, effective and simple power for launches on the market."[3] Frank declared the Compound Vapor Motor to be "the climax of all he had invented, as it was lighter, safer and more reliable than any of the other inventions."[4]

The new engine's working fluid was alcohol, and the fuel could be either kerosene or naphtha, evidence that Frank had reined in his fulminations against the dangers of naphtha.[5] Unlike his previous inventions, this engine was compound. In fact it would be accurate to describe it as a compound alco-vapor engine.

In his patent application, Frank described "a compact and light running engine more particularly adapted for use in connection with launches in which vapor is used as the motive power." In the original configuration there were two sets of high and low pressure cylinders, angled at 90 degrees.[6]

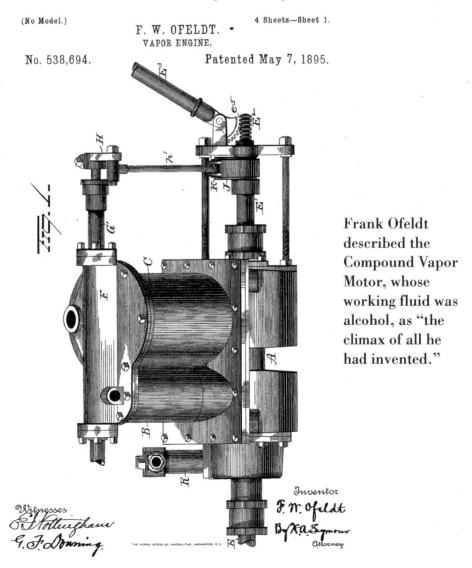

Frank Ofeldt described the Compound Vapor Motor, whose working fluid was alcohol, as "the climax of all he had invented."

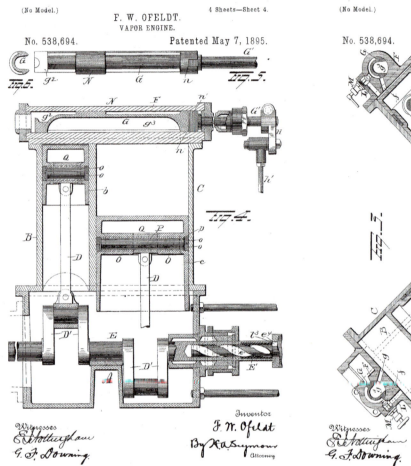 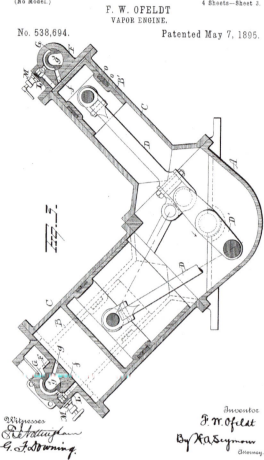

In a compound engine, the vapor begins its expansion in a small cylinder, and is then transferred to a larger cylinder where the expansion is completed.

The Improved Compound Vapor Motor had cylinders angled at 90 degrees. The patent drawings showed two pairs of cylinders, but the claims included a two-cylinder alternative, and that is the version that first went into production.

Chapter 18

In November 1896, Frank's invention was announced in a year-old publication, *The Horseless Age*: "The new and improved vapor motor, invented by F. W. Ofeldt, foot of Twenty-Fifth Street, South Brooklyn, N. Y., being now in shape for inspection, the editor of *The Horseless Age* paid a visit to the works recently to see it. Several sizes were exhibited, the smallest of three horse-power, and the largest of 50 horse-power, the former weighing 160 pounds complete and the latter 1600 pounds....The motor consists of two separate engines, each consisting of two separate cylinders one twice as large as the other, thus forming a compound engine....The motor has a double crank house, no dead center, and will start in two minutes. Any desired horsepower can be built under this system, the consumption of fuel averaging one quart per horsepower per hour."[7]

Frank soon simplified the configuration by eliminating the second pair of cylinders. The company's catalog also explained that "the crank is made in one piece with crank pins opposite to each other and of the same weight. This makes a perfectly balanced engine, capable of running at a very high rate of speed, without the slightest vibration."

The catalog also explained how Frank had made the mechanism even lighter than his previous motors: "Time and practical experience make decided changes in many things and this is especially true with the Improved Compound Vapor Motor for launches. In the past it was considered quite the right thing to construct an engine and place all the working parts within a cast casing, so that there were very few if any of the moving parts exposed to view, and while this style of engine appeared to be simplicity itself it was in reality very complicated when the casing was removed. Our new motor is constructed on modern lines and although it appears to the novice to be more complicated than the old style motors it is a fact that there are only about half the number of working parts, the difference being that they are exposed and easily accessible instead of encased by a cast box. By discarding half the number of working parts and the iron casing we have greatly reduced the weight of the complete outfit, so much so that it is possible to build a 10 horse power motor which weighs less than the old style 6 horse power."[8] In consequence, while a 10-hp naphtha engine weighed 700 pounds, a 10-hp Ofeldt compound engine weighed only 400.[9]

The company declared that "This new motor embodies many of the advantages of [Frank Ofeldt's] previous inventions with additional ones and is by far the most compact, complete, effective and simple power for launches on the market. The energy is obtained by expanding alcohol of a very low grade – wood alcohol diluted – in a retort or boiler constructed of small coils of pipe.

"A powerful fire, retorted from naphtha or kerosene is used to heat the coils. The alcohol is pumped in and flashes into vapor—pressure—by its contact with the heated coils passing from there to do its work in the motor, and is afterwards condensed by passing through copper pipes, arranged along the keel of the boat, returning to [the] supply tank, in its original state, ready to be used over again." The fuel tank was also placed in the bow. As in the naphtha launch, seawater washed around the tanks keeping their contents cool.

"Our engines are controlled entirely by the reversing lever and can be run at any rate of speed for hours according to the will of the operator; *it can be reversed at full speed*. We do not use naphtha or kerosene under pressure. We have no stuffing boxes subject to fuel pressure. If alcohol should leak out, being of a very low grade it will not burn. *No licensed engineer required....* Can be started in three minutes."[10]

Naphtha

The production version of the Improved Compound Vapor Motor.

The boiler's copper coils. By means of a distributing valve, each pulsation of the pump fed alcohol into one row of coils.

A 10-hp Compound Vapor motor weighed only 400 pounds, while an equivalent naphtha motor weighed 700 pounds.

Chapter 18

Lillian Russell

As Frank well knew, the best way to sell boats was by having celebrities as customers. According to his descendants, the company designed and built a launch for Lillian Russell, then the toast of the American musical stage.[11] A.J. Liebling wrote that Lillian Russell was "the reigning American Beauty, on and off stage, since about 1885. She was a butterscotch sundae of a woman, as beautiful as a tulip of beer with a high white collar. If a Western millionaire, one of the Hearst or Mackay kind, could have given an architect carte blanche to design him a woman, she would have looked like Lillian. She was San Simeon in corsets."[12]

Lillian Russell, the toast of Broadway, owned one of the first Compound Vapor launches.

Naphtha

Powerful Engines

Nautilus was powered by two 40-hp Improved Compound Vapor Motors. Frank Ofeldt's competitors were unable to build vapor engines of comparable power.

For small boats, Frank Ofeldt's prices more or less matched the competition. For bigger boats Frank specified more powerful engines than did his competitors, which makes it difficult to compare prices.[13]

Frank's ability to build powerful engines opened up the market for larger boats, and he built the 70-ft. yacht *Nautilus*, powered by two 40-hp engines, for Garrett B. Linderman of South Bethlehem, Pennsylvania.[14] It was not uncommon for builders to use each other's engines. Frank replaced the alco-vapor engine in *Curlew* with one of his own,[15] and, conversely, built the 52-ft. launch, *Canvas Back*, for W.A. Wadsworth of New York, but powered her with two 10-hp alco-vapor engines.[16] Surprisingly, Frank even installed one naphtha engine. In the spring of 1897, the *Brooklyn Eagle* reported that he had sold a 12-ft. launch with a 1-hp naphtha engine to a resident of Canarsie. *Brownie* was "the smallest craft of her class ever constructed, [but with] buoyancy enough to carry six people."[17] Frank probably had no choice; his company never made a 1-hp engine.

Vapor engines had their limits. As we have noted, starting in 1892 the Gas Engine and Power Company offered steam engines to those who wished them for yachts of 50 ft. and longer.[18] Frank came to the same conclusion, and began to manufacture compound and triple-expansion steam engines and boilers.

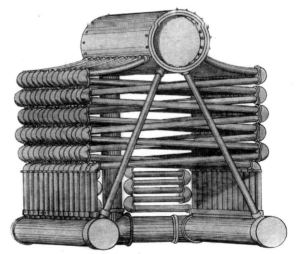

Yacht Boiler.
This boiler is built in all sizes from 20 horse power up and is specially adapted for yachts of large dimensions.

F.W. Ofeldt & Sons also built steam engines.

218

Chapter 18

William Gillette

Another prominent Ofeldt customer was the celebrated actor, William Gillette, famous for bringing Sherlock Holmes to the stage. Gillette owned a very unusual houseboat which the *Brooklyn Eagle* called an "aquatic freak,…one of the queerest specimens of a yacht seen in these waters for many a day,…driven by two gasoline explosion engines of eleven indicated horse power each." Christened *Holy Terror*, she had been built by James Lenox and launched in 1896.[19]

The *New York Dramatic Mirror* said that Gillette was "a daring navigator," and reported that "the *Holy Terror*, which joyous craft careered for some time in these waters and Long Island Sound…lived up to its name with such vim and bounce that accident insurance companies cancelled policies held by its passengers, the while other vessels ran up on assorted shores to get out of its way."[20] According to the *Brooklyn Eagle*, "One Sunday Gillette stopped on the Hudson, just below Grant's tomb, to take on some guests. When he started away the machinery of his Holy Terror got awry and the houseboat ran amuck through a lot of little catboats and rowboats anchored along shore, tearing away rigging, dories and everything in sight. Gillette stopped to ascertain the damage and make promises to pay. 'Say,' exclaimed one man, who rented boats, 'If you're goin' to build another thing like that I wish you'd name her the Merry H_ _ l.'"[21]

Gillette's choice of gasoline power proved premature. Finding his engines to be unreliable, he replaced them with two of Frank Ofeldt's Compound Vapor engines, each of 25 hp.[22]

William Gillette, who brought Sherlock Holmes to the stage, purchased two Ofeldt compound vapor engines to replace the unsatisfactory internal combustion engines in his first houseboat, the *Holy Terror*. He then asked Frank Ofeldt to build him a much larger houseboat, which Frank agreed to do.

Aunt Polly

Gillette soon felt cramped aboard his 62-foot houseboat and, having concluded that F.W. Ofeldt & Sons was the best boat builder around, placed an order with them for a vessel whose grandeur would suitably signal the actor's status. In May 1899 the *Brooklyn Eagle* announced that, "When William Gillette of 'Secret Service' fame returns from abroad in the latter part of July, he expects to find a new steam yacht ready for him in South Brooklyn. Ofeldt, the builder…has already laid the keel of a 100-foot craft, which when completed, will embody the actor's idea of what a steam yacht should be."[23]

As the houseboat was to weigh 100 tons,[24] compound vapor engines would be inadequate, so Frank chose steam, which would also be convenient in heating and lighting the boat.[25] F.W. Ofeldt & Sons designed and built a 150-hp triple expansion steam engine and a water tube boiler, calculated to give a speed of 12 miles an hour.[26]

Gillette named his boat *Aunt Polly*, "after a dear old lady I used to know down in South Carolina. They resemble each other. The original Aunt Polly couldn't move very fast and she was mighty good to me."[27]

Aunt Polly was built by F.W. Ofeldt and Sons for William Gillette. She was not powered by compound vapor, but by an Ofeldt 150-hp triple expansion steam engine.

Gillette lived aboard his houseboat for extended periods of time.

Gillette wryly described his houseboat as "a cumbersome craft, 98 feet long, propelled by a sewing machine motor and in a fair wind able to make two and a quarter knots,"[28] but *Aunt Polly* pleased him, and on September 30, 1902 he wrote to F.W. Ofeldt & Sons: "It gives me pleasure to testify to the excellence of your work. The engine you built for the 'Aunt Polly' has operated for three seasons with entire satisfaction."[29]

In fact, Gillette was not yet fully satisfied. Again he felt cramped, so he decided to lengthen *Aunt Polly* by some forty feet.[30] The Ofeldt yard could not handle such a behemoth, so the job was turned over to the Greenport Basin & Construction Co. at Greenport, Long Island, and Frank increased the engine power to 250 hp.[31]

Steam Cars

By this time the Ofeldt sons had become intrigued by the possibility of inventing a steam automobile. Clearly their father's design for a compound vapor engine was well suited to such a use. Frank did not even have to apply for a new patent; his sons simply put a version of Frank's compound vapor engine into two experimental cars. This was not the two-cylinder engine, but the configuration depicted in his patent, with two pairs of cylinders set at right angles.[32] Like the nautical version, the fuel could be either naphtha or kerosene, but this time the working fluid was water.

Frank's second son, Ernest, designed one of the cars, a "naphtha-steam vehicle," and he and George drove it from Brooklyn to Nyack to demonstrate it to their brother August, who was building the other car. Their arrival was celebrated in the *Nyack Evening Journal* of May 8, 1899, under the heading, "A HORSELESS CARRIAGE: THE FIRST ONE TO MOUNT THE NYACK HILLS. Its Maker and Owner is Mr. Ernest Ofeldt, Brother of A. W. Ofeldt, the Main Street Machinist—The Carriage Seen by Many Here Sunday.

"The first horseless carriage to mount the hills and descend into the vales of conservative Nyack made its appearance here yesterday afternoon….With his strange vehicle, Mr. Ernest Ofeldt left his naphtha launch plant in Brooklyn at about 7 a.m., and steaming up through the sands of New Jersey arrived at Nyack in time to dine here in the early afternoon. The carriage is a naphtha-steam vehicle, very compact and not nearly so clumsy looking as the electric carriage now so familiar a sight in New York City. The heating apparatus and boiler are located in the dash-board, giving the same a somewhat swollen appearance. A double engine works quite noiselessly under the seat. Its weight is three hundred pounds. The peculiar looking conveyance attracted general attention, and wherever it stopped was at once surrounded by the curious."[33]

The Horseless Age provided more information about the power plant. "The motor is a compound vapor engine similar to the one used by this firm in its launches. The generator is placed across the carriage body behind the dashboard and really forming part of it. It is constructed of coils of copper pipe, brazed together and arranged in such a manner that great heating surface is obtained. The generator has been tested to 1,000 lbs. pressure. The fuel is stove gasoline burned in an atmospheric burner, producing a blue Bunsen flame of high intensity. The engine consists of two compound engines, having cylinders 1½ x 3 x 3 in. stroke, and cranks set at 90 deg. All the bearings and working parts are extremely large and ample wearing surface is provided. The engine is fitted with a reversing attachment and is fully under control of the operator at all times. Speeds ranging from 3 to 25 miles an hour are obtainable at will, and can be maintained for hours. The wheels are 28 x 2½ in., with ordinary tandem tires.

"Enough fuel and water can be carried, it is claimed, for a run of 45 miles.…It is not a thing of beauty, but was constructed merely to demonstrate the practicability of the power. Its total weight is 400 lbs. Carriages of more elaborate design are now being constructed and will be on exhibition in a few months.

"The machinery has been subjected to all kinds of hard usage, and Mr. Ofeldt assures us that under all conditions of road and weather it has performed all that was expected."[34]

In 1964 August's second son, Ernest, reminisced about the very different car his father constructed: "That car was built from a horse-drawn surrey body and we didn't bother to change it. Anyway we wanted to have the car look as much like a horse-drawn vehicle so that it wouldn't scare horses. It contained the first V-type steam motor ever built, had a five-gallon fuel tank and a 15-gallon water tank, and generated 250 pounds of pressure. The fuel was kerosene or gasoline and the car would travel 20 miles on one filling of fuel and water."[35]

Ernest and George Ofeldt in Ernest's automobile, the first horseless carriage to arrive in Nyack.

Frank Ofeldt's first son, August, in his steam car, with his eldest son Frank by his side.

Chapter 18

The third son, Frank A., also built a steam car that earned him a ticket for speeding at 10 mph.

Frank A. and his wife Johanna are in the back, with their daughters, Lotta and Jennie, and a neighbor in front.

Frank A. Ofeldt, Frank W.'s third son, also built cars, one of which was described by his daughter, Jennie (Ofeldt) Russell: It "used bicycle wheels, had two brass headlights illuminated by gasoline, and a snake horn. The boiler was under the seat. The front folded up, making it a runabout when only two seats were required....It had a pilot light that spurted a flame out at the rear. It was the forerunner of the 1907 Stanley Steamer....I never remember that old steamer breaking down or our having any trouble with it. And, seat belts were around back then. Take a look at the picture of my sister Lotta and I. We were both always strapped in when we went out in the car with Dad." In Jennie's opinion, that was wise, for Frank A.'s driving secured him a ticket for speeding in Prospect Park at 10 mph.[36]

Back in 1893, while Frank Ofeldt was inventing his alco-vapor and compound vapor engines in New Jersey, August had joined him there, and applied for a patent on his own compound engine. Like his father's alco-vapor engine, August's had a radial configuration, but with four, rather than three, cylinders. On May 22, 1901, *The Horseless Age* announced the formation of the *Ofeldt Automobile and Steam Launch Company*, 111 Academy Street, Newark, N.J., with August W. Ofeldt as engineer. The company's objective was to manufacture August's four-cylinder engine in 5, 8, and 15-hp sizes, for both automobile and launch use, and also to manufacture boilers and burners of August's design. A light runabout carriage was almost complete.[37]

Naphtha

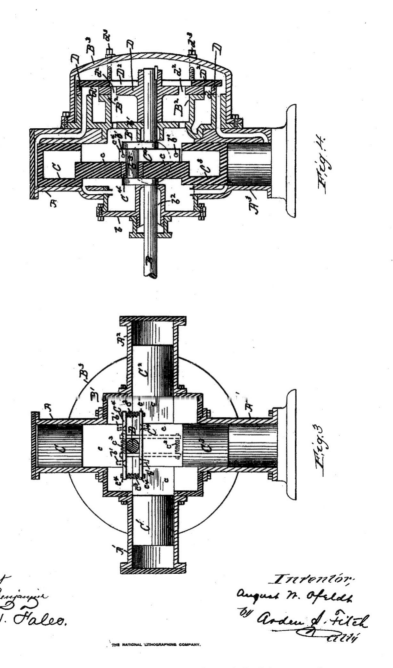

All the Ofeldt sons were inventors, and each held several patents. This four-cylinder compound steam engine was designed by August for use in automobiles and boats.

Chapter 18

The company did produce at least one steam car and one large express wagon, but the enterprise was not a success, and soon folded.[38] However, August's brothers continued to build vehicles at the boat works in Brooklyn, where they concentrated on trucks.

The F.W. Ofeldt catalog shows a one-ton delivery wagon, "using kerosene for fuel, built by us for and in constant use by Messrs. Minck Bros. of Brooklyn."[39] Another design was for a two-ton truck fueled by gasoline, which had a steering wheel, and rode on the new Timken roller bearings.[40] For their ¾-ton delivery wagon, the Ofeldts moved the engine to the front, freeing up the body of the vehicle for cargo. That vehicle had another innovation, a gas gauge, and the water supply, with the aid of a condenser, was designed to last five hours.[41] According to Frank A., they built two delivery trucks for Macy's, the first ever used by that store.[42]

Steam Delivery Wagon, with a carrying capacity of one ton, built by F.W. Ofeldt & Sons for the Minck Brothers.

"A Great and Prolific Mind"

Frank W. Ofeldt with his sons and workmen. According to Robert Ofeldt, who supplied the photo, George (wearing a bowler hat) is standing beside Frank. Ernest is in the second row, left, and Frank A. (Bob's great-great grandfather) is behind Ernest.

It was now more than thirty years since Frank Ofeldt had left Sweden. He had come to America in search of opportunity, and had found it. As an inventor he had fulfilled Ericsson's dream – to surpass the steam engine. True, he had been smacked down by partners he had put his trust in, but he had risen from the canvas and gone on inventing.

Fame eluded Frank, but did his inventions change the world? Absolutely.

Frank Ofeldt died on September 29, 1904, and *Popular Mechanics* carried an obituary headed, "The Story of the Inventor of the Naphtha Launch," which concluded with an appropriate accolade: "His was a great and prolific mind, leaving tangible results to the world."[43]

Frank was buried in Brooklyn's Greenwood Cemetery alongside Matilda, who had died seven years earlier.[44]

In telling Frank Ofeldt's story, we have been hampered by the dearth of sources. Not a single word that he wrote has come to light, outside of patents. No diaries, no letters, nor have we found any contemporary description of him. Was he as cantankerous as Ericsson, or consumed by self-loathing like Nobel, or was he prickly, like Van Syckel? Ericsson and Nobel had dysfunctional family lives, but the Ofeldt family appears to have been happy. We hear of no estrangements, and we are told that Frank and his sons collaborated on their inventions. One can only conclude that Frank, unlike Ericsson and Nobel, was comfortable in his skin.

Chapter 18

Nyack

Frank left his business to Ernest and Frank A., the two sons who had been managing it. The company did not stay long in Brooklyn. Less than a year after their father's death, the sons purchased the buildings and ways of the former Seabury Company. Then they loaded all the Ofeldt machinery and stock onto a covered barge, and floated it to Nyack.[45]

Motor Boat explained their plan: "F. W. Ofeldt & Sons, for years located at the foot of Twenty-fifth Street, Brooklyn, N. Y., purchased the Chas. L. Seabury property at Nyack, on the Hudson, and removed there September 1. The concern are well known as yacht and launch builders. They intend to rebuild the ways used by Mr. Seabury, and will haul, store and repair yachts and launches of all sizes at their new quarters. They also intend to build a large basin for the laying up of yachts. They believe that a basin at this point will be particularly welcomed by yachtsmen of New York and vicinity. It is said that Ofeldt & Sons are the oldest firm in the motorboat business, as the late F. W. Ofeldt was the inventor of the naphtha and alco-vapor launches."[46]

By the time of the move, the Ofeldts had given up on building automobiles. With 125 manufacturers of steam cars, the business had turned into a free-for-all.[47] However, some of the steam car builders were not very good at boilers, and that was where the Ofeldts had an edge. According to August's son, Ernest, car owners were having so much trouble with burnt-out boilers that the Ofeldts decided to manufacture boilers to replace those that went bad.[48]

By 1908 the Ofeldt sons had patented a burner, a boiler, a fuel regulator, and had applied for a patent on an automatic fuel feed, "which makes the car the easiest of all to start, for it will start every time."[49] This was a dig at gasoline engines, which had to be hand-cranked until Charles F. Kettering patented the self-starter in 1911.

After Frank Ofeldt's death, his sons moved the company's works to the site of the former Seabury shipyard in Nyack.

The Double-Acting Engine

OFELDT'S
BLUE FLAME KEROSENE BURNER
SAFETY WATER TUBE BOILER
AUTOMATIC WATER REGULATOR
AUTOMATIC FUEL REGULATOR
FEED WATER HEATER
AUTOMATIC FUEL FEED
AUTOMATIC AIR PUMP
HAND WATER PUMP
COMPOUND STEAM ENGINES
FOR
STEAM AUTOMOBILES

Copyrighted, 1908,
By F. W. Ofeldt & Sons

PATENTED AND MANUFACTURED
BY
F. W. OFELDT & SONS
NYACK-ON-THE-HUDSON, N. Y.

*The Old Firm
In A New Location*

While the Ofeldt company's 1908 catalog introduced a new line of products, it stressed the continuity of the enterprise.

The company's 1908 catalog makes clear that the Ofeldts were still doggedly fighting the internal combustion engine: "Thirteen years have elapsed since we built our first steam automobile, hence we claim to be among the pioneers of the automobile industry in America. From the first we pinned our faith on steam as the ideal power for automobiles and we believe, when properly applied, it will become the leading motive power for horseless vehicles."[50]

In the face of the industry preference for water as the working fluid, the Ofeldts gave up on alcohol. However, for fuel they recommended kerosene, even though most steam automobiles burned naphtha or gasoline, and they warned: "The dangers from burning naphtha are numerous and well known, chief among them being its volatility, for it readily unites with air under atmospheric pressure and forms one of the most powerful explosives known."[51]

In the 1908 catalog, the Ofeldts were at pains to remind the readers of their family's illustrious history: "We were the pioneers of the Motor Boat industry, being the first to create a demand for gasolene, which was at that time a waste product. We were the inventors of the famous Naphtha Launch, the Alco-Vapor Launch, and of the Improved Compound Vapor Launch which is the peer of all. During the past twelve years we have designed and built, from the keel up, a large number of yachts and launches, some as large as one hundred feet in length. We have also designed and built triple-expansion and compound steam engines of from 40 to 200 H.P. Our automobile engines are the outcome of our wide experience in engine designing and building. They are built on up-to-date lines and combine all the modern and best principles of steam engines."[52]

To provide evidence of their leadership, the Ofeldts announced another advance: a double-acting compound engine.[53]

Chapter 18

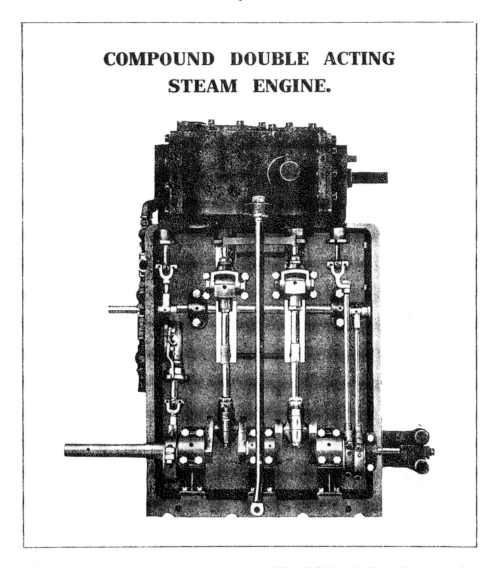

The compound double-acting engine. The Ofeldts believed that with this engine the steam car would prevail over gasoline-powered cars.

The company announced that its compound double-acting engines were "suitable for runabouts, light and heavy touring cars, racing machines and trucks and are the only engines yet offered which have sufficient horse power to put the high powered steam car on an equal with the large gasolene car." Further, the company predicted that a 30-hp version of this engine with an extra-light boiler 28 to 30 inches in diameter, in a car geared 2 to 1, "would readily make a mile in 30 seconds" (120 mph).[54]

With the Ofeldts busy improving steam cars, Gillette became miffed at the slowness of their service. On January 12, 1907, he wrote to Mr. Monsell, *Aunt Polly*'s engineer: "All right – I am very glad to have the "Polly" thoroughly overhauled & put in good shape. I wrote because I thought the delay might be in waiting for Ofeldt to send machinery & tubes ordered – and I knew that would mean many years."

He also asked Monsell to go to the auto exhibition and look at "the most *serviceable* and *durable* and not-break-downable car. I want you to look especially at the *White Steamers*. I like their mechanical work – and I like a *Steam Engine*.[55]

Gillette Castle

Gillette moored *Aunt Polly* in the Connecticut River and lived aboard sporadically for five years while he constructed a million dollar mansion on the cliff above.[56] Now known as the *Gillette Castle State Park,* it is one of Connecticut's most popular tourist attractions.

Gillette's Castle, designed by the actor himself, is now one of Connecticut's most popular tourist attractions.

The hull of Aunt Polly still lies in the river below, and is protected by the State of Connecticut as the *Aunt Polly Archaeological Preserve.*[57] For those who would like to see the remnants of Frank Ofeldt's most ambitious vessel, it is advisable to consult a tide table, for more of the remnants are visible at low tide.

The remains of Frank Ofeldt's most impressive vessel are now protected as the *Aunt Polly Archaeological Preserve.*

Chapter 19

Ending the Naphtha Glut

"It is not always the easiest of tasks to induce strong, forceful men to agree."
John D. Rockefeller[1]

Skunk Oil

In 1885, just before the introduction of the naphtha launch, the Standard Oil Company produced nearly two million barrels of the naphthas. By 1897, in spite of every effort to minimize naphtha production in favor of kerosene, the company's naphtha output more than tripled, while kerosene production merely doubled. Why the disparity? The answer, *skunk oil*.[2]

In June 1885, Ben Faurot, drilling for gas in Lima, Ohio, struck oil, and it came in with a rush.[3] The field was phenomenal, and the number of dry holes was a mere five percent.[4] However, the crude was sulphur-laden and ill-smelling. "If you got a drop on you, you smelled like a rotten egg" or, as one newspaper put it, "a stack of pole cats."[5] Kerosene distilled from it crusted the wicks and clouded the chimneys of lamps.[6] Standard Oil's attempts to refine the oil into anything useful proved a miserable failure.[7] At a time when Pennsylvania crude commanded 70 to 80 cents a barrel, a barrel of Lima oil sold for only 15 cents.[8]

What the company needed was an inventor, and the only one they could find was a German immigrant who, in Ron Chernow's words, "conformed to the stereotype of the eccentric scientist." Herman Frasch was a genius, but also a vainglorious prima donna with an explosive temper.[9] He had worked for Standard Oil once before and, as Nevins recounted, had proven "a most uncomfortable critter to work with." The Standard men called him *the flying Dutchman*, or *the wild Dutchman*, so they must have known what they were getting into.[10] However, they had little choice. At that time Frasch was probably the only qualified petroleum chemist in the country.[11]

The Standard Oil men had little use for scientists, but the intractable problem of *skunk oil* forced them to turn to the "erratic, explosive genius," Herman Frasch.

Chernow explains that "the Standard Oil board faced an excruciating dilemma: Should they assume Frasch would succeed and buy up huge leases along the Ohio-Indiana border; or should they wait until Frasch had finished and risk losing the choicest properties?"[12]

231

For fifteen years the board had never made a decision except by unanimous agreement, but now it was bitterly split. Charles Pratt vehemently opposed the risky investment, estimated at three million dollars,[13] and he led a group who "held up their hands in holy horror" at the risk.[14]

John D. described the stormy meeting that settled the question: "Our old partner was obdurate, he had made up his mind not to yield, and I can see him standing up in his vigorous protest, with his hands in his pockets, his head thrown back, as he shouted 'No.' It's a pity to get a man into a place in an argument where he is defending a position instead of considering the evidence. His calm judgment is apt to leave him, and his mind is for the time being closed, and only obstinacy remains.... When the heat of our discussion had passed, the subject was brought up again. I had thought of a new way to approach it. I said: 'I'll take it, and supply this capital myself. If the expenditure turns out to be profitable the company can repay me; and, if it goes wrong, I'll stand the loss.' That was the argument that touched him. All his reserve disappeared and the matter was settled when he said: 'If that's the way you feel about it, we'll go it together. I guess I can take the risk if you can.'"[15]

Once the decision was made, Daniel O'Day acted with characteristic promptness. While announcing publicly the "complete failure" of Standard Oil's attempts to distill marketable kerosene from Lima petroleum, he set out to corner the productive land.[16] As Frasch continued to experiment, the company's storage tanks soon held over forty million barrels of Lima crude.[17]

In 1888 the inventor succeeded in devising the "Herman Vapor Process," which involved the use of a revolving brush to stir a patentable compound into the oil. The Standard could make a profit even from oil at 15 cents a barrel.[18] The company then built the largest refinery in the United States, at Whiting's crossing, near Chicago, capable of distilling 36,000 barrels of Lima crude a day.[19] Because of O'Day's aggressive purchases, Standard Oil controlled 85-90 percent of the Ohio-Indiana fields.[20] The Frasch patents provided the Standard with a 17-year advantage over its competitors,[21] and reputedly produced a profit of half a billion dollars.[22] Frasch was paid in Standard Oil shares, which made him very rich.[23]

Herman Frasch soon left the company, but the Standard Oil men, after years of antipathy to science, established laboratories in a number of their facilities. That was the good news. The bad news was that Lima oil yielded a much higher percentage of the naphthas than did Pennsylvania oil, as evidenced by the fact that the Standard's naphtha yield increased from 10.37 percent in 1885 to 14.23 in 1890.[24] This is why the naphtha glut increased, rather than decreased, during the time of the naphtha launch.[25]

Dismantling the Trust

In 1890 David E. Watson, the idealistic Attorney-General of Ohio, came to the conclusion that Standard Oil had broken the law by handing over its business to the nine trustees. On May 8, 1890, he filed a petition asking that the company be dissolved.[26]

Within two years the Supreme Court of Ohio handed down its decision on the trust: "All such associations are contrary to the policy of our state and void."[27] However, the men of Standard were undeterred. New Jersey had just altered its law to permit the incorporation of holding companies that could do business outside the State,[28] exactly what businesses had needed all along. The Trust simply metamorphosed into Standard Oil of New Jersey. In Nevins' words, "This reorganization of course had no effect whatever on the continuity of the Standard Oil management. The same men remained in the same control, carrying out the same policies in the same way."[29]

But the company did change, and the cause was John D's stomach. He began to suffer digestive troubles, and in 1891 was seriously ill.[30] That same year Charles Pratt suddenly died. The time had come to end consensus decision-making, and to select one executive to take charge – what we would now call a C.E.O.

The job was handed to John D. Archbold, who had one overwhelming advantage: he had no business interest outside Standard Oil,[31] and he was the only partner who met that test.

Chapter 19

Export Oil

Soon Archbold turned his attention to the vexing naphtha problem. For several years the company had followed a somewhat dubious practice – exactly the strategy that professor Chandler had warned against – the dilution of kerosene with naphtha. They called the product *export oil*, and sold it only outside the United States. Hidy and Hidy, the company's historians, explained that standard kerosene, called *refined oil*, had a flash point of 110° F., while export oil was made by mixing naphtha into the kerosene to produce a flash point of 69.8° to 75.2° F.[32] That meant that if a lamp was lit in a room where the temperature exceeded 75 degrees, it could easily explode. As the residents of the British Isles were accustomed to living in cool homes, they made good customers, and in 1879 the British government had been induced to lower the legal flash point from 100° to 73° F.

However, during the summer of 1893, there were sixty days when the temperature exceeded 73° in London, and that year 19.3% of fires in London and 13.24% of the fires in Liverpool came from kerosene. In those cities the principal oil used was American export oil. In Glasgow, where most of the oil was of Scottish manufacture with a 100° flash point, the number of kerosene-related fires was less than 1.7%. In 1892, at a meeting of the Society of Chemical Industry in Great Britain, it was declared that about three hundred deaths a year occurred in England and Wales from lamp accidents due to the explosiveness of American oil.[33] Europeans were so antagonized that it soon became clear to Standard Oil that the naphtha glut could never be eliminated by increasing the sale of export oil.

Tilford's Campaign

Archbold handed the thorny problem to Wesley Hunt Tilford, whom Jabez Bostwick had brought into the oil business. Tilford's specialty was marketing and, starting at age 23, he had organized the whole Western market for Standard Oil products. According to Hidy and Hidy, he "had the foresight, organizing abilities, friendly personality, and vigor necessary for the rough game of domestic marketing. As we know, the men of Standard had appointed the 37-year-old as a trustee in place of Jabez. Then, after Jersey Standard became the operating company, Tilford was elected to that company's board.[34] The company's top policy makers were now William Rockefeller, Rogers, Flagler, Archbold, and Tilford. However, the first three were deeply involved in other businesses, so only Archbold and Tilford were able to devote their full attention to Standard Oil.[35]

Tilford concluded that the only way to get rid of the naphthas was to defy another of professor Chandler's warnings, and put a naphtha stove in every home. New York and many other cities prohibited the sale of vapor stoves, but on the Great Plains, where wood was scarce, they were very popular. A kitchen with a gasoline stove was cooler in summer, and the average operating cost was only about a cent an hour.[36]

How could Standard Oil persuade housewives who lived in cities to switch to the naphthas? Tilford saw this as a straightforward marketing problem, and acted accordingly. First, he transferred Charles M. Higgins, who had been successful in expanding gasoline sales in the midwest and the south, to the naphtha department in New York. Next, the company encouraged stove manufacturers to make improved stoves, and persuaded eastern insurance companies to follow the example of western firms and not charge higher rates on buildings where vapor stoves were used. Then Standard Oil mounted a massive advertising campaign. The tools were already at hand, for the company had been advertising in trade papers, and now Tilford redirected the advertisements to the country's housewives. Standard Oil placed 20,000 ads in newspapers, 7,000 in trolley cars, and handed out thirty million circulars. Then an army of fifteen hundred special agents and salesmen went out to instruct consumers on the safe use of vapor stoves. The campaign cost the company $250,000.[37]

The Standard Oil Company mounted an extensive advertising campaign, at a cost of a quarter of a million dollars, to persuade housewives that vapor stoves were safe.

Soon vapor stoves were being sold in enormous numbers. The campaign was such a success that by the summer of 1899, the price of crude naphtha exceeded that of kerosene,[38] and Standard Oil actually ran short of the naphthas.[39] The company abruptly ordered Charles Higgins to discontinue the New England campaign – so abruptly that he had to persuade the Chicago stove manufacturers to take back a large consignment they had already shipped to him.[40]

It is an ironic testament to the power of marketing that thirty years after Frank Ofeldt first sought to invent a device to make use of surplus naphthas, the solution came, not from an invention, but from an advertising campaign.

Chapter 20

Benedict Folds

"Do unto others as they would do unto you—and do it first."
Henry Flagler's favorite motto, adapted from *David Harum*[1]

E.C. Benedict, from *The Stock Exchange in Caricature*.

235

Naphtha

The Gas Magnate

In 1895 E.C. Benedict purchased the Americus Club at Indian Harbor, Greenwich, which had once been the seaside hangout for Boss Tweed and his buddies. Dr. Horace Bassett, whose father had worked for E.C. Benedict, described the dining room as "a beautiful thing,…a curved, domed building…with lights in the windows up overhead….They had moved it down toward the edge of the water, and Benedict used it as a boathouse. It was the gaudiest boathouse that was ever built….He had put cranes or tracks up overhead, and they ran out over the water so that he could pull up the launches, drive them in or pull them into the boathouse."[2]

Indian Harbor was ideal for a yachtsman. E.C. could dock *Oneida* at the foot of his garden, and coal her right there. As Bassett recalled, it took forty or fifty people to run the estate, twenty-five or thirty in the house itself, plus sixty or seventy on the *Oneida*.[3]

To design his splendid villa, E.C. commissioned Carrère and Hastings, the architects for Flagler's Ponce de Leon Hotel, the Senate Office Building in Washington, and the New York Public Library.

Thomas Hastings was an Englishman, given to expressions such as "Bully day, Commodore." He married E.C.'s daughter Helen, "a noted horsewoman [and] among the best women whips of her period."[4] It was said that E.C.'s wedding present was a check for one million dollars, and the couple sailed away on their honeymoon voyage aboard *Oneida*, with a white satin slipper waving in the breeze. It had been hoisted to the top of her mast an hour before by a group of happy guests.[5]

As we have previously noted, E.C. Benedict made most of his fortune in illuminating gas, and that is what brought him into conflict with Standard Oil. *The New York Times* described the dust-up: "Brooklyn had seven gas companies. Of these J. Edward Addicks controlled the People's, the Metropolitan, and the Nassau, while the Standard Oil Company controlled the Brooklyn, the Fulton, and the Citizens'. The seventh, the Williamsburg Gas Light Company, was controlled by E.C. Benedict and his associates, and was the key to the situation. It was buying naphtha from the Manhattan Oil Company, in which Mr. Benedict was heavily interested….The Standard Oil people, with lists of stockholders, bought the Williamsburg Company from under Mr. Benedict, and had him beaten and captured before he knew what he was doing."[6]

The battleground moved to Chicago. The *Greenwich News and Graphic* reported that "when the Chicago Gas company became a bone of contention between stock operators, E.C. Benedict & Company arrayed itself against the Standard Oil Company and boomed the stock for all it was worth."[7] Grover Cleveland, who had invested in Chicago Gas, wrote to E.C., "I see some of them wicked bears have had to climb a tree after poking sticks at Chicago Gas. I am glad of it. I guess they'll learn to let it alone after awhile."[8]

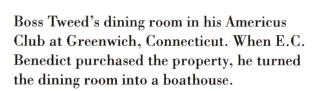

Boss Tweed's dining room in his Americus Club at Greenwich, Connecticut. When E.C. Benedict purchased the property, he turned the dining room into a boathouse.

236

Chapter 20

E.C. Benedict's villa at Indian Harbor near Greenwich, Conn., designed by the prominent architects, Carrère and Hastings. Thomas Hastings married Benedict's daughter, Helen.

E.C. Benedict in his alco-vapor tender, *Oneida II*. He reorganized the Marine Vapor Engine Company, gave it a new name, the *Marine Engine and Machine Company*, and took over the presidency himself.

The Reorganized Company

It appears that during these years the Marine Vapor Engine Company drifted, rudderless. When E.C. finally turned his attention to that company, he concluded that he had to reorganize it. He gave it a new name, the *Marine Engine and Machine Company*, and he invested heavily in a new plant in Harrison, N.J. He had not been an officer of the previous company, but now assumed the presidency, while J.B.M. Showell, the former president, was demoted to secretary.[9] Charles A. Wright, formerly credited as the inventor of the Wright Engine, was no longer mentioned, although the company continued to manufacture exactly the same engine.

Now that Charles Wright had gone the way of Frank Ofeldt, it is clear that E.C. Benedict, like Jabez Bostwick, saw inventors as disposable – to be separated from their inventions and flung aside.

The Marine Engine and Machine Company's plant in Harrison N.J., where alco-vapor launches were now built.

In its 1903 catalog, the Marine Engine and Machine Company vigorously attacked the internal combustion engine, now a serious competitor: "The 'Alco-Vapor' motor cannot and must not be compared with gasoline engines. It is as reliable for marine propulsion as is a steam engine. It is not burdened with the heavy or delicate parts found in explosive motors, or with the unreliable spark necessary in that class of motor.…The engine has a smooth, uniform, rotative motion.…The 'Alco-Vapor' motor is not placed on a foundation fastened to the flooring of the boat, but is securely bolted to the keelsons. This construction allows the engine to work at high speed, preventing vibration, and saving the boat from racking.…[It] has no water-jacket, with its liability to clog and cause overheating; no cumbersome fly-wheel to be started by hand: no puffing from exhaust.…One lever starts, stops and reverses. It has no dead centres, no reversible propeller blades.…The motor or engine is self-contained, all moving parts enclosed, preventing the throwing of oil in the bilges with its attendant disagreeable features."[10]

The catalog included a number of testimonials from owners who gave their reasons for preferring alco-vapor over naphtha or internal combustion.

"Not a penny has been spent on repairs, or a stop of a single second on account of the engine. The launch has met and defeated all comers, including about twenty launches of gasoline systems.

"I have used my 'Alco-Vapor' launch for all landings, in all weathers, and on three occasions I towed my 110-foot schooner with it for several miles. It was a great comfort to be relieved of fear of fire.

"I think the 'Alco-Vapor' is the best power for small boats. I have had over 2,000 miles of fun in mine, and in Egg Harbor alone, I had the pleasure of towing three disabled spark engines into harbor.

"My 5-hp 'Alco-Vapor' engine has never given me a minute of trouble or delay: always ready to go. I have owned six gas and gasoline launches and I must say there is no comparison between them and the 'Alco-Vapor'."[11]

E.C. Surrenders

From the catalog one would conclude that the alco-vapor launch had decisively trounced all competitors. Not only was it faster and safer than naphtha, but its engine was much more reliable than internal combustion.

E.C. Benedict was not fooled. He saw clearly that his real competitor was not just the gasoline engine, but gasoline itself, and his nemesis, the company that owned the gasoline business. It was Standard Oil that would profit most from the internal combustion engine, and he knew from experience that the men of Standard were relentless in stamping out competitors. He did not have the stomach to tangle with them again.

Some years later, E.C. said to an interviewer, "As I have told young men who have applied to me for advice, don't try to compete with The Standard Oil company; don't try to compete with the United States Steel Corporation. Turn your attention to places where these colossal corporations and people do business; hold your hat on the other side of the counter at which they spend their money.…They must spend their money. Hold your hat where it is going out."[12]

Shortly after the Marine Engine and Machine Company issued its 1903 catalog, E.C. Benedict made a stunning decision. Abruptly, and with no explanation, he handed over the marketing of alco-vapor launches to his competitor. On August 16, 1903, New York newspapers carried an announcement that the Gas Engine & Power Company and Charles L. Seabury & Company, Consolidated were now the "sole sales agents for Alco-Vapor engines and Launches."[13] The Marine Engine and Machine Company then reissued its 1903 catalogue with a new cover, confirming the capitulation.

The original cover for the Marine Engine and Machine Company's 1903 catalog.

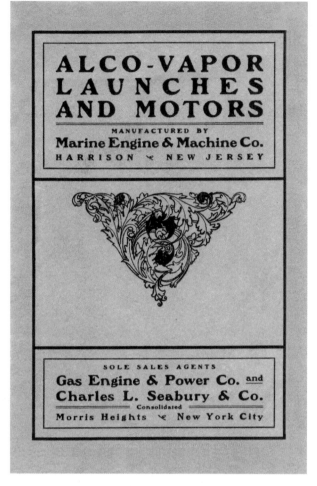

The revised cover revealed that E.C. Benedict had capitulated, and handed over the marketing of alco-vapor launches to his arch-competitor.

The new alliance soon resulted in Consolidated's installing alco-vapor engines in some of their own boats. In 1905 Consolidated built a 36-ft. boat with a 12-hp alco-vapor engine for the U.S. Navy Pay Office, and shortly after that delivered two unusual craft to the Marine and Fisheries Department in Quebec. As these boats were meant for shallow water use, their propellers were protected by tunnels. Again, the engines were not naphtha, but alco-vapor.[14]

The Marine Engine and Machine Company continued in business, but E.C. took his own advice and stopped trying to compete with Standard Oil. Instead he found something that couldn't be powered by gasoline, and gradually switched his boatworks to the manufacture of elevators.[15]

Chapter 21

Speed

"As if in a dream he found himself, somehow, seated in the driver's seat; as if in a dream, he pulled the lever and swung the car round the yard and out through the archway; and, as if in a dream, all sense of right and wrong, all fear of obvious consequences, seemed temporarily suspended. He increased his pace, and as the car devoured the street and leapt forth on the high road through the open country, he was only conscious that he was Toad once more, Toad at his best and highest, Toad the terror, the traffic-queller, the Lord of the lone trail, before whom all must give way or be smitten into nothingness and everlasting night."

Kenneth Grahame, *The Wind in the Willows*[1]

Driving

Jabez Bostwick's son, Albert C. Bostwick, was a sportsman. His mansion in Mamaroneck contained no library, but his carriage house had room for 20 carriages, and was "so clean you could eat off the floor."[2]

Jabez Bostwick's son, Albert, loved driving fast horses, boats, and cars.

For young bucks like Albert, *driving* was the favorite sport. Further, the ownership of a fast horse was a mark of success. Matthew Hale Smith described the phenomenon: "A man is 'nowhere' in Wall Street unless he keeps a fast team. What racing is to the English, trotting is to New York. Fabulous prices are paid for a fast horse.… The great stock men, speculators, dry goods men, and eminent New Yorkers can be found [in Harlem Lane] any afternoon. The exhilaration on the road is intense, for every steed is put to his best ability. Excitement and peril unite. Every man for himself. The teams are quite as much excited as the drivers. Flying, dashing, cutting across, moving in opposite directions, with unearthly yellings, make a scene indescribably exciting. Men of seventy compete with men of thirty. Lads of sixteen give an octogenarian all he can do. Bankers, brokers, speculators, old men and young men, clerks, draymen, cartmen, butchers, merchants, doctors, counsellors, ministers, in pell-mell New York style, are tearing up and down the road....A horse that can outspeed the fleet ones on the road can command any price – thirty or fifty thousand dollars even."[3]

Allan Nevins tells us that, to John D. Rockefeller, horses became almost a passion. After work he would don goggles and after an hour's fast driving – "trot, pace, gallop, everything," would feel rejuvenated. "Once Rockefeller, driving a favorite pair, was racing pell-mell on Euclid...when a heavy dray loaded with scrap-iron loomed in sight. Without hesitating, he plunged by it. [His companion] recalled years later that they had so little room that Rockefeller's hub-caps grazed in rapid succession those of the dray, giving two sharp reports: 'Tzing! tzing!' The president of the Standard...was delighted with his bold exploit. 'George,' he said with a happy smile, 'did you hear that *Tzing*? That was pret-t-y clo-o-se'!"[4]

Speedy Naphthas

If men were so passionate about fast horses, why not fast boats? As we know, in 1891 the Gas Engine and Power Company built the *Racer*, "The fastest boat of her size in the world."[5] However, the 1894 catalog stated that, "Our aim is to build pleasure boats, not racing machines, giving all the beam necessary for comfort and stability. Yet undoubtedly even then our boats attain greater speed than any other build of equal size and power, the lightness of the Naphtha Motors more than compensating for the extreme beam."[6]

The founder's son had other ideas, so the company built for him a 32-ft., 12-hp naphtha launch named *The Bostwick*, after his father. According to *The New York Times*, in the Larchmont races of 1902 *The Bostwick* "attracted the most attention. She completely outclassed all her competitors...and she walked quite away from her racing companions....The Bostwick, although being obliged to give big allowance, was easily the winner."[7]

That year the Consolidated catalog showed a 40-ft., 12-hp high-speed naphtha launch which, because of her length, must have been even speedier than *The Bostwick*.[8]

A 40-ft., 12-hp high-speed naphtha launch was featured in Consolidated's 1902 catalog.

Chapter 21

The Fastest Yacht

Seabury's return had made the company aware of the importance of speed. As we know, Consolidated constructed the fastest vessel in the U.S. Navy, and now was called upon to build the fastest steam yacht. John P. Duncan had commissioned the first *Kanawha* from Seabury, but she was called into service during the Spanish-American War, and Duncan asked Consolidated to construct a second *Kanawha*.[9] The *Brooklyn Eagle* announced, "This yacht is the fastest in the country, having beaten Commodore J. P. Morgan's new yacht Corsair in a race, also the Sandy Hook flyer Monmouth, and the fast Sound steamers Richard Peck and City of Lowell, a thing no other yacht in the fleet has done or is capable of doing."[10]

The Standard Oil partner, Henry H. Rogers, needed a fast yacht to commute between his 85-room mansion in Fairhaven, Massachusetts and his office in New York, so in 1901 he purchased *Kanawha* from Duncan. *Kanawha* was capable of 20 knots, and won the Lysistrata Cup in 1903 and 1904, but her owner's wealth gave her an advantage. Rogers was building the Virginian Railroad to carry West Virginia coal to Norfolk, and was able to have his workmen hand-pick the hard coal for his yacht.[11]

The second *Kanawha*, built by Consolidated, was the fastest steam yacht in the country.

Commuters

In 1902 Alfred Yarrow built the 153-ft. *Tarantula* for William K. Vanderbilt. She was one of the first high-speed commuters, and was patterned on the famous *Turbinia*. *Tarantula*'s three steam turbines turned nine propellers (three on each shaft), which drove her at 25 knots. Like her owner's palatial steam yacht *Valiant*, she carried a naphtha tender. Vanderbilt used her to commute to his office in Manhattan, and her heavy wake caused so much damage that a court case was decided against *Tarantula*, making William K. responsible.[12]

William K. Vanderbilt's *Tarantula*, designed by Alfred Yarrow, was capable of 25 knots. In this photo the crew is preparing to lower her naphtha tender.

Duels

With the intensifying desire for speed, the owners of launches were increasingly prone to challenge each other to races. In 1902, the *Brooklyn Eagle* reported on the duels: "Never before in the history of Shelter Island have there been so many naphtha, steam and gasoline launches in the harbor. One of the fastest of all the launches…is the naphtha launch Spray, belonging to Sinclair Smith of Brooklyn. She has more than once shown her mettle in a number of contests with similar craft.…Tot, belonging to C.F. Wildey of New York, claims to be among the fastest gasoline motor boats.… Spray and Tot often have tests of speed, with the result that Spray comes out the winner, although somewhat the smaller of the two boats."[13]

Until the turn of the century, Consolidated denied that there was any viable alternative to naphtha. In its 1899 catalog, the company noted, "The immense popularity of the Naphtha Launch as introduced by us, had its consequence in the springing into existence of several would-be substitutes and competitors, eagerly taken up by speculators, and advertised as equal to, better, or at least cheaper than our product. But in all sincerity we can say, after persistent and careful investigation…that there is not one motor among them all that is worthy of being classed as a rival, and hardly as a competitor."[14]

Chapter 21

The Speedway Engine

However, as Michael Dixon points out, "The ultimate weakness of the vapor engines was probably their speed."[15] *Spray* was the end of the line. In 1902 John J. Amory saw what was to come, and gave up the battle against internal combustion. That year's catalog announced the company's grudging capitulation: "While we advocate the naphtha engine for its many advantages, there are features about the gasoline engines worthy of consideration for working boats, where weight and noise are not objectionable and where very cheap operation is essential; also for auxiliaries where smokestacks cannot well be used. Undeniably there are thousands of gasoline engines in use, more or less successfully, and a long experimental stage has corrected many of the primary incongruities. A well-made gasoline engine (unfortunately they are few and far between), intelligently managed by a person who has patience and is familiar with the eccentricities of the motor he has to run, can be made a very satisfactory possession."[16]

Amory's new strategy was simple: not just to build a gasoline engine, but to build a better one. Introduced in 1903, the new engine was named the *Speedway*.[17] In L. Francis Herreshoff's opinion, it was "one of the best gasoline marine engines,…noted for its long life, quietness and reliability."[18]

After Consolidated surrendered and began building gasoline engines, the 1905 catalog contrasted one of the first naphtha launches to the new *Speedway* launch.

1885

Twenty Years Later

245

Speed Demons

The gasoline engine made possible the use of the planing hull, invented by the Rev. C.M. Ramus, Rector of Playden in Sussex, England. Back in 1872 he had written to the Admiralty proposing that the speed of steam vessels could be at least doubled by adopting his invention. He calculated that 1,500 hp would easily drive an 1,100-ton ship at 30 knots, and under some circumstances 50-60 knots.[19]

Although the Reverend's numbers seemed improbable, the concept lingered. In 1906 Alfred Yarrow was able to test an internal combustion engine in a motor launch. As Lady Yarrow explained, "The remarkable speed obtained by this particular launch was in a great measure due to the fact that the bottom of the hull was perfectly flat, and when travelling at very high speed was actually lifted on to the surface of the water instead of passing through it. In this way the resistance was enormously diminished."

The boat caught the attention of the First Sea Lord, "Jacky" Fisher, famous for forcing new ideas on the hidebound Royal Navy. According to Lady Yarrow, it was Fisher who turned the Queen of England into a speed demon: "Lord Fisher telegraphed to Yarrow that His Majesty King Edward expressed a wish to see the boat perform some manoeuvres. The following day the motor-launch came alongside the royal yacht, and King Edward, Queen Alexandra, Princess Victoria, and the King and Queen of Spain, accompanied by Lord Fisher, made a short trip. The King suggested that the boat should be driven at its highest speed, but Queen Alexandra added hastily: 'No, not whilst the King is on board. Do not run the slightest risk. I will go again later.' After King Edward and some of the party had left the boat, the Queen had a further trip at the maximum speed, the little vessel travelling at a rate previously unknown in a craft of so small a size."[20]

After the turn of the century, the internal combustion engine enabled every young buck to unleash his passion for speed. Albert Bostwick set several land speed records in the U.S. and Europe,[21] and in 1901 E.C. Benedict's son, Frederick, was one of the first to be killed in a car accident. In those days cars were top-heavy, and Frederick tried to go around a corner too fast.[22]

The twentieth century would indeed be Mr. Toad's.[23]

Chapter 21

King Edward VII and the Royal Party aboard Alfred Yarrow's experimental planing launch.

Chapter 22

Conclusion

After forty years, Standard Oil achieved its objective. Not only had the naphtha glut ended, but in 1911, with 618,727 cars and trucks registered, sales of gasoline and naphtha finally exceeded those of kerosene.[1] The Standard's new problem was a severe shortage of gasoline, but in 1913 Dr. William Burton, who had been Herman Frasch's assistant, invented "thermal cracking under pressure" (also called *catalytic cracking*), which enormously increased the yield of gasoline, and substantially reduced the cost of production. According to Williamson, it "was undoubtedly the greatest windfall in the history of petroleum refining."[2] It is no wonder that Hidy and Hidy, the company's historians, observed that "Divine Providence surely smiled upon the petroleum industry?"[3]

In our introduction, we stated that Frank Ofeldt's inventions ignited a transportation revolution. Before the naphtha launch there was no user-operated motor vehicle of any sort. Once people became accustomed to the convenience of operating their own motorboats, and going where they wanted when they wanted, they were ready to get their hands on the wheel of a motorcar.

The revolution was not merely in transportation, but in *empowerment*. During the course of the twentieth century, inventors would find many other ways to empower people, including the personal computer and the internet. Access to each of these innovations was another step in the advancement of individual freedom. As we now know, the first step was Frank Ofeldt's useful little naphtha launch.

As we now can clearly see, the story of the naphtha engine has another ending – one that is yet to be revealed. Frank Ofeldt's invention ushered in the age of petroleum as a fuel, and that age is drawing to a close.

One of the first visionaries to discern the inevitability of this was Frank Ofeldt's fellow Swede, John Ericsson.

In 1868, Ericsson became concerned about the depletion of fossil fuels. As Frank Ofeldt had not yet invented his naphtha engine, the hydrocarbon that Ericsson focused on was coal, but his argument applies even more forcefully to petroleum.

In Ericsson's words, "Already Englishmen have estimated the near approach of the time when the supply of coal will end…. I cannot omit averting to the insignificance of the dynamic energy which the entire exhaustion of our coal fields would produce, compared with the incalculable amount of force at our command, if we avail ourselves of the concentrated heat of the solar rays."[4]

Ericsson was so certain of this inevitability that he devoted his latter years to inventing a solar engine.

Ericsson was probably correct. With ingenuity and determination, our dependence on fossil fuels will come to an end.

When the whole story is finally told, Frank Ofeldt will assume his rightful place as one of the inventors who not only empowered our lives, but enhanced and enriched the lives of all who inhabit our planet.

Chapter 23

Epilogue

"So don't expect to see again one of those sweet little plum-bowed, fantail-stern launches with her warm brightwork, her shining brass funnel, her scalloped canopy and her lazy flags. There's a kind of charm about her like that of a pretty girl with all her clothes on, her head held high, dainty, refined; and yes, I'll say it, adorable."

Malcolm MacDuffie, *Naphtha Launch – The Missing Link*[1]

The Last Naphthas

Albert Bostwick hoped that his schooner *Vergemere* would be the fastest sailboat in the world, but in 1904 she was repeatedly beaten by Wilson Marshall's *Atlantic*. In 1905, Emperor Wilhelm II, an honorary member of the Larchmont Yacht Club, offered the *German Emperor's Cup* for a sailing race from New York to England. Eleven yachts entered, and Marshall hired Charlie Barr to skipper *Atlantic*. With three America's Cup victories, Barr was probably the best professional sailor in the world.[2]

In 1887, *Dauntless* had set the record for sailing 328 nautical miles in one day, but after eighteen years, *Atlantic* broke that record by sailing 341 nautical miles. The Larchmont Club's history recorded that "jubilation spread through the ship," and the crew was rewarded with a double ration of grog.

On the ninth day, *Atlantic* "was plunging before a whole gale with only a squaresail and fore trysail still set, and it was a wild and frightening ride.... Two men had to be lashed to the wheel to control the corkscrewing hull."[3] Barr crossed the finish line a full day ahead of the next competitor, and set a transatlantic record that endured for seventy-five years.[4]

Atlantic's naphtha tender was also a champion in 1907, winning the last Larchmont naphtha race. That year gasoline launches raced separately, but after 1908 Larchmont held no power boat races.[5]

Sales of naphtha launches declined, but slowly. In 1907 Consolidated still had fifty naphtha launches in stock ready for delivery, and the company advertised, "Many people are still recommending *The Only Naphtha Launch*. Many people believe that because we are also building Speedway Gasolene Launches that the Old Reliable is relegated simply to past memories. This card will disabuse inquiring minds of such a mistake."[6]

In his 1912 book, *Motor Boats: Construction and Operation*, Thomas H. Russell stated, "For use in launches of 16 to 30 feet, and especially for tenders on large yachts, the naphtha engine is still much in evidence."[7] That year Escher Wyss & Cie. still manufactured a range of naphtha launches, which they described as "the simplest, longest established and most proven motor boat, the simplest to service and the one needing the least maintenance."[8] L. Francis Herreshoff recalled that his family shipyard built its last naphtha launch around 1915.[9]

The decline in naphtha sales had little effect on Consolidated. The company now found a product that made excellent use of Seabury's talent – the express yacht, or commuter. Their first was the 60-foot *Dark Island*, powered by a 210-hp, six-cylinder Speedway engine, "longer than the average three-cushion sofa," that drove the flyer at 22 mph. This was followed by a series of commuters powered by twin 300-hp Speedway engines, and capable of 30 mph. According to C. Philip Moore, "The Speedway series of commuters were considered by many yachtsmen the finest express yachts of their time." During the First World War, the company built 175 flying boat hulls, and five minesweepers. By then the Consolidated yard had no less than thirteen ways, which made it possible to build vessels up to 300 feet.[10]

"Old Number One"[11]

For a dozen years no one gave much thought to the naphtha launch, but one man had not forgotten. Henry Ford was planning a new museum in Dearborn where he would exhibit important examples of American technology. In 1928 he asked Consolidated for *Old Number One*, but John Armory declined, as he had already decided to present her to the Smithsonian Institution. On August 2, Mr. Seyffer in Ford's New York office wired Frank Campsall, Henry Ford's Assistant Secretary: "IMPOSSIBLE OBTAIN NAPTHA LAUNCH FROM CONSOLIDATED BUILDING CORPN THEY VERY COURTEOUSLY PUT US ON LEAD FOR ANOTHER ONE OWNED BY FRANK PATTERSON LAKE MAHOPAC NY WHO WILL DONATE SMALLER ONE IN MUCH BETTER CONDITION TO MR FORD WE ARE TO SEND FOR AND SHIP THIS LAUNCH TO YOU PLEASE WIRE IF ACCEPTABLE TO YOU."[12]

After receiving the launch, Campsall wrote to John Amory: "We are very glad to be able to write you and advise that the Naphtha launch from Lake Mahopec, has been received from Mr. Patterson the owner and we wish to thank you for the assistance you have been in securing this for Mr. Ford's museum. Of course the boat we have received is a valuable piece for Mr. Ford to have but we are still hoping to get the first one that you contemplate presenting to the Smithsonian Institute."[13]

In 1935 *The New York Times* celebrated the fiftieth birthday of *Old Number One*. At that time the president of Consolidated was Eugene H. Amory, John Amory's son, and the vice president and manager was William K. Parslow, a nephew of William J. Parslow. The story's subtitle read: "Craft Built Half Century Ago Regarded as a Priceless Relic by Owners."[14]

Priceless or not, *Old Number One* seems to have disappeared, along with most of Consolidated's records. Jim Wright recounts that when the plant closed, an alert passer-by noticed that the company's blueprints had been put out for the trash man, so he loaded as many as he could into his car, and took them to the library at Mystic Seaport. When he returned for the remainder, they were gone.[15] Needless to say, Mystic carefully preserves the ones that they did acquire.

Chapter 23

In 1935 the Consolidated Shipbuilding Corporation celebrated the 50th anniversary of "Old Number One."

Survivors: *Chiripa*

The launch that Henry Ford acquired in place of "Old Number One" remained on display in the Henry Ford Museum for many years, but is now in storage. In 2002, Rodney (Pat) Spurlock arranged for a private viewing, and Bill Shaw and I accompanied him. Pat has done extensive research into the history of naphtha launches, and has published a number of nautical books. Bill was the inventor of the IMAX projector.

The launch is named *Chiripa*, and is 21 feet long, possibly the smallest remaining with a fantail hull.[16] Her hull is number 1329, and she was built about 1899.[17] She still has her original engine and is in very good condition, except that the pressure gauge has disappeared.

Chiripa was built about 1899 and is in excellent condition. She is owned by the Henry Ford Museum in Dearborn, but is currently in storage.

Pat Spurlock and Bill Shaw show us where to find the hull number in a naphtha launch.

Chapter 23

In the outboard condenser, seawater cooled the naphtha vapor, and returned it in liquid form to the fuel tank in the forepeak.

Holes in the hull allowed seawater to wash around the naphtha tank, keeping it cool. Also, if the tank should leak, the fuel could escape through these holes.

Lillian Russell

The public has not been able to examine *Chiripa* for some years, but other naphtha launches are readily accessible.

For nearly a century, the Peck family of Chicago has summered on the Lake of Bays, where my wife and I live. Cameron Peck was a passionate collector of boats and cars, and I remember seeing his elegant steam yacht *Naiad* here during the 1940s. Frank H. Miller described a visit to the Lake of Bays in 1948: "Our host, Cameron Peck, had seven steamers in commission, including a 100-foot express yacht. We rode in all of them, and brought the 50-foot *Phoebe* home with us. He was also converting the 135-foot *Magedoma* from hard coal to oil at that time….I had a delightful ride in the Naphtha launch *Lillian Russell*."[18]

Lillian Russell's hull number is 1973 and she is 21'3" long. She has a square stern and two lifting eyes, so was probably built as a yacht tender. However, she spent much of her life in storage before being reactivated by John Hahn, who gave her the name *Lillian Russell*.[19] John Hahn's name is written on the cover of her 1907 instruction book, which was copied for me by Cameron Peck's nephew, John Peck.

After Cameron Peck sold his collection, *Lillian Russell* was purchased by P.R. Mallory, and donated to Mystic Seaport in 1953.

Lillian Russell on the Lake of Bays, when she was part of Cameron Peck's collection.

The handle in front of *Lillian Russell*'s engine was a tiller. Now that the launch is at Mystic Seaport, the handle has been removed.

Chapter 23

The Vanderbilt Launch

The Adirondack Museum, Blue Mountain Lake, N. Y., has a 21'6" naphtha launch with no name, sometimes referred to as *The Vanderbilt Launch*, because Alfred Gwynne Vanderbilt and his family used her in the Adirondacks. She was built in 1906, and converted to gasoline power soon after, so the naphtha engine now in the boat is from another launch.[21] The Vanderbilt launch, like *Lillian Russell*, is clinker built, with a square stern. Her hull number is 1806.[22]

Frieda

In 1959 E.F. Coleman of Fargo, North Dakota, owned a 22-foot naphtha launch, named *Frieda* in honor of his wife. That November, Wilbur J. Chapman described her in *Model Engineer*:

"We found her docked at Pelican Lake [in Western Minnesota] in 'shipshape and Bristol fashion,' woodwork sparkling, brassware gleaming and flags flying at bow and stern. A 40-gallon fuel tank in the bow needs filling only once or twice a season. She has a red canopy with a fringe on top. I was curious to see how long it took to fire up *Frieda* and get under way. Two or three strokes on the air pump put a little naphtha in the priming cup which was then lit with a match. In about one minute, by working the naphtha pump, the retort was filled. Then the burner valve was opened. Two or three minutes later we had 25-lb. pressure, and turning the handwheel for reverse my host backed out of the dock. Total time was three or four minutes. I am sure most of us have cranked an outboard motor longer than that.

"We took a long leisurely cruise at a speed of 6 to 8 knots. Speed control is by turning the burner valve so that the launch can be slowed down to a crawl for docking. A pull on the handwheel operates the slip eccentric which reverses the engine instantly, giving perfect control."[23]

In 1974 *Frieda* was at the Ferguson Museum, Gallatin Gateway, Montana,[24] but she subsequently was moved to the Minnesota Lakes Maritime Museum, in Alexandria, Minnesota, where she is now on display.

Frieda can be seen at the Minnesota Lakes Maritime Museum, in Alexandria, Minnesota.

Naphtha

Bruce Trudgen, author of *The Naphtha Launches*, noted that, although *Frieda*'s engine carries a Gas Engine and Power Company logo, there is also a plaque on board listing the builder as Horace J. Conley. In 1900 Conley advertised in *The Rudder* as "Western Builder of the Only Naphtha Launch, Using Morris Heights N.Y. Motor."[25]

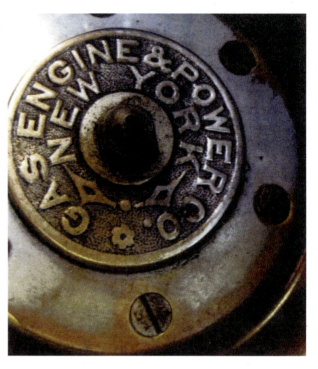

A plaque in *Frieda* indicates that Horace J. Conley was her builder.

The corporate logo on *Frieda*'s engine.

Conley's advertisement in *The Rudder*, December 1900.

Chapter 23

Anita

Another naphtha launch now on display is *Anita*. Like the Vanderbilt launch, she is an amalgam of two boats.

Roman Woodzicka homesteaded on Lake Tomahawk, Wisconsin in 1890, and established the Sunflower Cottage Resort there. He added a fleet of 15 rowboats and 6 launches, most of them built by his son Fabian. In 1914 Fabian opened a boat factory and in 1924 named it the *Sunflower Boat Works*. Fabian loved motors, and collected so many antique cars that he soon had his own museum, which by the time of his death in 1970 included 62 working cars.[26] That winter, heavy snow collapsed the roof of the museum, and Fabian's wife, Belle, sold the collection.[27] For many years Fabian had been hoping to restore an 18-ft. naphtha launch, which was in partly dismantled condition, but, according to Wilbur Chapman, he needed help to assemble it.[28]

In 1971 William H. Richardson Jr. and his father purchased three boats from the Sunflower Museum, and one contained a 6-hp naphtha engine. Two years later they found a 25-ft. 1902 naphtha launch, hull #1754, on Big Cedar Lake near their home in Sheboygan Falls. Supposedly that launch had been exhibited at the 1904 St. Louis World's Fair.[29] They put Fabian's engine into that hull, and took the boat, newly christened *Anita*, to the 1977 Antique Boat Show and Parade in Clayton, N. Y. As *Anita* was the first operating naphtha launch that anyone had seen for nearly twenty years, she caused a sensation.[30] In 1982 the Richardsons donated her to the Antique Boat Museum in Clayton, where she is very nicely displayed today.

When the Richardsons brought *Anita* to Clayton in 1977, it was the first time in almost a generation that anyone had seen a naphtha launch operating.

Anita is now displayed at the Antique Boat Museum in Clayton. Her original naphtha engine had disappeared, but the Richardsons acquired this 6-hp engine from the Sunflower Museum in Wisconsin.

The fireproof lining in *Anita*'s engine compartment.

Chapter 23

Anne and *Ada*

At least two other naphtha launches are on public display. *Anne*, hull #1744, can be seen at the Independence Seaport Museum in Philadelphia. According to Bill Richardson, she is a sister to *Anita*.[31] *Ada*, at the Mariners' Museum in Newport News, was converted to steam in the 1950s. Her aft compartment is still copper-lined, but has been converted to lockers for the storage of coal. The Mariners' Museum also possesses a naphtha engine, which dates to about 1899.

Papillon

A few naphtha launches are in private hands, most being restored or awaiting restoration. However, *Dorcas*, 28 ft., built in 1896, is in service. Around 1912, F.L. Brigham operated her in the Thousand Islands, and after that her naphtha engine was replaced by a gasoline engine.[32] About 1967 she was purchased by Harold McCarney of Gananoque, Ontario, who renamed her *Kallie M* (or *Kally M*).[33] Later she was repowered with an electric motor from Elco. In 2000 McCarney sold her to Richard McGinn, who changed her name to *Papillon*, and had her restored by St. Lawrence Restoration, Clayton, N.Y.

Papillon (ex-*Dorcas*) during restoration in 2000. Several years ago, she was repowered with an Elco electric motor, which is still functioning.

Naphtha

Heather Belle

There is one other launch that was once powered by a Frank Ofeldt engine, and is still in service. This is her story:

Some twenty years ago, Tim Butson, a prominent Muskoka boatbuilder, told me of an antique boat that was for sale because its owner's health was failing. The craft was a cabin launch. You may wonder, why would anybody want one of those? Well I did.

When I was five, my family summered near Sturgeon Falls on Lake Nipissing, and my greatest pleasure was to visit the town dock where I could marvel at the cabin launches, with lace curtains in their windows, and their tables set for tea. A cabin launch is not only esthetically pleasing, but practical. You always have shade, the windows slide open, you can picnic aboard, and your guests are not confined to their seats, so everyone can wander about and chat. Best of all, a cabin launch is built on a displacement hull – a design perfected by the time of the Viking longboat. Your boat doesn't hammer across the tops of waves, but knifes silently through them at a perfect speed. Modern boats whiz about, scaring loons, and battering the occupants until the scenery becomes a blur. Only in a boat with a displacement hull can you properly enjoy an outing on the water.

When my wife and I inspected *Heather Belle*, she fulfilled my childhood dreams. Before we took possession, the previous owner, Donald Davis, told us that she had once been powered by a naphtha engine. We were curious about that, and set out to learn something about naphtha launches. The first thing we discovered was that the inventor, Frank Ofeldt, was born in Sweden. That was good news: in my younger days I had served as assistant director on a Swedish feature film, Arne Sucksdorff's *En Djungelsaga*, and I still have good friends in that country. I immediately phoned my colleague Åke Bäcklund, and asked his assistance, which he provided unstintingly.

The author's filmmaking colleague, Åke Bäcklund (left), undertook the task of researching Frans Åfeldt's early years in Sweden. Here he looks through Norrköping's tax register with Rolf Sjögren, the city's archivist. Inset is an entry from 1866.

Chapter 23

Next we learned that the Museum of the Great Lakes in Kingston possessed copies of registration documents, which could be accessed on-line. My wife, Phyllis, entered the name *Heather Belle*, and to our surprise up came the registration for our launch.

Heather Belle had been delivered to Canada by the Marine Engine and Machine Company of Harrison, New Jersey, on August 16, 1902, at which time she was powered, not by naphtha, but by a 12-hp alco-vapor engine. We had been looking for the right inventor, but the wrong invention.

Rutgers University has a copy of the Marine Engine and Machine Company's 1903 catalog, and in it I found a remarkable picture of *Heather Belle*'s interior as it appeared in 1902: a Victorian drawing room afloat, with velvet drapes, sliding windows, carved mahogany pillars and panels, cushioned benches, wicker chairs, and in the latest style, linoleum flooring.

The alco-vapor launch *Heather Belle* in 1902, from the Marine Engine and Machine Company's catalog. Except for the linoleum floor, the interior has changed very little in more than 115 years.

Naphtha

This composite photograph by Tim Du Vernet represents *Heather Belle* as she appeared when she arrived in Canada.

Heather Belle was purchased by Sidney Finlay McKinnon, a prosperous Toronto merchant, for his daughter, Elizabeth Miles, to use at the family cottage on Tobin Island in the Muskoka Lakes. In 1914, Mrs. Miles sold the boat to George R. Thorel who needed a hotel boat for his new summer resort, Thorel House, on Lake Rosseau. By then the alco-vapor engine had been replaced by an internal combustion engine.

Heather Belle served as the Thorel House hotel boat, or "jitney," for 54 years. Throughout her long life, *Heather Belle* has probably spent every night in a boathouse, which explains her pristine condition.

Heather Belle must have fulfilled her duties well, for she continued at Thorel House for 54 years. Norman Stripp, who skippered *Shirl Evon*, another hotel boat, recounted, "The Thorels looked after the boat like a baby. They wouldn't let you near her." George R.'s son (George H.S.) was her only skipper. Sometimes he would let other people steer, but never let anyone else dock her.

After her long service at Thorel House, *Heather Belle* spent three years at Santa's Village, a theme park on the Muskoka River, and was then purchased by the actor, Donald Davis, from whom we acquired her in 1997.

At that time *Heather Belle* was powered by a 135-hp, six-cylinder Chrysler Crown gasoline engine, which took up quite a lot of room in the cabin, and was always in the way. We considered alternative propulsion systems, and discovered that Charles G. (Chuck) Houghton had revived Elco, the company that, in its first iteration, had supplied the electric boats for the 1893 Chicago Exposition. Elco provided us with an 8-hp Kostov motor, made in Bulgaria, which is so small that it fits out of sight beneath the floor, as do the twelve lead-acid batteries. The batteries weigh one ton, which adds to the boat's stability.

Heather Belle on the Lake of Bays, after she was converted to electric power.

Naphtha

Does *Heather Belle* meet my lifelong expectation of having my own cabin launch? The main requisite was that she have a displacement hull, which she certainly does. Displacement hulls are so efficient that they reach hull speed, effectively their maximum, with very little effort. Although *Heather Belle*'s alco-vapor engine was 12 hp, the 8-hp electric motor is adequate, for it can drive the boat at 7½ knots, her hull speed.

The fine lines of *Heather Belle*'s displacement hull are easily discerned from above.

Chapter 23

Heather Belle is the perfect size to take friends and family for a cruise.

Yes, *Heather Belle* fully confirms my opinion that the most pleasurable boating is done in a spacious cabin launch with a displacement hull.

Acknowledgments

Let me begin in Sweden, where Frans Åfeldt was born.

First, I am indebted to my old filmmaking colleague, Åke Bäcklund, who undertook much of the research, and who was ably assisted by his wife, Britta. Åke ferreted out the details of the Åfeldt family's life in Ivetofta and Norrköping, and then introduced me to the latter city, where we were able to examine documents in the City Archives (Norrköping Stadsarkivet). The City Archivist, Rolf Sjögren, was endlessly patient, and we also received support from staff members, Björn Wahrby and Rolf Jonsson. We did research at the City Museum (Norrköpings Stadsmuseum), where Jåken Andersson helped us, and at the Museum of Work (Arbetets Museum) we were assisted by the Librarian, Ann-Charlotte Persson. We also made good use of the City Library (Norrköpings Stadsbibliotek).

Among other Swedish sources, I should like to highlight the Royal National Archives (Riksarkivet Sverige), the Swedish National Library (Kungliga Biblioteket), the Stockholm City Archives (Stadsarkivet), and the City Museum (Stadsmuseet), where we were assisted by Ingrid Åkerind. Åke Bäcklund also found useful material in the Nobel archives and at the Nobel Foundation, and received advice from Professor Barany at the Nobel Museum. I very much enjoyed the exhibits in the National Museum of Science and Technology (Tekniska Museet), where we were given helpful information by the Curator, Gert Ekström. At the Museum of Maritime History (Sjöhistoriska Museet), we were assisted by a number of people, including Cege Olsson and Martin Lindberg. Both the Sjöhistoriska Museum and the Nordic Museum (Nordiska Museet) contributed valuable pictures. Additional Swedish sources were the House of Genealogy (Släktforskarnas) in Leksand, and the Emigrants' House (Utvandrarnas Hus) in Växjö.

A great deal of information was provided by Lars Bråthe, who had already been conducting his own research into the Åfeldt family, as had Gunbritt Åhfeldt. Brita Åsbrink (author of *Ludvig Nobel: "Petroleum har en lysande framtid!"*) and Gunnar Sillén both supplied important pictures. We also received advice from Per Gillbrand and Lars Porne, and assistance in translating from Frank Asplund.

Now let me turn to the United States, where Frans took the name Frank Ofeldt, and where he became an inventor.

Not long after I started my research, I encountered Rodney (Pat) Spurlock, the proprietor of *Boathouse*, the well-known publisher of nautical books. Pat also supplies kits that enable steam buffs to build their own engines. One of Pat's publications, *Elliott Bay Classics*, had reprinted the magazine, *Steamboats and Modern Steam Launches*, published by Bill Durham in the 1960s. Bill and Pat shared a curiosity about the naphtha engine, and they amassed a considerable collection of clippings and catalogs, with the intention of turning their findings into a book. Pat also enlisted Charles Wells to supply an analysis of Ofeldt's patents.

When I came along, I offered to do some research for them, but shortly thereafter, Durham, who had reached the age of eighty, decided that it was time to retire from the project. Pat then turned his files over to me, and I attempted to become an author. I was still making films, so the book progressed sporadically, but I went to Sweden twice, and also visited several archives in the United States and Canada. Pat, too, continued to do research, and paid visits to Europe, where he found information on Escher Wyss. Pat's contribution has been inestimable, but as it has fallen to me to write the story down, I take full responsibility for the result, warts and all.

Anyone who has delved into nautical history will have learned that the motherlode of information resides in the archives of maritime museums. I first discovered this when my wife and I visited the Antique Boat Museum in Clayton, New York. The Librarian, Phoebe Tritton, pulled out a scrapbook that she had personally assembled, containing clippings on naphtha launches, and she photocopied several of her gems for us. Alas, Phoebe has passed on, but her colleagues at the Antique Boat Museum continue to share their treasures. I have received good assistance from Barton Haxell and Brooke Hartle, among others.

Another gold mine is the Mystic Seaport Museum. Paul O'Pecko, V.P., Research Collections, has been particularly helpful over the years, and has enabled me to spend several days in the G.W. Blunt White Library, poring through their files, which include the records of Seawanhaka Corinthian Yacht Club, of which E. C. Benedict was Commodore. Mystic also possesses a unique trove, the Rosenfeld Collection, the repository of many 8"x10" glass negatives, and some of those beautiful images are reproduced in this book. I have leaned heavily on others of the Museum's staff, including Louisa Alger Watrous and Carol Mowrey.

Several other museums have important possessions. The Henry Ford Museum's naphtha launch, *Chiripa*, is in storage, but the Museum kindly permitted Pat Spurlock, Bill Shaw (the inventor of the IMAX® projector), and me to inspect her. Since then, Jim Orr has been most helpful in scanning photos from their collection. I also visited M.I.T.'s Francis Russell Hart Nautical Museum, whose curator, Kurt Hasselbalch, supplied several illustrations. The Archibald S. Alexander Library at Rutgers University is a repository of alco-vapor catalogs, and David Kuzma's scans have been most useful. Even though the Mariners' Museum in Newport News was undergoing renovations, Lisa Williams was able to to scan a number of images from a rare copy of the 1887 *Gas Engine & Power Company.* catalog. At the South Street Seaport in Manhattan, Norman Brouwer helped me to browse their library, and copy photos of interest.

When I was making the IMAX film, *The Dream Is Alive,* I worked with Fred Durant at the Smithsonian Institution's National Air and Space Museum, so was able to go back to Fred for assistance in procuring the picture of the Durant family in their naphtha launch, *Mugwump*. The photo, which was previously published in Kenneth Durant's *The Naphtha Launch,* is now in the collection of *The Adirondack Experience, The Museum on Blue Mountain Lake,* whose registrar, Hanna E. Person, supplied a scan.

A number of historical societies have responded to my requests. At the Greenwich Historical Society, Amy Braitsch was helpful, and Christopher Shields, the Curator of Library & Archives, provided the photo of E.C. Benedict's impressive mansion at Indian Harbor. At the Newport Historical Society, Molly Bruce Patterson, Collections Team Coordinator & Manager of Digital Initiatives, supplied the photograph of *Conqueror*'s naphtha tender from their Henry O. Havemeyer Collection. This picture had been published previously in Ed Holm's *Yachting's Golden Age*. At the New Jersey Historical Society, I received help from both the Reference Librarian, James Lewis, and Reference Assistant, Brenna King.

When Cece Saunders and Richard Schaefer were assembling the book, *His Beloved Aunt Polly*, we exchanged information and photographs, and later, when I visited Gillette Castle, Joan Lindeen copied several photos of Frank Ofeldt's *Aunt Polly* from the State Park's collection.

I feared that the Library of Congress might be a Kafkaesque bureaucracy, but during two visits I was welcomed warmly, my requests received careful attention, and I was provided unstinting assistance. This enabled me to quote extensively – and include illustrations – from Professor C.F. Chandler's *Report on Petroleum as an Illuminator*. Ellen Terrell found other material, and Melissa Lindberg, a Reference Librarian in the Prints and Photographs Division, was able to discover the wonderful photograph of the actress, Lillian Russell, resting on a tiger skin (previously published in *The Nineties, An American Heritage Extra*). I could not have been better served, and have nothing but admiration for the Library's staff.

I had an equally enjoyable experience in dealing with a National Park. At the Perry's Victory and International Peace Memorial, the Park Ranger (Interpretation) and Historic Weapons Supervisor, Robert Whitman, searched through the photographic albums in their collection, and unearthed the photo of Granville Henchele and friends in his naphtha launch on Lake Erie (previously published in James P. Barry's, *American Powerboats: The Great Lakes Golden Years*).

I received very fine assistance from Margaret Vollmer at the New York Public Library, where Richard Foster and Maurice Klapwald kindly copied several days' testimony from the Hepburn Commission's hearings. And at the Greenwich Library, Richard Hart, Cathy Ogden, and Isabel Maddox provided useful help.

A special case is the invaluable archive of the *Brooklyn Eagle*. Fortunately every page of this daily newspaper is available on-line, so that although I have quoted extensively from its articles, I never interacted with a real person. Anyway, whoever you are, many thanks.

A number of valuable archives are in the possession of yacht clubs, and one of the most extensive is held by the New York Yacht Club. Timothy M. James, who is a member, copied several documents for me, and invited me to browse the library, where I received assistance from Librarian William Watson. Timothy James also arranged for me to stay at the Larchmont Yacht Club, where I was generously allowed to go through the Club's files, and where Lucian J. Leone and Nicholas Langone enabled me to photograph the exquisite model of the naphtha launch that the Gas Engine and Power Company had presented to the Club.

As well as visiting museums and yacht clubs, I have had the pleasure of interacting extensively with a number of individuals. Apart from Pat Spurlock, the principal American contributor is Robert Francis Ofeldt. A great-great grandson of Frank W., and great-grandson of Frans Axel (Frank A.), Bob has unstintingly supplied the historic family photographs that grace this publication. Another descendant of Frank W. is Sandra Brockel (a great-granddaughter of Ernest), who has provided constant encouragement.

Outside the Ofeldt family, a principal supporter is Whitney Moore, who wrote an excellent article about E.C. Benedict for *Nautical Quarterly*. She also authored a full-length biography of the Commodore, entitled *Some Things Never Change*. Although it is still unpublished, Whitney made the manuscript available for my research. Additionally, Whitney supplied information that she had obtained from her interviews with Chalmers Benedict (Ben) Wood, E.C.'s great-grandson. I was also helped by Ben's wife, Dr. Patricia Wood, and by their daughters, Penelope and Felicity.

When Charles G. (Chuck) Houghton was the proprietor of Elco, he not only supplied the electrical system that now powers *Heather Belle*, he also provided information from William C. Swanson on the history of electric boats. Swanson himself then gave me useful advice. One of Chuck Houghton's customers, Richard McGinn, owner of *Papillon*, was helpful too. I also received the co-operation of Donald Price, proprietor of St. Lawrence Restoration, who enabled me to photograph *Papillon*.

In 1946, when I first visited the Lake of Bays, I was amazed to see Cameron Peck's elegant steam yacht, *Naiad*. Now that my wife and I live on the Lake of Bays, it is our pleasure to visit with John and David Peck, Cameron's nephews. John has done the world a great favor by scanning every picture in Cameron's collection, including the photos of *Lillian Russell* that he provided for this book.

Undoubtedly, the most dedicated naphtha enthusiasts have been William H. Richardson and his son, who restored *Anita* (the only naphtha launch to have seen service in recent years), which is now on display at the Antique Boat Museum in Clayton. William H., Jr. sent me the photo that appears in this book's epilogue. Another naphtha aficionado is Jim Wright. When I visited Mystic Seaport, I stayed at Jim and Sandra's charming hostel, *Another Second Penny Inn*, and saw – in Jim's workshop – the two naphtha launches that he was then hoping to combine into one.

I have been delighted to connect with a number of collectors of naphtha memorabilia, and thrilled that they have been willing to provide treasures for this book. Tim James, who collects hardware from naphtha launches, discovered the rare 1889 Ofeldt advertisements that are included in chapter ten. Karl A. Petersen sent me several articles, including the one from the *Syracuse Daily Standard* on the Star Gas Machine, and the account of the naphtha torpedo boat from the *Wayne County Review*. Richard Durgee supplied historic images from *The Rudder*, and Charles S. Purinton provided information from *Model Engineer*.

I am also very pleased at the willingness of nautical historians to share information. These include John Rousmaniere, Benjamin A.G. Fuller, and Michael M. Dixon. Most particularly, the late Bruce Trudgen, author of *The Naphtha Launches*, was very generous. I have quoted liberally from his book, and used some of his photos. I was especially delighted that Bruce and his wife, May, came to the Lake of Bays to enjoy a ride in *Heather Belle*.

Now to Canada.

I have received a good deal of assistance from Canadian archives. It is a particular convenience that the Marine Museum of the Great Lakes in Kingston has digitized the registrations of Canadian ships, including steam yachts. Similarly, the Muskoka Steamship and Historical Society has amassed a comprehensive record of Canadian pleasure craft, including thousands of

Muskoka-built boats, and hundreds of American-built craft that, like *Heather Belle*, ply Canadian lakes. At the Muskoka Lakes Museum in Port Carling, I spent days going through the photo collection, and I also obtained useful information from the Royal Canadian Yacht Club. Local public libraries in Baysville and Huntsville were helpful, and the latter procured from the University of Alberta the complete Cleveland-Benedict correspondence that the Library of Congress had transferred to microfilm. The historical researcher, Grace Nesbitt Fulford, uncovered the story of Sidney Finlay McKinnon, who in 1902 purchased the alco-vapor launch *Heather Belle* for his daughter, Elizabeth Miles.

Many Canadians were more than willing to share their knowledge of antique boats, including Tim and Sharon Butson, and Tim's father, the veteran boatbuilder, Ron Butson. Others with deep experience of boating history included Ed Skinner, Ian Turnbull, Norman Stripp, Everett MacFarlane, John Mills, Roger Dyment, Dr. Jacques Valiquette, and a number of members of the Thorel family, particularly the late George R. (Geordie) Thorel, whose father, George H.S. Thorel, operated *Heather Belle* as a hotel boat for 54 years. Other Canadians who lent assistance included Donald Davis, Rick Terry, Liz Lundell, Ted and Suzanne Currie, Guy Boisjoli, Jonathan Killing, and Nancy Button.

Two of my high school classmates, and IMAX partners, Robert Kerr and William C. Shaw, were wooden boat owners. Robert, who built a beautiful replica of a Victorian-era Thames launch, observed that "hull design peaked in 1900, and has gone downhill ever since." Bill, an engineering genius, guided *Heather Belle*'s conversion to electric power, and even went to Bavaria to conduct research into the performance of electrically-powered craft. Another colleague, Creighton Douglas, contributed his expertise in translating from French. Some Swedish translation was done by Leif Axbåge, and German by Paul Ehnes. I have also benefited from the assistance of several members of my own family, including the theatrical designer, Eo Sharp, my grandson Lucas Ferguson-Sharp, Steven Lidster at Rutgers University, the Reverend George Fairlie in Scotland, and Tina Leyds in the Netherlands.

So much for research; now let me turn to the creation of this book.

The one person who has made the greatest contribution is my longtime IMAX colleague, Gayle Bonish. Gayle made all the artistic decisions. She designed the book, chose the typefaces, conquered the intractable problems of layout, and even typed the complete text. Her greatest achievement is invisible: she enhanced most of the photographs, some of which were in abominable condition. I would not have dreamt of embarking on a project such as this without Gayle's wisdom and guidance.

Many thanks as well to publishing executive Vicki Pasternak who became a key advisor and helped us make wise decisions. She was an invaluable guide through the many challenges of publishing a book in a COVID-19 environment.

Proofreading services were provided by Moveable Inc., who saved me from a number of embarassing mistakes.

Other people who contributed their imaging expertise were Randy Foster and the accomplished nautical photographer, Tim Du Vernet.

A special thanks to my many friends, colleagues and family members who made thoughtful and useful recommendations to the advanced edition of the book; some of these are reflected in this edition.

This project has stretched over twenty years, so the patient support provided by my wife, Phyllis, has been crucial. However, she contributed in other ways. She too is a filmmaker, and was my colleague in making the first IMAX films in space. She is particularly adept at mastering the mysteries of technology, so it was no surprise to me that she discovered that *Heather Belle*'s registration can be found on the internet. That discovery is what got this book started.

Finally, in spite of racking my brain, I have probably omitted other people who have made significant contributions. If you, dear reader, are among them, please accept my deepest apologies.

My colleague, mentor and friend Graeme Ferguson died in May, 2021; his beloved wife Phyllis Ferguson had died eight weeks earlier.

Making sure *The Naphtha Revolution* was published was one of Graeme's final wishes. I sincerely thank Munro Ferguson, Stephen Low, Vicki Pasternak, Sue Avis and Barlow Books for their unstinting efforts to get us over the finish line.   Gayle Bonish, Artistic Director/Designer

Abbreviations

Consolidated: Gas Engine & Power Company and Charles L. Seabury & Company, Consolidated
Elco: Electric Launch Company
Garfield Report: Investigation Into the Causes of the Gold Panic
GEPC: Gas Engine and Power Company
Hepburn Report: Report of the Special Committee on Railroads, New York Assembly
MEMC: Marine Engine & Machine Company
MVEC: Marine Vapor Engine Company

Notes

Introduction

1. *The Rudder*, July 1890, p. 5

Chapter 1: The Naphtha Problem

1. Chandler, C. F., p. 32. Chandler's use of "inflammable" from "inflame" has the same meaning as "flammable."
2. Ibid., p. 35
3. Ibid., p. 43
4. Sweet, p. 78. In 1878 E.T. Sweet stated that gasoline boils at 120 °F, naphtha at 180 °F, benzine at 216 °F, and kerosene at 350 °F. In 1959 Harold F. Williamson and Arnold R. Daum listed average boiling points for gasoline as 110 °F, naphtha as 180 °F, benzine, 300 °F, and kerosene, 350 °F, but they pointed out that the numbers are imprecise, because petroleum contains thousands of hydrocarbon compounds. (Williamson, vol. I, pp. 207, 208)
5. Kerosene had recently replaced whale oil and coal oil (made from coal) as fuel for lamps. The Standard Oil Company called kerosene "refined oil." (Hidy and Hidy, p. 124), and it was also known as "refined petroleum." However, as long as the lamps continued in use – about a century – people doggedly called the fuel "coal oil," which it wasn't.
6. Chandler, C. F., p. 9
7. Ibid., pp. 32, 35. Naphtha stoves were also called gasoline stoves or vapor stoves.
8. Ibid., pp. 7, 14. In the early years some operators increased their yields to as much as 70 percent by destructive distillation (cracking), which used higher temperatures and much longer distillation times to break down the larger molecules into smaller ones. However, heavy uncontrolled cracking yielded an "abominable" kerosene, "malodorous, badly colored, unstable." This early form of cracking is not to be confused with modern cracking under pressure, invented by Dr. William Burton in 1912 to increase the yield of gasoline. (Williamson, vol. I, pp. 219, 229, and vol. II, pp. 136-150)
9. Williamson, vol. I, p. 238
10. Arter, Frank, quoted in Nevins, *Rockefeller*, vol. I, p. 269
11. Chandler, C. F., p. 14; Williamson, vol. I, p. 238
12. Chandler, C. F. pp. 16, 17
13. *Oil, Paint & Drug Reporter*, Nov. 1881, quoted in Williamson, vol. I, p. 524
14. MVEC catalog, 1896, p. 8
15. Sweet, p. 79
16. Chandler, C. F., pp. 48-51
17. Ibid., pp. 15, 39, 42, 47
18. Ibid., pp. 15, 16, 43
19. Ibid., p. 17

Chapter 2: The Inventor

1. Stuart, *Anecdotes*, Vol. I, p. 216. Stuart paraphrased Bacon's words, which were written in Latin. The original English text can be found in *Novum Organum*, First Book, Section 129, published by *Encyclopaedia Britannica*.
2. Tolf, p. 6
3. Church, vol. II, pp. 122, 123
4. Olsson & Ekström, pp. 6-8. The vevslup was not a Swedish invention; Leonardo da Vinci had proposed such a boat, and they had been used in Germany for some time.
5. St. Olai Church records
6. Bråthe, Lars, email to Bob Ofeldt, March 14, 1999. Herr Bråthe explains that, "å is pronounced like 'o' when a highbrow Englishman says 'more.'"
7. St. Olai Church records, Gunbritt Åhfeldt, email to Bob Ofeldt, May 21, 1999
8. *Popular Mechanics*, November, 1904, "The Story of the Inventor of the Naphtha Launch"
9. Jämshög *Household Examination Record*. AI: 14, 1853-65, p. 140, quoted by Lars Bråthe, email to author, January 9, 2005
10. Mokyr, p. 145
11. Bråthe, Lars, email to Bob Ofeldt, Dec. 1, 2002
12. Bråthe, Lars, email to author, Jan. 9, 2005
13. Emails, Gunbritt Åhfeldt to Bob Ofeldt, May 21 and 27, 1999, and Lars Bråthe to author, January 9, 2005
14. St. Olai Church records: Lars Bråthe, email to Bob Ofeldt, December 1, 2002
15. Norrköping City Archives, City Registration of Taxes, 1860: Bråthe, Lars, email to author, January 12, 2005. Herr Bråthe says that jernarbetare is "nowadays an unusual word in Swedish." Literally, it translates as "iron worker, but "metal worker" might be an alternative.

16 Bäcklund, Åke, to author, January 23, 2003
17 Dott, p. 22
18 Ibid., p. 18, summarized by Leif Axbåge
19 Bäcklund, Åke, to author, November 14, 2002 and January 23, 2003
20 St. Olai Church records
21 Bråthe, Lars, email to Bob Ofeldt, December 1, 2002
22 Church, vol. I, pp. 35, 36, 40
23 Ibid., pp. 201, 202, 204
24 Ibid., pp. 192, 193
25 Ericsson, John, quoted in Church, vol. I, pp. 195, 196
26 Cardwell, *The Norton History of Technology*, p. 282, and *Turning Points in Western Technology*, p. 163. In *From Watt to Clausius*, p. 152, Cardwell states that, "A cubic foot of air expands by about one-third between the freezing- and boiling-points of water while a cubic foot of steam expands 1,800-fold."
27 Church, vol. I, pp. 192, 193
28 Ericsson, John, to G.V. Fox, quoted in Church, vol. I, p. 262
29 Rosen, p. 322. Thomas Jefferson was also an inventor, but declined to apply for patents. (Freeberg, p. 147)
30 Church, vol. I, pp. 249-251
31 MacCord, Professor C.W., quoted in Church, vol. I, p. 256
32 Church, vol. II, pp. 233, 234
33 Ibid., vol. II, pp. 245, 246
34 Ibid., vol. I, pp. 279, 280
35 Ibid., vol. II, pp. 96, 219, footnote
36 Wilson, vol. IV, p. 239
37 Church, vol. II, pp. 76, 120
38 St. Olai Church records
39 Bråthe, Lars, email to Bob Ofeldt, December 1, 2002. The author may have misunderstood the order of these moves.
40 *Norrköping Tidningar*, September 6, 1864 (translated by Frank Asplund)
41 Bergengren, p. 28
42 Frängsmyr, pp. 9, 10
43 Bergengren, p. 112
44 Norrköping City Archives, 1865; Bråthe, Lars, email to author, January 12, 2005
45 Norrköping tax roll
46 Lindberg, pp. 56, 212
47 Church, vol. II, pp. 231-232
48 St. Olai Church records, Bäcklund to author, November 14, 2002
49 St. Olai Church records

Chapter 3: Everything He Touched Turned to Gold

1 Gale, pp. 50, 51
2 Boyle, vol. I, p. 918
3 *New York Times*, August 18, 1892. The other Baptists were John D. Rockefeller, Charles Pratt, and John D. Archbold.
4 Boyle, vol. I, p. 918
5 Nevins, *Rockefeller*, vol. I, p. 512
6 Josephson, p. 50
7 Hidy and Hidy, pp. 27, 315
8 Nevins, *The War for the Union*, vol. III, p. 352
9 Van Deusen, pp. 288, 289
10 Nevins, *The War for the Union*, vol. III, pp. 343-372
11 Hidy and Hidy, pp. 27, 315
12 Chandler, C.F., pp. 3, 22
13 Williamson, vol. I, pp. 44-48
14 Booth, James C. and Garrett, Thos. H., "Experiments on Illumination with Mineral Oils" (J. Franklin Institute, vol. XLIII, 1862, pp. 373-380, quoted in Forbes, *More Studies in Early Petroleum History*, p. 130); Gale, p. 53
15 *The Living Age*, September 1860, quoted in Nevins, *Rockefeller*, vol. I, p. 167
16 McLaurin, pp. 178, 346
17 Wright, pp. 213, 215, 216
18 Tarbell, vol. I, p. 22
19 Wright, p. 236
20 Tarbell, vol. I, p.10; McLaurin, p. 74
21 Dolson, p. 100
22 Tarbell, vol. I, p. 31
23 Wright, p. 106
24 Tarbell, vol. I, p. 22
25 Ibid, vol. I, pp. 18, 19
26 Gale, p. 40. For an analysis of the costs of building and operating refineries, see Williamson, vol. I, pp. 282-286
27 Williamson vol. I, p. 287
28 McLaurin, pp. 314, 315
29 Ibid., pp. 311-313
30 Tarbell, vol. I, p. 18
31 Hidy and Hidy, vol. I, p. 27
32 Hepburn Report, p. 2679 (Testimony of Jabez Bostwick)
33 Ibid.
34 Chandler, C.F., p. 7
35 Tarbell, vol. I, p. 21, footnote
36 Hepburn Report, p. 2677 (Testimony of Jabez Bostwick)
37 Tarbell, vol. I, p. 28
38 Nevins, *Rockefeller*, vol. I, p. 512
39 Boyle, vol. I, p. 931
40 Tarbell, vol. I, p. 181
41 Chernow, *Titan*, p. 171
42 Boyle, vol. I, p. 921
43 Ibid., p. 134
44 Ibid., p. 139
45 Nevins, *Rockefeller*, vol. I, p. 339
46 Boyle, vol. I, p. 140
47 Nevins, *Rockefeller*, vol. I, p. 436; Hidy and Hidy, p. 27; Chernow, *Titan*, p. 134; Williamson, vol. I, p. 353

Chapter 4: The Star Gas Machine

1. Nevins, *Ordeal Of The Union*, vol. II, p. 251
2. Strong, vol. III, p. 304
3. Roper, pp. 21-34, 84, 86, 87
4. Olmsted, F.L., "Yeoman," *New York Daily Times*, February 19, 1853, quoted in Roper, p. 89
5. Roper, pp. 129, 137
6. *Appleton's Annual Cyclopedia*, 1862, p. 20, quoted in Lee, p. 57
7. Maxwell, William Quentin, p. 5, quoted in Roper, p. 159
8. Nevins, *The War For The Union*, vol. III, p. 317
9. Nevins, *Ordeal Of The Union*, vol. I, p. 58
10. *Popular Mechanics*, November 1904, "The Story of the Inventor of the Naphtha Launch"
11. *Brooklyn Eagle*, July 15, 1867, "Trouble at Prospect Park"
12. Roper, p. 140
13. *Popular Mechanics*, November 1904, "The Story of the Inventor of the Naphtha Launch"
14. Gale, pp. 44, 45
15. Forbes: *More Studies in Early Petroleum History*, pp. 167-169
16. Williamson, vol. I, pp. 241, 242
17. *Chemical News*, vol. XVII, 1868, pp. 224, 225, "Petroleum Fuel for Steamships," quoted in Forbes, *More Studies in Early Petroleum History*, pp. 164, 165
18. *Popular Mechanics*, November 1904, "The Story of the Inventor of the Naphtha Launch"
19. Åhfeldt, Gunbritt, email to Bob Ofeldt, May 21, 1999
20. Svenska Emigrantinstitutet Växjö, February 20, 2002, Bäcklund to author, January 23, 2003
21. Patent 131, 369, September 17, 1872, *Improvement in Carbureters*, p. 1
22. Marvin, pp. 255, 256
23. Boyle, vol. I, p. 131
24. Patent 131, 966, October 8, 1872, *Improvement in Oil-burning Steam-Boilers*, p. 1
25. Josephson, *Edison*, p. 180
26. Hidy and Hidy, p. 116
27. Williamson, vol. I, pp. 235-238
28. Forbes, *More Studies in Early Petroleum History*, pp. 130, 131
29. Ford, William M.
30. Patent 131,966, October 8, 1872, *Improvement in Oil-Burning Steam-Boilers*, p. 1
31. *Old Timers News*, February 1950, p. 9
32. *Syracuse Daily Standard*, June 6, 1873, "Star Gas Machine"
33. *Old Timers News*, February 1950, p. 9, "Built Car Like Carriage for Sake of Horses"
34. Ford, William M.
35. Patent 162,848, May 4, 1875, *Improvement in Gas Apparatus for Carbureting Air*, p. 1
36. Patent 184,049, November 7, 1876, *Improvement in Automatic Heat-Regulators for Gas-Machines*, p. 2
37. Patent 189,873, April 24, 1877, *Improvement in Gas-Machines*, p. 1
38. Patent 162,848, May 4, 1875, Patent 184,049, November 7, 1876, Patent 189,873, April 24, 1877
39. Williamson, vol. I, p. 238
40. Williamson, vol. I, p. 682; Nevins, *Rockefeller*, vol. II, pp. 20, 21. Dr. W. M. Burton told Allan Nevins that "the popular name for gasolene was 'gas-house naphtha,' for much of (it) was sold to gas manufacturers" to make carbureted water gas. (Nevins, *Rockefeller*, vol. I, p. 270)
41. *New York Tribune*, September 28, 1878, quoted in Josephson, *Edison*, p. 181
42. *Edison Laboratory Notebook*, No. 184, 1878, quoted in Josephson, *Edison*, p. 181
43. Josephson, *Edison*, pp. 181, 222
44. *Newark City Directory*, 1881-1882, p. 652

Chapter 5: Taking the Fifth

1. Hepburn Report, vol. II, pp. 1668-1669, quoted in Tarbell, vol. II, p. 388
2. Chernow, p. 130
3. Tarbell, vol. I, p. 42; Nevins, *Rockefeller*, vol. I, pp. 178, 179
4. Hidy and Hidy, p. 13
5. Flynn, p. 177
6. Rockefeller, p. 13
7. Chandler, David Leon, pp. 78, 79
8. Nevins, *Rockefeller*, vol. I, pp. 438, 439
9. Williamson, vol. I, pp. 303-306
10. Chernow, p. 135
11. Flynn, p. 155; Lloyd, pp. 46, 47
12. Nevins, *Rockefeller*, vol. I, p. 324
13. Flynn, p. 156
14. Nevins, *Rockefeller*, vol. I, pp. 324, 325, 335
15. Chernow, *p. 138*
16. Tarbell, vol. I, p. 58
17. Hidy and Hidy, p. 27
18. Swanberg, pp. 38, 39
19. Ibid., p. 39
20. Nevins, *Rockefeller*, vol. I, p. 362
21. Flynn, p. 157
22. Swanberg, pp. 21, 37
23. Williamson, vol. I, p. 344
24. Flynn, pp. 157, 158
25. Williamson, vol. I, p. 355. Colonel Payne was paid in Standard Oil stock.
26. Flynn, p. 238; Chernow, p. 144. According to John J. McLaurin, Jabez Bostwick had preceded Payne as treasurer. (McLaurin, p. 421)
27. Chernow, p. 144
28. Ibid., p. 134
29. Tarbell, vol. I, p. 63
30. Ibid., p. 67
31. Lloyd, p. 64
32. Tarbell, vol. I, p. 68

33. Ibid., pp. 57, 58
34. Ibid., pp. 68, 69
35. Ibid., p. 37
36. Flynn, pp. 165-167
37. Nevins, *Rockefeller*, vol. I, p. 352
38. Flynn, p. 168
39. *Titusville Herald*, quoted in Moore, Austin Leigh, p. 82
40. Tarbell, vol. I, p. 180
41. Nevins, *Rockefeller*, vol. I, p. 337; Tarbell, vol. I, p. 94
42. This was a reversion to what the Standard Oil men called "Our Plan," worked out by John D. Rockefeller and Henry Flagler before Jabez Bostwick joined the company. (Nevins, *Rockefeller*, vol. I, pp. 312-313)
43. Tarbell, vol. II, p. 252
44. *Scientific American*, May 18, 1872, pp. 341, 342, quoted in Forbes, *More Studies in Early Petroleum History*, p. 126. Professor C. F. Chandler also found Astral Oil to be the safest kerosene sold in New York.
45. Lawson, p. 17
46. Hidy and Hidy, p. 30; Williamson, vol. I, pp. 269-271
47. Nevins, *Rockefeller*, vol. I., pp. 477, 478
48. Tarbell, vol. II, p. 252
49. Chernow, p. 165
50. Flynn, p. 166
51. Moore, Austin Leigh, pp. 110, 111
52. Chernow, p. 166; Flynn, p. 190
53. Flynn, p. 189
54. Tarbell, vol. II, p. 251
55. Flynn, p. 221
56. Hepburn Report, p. 2688
57. Nevins, *Rockefeller*, vol. I, p. 448. Standard Oil also assisted the Erie by buying its tank cars, which at $700 cost almost twice as much as a boxcar. (Williamson, vol. I, pp. 414, 530)
58. Nevins, *Rockefeller*, vol. I, p. 652 (footnote), Hidy and Hidy, vol. I, p. 54
59. Hepburn Report, pp. 2690-2692
60. *New York Tribune*, June 24, 1879, reporting Hepburn Committee testimony, quoted in Nevins, *Rockefeller*, vol. II, p. 40
61. Tarbell, vol. I, pp. 156, 157
62. Nevins, *Rockefeller*, vol. I, pp. 544, 545
63. Tarbell, vol. I, pp. 210-212
64. Nevins, *Rockefeller*, vol. I, p. 552. In 1880-83 the Bradford field furnished the bulk of the world's consumption (Williamson, vol. I, p. 390)
65. Boyle, vol. I, p. 713
66. Tarbell, vol. I, p. 216,
67. Nevins, *Rockefeller*, vol. I, p. 554
68. Lloyd, p. 105
69. Tarbell, vol. I, p. 217
70. Nevins, *Rockefeller*, vol. I, p. 555
71. Chernow, p. 198; Tarbell, vol. I, p. 224
72. Tarbell, vol. I, p. 224
73. Flynn, p. 213
74. Lloyd, pp. 105, 106
75. Tarbell, vol. I, p. 224
76. Ibid., p. 239
77. Nevins, *Rockefeller*, vol. I, p. 570
78. Flynn, p. 218
79. Moore, Austin Leigh, pp. 115-118
80. Nevins, *Rockefeller*, vol. I, p. 486
81. Hepburn Report, p. 2709
82. Nevins, *Rockefeller*, vol. II, p. 42
83. Hepburn Report, pp. 2601, 2602
84. Ibid., p. 2683
85. Ibid., p. 2686
86. Ibid., p. 2705
87. Ibid., pp. 2694-2708
88. Ibid., pp. 2704-2705
89. Hepburn Report, p. 42, quoted in Lloyd, p. 473. The Standard Oil men again found an opponent they admired, and a few years later Rockefeller invited Hepburn to become a trustee of the Rockefeller Foundation, a position Hepburn was honored to accept. (Flynn, p. 218)
90. Flynn, p. 198
91. Rockefeller, pp. 65, 67
92. Schumpeter, p. 106
93. Nevins, *Rockefeller*, vol. 1, p. 676
94. Ibid., p. 237
95. Chernow, p. 223
96. Nevins, *Rockefeller*, vol. I, p. 674
97. Rockefeller, pp. 6, 10
98. Nevins, *Rockefeller*, vol. I, p. 612
99. Lloyd, p. 55
100. Flynn, p. 249
101. Lloyd, p. 55
102. Flynn, p. 251
103. Hidy and Hidy, p. 56. The other trustees were the Rockefeller brothers, Oliver Payne, Charles Pratt, Henry Flagler, John D. Archbold, W. G. Warden, and Benjamin Brewster, a Cleveland financier.
104. Nevins, *Rockefeller*, vol. I. p. 614
105. Tarbell, vol. II, p. 141
106. Nevins, *Rockefeller*, vol. I, p. 613
107. Flynn, p. 252
108. Nevins, *Rockefeller*, vol. I, p. 618

Chapter 6: The Naphtha Launch

1. Trollope, quoted in Ierley, p. 15
2. Babbage, Charles, *The Great Exposition of 1851,* quoted in Cardwell, *Turning Points in Western Technology,* p. 163
3. Stephens, William P., *Cassier's Magazine,* May-October, 1903, pp. 290, 291, "Modern American Launch Motors"
4. Birdsall, Edward T., M.E., *The Rudder,* May 1896, p. 129, "Gas and Vapor Marine Engines"
5. MacDuffie, Malcolm, *National Fisherman,* May 1971, p. 4B. "Naphtha Launch – the Missing Link." Weston Farmer described MacDuffie as "a naval architect who forsook M.I.T. engineering and the feast-or-famine yacht designing game to teach religion and do his praying in church." (Farmer, pp. 232, 233)
6. Harniman, Ken, *Nyack Journal-News* (1970?), "Remember? Get a Horse!"
7. "Ofeldt Patent Listing," website: Genealogy/Patents.xls
8. Lincoln, John W., *The Steam Automobile,* Fall 1980, p. 13, "The Naphtha Launch, The Steamless Steam Motorboat of 1885"
9. Mokyr, p. 249
10. Birdsall, Edward T., *The Rudder,* May, 1896, p. 129, "Gas and Vapor Marine Engines"
11. Hawkesworth, John, quoted in Stuart, *Anecdotes,* vol. II, p. 342.
12. Smiles, pp. 75, 80
13. Dr. John Robinson, quoted in Muirhead, p. 67
14. Rosen, pp. 99, 100
15. *James Watt and the Steam Engine* (author not identified), The Religious Tract Society, p. 70
16. Robison, Dr. John, quoted in Muirhead, p. 67
17. Hart, Robert, in *Transactions of the Glasgow Archaeological Society, 1859,* "Reminiscences of James Watt," quoted in Smiles, pp. 89-91
18. Smiles, p. 91
19. Haig-Brown
20. Patent 279,270, June 12, 1883
21. Uglow, p. 100
22. Stuart, *Anecdotes,* vol. II, pp. 585, 599
23. Cardwell, *Norton History of Technology,* p. 213
24. *Modern Mechanisms,* a supplementary volume to *Appletons' Cyclopaedia of Applied Mechanics,* p. 272
25. Durham, March-April 1961, p. 14
26. Patent 279,270, *Naphtha Engine,* June 12, 1883, p. 1
27. Ibid., p. 2
28. Birdsall, Edward T., *The Rudder,* May, 1896, p. 129, "Gas and Vapor Marine Engines"
29. "Powered by Boiling Petrol," *The Museum of Retro Technology* (website), p. 7, quoting unnamed source.
30. Forbes, *More Studies in Early Petroleum History,* pp. 68, 69
31. Escher Wyss catalog, 1897, p. 10
32. GEPC catalog, 1887, p. 3. "Unless deodorized, [naphtha] has a vile organic smell." (Fostle, p. 21)
33. Durant, p. 11
34. Farmer, Weston, *Yachting,* July 1973, p. 38, "Those Wonderful Naphtha Launches"
35. Kunhardt, p. 90
36. Fuller, Benjamin A. G., *Log of Mystic Seaport,* Autumn 1993, p. 36, "The Coming of the Explosive Engine, 1885-1910"
37. Muirhead, pp. 257, 258
38. Smiles, pp. 439-431 and 334, footnote
39. Rockefeller, p. 88
40. Hidy and Hidy, p. 116
41. American Biographical Library
42. Summerscale, p. 10
43. *New York Times,* August 18, 1892, "Jabez A. Bostwick's Death"
44. Chandler, David Leon, p. 91
45. Rousmaniere, *The Golden Pastime,* p. 111
46. Parkinson, vol. I, p. 111
47. *The Manufacturer and Builder,* vol. 16, Issue 3, March, 1884, p. 57
48. *Industries and Wealth of the Principal Points in Rhode Island,* 1882, quoted in *Providence Directory,* 1889
49. *Industries and Wealth of the Principal Points in Rhode Island,* 1882
50. *The Manufacturer and Builder,* March 1884, p. 57 and December 1891, p. 269. A 3-hp single cylinder double-acting Shipman engine was rebuilt by Everett MacFarlane, who added an outboard condenser. Everett told the author, "It runs well." The engine was in a boat offered for sale in *Classic Boat* (published by the Antique and Classic Boat Society, Toronto), April 2008. There are also three Shipman engines at the New England Wireless and Steam Museum.
51. *Forest and Stream,* December 31, 1885, quoted by Stephens, William P., *Motor Boating,* 1939, "Traditions and Memories of American Yachting, part 42, The Herreshoffs of Bristol – Continued" (reprinted 1981 and 1989 by Wooden Boat Publications). In the same article Stephens stated that, "The name 'Gas Engine & Power Company' was originally chosen for a proposed organization for the manufacture of gas engines for land use." Both stories could be true, but *Forest and Stream,* being contemporary, carries more weight. Also, we should take Stephens' recollections with a pinch of salt; in the same article he described Frank Ofeldt as a "clever German." L. Francis Herreshoff used Stephens' account as a source for his article, "Naphtha Launches," in *The Rudder,* November 1965, including the story that Ofeldt was German.
52. Lincoln, John W., *The Steam Automobile,* Fall 1980, pp. 12, 13, "The Naphtha Launch, the Steamless Steam Motorboat of 1885"
53. Prouty, W.A., *Asbury Park Press,* quoted in *Old Timers News,* February, 1950, p. 9
54. *New York Times,* August 18, 1892, "Jabez A. Bostwick's Death." The first reference we have found to his connection with GEPC was in the *Columbus* (Georgia) *Daily Enquirer,* August 24, 1890, which mentioned that, "J.A. Bostwick, Clement Gould, John J. Amory, Edward V. Cary, and others with capital took up the invention." Actually Gould, Amory, and Cary were officers of the company, and may not have been original investors.
55. GEPC Catalog, 1886, p. 1; *New York Times,* August 18, 1892 "Jabez A. Bostwick's Death"
56. Stephens, William P., *Motor Boating,* (1989 reprint of 1939 article), p. 191, "Traditions and Memories of American Yachting," part 42, "The Herreshoffs of Bristol – Continued"

57 GEPC catalog, 1886, p. 1
58 *Power Boating,* (date unknown), p. 53, "Building up the Industry"
59 Herreshoff, L. Francis, *The Rudder,* November 1965, p. 72, "Naphtha Launches"
60 Farmer, p. 346
61 *The Rudder,* May 1922, "Charles Lincoln Seabury"
62 *Power Boating,* (date unknown), p. 53, "Building up the Industry"
63 Patent 356,419, *Gas Engine,* January 18, 1887, pp. 1, 2
64 Ofeldt, Frank W. II, quoted in Lincoln, John W., *The Steam Automobile,* Fall, 1980, p. 10, "The Naphtha Launch, the Steamless Steam Motorboat of 1885." Max F. Holmfield explains that, "Since the force is always down, no provision was needed to retain the ball in the piston. There is a knuckle joint between the lower end of each rod and its bearing, so rod alignment is automatic." *The Weather Guage* (sic), 1991, "The Age of the Wonderful Naphtha Launch."
65 *Forest and Stream,* December 8, 1887, "A New American Industry – the Naphtha Launch"
66 Johnston and Kerlin, p. 33
67 Durant, p. 11
68 *Scientific American,* Mar. 16, 1895, "The Naphtha Launch of the Gas Engine and Power Company of New York City"
69 Lincoln, John W., *The Steam Automobile,* Fall 1980, p. 10, "The Naphtha Launch, the Steamless Steam Motorboat of 1885"
70 Patent 356,419, *Gas Engine,* January 18, 1887 p. 3. See also Trudgen, first edition, p. 23, second edition, p. 19: "A camshaft operated slide valves. The valves moved transversely across the cylinder heads, using a scotch yoke mechanism. The camshaft was gear-driven, turning at the same speed and in the same direction as the crankshaft. A wood-rimmed wheel was attached to the forward end of the crankshaft. Using a slip eccentric, a quarter turn of free play of this wheel would shift the valves, so slapping the wheel at any engine speed would slow the wheel enough to pick up the quarter turn of free play, shifting the valves, and instantly reversing the engine's direction of rotation."
71 *Consolidated* catalog, 1899, p. 19
72 Herreshoff, L. Francis, *The Rudder,* November 1965, p. 70, "Naphtha Launches." W. J. Chapman called the device a *slip eccentric.* (Chapman, Wilbur J., *Motor Boating,* December 1960, p. 123, "The Naphtha Launch, Relic of the 90's." The Mariners' Museum in Newport News has a naphtha engine with the inscription, "Pat. Sept. 22, 1881," on the top gear. Presumably the Gas Engine and Power Company acquired a license from the inventor to incorporate this feature in the naphtha engine.
73 Trudgen. On p. 43 of the first edition (p. 48 of the second edition) he lists all the changes.
74 Fostle, p. 23
75 Johnston and Kerlin, pp. 2, 5, 6
76 Chamberlain, p. 35
77 GEPC catalog, 1894, p. 15
78 *Forest and Stream,* December 8, 1887, "A New American Industry — The Naphtha Launch"
79 GEPC catalog, 1887, p. 17
80 *Scientific American Supplement,* No. 1104, February 27, 1897, p. 17650
81 Farmer, Weston, *Yachting,* July 1973, p. 39, "Those Wonderful Naphtha Launches," part I
82 *Scientific American,* Mar. 16, 1895, "The Naphtha Launch of the Gas Engine and Power Company of New York City"
83 Lincoln, John W., *The Steam Automobile,* Fall, 1980, p. 10, "The Naphtha Launch, The Steamless Steam Motorboat of 1885"
84 Herreshoff, L. Francis, *The Rudder,* November, 1965, p. 71, "Naphtha launches"
85 Farmer, Weston, *Yachting,* July, 1973, p. 88, "Those Wonderful Naphtha Launches"
86 *New York Times,* June 9, 1935, Sports Section, p. 6, "Yachtsmen Plan Ceremonies to Mark the Anniversary of Unique Craft"
87 Chapman, Wilbur J. *Motor Boating,* December 1960, p. 24, "The Naphtha Launch – Relic of the 90's,"
88 *The Manufacturer and Builder,* March 1881, p. 57
89 *Industries and Wealth of the Principal Points in Rhode Island,* 1882,

Chapter 7: The Steam Regulations

1 Farmer, Weston, *Yachting,* August, 1973, p. 46, "Those Wonderful Naphtha Launches, Part II"
2 Strong, Vol. IV, p. 377
3 Dixon, p. 33
4 Kunhardt, p. 108
5 Herreshoff, L. Francis, *The Rudder,* November 1965, p. 35, "Naphtha Launches"
6 MacDuffie, Malcolm, *National Fisherman,* May 1971, p. 4-B, "Naphtha Launch – The Missing Link"
7 Herreshoff, L. Francis, *The Rudder,* November 1965, p. 35, "Naphtha Launches"
8 Fostle, p. 23
9 MacDuffie, Malcolm, *National Fisherman,* May 1971, p. 19-B, "Naphtha Launch — The Missing Link"
10 Durham, March-April, 1961, p. 14
11 Farmer, Weston, *Yachting,* August 1973, p. 46, "Those Wonderful Naphtha Launches, Part II"
12 Kunhardt, p. 107,
13 Muirhead, pp. 247, 248
14 Yergin, p. 104
15 Chernow, pp. 212, 213
16 Whitney, William, to Joseph Pulitzer, December 19, 1883, quoted in Hirsch, p. 232
17 Hirsch, p. 11

18 Ibid., p. 34
19 Swanberg, p. 44
20 Hirsch, pp. 55, 91
21 Nevins, *Cleveland*, p. 97
22 Milburn, John G., *Scribner's Magazine*, April 1927, p. 346, "Cleveland's View of Public Life"
23 McElroy, p. 26
24 Armitage, p. 141
25 Brooks, p. 335
26 Armitage, p. 158
27 Hirsch, p. 184
28 Nevins, *Cleveland*, p. 103
29 Graff, p. 27
30 Hirsch, p. 190; Parker, p. 55
31 Lynch, p. 115
32 Parker, p. 55
33 Nevins, *Cleveland*, pp. 113, 132, 194
34 Ibid., pp. 320, 325
35 Josephson, *The Politicos*, p. 383
36 Nevins, *Cleveland*, pp. 125, 320, 325
37 Hirsch, pp. 204, 205
38 *New York Times*, July 8, 1884, quoted in Lynch, pp. 182, 183
39 Merrill, p. 53
40 Hirsch, p. 235
41 Nevins, *Cleveland*, p. 160
42 Hirsch, p. 238; Nevins, *Cleveland*, p. 178
43 Graff, p. 57; Nevins, *Cleveland*, p. 177
44 Hirsch, p. 170
45 Chernow, p. 291. Some of the money came from Oliver Payne's father, Senator Henry B. Payne.
46 Yergin, p. 104
47 Lynch, p. 284
48 Ford, Henry Jones, p. 42
49 Milburn, John G., *Scribner's Magazine*, April 1927, p. 344, "Cleveland's View of Public Life"
50 Tugwell, pp. 99, 128
51 Nevins, *Cleveland*, p. 194
52 Chernow, p. 291
53 *Springfield* (Mass.) *Republican*, quoted in Swanberg, p. 78
54 *Philadelphia Press*, January 3, 11, 1885, quoted in Hirsch, p. 250
55 Lynch, p. 296
56 Hudson, p. 243
57 Hirsch, p. 252
58 *Washington Post*, February, 19, 26, 1885, quoted in Hirsch, p. 252
59 Hirsch, p. 253.
60 Swanberg, p. 9
61 Nevins, *Cleveland*, p. 217
62 Mahan, Vol. I, p. 544, quoted in Zimmerman, p. 87
63 Hirsch, pp. 292, 308, 309
64 Josephson, *The Politicos*, p. 378
65 Swanberg, p. 15
66 Chandler, David Leon, pp. 98, 100,

67 Lloyd, p. 402: "It is the Secretary of the Navy who passes upon the speed of the ships receiving subsidies; and his findings are binding upon the Post-office Department which awards the contracts and upon the Treasury Department which pays."
68 Swanberg, p. 163
69 Some writers have suggested that it was a desire to get around the steam regulations that gave Frank Ofeldt the idea of inventing the naphtha launch. L. Francis Herreshoff wrote that, "The real, and possibly the only reason, for the naphtha launch was to get around the law that required a licensed engineer on a steam launch." (*The Rudder*, Nov. 1965, pp. 34, 35, "Naphtha Launches.") Herreshoff's information is questionable, as he was born in 1890 and probably never met Frank Ofeldt. As we have noted previously, in the same article he said that Frank Ofeldt was a German (an idea he copied from William P. Stephens' "Traditions and Memories of American Yachting," in *Motor Boating*, 1939), another indication that he relied on hearsay. Another source of this theory about Frank's motivation was Frank's grandson, Frank W. Ofeldt II. On April 10, 1945 he wrote to John W. Lincoln: "The basic reason for (the naphtha engine) was to avoid the restrictions of the steam boiler and steam navigation laws so as to enable the average person to obtain the benefits and pleasures of motor boating." (Lincoln, John W., *The Steam Automobile*, vol. 22, No. 4, Fall 1980.) On the other hand, as we have noted in chapter four, Frank II's brother, Ernest, explained: "In those days gasoline was a by-product in the manufacture of kerosene and was considered worthless by the big oil companies. This posed a challenge to grandfather and soon he began to experiment with this waste product. The first results of his work took the form of a machine for lighting homes with gasoline." I am inclined to believe Ernest. All through their lives members of the Ofeldt family had heard about the naphtha engine's success in evading the steam regulations, so it is hardly surprising that over the decades some of them came to believe that Frank had cleverly designed the engine just to achieve that purpose. It appears that the inventor's single-minded motivation, since he had begun the invention of the Star Gas Machine, was to find a use for the low-price naphthas. In inventing the naphtha engine, he simply continued that quest. We have found no evidence that he thought about the steam regulations until after he rotated the engine to give the skipper access to the controls. Even then, the evasion of regulations may have been Jabez Bostwick's idea, not Frank's.

Chapter 8: Bostwick's Strategy

1. Veblen, p.191
2. Fostle, p. 29
3. GEPC catalog, 1886, p. 5
4. Patent 356,419, *Gas Engine,* January 18, 1887. It was prudent to broaden the uses of the invention, so four months later Frank filed a companion application, *Pressure-Generator for Naphtha-Engines,* in which "the apparatus...is the same [but] the vapor thus obtained [is utilized] either as the motive power in an engine or for producing an illuminating and heating gas, or both...or for other purposes." (Patent No. 356,420, Jan. 18, 1887)
5. *Forest and Stream,* December 31, 1885, "A New Gas Engine," quoted in Stephens, William P., *Motor Boating,* 1939, re-published 1981 and 1989, "Traditions and Memories of American Yachting"
6. GEPC catalog, 1886, cover, pp. 1, 3
7. Parkinson, vol. I, pp. 56, 57, 64, 68, 533
8. Cookman, p. 37
9. Parkinson, vol. I, p. 127
10. Ibid., pp. 127, 128
11. Holm, p. 72
12. Parkinson, vol. I, p. 127
13. *Forest and Stream,* December 8, 1887
14. GEPC catalog, 1887, p. 22
15. Ibid., p. 11
16. Ibid., p. 7
17. Chamberlain, p. 38
18. Ibid., p. 27: "The ordinary stove gasoline, now in common use everywhere, may take the place of the naphtha when the grade mentioned is not to be conveniently had."
19. GEPC catalog, 1887, cover, pp. 10, 12, 13, 16, 17, 23
20. GEPC catalog, 1886, p. 2
21. Durant, p. 11
22. MacDuffie, Malcolm, *National Fisherman,* May, 1971, p. 4-B, "Naphtha Launch – the Missing Link"
23. The valve was also termed a damper. (GEPC 1892 catalog, p. 55)
24. McConnell, Chrystie, *The Ensign,* Feb. 1967, p. 21, "The Redoubtable Naphtha Launch." For alternative instructions, see Chamberlain, p. 37, or Trudgen, first edition p. 32, second edition p. 37.
25. Chamberlain, p. 28
26. Trudgen, Bruce, *The Ensign*, November/December, 2008, p. 21, "The Naphtha Launch"
27. *Consolidated* catalog, 1897, p. 51
28. McConnell, Chrystie, *The Ensign,* February, 1967, p. 21, "The Redoubtable Naphtha Launch"
29. GEPC catalog, 1887, pp. 15, 19; Chamberlain, back page
30. *Forest and Stream,* Dec. 8, 1887, "A New American Industry – The Naphtha Launch"
31. Rosen, p. 235
32. Josephson, *The Robber Barons*, p. 101
33. Gladwell, pp. 116-117
34. Church, vol. II, p. 160
35. Church, vol. I, p. 86, in part quoting Du Chaillu
36. Nevins, *Rockefeller*, vol. I, p. 394
37. Flynn, p. 236
38. Winkler, p. 67, quoted in Chernow, p. 180
39. Lloyd, p. 184. For an account of other inventors who had tried continuous distillation see Williamson, vol. I, pp. 266-268.
40. Hidy and Hidy, pp. 51, 206
41. Lloyd, pp. 187-195
42. McLaurin, p. 422
43. Josephson, *The Robber Barons*, p. 101
44. GEPC catalog, 1887, p. 1

Chapter 9: Nobel's *Mignon*

1. Bergengren, p. 182
2. Bergengren, pp. 37-41
3. Tolf, pp. 26, 30, 31, 39, 45
4. Tolf, pp. 40, 41
5. Forbes: *Bitumen and Petroleum in Antiquity*, Table I
6. Tolf, pp. 43, 44; Fant, p. 205
7. Forbes, *Studies In Early Petroleum History*, p. 162
8. Tolf, pp. 34, 45, 46, 47, 49
9. Yergin, p. 116
10. Tolf, p. 54
11. Marvin, p. 283
12. Nevins, *Rockefeller*, vol. II, p. 30
13. Isaacson, p. 105
14. Tolf, p. 55, 56; Marvin, p. 283
15. Fant, p. 223; Marvin, p. 287
16. Tolf, pp. 66, 67, 74, 75. According to Williamson and Daum, It may have been Alfred Nobel who suggested trying continuous distillation. (Williamson, vol. I, p. 517)
17. Marvin, p. 294
18. Tolf, p. 98
19. Marvin, p. 294
20. Marvin, pp. 234-236, 239, 246-249
21. Tolf, pp. 56, 61, 62, 64, 80
22. Williamson, vol. I, p. 516
23. Marvin, p. 300
24. Tolf, p. 80
25. Bergengren, p. 155
26. Sohlman, p. 34
27. Lindqvist, p.36
28. Bergengren, pp. 108, 109
29. Hellberg and Jansson, p. 9
30. Strandh, *Aluminium*, pp. 29, 30
31. Strandh, *Alfred Nobel*, p. 248
32. Strandh, *Aluminium*, p. 30
33. *100 Jahre Escher Wyss Ravensburg*
34. Escher Wyss catalog, 1912, p. 13

35 Escher Wyss catalog, 1897, p. 19
36 Ibid., p. 20, quoting *Nouvelle Gazette de Zurich*, July 21, 1891
37 Ibid., p. 10, 20, 31, 32
38 *Rudder, Sail and Paddle*, February 1892, p. 54, "A Boat Built of Aluminium"
39 *Frankfurt Gazette*, July 26, 1891, quoted in Escher Wyss catalog, 1897, p. 20
40 Martin and Sachs, p. 1
41 Hawthorne, p. 7, quoting, in part, *The Times*
42 Hawthorne, p. 10
43 Martin and Sachs, p. 13
44 Barnes (Lady Yarrow), p. 166
45 Martin and Sachs, p. 14
46 Hawthorne, p. 26
47 Strandh, *Aluminium*, p. 30
48 Fuller, Benjamin A.G., *The Log of Mystic Seaport*, Autumn 1993, p. 35, "The Coming of the Explosive Engine"
49 Dixon, p. 82; Grayson, pp. 4, 5
50 Simms, Frederick P., to Alfred Nobel, November 10, 1891, Nobel Archives (Courtesy Åke Bäcklund), translated by Paul Ehnes
51 Ibid., November 12 and 17, 1891
52 Strandh, *Alfred Nobel, Mannen, Verket, Samtiden*, p. 249
53 Bergengren, p. 182
54 Fant, p. 334
55 *Engineering*, September 9, 1892, p. 320, "Aluminium Naphtha Yacht 'Mignon' "
56 *Nouvelle Gazette de Zurich*, September 12, 1892, quoted in Escher Wyss catalog, 1897, p. 27
57 Hellberg and Jansson, p. 61
58 Bergengren, pp. 191, 192
59 Fant, p. 334
60 Bergengren, p. 194
61 Ibid., pp. 189, 190, 195
62 Lindqvist, p. 27
63 Bäcklund, Åke, to author, Jan. 7, 2007

Chapter 10: Starting Over

1 Nevins, *Rockefeller*, vol. II, p. 712
2 Ofeldt catalog, 1903, p. 4
3 *Popular Mechanics*, November 1904, "The Story of the Inventor of the Naphtha Launch"
4 Ibid.
5 *Outing*, September 1888, p. 575, "Our Monthly Record"
6 Parkinson, vol. I, pp. 120, 121
7 *Brooklyn Eagle*, April 20, 1884, p. 2, "Yachting Affairs"
8 *New York Times*, September 25, 1890
9 *The Rudder*, February 10, 1891, p. 7, "Personal"
10 *Outing*, September 1888, p. 575, "Our Monthly Record"
11 *Popular Mechanics*, November, 1904, "The Story of the Inventor of the Naphtha Launch"
12 *Brooklyn Directory*, 1889, in Ancestry.com
13 Ofeldt, Bob, to Karl Petersen, October 8, 2000
14 Nyack newspaper (unidentified), September 16, 1954, "Frank A. Ofeldt, Builder of Cars in Days of Steamers, Dies at his Nyack Home"
15 *Brooklyn Eagle*, April 15, 1889, p. 1, "Preparing the Yachts"
16 Ibid., May 23, 1889, p. 1, "Among the Yachts"
17 Chamberlain, p. 31
18 *Brooklyn Eagle*, April 19, 1890, p. 1, "News of the Yachts"
19 Ibid., May 1, 1890, p. 6, "The Steam Launch Crescent"
20 U. S. Coast Guard web site
21 Benedict, vol. I, p. 126
22 Summers, Captain James C., *The Rudder*, June 1916, pp. 261, 265
23 Stedman, p. 468
24 Summers, Captain James C., *The Rudder*, June 1916, p. 265
25 Sobel, *Panic on Wall Street*, p. 114
26 Clews, p. 6
27 Sobel, *The Big Board*, p. 63
28 Moore, Whitney, *E.C.B Brief Bio*
29 Fowler, pp. 185, 187
30 Carpenter, p. 107. Andrew Greg Curtin was Governor of Pennsylvania.
31 Medbery, p. 251
32 Fowler, p.75; Summers, Captain James C., *The Rudder*, June 1916, p. 265
33 Garfield Report, p. 56 (Testimony of Henry M. Benedict)
34 Smith, M.H., pp. 62, 63, 83
35 Ackerman, p. 48
36 Sobel, *Panic on Wall Street*, pp. 135, 136
37 Adams, p. 113
38 Fowler, p. 515
39 Adams, p. 114
40 O'Connor, p. 39
41 Garfield Report, p. 358, (Testimony of George Boutwell)
42 Clews, p. 193
43 Garfield Report, p. 358, (Testimony of George Boutwell)
44 Ackerman, pp. 88, 171; Garfield Report, p. 14
45 Stedman, pp. 227, 228
46 Ackerman, pp. 214, 222
47 Fowler, p. 525
48 Ackerman, p. 238
49 Summers, Captain James C., *The Rudder*, June 1916, p. 265
50 *New York Times*, November 24, 1920, "E. C. Benedict Dies in his 87th Year"
51 Summers, Capt. James C., *The Rudder*, June 1916, p. 263, "Com. E. C. Benedict, Veteran Yachtsman"
52 Chandler, David Leon, p. 105
53 Moore, Whitney, *Some Things Never Change*, p. 49
54 Benedict, E.C., *Valentine's Manual of Old New York*, No. 5, 1921, pp. 22, 23. Cleveland's companion was Daniel Lamont, who had been his right-hand man since his days as Governor of New York.
55 Ibid., pp. 22, 23, 44
56 Satterlee, p. 302
57 Moore, Whitney, *Nautical Quarterly*, No. 49, Spring, 1990, p. 107
58 Jeffers, p. 225
59 Benedict, E.C., *Valentine's Manual of Old New York*, No. 5, 1921, p. 23

60 Ibid., p. 38
61 Bassett, p. 112
62 Bergh, p. 155
63 Bassett, pp. 114-115
64 GEPC catalog, 1892, p. 24
65 Jersey City, N. J. Directory, 1893

Chapter 11: The Bostwick Legacy

1. Birdsall, Edward T., *The Rudder*, May 1896, p. 129, "Gas and Vapor Marine Engines"
2. *New York Times*, August 18, 1892, "Jabez A. Bostwick's Death"
3. Hidy and Hidy, pp. 56, 315; Nevins, *Rockefeller*, vol. I, p. 659
4. Chernow, p. 291
5. *New York Herald*, quoted in Nevins, *Rockefeller*, vol. II, p. 114 (and footnote)
6. *New York Times*, August 18, 1892, "Jabez A. Bostwick's Death"
7. Summerscale, pp. 10, 11; *New York Times*, Aug. 18, 1892, "Jabez A. Bostwick's Death"
8. *New York Times*, August 18, 1892, "Jabez A. Bostwick's Death"
9. McLaurin, p. 422
10. Summerscale, p. 55
11. *New York Times*, August 20, 1892, "Funeral of Jabez A. Bostwick"
12. Chernow, p. 134
13. Nevins, *Rockefeller*, vol. II, p. 454
14. *New York Times*, August 18, 1892, "Jabez A. Bostwick's Death"
15. American Biographical Library
16. Chernow, pp. 153, 154
17. Flynn, pp. 199, 200, 403
18. Tawney, pp. 200, 204
19. Playfair, John, *Monthly Magazine*, 1819, quoted in Stuart, *History*, p. 122.
20. Nature (the French journal), July 21, 1888, quoted in *The Museum of Retro Technology* (internet site)
21. Durham, July-August, 1961, p. 21, "Naphtha Launch Imitators"
22. GEPC catalog, 1892, pp. 58, 75
23. Seabury catalog, 1893, p. 49
24. Partelow catalog, 1891. Partelow described its boats as naptha (sic) launches.
25. *Columbus* (Georgia) *Daily Enquirer*, August 24, 1890, p. 11, "Naphtha Launches. The Remarkable Rapid Growth of this Novel Craft"
26. *Brooklyn Eagle*, July 13, 1891, p. 6, "Down to Death"
27. *Brooklyn Eagle*, July 15, 1891, p. 6, "Both Bodies Recovered"
28. GEPC catalog, 1892, pp. 10, 76, 77
29. See Trudgen, first edition p. 29, second edition p. 7: "Boat naphtha…wasn't available everywhere, so some owners substituted other naphtha products. Consequently, their engines didn't always put out their full rated horsepower, but as petroleum technology improved, the quality and consistency of their naphtha products improved. Eventually, the company advised owners, 'Our tests show that petroleum products under the names launch naphtha, deodorized naphtha, stove gas, motor gasoline, or red crown gasoline will give satisfactory results in our engines.'"
30. *Cautionary Notes*, 1890, inside front cover, pp. 1, 6, 30
31. *Oswego Palladium*, August 5, 1889, "A Buffalo Holocaust"
32. According to Chamberlain, p. 32, "The *Leo* was a steam launch, using kerosene oil for fuel." Perhaps the *Times* story was incorrect.
33. *New York Times*, Sept. 21, 1889
34. Chamberlain, p. 32
35. GEPC catalog, 1892, p. 2
36. Chandler, David Leon, p. 15
37. Chernow, p. 261
38. Flynn, p. 292
39. *New York World*, February 23, 1891, quoted in Lloyd, p. 401
40. *New York Times*, February 23, 1891, quoted in Lloyd, p. 400
41. *New York Press*, quoted in Lloyd, p. 400
42. MacTaggart, p. 15, quoting unknown source
43. Herreshoff, L. Francis, *The Rudder*, November 1965, p. 34, "Naphtha Launches"
44. *The Rudder*, July 1, 1890, p. 1, Editorial
45. Ibid., p. 5, "The Naphtha Launch" (signed J.J.A.)
46. Chamberlain, p. 23
47. GEPC catalog, 1892, p. 76
48. Chamberlain, p. 29
49. *Scientific American*, Mar. 16, 1895, "The Naphtha Launch of the Gas Engine and Power Company of New York City"
50. Trudgen, first edition, p. 25; second edition, p. 23
51. *Brooklyn Eagle*, August 11, 1889, p. 15, "The Talk of New York"

Chapter 12: Competitors

1. GEPC catalog, 1894, pp. 59, 60
2. *The Rudder*, July 1891, p. 10, "Launch Building and Launch Builders"
3. Roper, p. 426
4. Roper, p. 430
5. Larson, pp. 143, 144
6. Roper, pp. 432, 448
7. Larson, p. 144
8. Roper, p. 440
9. *Chicago Daily Tribune*, June 18, 1892, "Testing Launches for the Fair"
10. *Chicago Daily Tribune*, July 3, 1892, p. 11, "Test of Launches." The Electric Launch and Navigation Company, also known as the General Electric Launch Company, evolved into the Electric Launch Co., shortened to Elco. (Swanson, pp. viii, 122)
11. GEPC catalog, 1892, p. 77
12. Martin and Sachs, p. 7
13. GEPC catalog, 1894, pp. 86, 87
14. GEPC catalog 1896, p. 67
15. GEPC catalog, 1893, pp. 5, 13, 14, 16
16. GEPC brochure for Columbian Exposition, 1893
17. Fostle, pp. 17, 18

18 *The Rudder, Sail and Paddle*, March 1893, p. 80, "Daimler Motor"
19 Fostle, pp. 18, 19, 26
20 GEPC catalog, 1892, p. 14
21 Dixon, p. 73
22 Fostle, p. 20
23 *The Horseless Age*, 1896, quoted by Fuller, Benjamin A.G., *The Log of Mystic Seaport*, Autumn 1993, p. 38, "The Coming of the Explosive Engine, 1885-1910"
24 Monitor catalog, 1895. A 4-hp Monitor engine sold for $440. As we have noted, Steinway priced a 4-hp engine at $1,225, while a 4-hp naphtha engine cost $650.
25 The funnel's one use was to hide the exhaust pipe, but as Kenneth Durant pointed out, "The exhaust fumes could as well have been carried down and out through the stern." (Durant, p. 19)
26 Monitor catalog, 1895, p. 7
27 Escher Wyss catalog, 1897, pp. 2, 3, 30, 31, 34
28 GEPC catalog, 1894, pp. 10, 11
29 Monitor catalog, 1895, p. 7
30 GEPC catalog, 1894, p. 60
31 *Consolidated* catalog, 1897, p. 52
32 Fuller, Benjamin A. G., to author, January 11, 2005
33 Birdsall, Edward T., *The Rudder*, Vol. VII, No. 7, July 1896, p. 217, "Gas and Vapor Marine Engines, Part III"
34 Church, Vol. I, p. 205
35 *Consolidated* catalog, 1902, p. 4
36 Mitchell, p. 203
37 GEPC catalog, 1894, p. 14
38 Lincoln, John W., *The Steam Automobile*, Fall 1980, p. 8, "The Naphtha Launch, The Steamless Steam Motorboat of 1885"
39 Farmer, Weston, *Yachting*, July 1973, p. 38, "Those Wonderful Naphtha Launches"
40 Chapman, W.J., *Motor Boating*, December 1960, p. 123, "The Naphtha Launch, Relic of the 90s"
41 Durant, pp. 19, 24, 25
42 *Boating Business*, 1936, p. 8, "Consolidated Shipbuilding Has Long, Honorable Record"
43 GEPC brochure, 1895
44 *Scientific American*, March 16, 1895
45 GEPC catalog, 1894, pp. 7, 58
46 Matthew Walker's knot
47 *New York Times*, April 14, 1895, "Naphtha Launches"
48 Stephens, pp. 199, 218
49 Ogilvy, pp. 95, 96

Chapter 13: The Presidential Crony

1 Tugwell, pp. 200, 201
2 Benedict, E.C., *Valentine's Manual of Old New York*, No. 5, p. 30
3 Dunn, Vol. I, pp. 107, 108, quoting Hoke Smith, Secretary of the Interior
4 Josephson, *The Politicos*, p. 589
5 Bradley, p. 68; Clews, p. 689; Satterlee, p. 267
6 Sobel, *The Big Board*, p. 138
7 Grant, pp. 40, 41, 157
8 Morrison, Commager and Leuchtenburg, vol. II, p. 140
9 Merrill, p.111
10 Morrison, Commager and Leuchtenburg, vol. II, p. 180
11 Hovey, p. 153
12 Noyes, p. 184
13 Nevins, *Cleveland*, pp. 523, 526, 527
14 Ferrell, p. 4
15 Keen, pp. 30, 31
16 Nevins, *Cleveland*, p. 529
17 Algeo, p. 55
18 Tugwell, pp. 198, 200, 201. Tugwell wrote from experience, having been a member of Roosevelt's "Brains Trust" when FDR kept the full extent of his polio disability hidden from the public.
19 Algeo, pp. 54, 55
20 MacMahon and Curry, p. 55
21 Hoyt, p. 111
22 MacMahon and Curry, p. 44
23 Algeo, p. 64
24 Seelig, M. G., *Surgery, Gynecology and Obstetrics*, 85, 1947, pp. 373-376, "Cancer and Politics, The Operation on Grover Cleveland," quoted in Ferrell, p. 5
25 Keen, pp., 11, 12; Algeo, p. 83
26 Algeo, pp. 84, 85
27 Martin, John Stuart, *American Heritage*, October 1957, p. 12, "When the President Disappeared"
28 Keen, p. 32
29 Martin, John Stuart, *American Heritage*, October 1957, p. 12, "When the President Disappeared"
30 Algeo, p. 79
31 Keen, pp. 34, 35
32 Ferrell, p. 7
33 Algeo, pp. 104, 150
34 Given the dependence of Wall Streeters on inside information, it is natural to wonder whether Benedict profited from his access to the President. He knew that Cleveland was about to call a special session of Congress, and apparently he passed the information along to his nephew, Henry's son. The *New York Sun* reported, "One of the singular incidents connected with the calling of the special session of Congress is the remarkable guessing of James H. Benedict of E.C. Benedict & Co.…Mr. Cleveland intended to forestall speculation, but there was a leak somewhere, and more than one man was shrewd enough to guess with the Benedicts, and today they are congratulating themselves on their prescience." The *Sun* added that brokers on the Exchange had started a wild tumult of buying, as a result of the tip. A second report went on to say that "Wall Street men are putting this and that together and wondering who was close enough to Cleveland to get hold of such a secret that could be used to upset the market to the advantage of a few." E.C.'s great grandson Ben Wood stated flatly that it was not E.C.'s nephew but E.C. himself, along with his brother Henry, who

profited. "With advance knowledge and confidence that these plans would be put before and enacted at a special session of congress called for August 7, ECB and his older brother and partner Henry were buyers of stocks at panic prices. Their judgment was correct." (Moore, Whitney, *Some Things Never Change*, pp. 31, 32, in part quoting the *New York Sun* and Wood, p. 7.)

35 Dr. Keen diagnosed the lesion as *carcinosarcoma*, but recently experts have concluded that it was *verrucous carcinoma*, a low-grade tumor that does not spread to other parts of the body. First identified in 1948, it appears to the naked eye to be a cancer, but behaves like a wart. (MacMahon & Curry, p. 54)
36 Nevins, *Cleveland*, pp. 537, 543, 544
37 Merrill, pp. 180, 181
38 Nevins, *Cleveland*, p. 546; White, William Allen, quoted in Josephson, *The Politicos*, p. 555;
39 Noyes, p. 199
40 Algeo, p. 118
41 Jeffers, p. 280
42 Sobel, *The Big Board*, p. 138
43 Tugwell, p. 195
44 Hovey, p. 147
45 Noyes, p. 234; Josephson, *The Politicos*, p. 602
46 Myers, Vol. III, p. 224
47 Nevins, *Cleveland*, P. 665
48 Dunn, Vol. I, p. 108
49 Noyes, pp. 237, 241, 248, 249
50 Satterlee, p. 302
51 Ibid., p. 255
52 *New York Times*, May 10, 1894, "Some New Steam Yachts"
53 Allen, p. 55
54 Satterlee, pp. 302, 303
55 Gilder, pp. 157, 158

Chapter 14: Alco-Vapor

1 Stuart, *Anecdotes*, vol. II, pp. 416, 417
2 Patent 551, 226, filed April 20, 1894, issued December 10, 1895, pp. 1, 2, *Apparatus for Operating Vapor-Launches*
3 Ibid., p. 2
4 Patent 540, 757, filed January 18, 1893, issued June 11, 1895, *Vapor-Engine*, pp. 1, 2, 3
5 *The Rudder*, December, 1895, p. 306, "The Alco Vapor Launch Engine." A 2-hp, three-cylinder engine of similar configuration is on display at the Stockholm Technical Museum. It was manufactured in 1888 by J.E. Erikssons Mekaniska Verkstads AB in Stockholm to power a generator aboard the Royal Swedish Navy's Mine Boat no. 2
6 MVEC catalog, 1896, p. 31, letters from E.M. Townsend and J.W. Hamer
7 Wells, Charles, to Rodney Spurlock, p. 6
8 MVEC catalog, 1896, pp. 10, 11
9 Chapman, W. J., *Motor Boating*, December 1960, p. 24, "The Naphtha Launch"
10 MVEC catalog, 1896, p. 25
11 MVEC catalog, 1896, p. 8
12 Ofeldt catalog, 1903, p. 4
13 MVEC catalog, 1896, p. 9
14 MVEC catalog, 1896, p.1
15 Cleveland to Benedict, June 23, 1895, Library of Congress. In *Letters*, Nevins mis-dated this as June 30, 1895.
16 *The Rudder*, January 1896, p. 31, "Some Alco-Vapor Launches"
17 MVEC catalog, 1896, pp. 3, 4, 6, 7
18 GEPC catalog, 1892, p. 10; MVEC catalog, 1896, p. 3
19 MVEC flyer, 1897; MVEC catalog, 1897, p. 6. The company sometimes referred to the alco-vapor motor as the *Alco Motor*, and just as naphtha launches were nicknamed *naphthas*, an alco-vapor launch was also called an *alco*. At first the company did not hyphenate the name of its product, but starting in 1897 it added a hyphen, so we have done so, consistently.
20 MVEC catalog, 1896, p. 7
21 Cleveland to Carlisle, May 18, 1890, Nevins, *Letters*, p. 224
22 Cleveland to Olney, September 23, 1895, Nevins, *Letters*, p. 409
23 *The Rudder*, May 1896, pp. 164, 165
24 *The Rudder*, Dec. 1899
25 Scrapbook, 1898-1908, *Seawanhaka Corinthian Yacht Club Archives*, Coll. 198, Box 4, vol. 22, Mystic Seaport Manuscript Collection
26 MVEC catalog, 1896, p. 20. By 1897 the price of alcohol had dropped to 75 cents a gallon.
27 Herreshoff, L. Francis, *The Rudder*, November 1965, p. 71, "Naphtha Launches"
28 MVEC catalog, 1897, p. 20
29 GEPC catalog, 1894, pp. 31, 33
30 GEPC catalog, 1894, p. 17
31 GEPC catalog, 1896, pp. 16, 17; MVEC catalog, 1896, pp. 22, 26
32 McConnell, Chrystie, *The Ensign*, Feb. 1967, p. 21, "The Redoubtable Naphtha Launch"
33 MVEC catalogs, 1896, p. 31; 1897, pp. 19, 30
34 Cleveland to Benedict, April 30, 1896, Nevins, *Letters*, p. 437
35 Benedict to Cleveland, June 17, 1896, Library of Congress
36 Cleveland to Benedict, June 19, 1896, Nevins, *Letters*, p. 442
37 Cleveland to Benedict, July 17, 1896, Nevins, *Letters*, p. 449
38 Cleveland to Benedict, July 18, 1897, Nevins, *Letters*, pp. 479, 480. Richard Olney was Attorney General.
39 Cleveland to Benedict, September 16, 1897, Library of Congress
40 Ibid., February 6, 1898, Nevins, *Letters*, p. 493
41 Ibid., May 8, 1899, Library of Congress
42 Ibid., Sept. 3, 1899, Library of Congress
43 MVEC catalog, 1897, p. 22. At that time a barrel held 42 gallons.
44 Cleveland to Benedict, September 13, 1900, Library of Congress
45 Ibid., June 4, 1901, Library of Congress
46 MVEC catalogs, 1896, p. 31; 1897, pp. 28, 30
47 *Brooklyn Eagle*, July 19, 1899, p. 6
48 MEMC catalog, 1903, p. 12
49 Ofeldt catalog, 1903, p. 4; *Popular Mechanics*, November 1904, "The Story of the Inventor of the Naphtha Launch"

Chapter 15: The Height of Fashion

1. Veblen, p. 29
2. Hofman, p. 3
3. *New York Times*, May 9, 1894, "Launch of the Eleanor"
4. *Brooklyn Eagle*, Feb. 26, 1899, "Colonel O. H. Payne's *Aphrodite*;" *The Rudder*, Dec. 1898, p. 410, "Our Builders: Where Naphtha Launches Grow"
5. Chamberlain, p. 27
6. GEPC catalog, 1887, p. 22
7. *Brooklyn Eagle*, August 5, 1888, p. 7, "Yachting"
8. *New York Times*, July 29, 1888, "Naphtha Launch Race"
9. *Brooklyn Eagle*, August 5, 1888, p. 7, "Yachting"
10. *New York Times*, July 18, 1891, "Race of Naphtha Launches"
11. GEPC catalog, 1896, p. 45
12. *Seaboard*, May 24, 1894, p. 611
13. *Consolidated* catalog, 1899, p. 36; Mayhew, Augustus, New York Social Diary, www.newyorksocialdiary.com, "Oil Swells: The Standard Oil Crowd in Palm Beach"
14. GEPC catalog, 1893, p. 14
15. Stephens, p. 201
16. *Brooklyn Eagle*, June 15, 1902, p. 16
17. Farmer, Weston, *Motorboat*, January 1975, pp. 49, 50, "Halcyon Days, Part I"
18. Gates, p. 113
19. Astor, pp. 35, 47-49, 54-56, 61-64, 80
20. Martin and Sachs, pp. 16, 19
21. Swanson, p. ix. According to Wikipedia, Czar Nicholas II was Grand Duke Alexander's brother-in law.
22. Martin and Sachs, p. 20
23. *Rudder, Sail and Paddle*, Aug. 1893, p. 145
24. *The Rudder*, October 1896, pp. 287-289, "J.J. Astor's Electric Yacht"
25. *New York Times*, July 20, 1902, "The News of Newport." (D.W. Fostle, in *Speed Boat*, p. 41, stated that, "In September of 1897 she was hit and sunk by the *Mary Powell*. Mr. Astor's boat was never recovered from the waters of the North River." This is inconsistent with the *Times*' report from 1902).
26. *Brooklyn Eagle*, November 11, 1901, p. 8, "From Maryland to Florida in a Launch"
27. *Brooklyn Eagle*, July 20, 1902
28. GEPC catalog, 1894, p. 53
29. *New York Times*, Dec. 1, 1895, "Twin-Screw Naphtha Yacht;" *The Rudder*, Feb. 1896, "Power Yachting"
30. *New York Times*, January 26, 1896, "Several New Steam Yachts"
31. *The Rudder*, February, 1896, p. 58, "Power Yachting"
32. *Brooklyn Eagle*, May 12, 1896, p. 1, "Trial Trip of the Thelma," May 17, 1896, p. 15; *New York Times*, January 26, 1896, "Several New Steam Yachts"
33. *Brooklyn Eagle*, July 8, 1896, p. 4, "May Raise the Thelma"
34. *Brooklyn Eagle*, June 19, 1896, p. 3, "Bay Shore Yachtsmen"
35. *Brooklyn Eagle*, July 8, 1896, p. 4, "May Raise the Thelma"
36. *Brooklyn Eagle*, July 9, 1896, p. 7, "The Thelma's Accident"
37. *Consolidated* catalog, 1902, p. 27

Chapter 16: Kapowie!

1. Farmer, Weston, *Yachting*, August 1973, p. 105, "Those Wonderful Naphtha Launches," Part II
2. Millar, Gordon H., P.E., *Classic Boating*, May/June, 1995, p. 14, "The Heritage of Early Marine Engines"
3. Mitchell, p. 203
4. Irwin, pp. 50-58, (Courtesy Phoebe Tritton, Antique Boat Museum)
5. *New York Times*, July 24, 1900, "Naphtha Launch Blows Up in Sound"
6. *New York Times*, July 10, 1897, "Naphtha Launch Builders' Views"
7. *Brooklyn Eagle*, April 20, 1895, p. 14, "Explosion on Naphtha Launch;" April 23, 1895, p. 5, "Badly Wrecked Launch;" *New York Times*, April 21, 1895, "Yacht Reva Wrecked"
8. *New York Times*, July 31, 1901, "Leaped, Ablaze, From a Burning Launch"
9. *Brooklyn Eagle*, July 6, 1900, p. 18, "Dr. and Miss Evans Burned"
10. *New York Times*, September 5, 1910, "Hurled Into Water by Boat Explosion"
11. GEPC catalog, 1896, p. 12
12. GEPC catalog, 1892, P. 10
13. GEPC catalog, 1899 p. 17
14. Herreshoff, L. Francis, *The Rudder*, Nov. 1965, p. 34, "Naphtha Launches"
15. Durant, p. 20
16. Holmfield, Max F., *The Weather Guage* (sic), 1991, "The Age of the Wonderful Naphtha Launch"
17. Farmer, Weston, *Yachting*, August, 1973, p. 46, "Those Wonderful Naphtha Launches"
18. Hartford, W. P., *Motor Launch* magazine, 1905, quoted by Dr. Marcus Rooks, *Model Engineer*, July 14, 2000
19. McConnell, Chrystie, *The Ensign*, February, 1967, p. 20, "The Redoubtable Naphtha Launch"
20. Peabody, Cecil H., M.E., *Engineering*, June 1898, p. 6, "Marine Gasoline and Gas Engines as Used in Modern Motor Boats – I"
21. JHS of Portsmouth, *Industries*, 1891, "The Second Law of Thermodynamics and Naphtha Launches," quoted in "Powered by Boiling Petrol," p. 9, *The Museum of Retro Technology* (web site)
22. *The Horseless Age*, Jan. 1896, p. 4, "Legislation against Petroleum Boats," (courtesy Karl Petersen)
23. GEPC catalog, 1896, p. 5
24. *New York Times*, Jan. 23, 1901, "Launch Owners Warned"
25. Gardner, John, *National Fisherman*, February, 1977, "Naphtha Launch Project Lacks Authentic Engine"

Chapter 17: Combat

1. *Wayne County Review*, May 19, 1904, "First Russian Naval Success"
2. GEPC catalog, 1893, p. 5
3. *New York Times*, June 1, 1896, quoted in GEPC catalog, 1896, pp. 61, 63
4. Consolidated catalog, 1899, p. 1
5. Farmer, Weston, *Yachting*, August, 1973, p. 104, "Those Wonderful Naphtha Launches, Part II"
6. *The Rudder*, December 1898, pp. 409, 410, "Our Builders: Where Naphtha Launches Grow"
7. *New York Times*, June 1, 1896, quoted in GEPC catalog, 1896, p. 63
8. Moore, C. Philip, p. 47
9. *Scientific American Supplement*, Special Navy Edition, vol. XLV, No. 1165, April 30, 1898
10. *The Rudder*, December, 1898, p. 411, "Our Builders: Where Naphtha Launches Grow"
11. *Brooklyn Eagle*, February 26, 1899, p. 8, "Palatial Steam Yachts for Prominent Clubmen"
12. Davis, Charles G., *The Rudder*, 1899, "The Steam Fleet of 1899"
13. *Brooklyn Eagle*, April 8, 1900, "Many Launches Being Built at Morris Heights"
14. Moore, C. Philip, p. 47
15. Escher Wyss catalog, 1897, p. 25
16. Escher Wyss catalog, 1897, pp. 22, 23
17. Escher Wyss catalog, 1897, pp. 13, 14, 22, 39, 40, quoting *Nouvelle Gazette de Zurich*, December 4, 1895, and *Journal de Neuwied*, November 30, 1895
18. MacMillan, p. 359
19. Rousmaniere, *The Luxury Yachts*, p. 124
20. Buckle, Vol. III, p. 441, quoted in Massie, pp. 208, 209
21. Wikipedia
22. GEPC catalog, 1892, p. 20
23. Massie, pp. 155, 156
24. Magnus, p. 250, quoted in Massie, p. 106
25. Balfour, p. 265, quoted in Massie, p. 106
26. Rousmaniere, *The Luxury Yachts*, p. 124
27. *Rudder, Sail and Paddle*, Nov. and Dec. 1893, "German Emperor's New Yacht"
28. Escher Wyss catalog, 1896, p. 1
29. Headrick, pp. 17, 53, 54
30. *Indicateur Journalier* (Zurich), February 1894, quoted in Escher Wyss catalog, 1897, p. 28
31. 550 pounds
32. *Indicateur Journalier* (Zurich), April 4, 1895, quoted in Escher Wyss catalog, 1897, p. 28
33. Leeuw, p. 190
34. Escher Wyss catalog, 1897, pp. 16, 31
35. Kennedy, p. 197
36. Escher Wyss catalog, 1897, pp. 30, 31, 35, 36
37. *Wayne County Review*, May 19, 1904, "First Russian Naval Success"

Chapter 18: Compound Vapor

1. Ofeldt catalog, 1903, p. 4
2. Frank originally called this invention the *Improved Naphtha Launch*, but we have called it the *Ofeldt Improved System*. See chapter 10.
3. Ofeldt catalog, 1903, p. 4
4. *Popular Mechanics*, Nov., 1904, "The Story of the Inventor of the Naphtha Launch"
5. Ofeldt catalog, 1903, p. 4
6. U.S. Patent 538, 694, *Vapor-Engine*, filed December 21, 1893, issued May 7, 1895.
7. *The Horseless Age*, November, 1896, "The Ofeldt Marine Vapor Motor"
8. Ofeldt catalog, 1903, pp. 1, 7
9. Ibid., p. 10; GEPC catalog, 1896, p. 10
10. Ibid., pp. 4, 5
11. Parkhurst, Virginia, unidentified Nyack newspaper, March 14, 1964, "1898 Steamer Sported Surrey Chassis so Nags Would Feel at Home on Road;" Harniman, Ken, interview with Jennie Ofeldt Russell, daughter of Frank A. Ofeldt, *Nyack Journal-News*, circa 1970, "Remember? 'Get a Horse'"
12. Liebling, p. 25
13. About 1902 a customer could buy a 21-ft. naphtha launch with a 2-hp motor from $850 or an alco-vapor motor for $750, but the Ofeldts' 21-ft. launch came only with a 5-hp motor at $1,075. For a 25-ft. launch with a 4-hp motor, Consolidated's prices started at $950. There was no 4-hp alco-vapor motor, but for a 5-hp motor the price was $1,000. For a boat of that length with a 10-hp motor, the only one offered, the Ofeldts charged $1,350. The Ofeldts even offered a 35-ft. open launch with a 20-hp motor for $3,200, but the other builders could not manufacture anything comparable. (*Consolidated* catalog, 1902, p. 18; MEMC. catalog, 1903, p. 7; Ofeldt catalog, 1903, p. 9)
14. Ofeldt catalog, 1903, p. 13 (Per *Lloyd's Register of American Yachts*, 1904, *Nautilus* was 64 ft. long)
15. *Lloyd's Register of American Yachts*, 1915, p. 79
16. *Brooklyn Eagle*, April 1, 1898, p. 13, "New Alcho-Vapor Yacht" (sic)
17. *Brooklyn Eagle*, May 17, 1896, and May 11, 1897, p. 4, "Yachting Notes"
18. GEPC catalog, 1892, p. 58
19. *Brooklyn Eagle*, July 7, 1896, p. 8, "It's an Aquatic Freak"
20. *New York Dramatic Mirror*, August 5, 1899, "Gillette, Play and Ship Builder"
21. *Brooklyn Eagle*, August 3, 1902, p. 33
22. *Brooklyn Eagle*, March 23, 1897, p. 4, "Yachting Notes;" *Marine Engineering*, Sept. 1897, p. 42

23 *Brooklyn Eagle*, May 19, 1899 p. 13, "Yachting at Bay Shore: Actor Gillette's New Boat"
24 *New York Times*, June 4, 1899
25 Field, Edward P., in Hunt, p. 88
26 *Brooklyn Eagle*, May 19, 1899, p. 13, "Yachting at Bay Shore: Actor Gillette's New Boat"
27 Sheet #29 from Gillette Castle State Park
28 Caption on an exhibit at Gillette Castle State Park
29 Ofeldt catalog, 1903, p. 19
30 Schaefer, p. 12
31 Field, Edward P., in Hunt, p. 91
32 Kimes and Clark, p. 1054
33 *Nyack Evening Journal*, May 8, 1899, "A Horseless Carriage"
34 *The Horseless Age*, December 6, 1899, p. 51, "The Ofeldt Steam Carriage"
35 Prouty, W. A., *Asbury Park Press*, quoted in *Old Timers News*, February, 1950, p. 9, "Built Car Like Carriage for Sake of Horses"
36 Harniman, Ken, *Nyack Journal-News*, c. 1970, "Remember? 'Get a Horse'!"
37 *The Horseless Age*, May 22, 1901, p. 167, "The Ofeldt Automobile and Steam Launch Company's Engines and Boilers"
38 Kimes and Clark, p. 1054
39 Ofeldt catalog, 1903, p. 27
40 *The Horseless Age*, March 20, 1901, pp. 23, 24, "The Ofeldt Steam Truck"
41 Ibid., Vol. 8, No. 22, p. 464, "The Ofeldt Delivery Wagon"
42 Unidentified Nyack newspaper, Sept. 16, 1954, "Frank A. Ofeldt, Builder of Cars in Days of Steamers, Dies at His Nyack Home"
43 *Popular Mechanics*, November 1904, "The Story of the Inventor of the Naphtha Launch"
44 Sandra Brockel, Frank W. Ofeldt's great-great granddaughter, (and Ernest's great-granddaughter), sent the author a photograph of Frank and Augusta's tombstone, which is in Public Lot 8899, Greenwood Cemetery, Brooklyn.
45 Unidentified Nyack newspaper, Sept. 16, 1954, "Frank A. Ofeldt, Builder of Cars in Days of Steamers, Dies at his Nyack Home"
46 *Motor Boat*, September 10, 1905, "Ofeldt & Sons Move"
47 Harniman, Ken, *Nyack Journal News*, c. 1970, "Remember? 'Get a Horse'!"
48 Parkhurst, Virginia, unidentified Nyack newspaper, March 14, 1964, "1898 Steamer Sported Surrey Chassis so Nags Would feel at Home on Road"
49 Ofeldt catalog, 1908, p. 22
50 Ibid., Folio Seven
51 Ibid., Folio Eight
52 Ibid., Folio Nine
53 In a double-acting engine the working fluid acts alternately on both sides of the piston. While internal combustion engines are normally single-acting, most modern steam engines are double-acting.
54 Ofeldt catalog, 1908, Folios Twenty-five and Twenty-eight. This was not an outlandish suggestion. Two years earlier a Stanley Steamer driven by Fred Marriott had reached 127 mph, a record that stood for over 100 years. (Wikipedia)
55 Gillette to Monsell, January 12, 1907. (Courtesy Gillette Castle State Park)
56 Schaefer
57 Ibid.

Chapter 19: Ending the Naphtha Glut

1 Rockefeller, p. 6
2 Hidy and Hidy, pp. 160, 188, 289. It was also called *Stink*. (Williamson vol. I, p. 618, footnote)
3 Boyle, vol. I, p. 926
4 Williamson vol. 1, p. 593
5 Nevins, *Rockefeller*, vol. I, p. 650, and Packard, p. 131, quoted in Chernow, p. 284
6 U.S. Geological Survey, 1886, quoted in Williamson. vol. I, p. 591
7 Hidy and Hidy, p. 158
8 Nevins, *Rockefeller*, vol. II, p. 298
9 Chernow, p. 286
10 Nevins, *Rockefeller*, vol. II, pp. 7, 8
11 Chernow, p. 287
12 Ibid., p. 285
13 Rockefeller, p. 7
14 Nevins, *Rockefeller*, vol I, p. 680; vol. II, p. 189
15 Rockefeller, pp. 7-9
16 *Toledo Bee*, reprinted in *Titusville Morning Herald*, July 12, 1887, quoted in Williamson, vol. I, p. 600
17 Chernow, p. 286
18 Williamson, vol. I, p. 606
19 Hidy and Hidy, p. 164
20 Williamson, vol. II, pp. 174-175
21 Nevins, *Rockefeller*, vol. II, pp. 8, 11
22 Barron, p. 191
23 Wikipedia
24 Hidy and Hidy, p. 193
25 Undoubtedly manufacturers of illuminating gas purchased more naphtha than did naphtha launch owners, but we do not have the figures.
26 Nevins, *Rockefeller*, vol. II, pp. 142-144
27 Hidy and Hidy, p. 219
28 Ibid., p. 225
29 Nevins, *Rockefeller*, vol. II, p. 356
30 Hidy and Hidy, p. 228
31 Nevins, *Rockefeller*, vol. II, p. 433
32 Hidy and Hidy, pp. 124, 192
33 Lloyd, pp. 408-410
34 Hidy and Hidy, pp. 224, 269, 315, 316
35 Ibid., p. 230
36 Nevins, *Rockefeller*, vol. II, pp. 18, 19
37 Hidy and Hidy, pp. 298, 299
38 Williamson, vol. I, p. 680
39 Hidy and Hidy, p. 299
40 Nevins, *Rockefeller*, vol. II, pp. 19, 20

Chapter 20: Benedict Folds

1. Chandler, David Leon, p. 82. Chandler, Henry Flagler's biographer, wrote that Flagler kept the axiom, *Do unto others as they would do unto you – and do it first*, on his desk. For the original text, see Westcott, *David Harum*, p. 155. The protagonist of the best-selling novel was a homespun country banker and horse trader who always got the best of every deal. In the book Harum was not expressing his own opinion, but one held by many of his contemporaries. The actual quote was, "Bus'nis is bus'nis' ain't part of the golden rule, I allow, but the way it gen'ally runs, fur's I've found out, is, 'Do unto the other feller the way he'd like to do unto you, an' do it fust'." *David Harum* was one of the few books, besides the Bible, that John D. Rockefeller ever read. (Nevins, *Rockefeller*, vol. II, p. 449). Grover Cleveland advised E.C. Benedict that "It seems to have been written for just such country bred chaps as you and I." (Cleveland to Benedict, Jan. 18, 1899, Library of Congress).
2. Bassett, pp. 75, 102, 127
3. Ibid., pp. 113, 114. Bassett was probably referring to the crew on E.C.'s second yacht, the *"Big" Oneida*.
4. Moore, Whitney, *Some Things Never Change*
5. Holch, pp. 26, 27
6. *New York Times*, August 27, 1897, "Owns Nearly all the Gas; Standard Oil Co. Controls the Supply of Almost Every Large City in the Country"
7. *Greenwich News and Graphic*, quoted in Holch, p. 16
8. Cleveland to Benedict, July 17, 1896, Nevins, *Letters*, p. 449; Cleveland to Benedict, September 16, 1897, Library of Congress
9. MEMC catalog, 1903, p. 1
10. Ibid., 1903, pp. 4, 6, 7. Pat Spurlock explains: "Early internal combustion engines throw oil off their flywheels when crank case oil flows out of loose main bearings. Wired-on tin skirts help. Latter-day old boat restorers throw these in the trash first thing, only later they re-fashion them by necessity. Suede shoes not a good choice." (Spurlock to author, May 14, 2010.)
11. MEMC catalog, 1903, p. 11
12. Bigelow, Edward F., *The Guide to Nature*, February, 1911, p. 413
13. Unidentified New York newspaper, Aug. 16, 1903
14. List of *Consolidated*'s deliveries, courtesy Mystic Seaport. The hull of the boat for the U.S. Navy was #1953. The hull numbers of the two boats for Canada were #1955 and #1960.
15. *Industrial Directory of New Jersey*, 1906, p. 155: "Marine Engine and Machine Company, makers of vapor launches, elevators, etc., employ 200 persons."

Chapter 21: Speed

1. Grahame, pp. 138, 139
2. Ogilvy, p. 119, quoting unknown source
3. Smith, pp. 258, 259
4. Nevins, *Rockefeller*, vol. I, p. 638
5. GEPC catalog, 1892, pp. 26, 27
6. Ibid., 1894, pp. 37, 39
7. *New York Times*, July 23, 1902, "Yacht Sailors in Race." In 1905 Albert Bostwick, at the early age of 27, was elected Commodore of the Larchmont Yacht Club. At that time he also owned a large schooner and a steam yacht, both named *Vergemere* (Ogilvy, p. 119)
8. *Consolidated* catalog, 1902, p. 2
9. *Brooklyn Eagle*, February 26, 1899, p. 3, "The New Kanawha"
10. Ibid., March 15, 1900, p. 2
11. MacTaggart, p. 48; Hofman, p. 124
12. Moore, C. Philip, pp. 50, 51; Johnston et al, p. 270
13. *Brooklyn Eagle*, July 25, 1902, p. 13, "Boom in Yachting on Long Island"
14. *Consolidated* catalog, 1899, p. 13
15. Dixon, p. 47
16. *Consolidated* catalog, 1902, p. 8
17. *Power Boating*, date unknown p. 53, "Building up the Industry"
18. Herreshoff, L. Francis, *The Rudder*, November 1965, p. 72, "Naphtha Launches"
19. Brown, pp 204, 205
20. Barnes, p.179
21. Mayhew, Augustus, *New York Social Diary*, www.newyorksocialdiary.com, "Oil Swells: The Standard Oil Crowd in Palm Beach"
22. Wood; Bassett, p. 135
23. The real speed demon was Jabez Bostwick's granddaughter, Marion Carstairs. Known as "Joe," in the 1920s she became the fastest female speedboat racer. (Summerscale, front dust cover)

Chapter 22: Conclusion

1. Hidy and Hidy, p. 454
2. Williamson, vol. II, pp. 146, 150
3. Hidy and Hidy, p. 454
4. Church, vol II, p. 265

Chapter 23: Epilogue

1. MacDuffie, Malcolm, *National Fisherman*, May 1971, p. 19-B, "Naphtha Launch — The Missing Link"
2. Ogilvy, p. 120; Holm, p. 79
3. Robinson, p. 141
4. Holm, p. 79
5. Ogilvy, p. 133
6. *The Rudder*, (month unknown) 1907, inside front cover, from Dixon, p. 48
7. Russell, p. 29
8. Escher Wyss catalog, 1912, p. 2
9. Herreshoff, L. Francis, *The Rudder*, Nov. 1965, p. 72, "Naphtha Launches"
10. Moore, C. Philip, pp. 48, 49, 66, 67
11. *Antique Boating*, Vol. IV, Nos. 4&5, Fall/Winter 1977. This is the only reference we have found to any name for the boat, but it is obviously not the original one.
1. MacDuffie, Malcolm, *National Fisherman*, May 1971, p. 19-B, "Naphtha Launch — The Missing Link"
2. Ogilvy, p. 120; Holm, p. 79
3. Robinson, p. 141
4. Holm, p. 79
5. Ogilvy, p. 133
6. *The Rudder*, (month unknown) 1907, inside front cover, from Dixon, p. 48
7. Russell, p. 29
8. Escher Wyss catalog, 1912, p. 2
9. Herreshoff, L. Francis, *The Rudder*, Nov. 1965, p. 72, "Naphtha Launches"
10. Moore, C. Philip, pp. 48, 49, 66, 67
11. *Antique Boating*, Vol. IV, Nos. 4&5, Fall/Winter 1977. This is the only reference we have found to any name for the boat, but it is obviously not the original one.
12. Telegram, Seyffer to Frank Campsall, August 2, 1928 (courtesy Henry Ford Museum)
13. Campsall, Frank, to John J. Amory, August 29, 1928 (courtesy Henry Ford Museum)
14. *New York Times*, June 9, 1935, Sports Section, "Yachtsmen Plan Ceremonies to Mark the Anniversary of Unique Craft"
15. Jim Wright, in conversation with author
16. Richardson, William H., Jr. to Randy Mason, Henry Ford Museum, October 14, 1977 (courtesy Henry Ford Museum)
17. Mitchell, p. 205. The caption on *Chiripa's* display states "c. 1899," and also states that Frank H. Patterson had purchased her in 1901
18. Miller, Frank H., in Durham, September-October 1961, p. 13, "Corrections and Addenda on Naphtha Launches." *Phoebe*, originally owned by Dr. John Alfred Brashear of Pittsburgh, is now on display in Kingston, Ontario. *Magedoma* (ex *Cangarda*) was owned for 40 years by Senator George Taylor Fulford of Brockville, Ontario, and is now owned by Robert McNeil.
19. Mystic Seaport website
20. Ibid.
21. Bond, p. 290
22. Mitchell, p. 205
23. Chapman, Wilbur J., *Model Engineer*, November 5, 1959, pp. 364, 365, "Sixty years old, this naphtha launch has plenty of 'go' "
24. Richardson, William H. Jr. to Ernest T. Ofeldt, January 28, 1974 (courtesy William H. Richardson, Jr.)
25. *The Rudder*, December 1900, p. xiv
26. Laabs, Joyce, *Northwoods Nostalgia*, Vol. II, 1979, "The Woodzickas and the Sunflower Resort"
27. *Classic News*, October 31, 2007, p. 2
28. Chapman, Wilbur J., *Model Engineer*, November 5, 1959, p. 364
29. Richardson, William H., Jr. to Ernest T. Ofeldt, January 28, 1974 (courtesy William H. Richardson, Jr.)
30. Richardson, William H., Jr., *Antique Boating*, vol. IV, nos. 4&5, Fall/Winter 1977, pp. 5, 6
31. Richardson, William H., Jr. to Randy Mason, Henry Ford Museum, October 14, 1977 (courtesy Henry Ford Museum)
32. Mitchell, p. 210
33. Tritton, Phoebe, (Antique Boat Museum) to author, December 15, 1999

Bibliography

Books and Booklets

Ackerman, Kenneth D., *The Gold Ring,* Harper Business, 1888.
Adams, Charles F., *Chapters of Erie,* Boston, 1871.
Algeo, Matthew, *The President is a Sick Man,* Chicago, 2011.
Allen, Frederick Lewis, *The Great Pierpont Morgan,* New York, 1948-49.
Appleton's Cyclopaedia of Applied Mechanics.
Armitage, Charles H., *Grover Cleveland as Buffalo Knew Him,* Buffalo, 1926.
Arthur, Richard, *Ten Thousand Miles in a Yacht,* New York, 1906.
Åsbrink, Brita, *Ludvig Nobel: "Petroleum har en lysande framtid!"* Stockholm, 2001.
Astor, John Jacob, *A Journey in Other Worlds,* New York, 1894.
Babbage, Charles, *The Great Exposition of 1851,* London, 1851.
Bacon, Sir Francis, *Novum Organum,* 1620, republished by Encyclopaedia Britannica.
Balfour, Michael, *The Kaiser and His Times,* Boston, 1964.
Barnes, Eleanor C. (Lady Yarrow), *Alfred Yarrow, His Life And Work,* New York, 1923.
Barron, Clarence W., *More They Told Barron,* New York, 1931.
Barry, James P., *American Powerboats: The Great Lakes Golden Years,* St. Paul, 2003.
Bassett, Horace H., *Bruce Park and the Benedict Estate,* Greenwich, 1978.
Benedict, Henry Marvin, *The Genealogy of the Benedicts in America,* Albany, 1870.
Bergengren, Erik, *Alfred Nobel,* Thomas Nelson and Sons Ltd, 1960.
Bergh, Albert Ellery, *Grover Cleveland: Addresses, State Papers and Letters,* New York, 1908.
Bond, Hallie E., *Boats and Boating in the Adirondacks,* Syracuse, 1995.
Boyle, Patrick C., *The Derrick's Hand-Book of Petroleum,* Oil City, 1898.
Bradley, James, *The Imperial Cruise,* New York, 2009.
Brooks, Noah, *Men of Achievement: Statesmen,* New York, 1895.
Brown, David K., *The Way of a Ship in the Midst of the Sea,* Penzance, Cornwall, 2006.
Buckle, George Earle, *The Letters of Queen Victoria,* London, 1932.
Cardwell, Donald S. L., *From Watt to Clausius,* Cornell University Press, 1971.
----------, *The Norton History of Technology,* New York, 1995.
----------, *Turning Points in Western Technology,* New York, 1972.
Carpenter, Francis Bicknell, *Six Months at the White House With Abraham Lincoln,* New York, 1866.
Chandler, David Leon, *Henry Flagler,* New York, 1986.
Chernow, Ron, *Titan,* New York, 1998.
Church, William Conant, *The Life of John Ericsson,* New York, 1890.
Clews, Henry, *Fifty Years in Wall Street,* New York, 1908.
Cookman, Scott, *Atlantic,* New York, 2002.
Dixon, Michael M., *Motormen & Yachting,* Mervue publications, 2005.
Dolson, Hildegarde, *The Great Oildorado,* New York, 1959.
Dott, Robert, *Aktiebolaget Textilmaskiner Norrköping 100 År, 1848-1948.*

Du Chaillu, Paul Belloni, *The Viking Age,* 1889.
Dunn, Arthur Wallace, *From Harrison to Harding,* New York, 1922.
Durant, Kenneth, *The Naphtha Launch,* Adirondack Museum, 1976.
Durham, Bill, *Steamboats and Modern Steam Launches,* 1961-1963 and 1986. Republished by Boat House, Portland, Oregon, 1997.
Fant, Kenne, *Alfred Bernhard Nobel,* Stockholm, 1991.
Farmer, Weston, *From My Old Boat Shop,* 1979. Republished by Boat House, Portland, Oregon, 1996.
Ferrell, Robert H., *Ill-Advised,* Columbia, Missouri, 1992.
Flynn, John T., *God's Gold,* New York, 1932.
Forbes, R. J., *Bitumen and Petroleum in Antiquity,* Leiden, 1936.
----------, *Studies in Early Petroleum History,* Leiden, 1958.
----------, *More Studies in Early Petroleum History,* Leiden, 1959.
Ford, Henry Jones, *The Cleveland Era,* New Haven, 1919.
Ford, William M., *The Industrial Interests of Newark, N.J.,* New York, 1874.
Fostle, D. W., *Speedboat,* Mystic, 1988.
Fowler, William Worthington, *Ten Years in Wall Street,* Hartford, 1870.
Frängsmyr, Tore, *Alfred Nobel,* Stockholm, 1996.
Freeberg, Ernest, *The Age of Edison,* New York, 2013.
Gates, John D., *The Astor Family,* New York, 1981.
Gilder, Richard Watson, *Grover Cleveland: A Record of Friendship,* New York, 1910.
Gladwell, Malcolm, *David and Goliath,* New York, 2013.
Graff, Henry F., *Grover Cleveland,* New York, 2002.
Grahame, Kenneth, *The Wind in the Willows,* London, 1908.
Grant, James, *Mr. Speaker!,* New York, 2011.
Grayson, Stan, *Old Marine Engines,* Marblehead, 1994.
Haig-Brown, Valerie, *Ron Jones: Inventor and Gentleman* (manuscript), 2000.
Hawthorne, Edward, *Electric Boats on the Thames, 1889-1914,* United Kingdom, 1995.
Headrick, Daniel R., *The Tools of Empire,* New York, 1981.
Hellberg, Thomas, and Jansson, Lars Magnus, *Alfred Nobel,* Stockholm, 1986.
Hidy, Ralph W. and Hidy, Muriel H., *Pioneering in Big Business, 1882-1911,* New York, 1955.
Hirsch, Mark D., *William C. Whitney,* New York, 1948.
Hofman, Erik, *The Steam Yachts,* Tuckahoe, 1970.
Holch, Arthur, *Rich and Famous in Greenwich* (manuscript).
Holm, *Yachting's Golden Age,* New York, 1999.
Hovey, Carl, *The Life Story of J. Pierpont Morgan,* New York, 1911.
Hoyt, Edwin P., *Grover Cleveland,* Chicago, 1962.
Hudson, William C., *Random Recollections of an Old Political Reporter,* New York, 1911.
Hunt, Albert Bradlee, *Houseboats and Houseboating,* New York, 1905.
Ierley, Matthew, *Wondrous Contrivances,* New York, 2002.
Investigation Into the Causes of the Gold Panic, Washington, 1870 (Garfield Report).

Irwin, May, *May Irwin's Home Cooking,* 1904.
Isaacson, Walter, *The Innovators,* New York, 2014.
Jeffers, H. Paul, *An Honest President,* New York, 2000.
Johnston, William Cameron, et al., *The Seabound Coast,* Toronto, 2010.
Josephson, Matthew, *Edison,* New York, 1959.
----------, *The Politicos,* New York, 1938.
----------, *The Robber Barons,* Harcourt Inc., 1934.
Keen, William W., *The Surgical Operations on President Cleveland in 1893,* Philadelphia, 1917.
Kennedy, Paul, *Engineers of Victory,* New York, 2013.
Kimes, Beverly Rae, and Clark, Henry Austin, *Standard Catalog of American Cars, 1805-1942,* Motorbooks International, 1996 (?)
Kunhardt, C.P., *Steam Yachts and Launches,* New York, second edition, 1891.
Larson, Erik, *The Devil in the White City,* New York, 2003.
Lawson, Thomas W., *The Crime of Amalgamated,* New York, 1905.
Leeuw, De Bataafsche, *Tot in de Verste Uithoeken...,* Amsterdam, 1998.
Liebling, A. J., *Just Enough Liebling,* New York, 2004.
Lindberg, John S., *The Background of Swedish Emigration to the United States,* Minneapolis, 1930.
Lindqvist, Svante, *A Tribute to the Memory of Alfred Nobel,* Stockholm, 2001.
Lloyd, Henry Demarest, *Wealth Against Commonwealth,* New York, 1894.
Lynch, Denis Tilden, *Grover Cleveland: A Man Four-Square,* New York, 1932.
MacMahon, Edward B., and Curry, Leonard, *Medical Cover-ups in the White House,* Washington, 1987.
MacMillan, Margaret, *Paris 1919,* New York, 2001.
MacTaggart, Ross, *The Golden Century,* New York, 2001.
Mahan, Alfred Thayer, *Letters and Papers of Alfred Thayer Mahan,* Annapolis, 1975.
Martin, Thomas Commerford, and Sachs, Joseph, *Electrical Boats and Navigation,* New York, 1894. Republished by Boat House, Portland, Oregon, 2002.
Marvin, Charles, *The Region of the Eternal Fire: An Account of a Journey to the Petroleum Region of the Caspian in 1883,* W. H. Allen Co., 1891.
Massie, Robert K., *Dreadnought,* New York, 1991.
Maxwell, William Quentin, *Lincoln's Fifth Wheel: The Political History of the United States Sanitary Commission,* New York, 1956.
McElroy, Robert, *Grover Cleveland,* New York, 1923.
McLaurin, John J., *Sketches in Crude Oil,* Franklin, Pa., 1902.
Medbery, James K., *Men and Mysteries of Wall Street,* Boston, 1870.
Merrill, Horace Samuel, *Bourbon Leader: Grover Cleveland and the Democratic Party,* Boston, 1957.
Mitchell, Richard M., *The Steam Launch,* Boat House, Portland, Oregon, 1994.
Mokyr, Joel, *The Gifts of Athena,* Princeton University Press, 2002.
Moore, Austin Leigh, *John D. Archbold,* Macmillan, 193?
Moore, C. Philip, *Yachts in a Hurry,* New York, 1996.
Moore, Whitney, E. C. B. Brief Bio (manuscript).
----------, *Some Things Never Change* (manuscript).

Morrison, Samuel Eliot; Commager, Henry Steele; and Leuchtenberg, William E., *The Growth of the American Republic,* New York, 1969.
Mott, Henry A., *The Yachts and Yachtsmen of America,* New York, 1894
Muirhead, James Patrick, *The Life of James Watt,* London, 1858.
Myers, Gustavus, *History of the Great American Fortunes,* Chicago, 1907-09.
Nevins, Allan, *Grover Cleveland,* New York, 1941.
----------, *John D. Rockefeller,* New York, 1940.
----------, *Letters of Grover Cleveland,* Boston, 1933.
----------, *Ordeal of the Union,* New York, 1947.
----------, *The War For The Union,* New York, 1971.
The Nineties: An American Heritage Extra, New York, 1967
Norrköping och dess Omgifningar, 1861.
Noyes, Alexander Dana, *Forty Years of American Finance,* New York, 1909.
O'Connor, Richard, *Gould's Millions,* New York, 1962.
Ogilvy, C. Stanley, *The Larchmont Yacht Club,* Larchmont, 1993.
Olsson, Cege, and Ekström, Gert, *Alla Våra Ångslupar,* Stockholm.
Packard, Roy D., *Informal History of the Standard Oil Company (Ohio) (1870-1911),* manuscript in archives of British Petroleum (Cleveland).
Parker, George F., *Recollections of Grover Cleveland,* New York, 1911.
Parkinson, John, Jr., *The History of the New York Yacht Club,* New York, 1975.
The Religious Tract Society, *James Watt and the Steam Engine,* London, ca. 1852.
Report of the Special Committee on Railroads, New York Assembly, 1879 (Hepburn Report).
Robinson, Bill, *Legendary Yachts,* Norwalk, 1971-1987.
Rockefeller, John D., *Random Reminiscences of Men and Events,* New York, 1937.
Roper, Laura Wood, *FLO, A Biography of Frederick Law Olmsted,* Baltimore, 1973.
Rosen, William, *The Most Powerful Idea in the World,* New York, 2010.
Rousmaniere, John, *The Golden Pastime,* New York, 1986.
----------, *The Luxury Yachts,* Amsterdam, 1981.
Russell, Thomas H., *Motor Boats, Construction and Operation,* 1910.
Satterlee, Herbert L., *J. Pierpont Morgan,* New York, 1939.
Schaefer, Richard G., *His Beloved Aunt Polly,* Aunt Polly Archaeological Preserve, East Haddam, Connecticut, 2004.
Schumpeter, Joseph A., *Capitalism, Socialism and Democracy,* London, fifth edition, 1976.
Smiles, Samuel, *Lives of the Engineers: Boulton and Watt,* popular edition, 1904.
Smith, Matthew Hale, *Twenty Years Among the Bulls and Bears of Wall Street,* Hartford, 1870.
Sobel, Robert, *The Big Board,* New York, 1965.
----------, *Panic on Wall Street,* New York, 1968.

Sohlman, Ragnar, *The Legacy of Alfred Nobel,* London, 1983. Originally published in Swedish as *Ett Testamente,* 1950.

Souvenir of Indian Harbor.

Stedman, Edmund Clarence, *The New York Stock Exchange,* New York, 1905.

Stephens, W. P., *The Seawanhaka Corinthian Yacht Club: Origins and Early History,* New York, 1963.

Stone, Abram, *The Stock Exchange in Caricature,* New York, 1904.

Strandh, Sigvard, *Alfred Nobel, Mannen, Verket, Samtiden,* Stockholm, 1983.

Strong, George Templeton, *The Diary of George Templeton Strong,* New York, 1952.

Stuart, Robert, *A Descriptive History of the Steam Engine* (third edition), London, 1825.

----------, *Historical and Descriptive Anecdotes of Steam-Engines and of Their Inventors and Improvers,* London, 1829.

Summerscale, Kate, *The Queen of Whale Cay,* New York, 1997.

Swanberg, W. A., *Whitney Father, Whitney Heiress,* New York, 1980.

Swanson, William C., *Launches and Yachts: The 1902 Elco Catalog,* Waldorf, 1984.

Tarbell, Ida M., *The History of the Standard Oil Company,* New York, 1904.

Tawney, R. H., *Religion and the Rise of Capitalism,* London, 1926.

Tolf, Robert W., *The Russian Rockefellers,* Stanford University, 1976.

Trollope, Anthony, *North America,* London, 1862.

Trudgen, Bruce, *The Naphtha Launches,* 2010.

Tugwell, Rexford G., *Grover Cleveland,* New York, 1968.

Uglow, Jenny, *The Lunar Men,* London, 2002.

Van Deusen, Glyndon G., *Thurlow Weed,* Boston, 1947.

Veblen, Thorstein, *The Theory of the Leisure Class,* New York, 1899.

Westcott, Edward N., *David Harum,* New York, 1898.

Williamson, Harold F., and Daum, Arnold R., *The American Petroleum Industry,* vol. I: *The Age of Illumination,* Northwestern University Press, 1959.

----------; Andreano, Ralph L.; Daum, Arnold R.; Klose, Gilbert C., *The American Petroleum Industry,* vol. II: *The Age of Energy,* Northwestern University Press, 1963.

Wilson, Woodrow, *A History of the American People,* New York, 1901, 1902.

Winkler, John K., *John D.; A Portrait in Oils,* 1929.

Wormeley, Katharine Prescott, *The Other Side of War,* 1889.

Wright, William, *The Oil Regions of Pennsylvania,* 1865. Republished by Bibliobazaar.

Yergin, Daniel, *The Prize,* New York, 1991.

Zimmerman, Warren, *First Great Triumph,* New York, 2002.

100 Jahre Escher Wyss Ravensburg, 1956.

Articles

Booth, James C. and Garrett, Thos. H. *Experiments on Illumination With Mineral Oils,* J. Franklin Institute, 1862.

Chamberlain, J., *A Story of the Naphtha Launch,* Published by GEPC, 1889.

Chandler, C.F., *Report on Petroleum as an Illuminator, and the advantages and perils which attend its use; with special reference to the prevention of the traffic in dangerous kerosene and naphtha,* New York, 1871.

Gale, Thomas A, *Rock Oil in Pennsylvania and Elsewhere,* Erie, 1860.

Johnston, Archibald, and Kerlin, John Martin Sharpless, *The Naphtha Engine,* bachelor thesis, Lehigh University, 1889.

Lee, Brother Basil Leo, *Discontent in New York City, 1861-1865,* Washington, 1943 (dissertation).

Strandh, Sigvard, *Aluminium,* Stockholm Tekniska Museet, 1983.

Sweet, E.T., *On Kerosene Oil,* Wisconsin Academy of Sciences, Arts, and Letters, 1878.

Wood, Ben, *Benedict and Big Business* (manuscript).

Periodicals

Antique Boating
Appleton's Annual Cyclopaedia and Register of Important Events
Asbury Park Press
Boating Business
Brooklyn Directory
Brooklyn Eagle
Cassier's Magazine
Chemical News
Chicago Daily Tribune
Classic Boat (ACBS Toronto)
Classic Boating
Classic News
Columbus (Georgia) *Daily Enquirer*
Engineering
The Ensign
Forest and Stream
Frankfurt Gazette
Greenwich News and Graphic
The Guide to Nature
The Horseless Age
Indicateur Journalier (Zurich)
Industrial Directory of New Jersey
Industries and Wealth of the Principal Points on Rhode Island
Jersey City, N.J. Directory
Journal de Neuwied
The Living Age
Lloyd's Register of American Yachts
The Log of Mystic Seaport
The Manufacturer and Builder
Marine Engineering
Model Engineer

Monthly Magazine
Motor Boat
Motor Boating
Motor Launch
National Fisherman
Natur och Kultur
Nature
Nautical Quarterly
Newark City Directory
New York Dramatic Mirror
New York Herald
New York Press
New York Sun
New York Times
New York World
Norrköping Tidningar
Northwoods Nostalgia
Nouvelle Gazette de Zurich
Nyack Evening Journal
Nyack Journal-News
Oil, Paint & Drug Reporter
Old Timers News
Oswego Palladium
Outing

Philadelphia Press
Popular Mechanics
Power Boating
Providence Directory
The Rudder
Rudder, Sail and Paddle
Scientific American
Scribner's Magazine
Seaboard
Springfield (Mass.) *Republican*
The Steam Automobile
Surgery, Gynecology and Obstetrics
The Times
Titusville Herald
Toledo Bee
Transactions of the Glasgow Archaeological Society
U.S. Geological Survey
Valentine's Manual of Old New York
Vanity Fair
Washington Post
Wayne County Review
The Weather Guage (sic)
Yachting

Catalogs and Brochures

Electric Launch Company (Elco).

Escher Wyss & Co. (1897 catalog translated from French by Creighton Douglas, B.Sc., C. Tran.).

Gas Engine and Power Company.

----------, Cautionary Notes.

Gas Engine & Power Company and Charles L. Seabury & Company, Consolidated.

Marine Engine & Machine Company.

Marine Vapor Engine Company.

Monitor Vapor Engine and Power Company.

F. W. Ofeldt & Sons.

H. V. Partelow & Co.

Charles L. Seabury & Co.

Picture Credits

ii: **Frank W. Ofeldt with horn.** Courtesy Robert Francis Ofeldt.
Page 1: **Professor Charles F. Chandler.** Wikipedia.
2: **Vapor lamps.** Published in Chandler, C.F., p. 31. Courtesy Library of Congress.
3: **Vapor stoves.** Ibid., p. 33.
5: **Swedish dinghy gunboat.** Courtesy Sjöhistoriska Museet, National Maritime Museum of Sweden, Stockholm, and Åke Bäcklund.
6, top: **Stockholm water taxi.** Drawing by Hjalmar Mörner. Courtesy Stockholms Stadsmuseum.
6, bottom: **Vevslup (crank boat).** Courtesy Ibid.
7, top: **Frank W. Ofeldt as a young man.** Published in *Popular Mechanics*, Nov. 1904. Enhanced by Gayle Bonish. Courtesy Library of Congress.
7, bottom: **Norrköping Harbor.** Published in *Norrköping och dess Omgifningar*. Courtesy Norrköping Library.
8, top: **Steamship *Svea*.** Ibid.
8, bottom: **Textile mills on the Motala River.** Ibid.
9: **Gunnar Welander and Carl W. Kellner.** Published in Dott, p. 20. Courtesy Norrköping Library.
10: **Old houses in Block Lyckan.** Photograph by Frida Moberg, 1900. Courtesy Norrköping Stadsarkivet.
11: **Caloric ship, *Ericsson*.** Published in Church, Vol. I, p. 197.
13: **Battle of Hampton Roads.** Drawing by Julian Oliver Davidson. Ibid., opposite p. 288.
14: **John Ericsson with flags.** Repaired by Gayle Bonish. Courtesy Nordiska museets ämnesordnade arkiv, Ämnesordnade bildarkivet, Personhistoria, and Åke Bäcklund.
16: **St. Olai Church, ca. 1870.** Courtesy Norrköping Stadsarkivet.
18: **Jabez Bostwick.** Published in Boyle, Vol. I, p. 918.
21: **Teaming in the oil regions.** Published in *Frank Leslie's Illustrated Newspaper*, 1865. Republished in Flynn, p. 96.
22: **Pond freshet jam.** Mather Studio, Titusville, Pa. Published in Moore, Austin Leigh, opposite p. 30.
24: **Daniel O'Day.** Published in Tarbell, Vol. II, opposite p. 232.
26: **Frederick Law Olmsted.** Published in Wormeley, frontispiece.
28: Patent drawing, **"Improvement in Carbureters"** (Star Gas machine), #131, 369, Sept. 17, 1872. Courtesy Patent and Trademark Resource Center, New York State Library.
32, left: **John D. Rockefeller, 1872.** Published in *McClure's Magazine*, 1902. Republished in Tarbell, Vol. I, p. 40.
32, right: **Henry M. Flagler, 1870.** Courtesy Florida Memory.
36: **Pratt's refinery.** Published in Chandler, C. F., p. 54. Courtesy Library of Congress.
39: **Joseph Seep.** Published in Tarbell, Ida M., Vol. II, Opposite p. 232.
43: **Steam launch, *Mohawk*.** Published in Kunhardt, p. 185.
46, left: Patent drawing, **"Naphtha Engine"** (two-cylinder naphtha engine), #279, 270, June 12, 1883, Sheet 1. Courtesy Patent and Trademark Resource Center, New York State Library.
46, right: Ibid., Sheet 3.
47: **Ofeldt family in experimental naphtha launch.** Courtesy Robert Francis Ofeldt.

49, top: **Shipman engine.** Published in Kunhardt, p. 219.
49, bottom: **Shipman Launch.** Published in *Scientific American*. Republished in Kunhardt, p. 222.
51: Patent drawing, **"Gas Engine"** (three-cylinder naphtha engine), #356, 419, Jan. 18, 1887, Sheet 1. Courtesy Patent and Trademark Resource Center, New York State Library.
52: Ibid., Sheet 2.
54: **GEPC executives with the company's first naphtha launch.** Photographed Dec. 27, 1921. (c) Mystic Seaport, Rosenfeld Collection.
55: **Prototype three-cylinder naphtha engine.** (c) Mystic Seaport, Rosenfeld Collection.
58, left: **Col. Oliver Payne, c. 1890.** Marist website.
58, right: **William Collins Whitney.** Photograph by William Kurtz. Rephotographed by S.S. Burden. Published in Swanberg, p. 2.
61: **Daniel Manning, from $20 Silver Certificate.** The Bureau of Engraving and Printing – Restoration by Godot13.
63, left: **GEPC catalog, 1886,** front cover. Courtesy Rodney Spurlock.
63, right: Ibid. title page.
64: ***L'Hirondelle*, later *Dauntless*.** Painting by James E. Buttersworth. (c) Mystic Seaport.
65, top: **Commodore Caldwell H. Colt's quarters aboard *Dauntless*.** Photograph from a private collection. Published in Ogilvy, p. 75. Enhanced by Randy Foster.
65, bottom: **Colt's bunk.** Ibid.
66: **Commodore Caldwell H. Colt and Captain Samuel S. Samuels aboard *Dauntless*.** Photograph by Charles Foster. Courtesy Hart Nautical Collections, MIT Museum.
67, top: ***Dauntless* in gale.** Published in Mott, p. 50. Courtesy Ibid.
67, bottom: ***Dauntless'* tender, the first naphtha launch delivered.** Published in GEPC catalog, 1887, p. 6. Courtesy Mariners' Museum.
68: **Naphtha tender in davits.** Ibid., p. 14.
69, top: **GEPC catalog, 1887,** Ibid., front cover.
69, bottom: **GEPC catalog, 1887,** Ibid., p. 23.
72: **Naphtha engine.** Published in GEPC catalog, 1896, p. 14.
73: **"The Naphtha Launch, Every Man His Own Engineer!"** advertisement. Published in *Harper's New Monthly Magazine*, May 1887. Republished in *The Ensign*. Courtesy Antique Boat Museum.
75, top: **Samuel Van Syckel.** Published in Tarbell, Vol. II, opposite p. 4.
75, bottom: **Van Syckel's system of continuous distillation.** Published in Williamson and Daum, Vol. I, p. 27.
78: **Ludwig Nobel.** Wikipedia.
79, top: **Baku oil field.** Published in Åsbrink, p. 40. Courtesy Brita Åsbrink.
79, bottom: **Nobel refinery.** Published in McLaurin, p. 292.
80: **Alfred Nobel.** Wikipedia.
81: **Naphtha launch, *Sarcelle*.** Published in Escher Wyss catalog, 1912, p. 13. Reprinted as *Steamboat Catalog no. 6*. Courtesy Robert Kerr.
82: **Escher Wyss naphtha engines.** Ibid., p. 12.
83: ***Zephir*, the first aluminum boat.** Published in Escher Wyss catalog, 1896, opposite p. 10. Courtesy Rodney Spurlock.

84: **Alfred Yarrow's electric launch, 1883.** Published in Barnes, opposite p. 167. 85: **"The Immisch Electric Pleasure Launches,"** advertisement. Published in *Lock to Lock Times*, July 18, 1890. Republished in Hawthorne, p. 21.

86/87: *Mignon,* drawings. Published in *Engineering*, Sept. 9, 1892, p. 318. Courtesy Gunnar Sillén, and Åke Bäcklund.

88: *Mignon* **on trailer.** Courtesy Tekniska Museet, Stockholm, and Åke Bäcklund.

89: **Alfred Nobel in** *Mignon.* Courtesy Nobel Museum, Stockholm, and Åke Bäcklund.

90: **Bertha von Suttner.** Internet.

92/93: **Commodore Gerry's** *Electra,* **with Ofeldt Improved tender.** (c) Mystic Seaport, Rosenfeld Collection.

94: Patent drawing, **"Hydrocarbon furnace for Steam Boilers" (Ofeldt Improved engine),** #393, 850, Dec. 4, 1888. Courtesy Patent and Trademark Resource Center, New York State Library.

96, top: **"Improved Naphtha Launches,"** advertisement, part 1. Courtesy Tim James.

96, bottom: Ibid., part 2.

99: **"Ruined."** Drawing by C.G. Bush. Published in *Harper's Weekly*, Nov. 13, 1869, p. 729.

101, top: **Commodore E.C. Benedict at helm of** *Oneida.* Published in *Nautical Quarterly* #29, Spring 1990, p, 94. Courtesy Whitney Moore.

101, bottom: *Oneida* **sailing.** Photograph by Charles Edwin Bolles, c. Aug. 11, 1900. (c) Mystic Seaport, Rosenfeld Collection.

102: **Grover Cleveland and L. Clarke Davis.** Published in Gilder, p. 56.

104: **Race between naphtha launch and Ofeldt Improved launch.** Published in GEPC catalog, 1892, p. 25. Courtesy Mystic Seaport.

105: **Jabez Bostwick.** Published in Tarbell, opposite p. 232.

107: **Alfred Yarrow.** Internet, Grace's Guide.

108: **Alfred Yarrow's Petroleum Spirit Vapor launch,** *Zephyr.* Published in *The Engineer.* Republished in Durham, July-August 1961, p. 21.

109, top: **Seabury catalog, 1893,** front cover. Reconstructed by Gayle Bonish from two damaged versions. Courtesy Mystic Seaport and Rodney Spurlock.

109, bottom: **"The Only Naphtha Launch,"** advertisement. Published in *The Rudder*, July1890, Courtesy Mystic Seaport.

113: **Treasury Secretary Charles Foster.** Photograph by Matthew Brady. Wikipedia.

114: **Masthead,** *The Rudder.* Published in *The Rudder*, vol. I, No. 1, May 1890, p. 1. Retouched by Gayle Bonish. Courtesy Mystic Seaport.

115: **Thomas Fleming Day.** (c) Mystic Seaport, Rosenfeld Collection.

116: **Gas Engine and Power Company Boat Shop, 1892.** Published in GEPC catalog, 1892, p. 9. Courtesy Mystic Seaport.

117, top: **Craftsmen building naphtha launches.** Published in GEPC catalog, 1896, pp. 7-10.

117, bottom: **Machine Shop.** Published in GEPC catalog, 1892, p. 11. Courtesy Mystic Seaport.

118, top: **Framing Shop.** Published in GEPC catalog, 1896, p. 6.

118, bottom: **Naphtha engines.** Published in *Consolidated* catalog, 1899, p. 12. Courtesy Mystic Seaport.

119: **Show Room.** Published in GEPC catalog, 1892, p. 5. Courtesy Ibid.

120, top: **GEPC catalog, 1892,** Ibid., front cover.

120, bottom: **GEPC catalog, 1892,** Ibid., inside front cover.

121, top: **21-ft. naphtha launch.** Published in GEPC catalog, 1894, p. 22.

121, bottom: **30-ft. half enclosed, half standing roof, naphtha launch.** Ibid., p. 28.

122, top: **35' cabin cruising naphtha launch.** Published in GEPC catalog, 1892, p. 43. Courtesy Mystic Seaport.

122, bottom: Ibid., plan view, p. 45.

123, top: **42' naphtha yacht.** Published in GEPC catalog, 1894, p. 46.

123 bottom: **53' naphtha yacht.** Published in GEPC catalog, 1892, p. 49. Courtesy Mystic Seaport.

124, top: **30-ft. auxiliary naphtha yacht,** *Etcetera.* Ibid., p. 31.

124, bottom: *Etcetera,* drawings. Published in Kunhardt, p. 263.

125, top: *The Racer.* Published in GEPC catalog, 1892, p. 27. Courtesy Mystic Seaport.

125, bottom: **Naphtha Oyster boat.** Published in GEPC catalog, 1896, p. 29.

126, top: **Naphtha pumping engine.** Published in GEPC catalog, 1892, p. 78. Courtesy Mystic Seaport.

126, bottom: Ibid., section, p. 81.

127: **Young women in naphtha launch.** Enhanced by Randy Foster. Courtesy Ibid.

128: **Durant family in** *Mugwump.* Courtesy Adirondack Experience, The Museum on Blue Mountain Lake (Kenneth Durant Collection), and Frederick C. Durant III.

129, top: **Granville Henchele and companions in naphtha launch.** Courtesy Perry's Victory and International Peace Memorial, U.S. National Parks Service (K.K. Jennings Collection).

129, bottom: **Dog on bow of naphtha launch.** Published in *Consolidated* catalog, 1902, p. 7. From the Collections of The Henry Ford.

130: **Clay & Torbensen steam launch.** Published in *The Rudder*, July 1891, p. 10. Courtesy Mystic Seaport.

132: **Electric launch at Columbian Exposition.** *Yachting Magazine.com.*

133, top: **GEPC seashell brochure for Columbian Exposition,** cover.

133, bottom: Ibid., interior.

135, top: **Daimler Motor Company,** advertisement. Published in *Rudder, Sail and Paddle*, March 1893, p. 81. Courtesy Mystic Seaport.

135, bottom: **Monitor engine.** Published in Monitor Vapor Engine and Power Company catalog, 1898, p. 8. Courtesy Ibid.

136, top: **Monitor launch.** Ibid., p. 23.

136, bottom: **Double Monitor engine.** Ibid., p. 10.

140: *Scientific American*, March 16, 1895, front cover. Published in Mitchell, p. 214.

142: **Naphtha launch model at Larchmont Yacht Club.** Photograph by author. Enhanced by Randy Foster.

145: **President Grover Cleveland.** Published in *Harper's Weekly,* Nov. 19, 1892.

146: **President Cleveland,** caricature by Homer Davenport. Probably published in the *New York Morning Journal*, c. 1895. Republished in Tugwell, p. 252. Courtesy New York Historical Society.

148: **J.P. Morgan's second** *Corsair* **with naphtha tender.** Shutterstock.

151: Patent drawing, **"Apparatus for Operating Vapor Launches."** (Alco-Vapor System), #551, 226, Dec. 10, 1895. Courtesy Patent and Trademark Resource Center, New York State Library.

152: Patent drawing, **"Vapor Engine"** (Alco-Vapor Engine), #540, 757, June 11, 1895, Ibid.

153, left: **Charles Wright's single-lever control**, drawing. Published in MVEC catalog, 1896, p. 9, Courtesy Rutgers University Archibald S. Alexander Library.

153, right: **Alco-Vapor forward control lever,** published in MVEC catalog, 1897, p. 27. Courtesy Antique Boat Museum.

155: **Alco-Vapor engine,** published in MEMC catalog, 1903, p. 9. Courtesy Dr. Jacques Valiquette, and Rodney Spurlock.

156/157: **E.C. Benedict's yacht, *Oneida,* with alco-vapor tender, *Oneida II,* in davits.** Photograph by Charles Edwin Bolles, Aug. 11, 1900, (c) Mystic Seaport, Rosenfeld Collection.

158, top: **Mrs. Cleveland with daughters, Esther and Ruth.** Published in Gilder, p. 147. Enhanced by Gayle Bonish.

158, bottom: **President Cleveland's alco-vapor launch, *Esther.*** Published in *The Rudder,* Jan. 1896, opposite p. 28. Courtesy Mystic Seaport.

159: **MVEC 1896 catalog,** cover. Courtesy Rutgers University Archibald S. Alexander Library.

160: **Alco-Vapor launch for U.S. War Department.** Published in MVEC catalog, 1896, Ibid., p. 28.

161: **Alco-Vapor launch designed and built by John Stuart & Co.** Published in *The Rudder,* Dec. 1899. Courtesy Antique Boat Museum.

162, top: **Alco-Vapor launch for *S.S. Paris,*** drawing. Published in *Marine Engineering,* Mar. 1899. Courtesy University of Oregon Library, and Rodney Spurlock.

162, bottom: **E.C. Benedict's alco-vapor launch, *Oneida II,* in the Amazon River.** Published in Arthur, p. 109.

166: **Alco-Vapor launches win Larchmont 1900 race.** Published in MEMC catalog, 1903, p. 1. Courtesy Dr. Jacques Valiquette, and Rodney Spurlock.

168/169: **William A. Slater's steam yacht, *Eleanor,* with naphtha tender alongside.** Photograph by Charles Edwin Bolles, Oct. 16, 1894. (c) Mystic Seaport, Rosenfeld Collection.

170: (new 170) **Col. Oliver Payne's steam yacht, *Aphrodite,* with naphtha tender alongside.** Enhanced by Gayle Bonish. Courtesy Rodney Spurlock Collection.

171: **Frederick W. Vanderbilt's steam yacht *Conqueror's* naphtha tender.** Courtesy, Collection of the Newport Historical Society (Henry O. Havemeyer scrapbook, 1894-1897, p. 11).

172: **Alfred Van Santvoord's side-wheel yacht, *Clermont,* with naphtha tender alongside.** (c) Mystic Seaport.

173: ***Clermont* at speed.** Photograph by Charles Edwin Bolles. (c) Mystic Seaport, Rosenfeld Collection.

174: **Naphtha tender in waves.** Published in Ogilvy, p. 94. Enhanced by Randy Foster.

175: **Naphtha race at Larchmont Yacht Club.** Published in *The Rudder,* May 1901. Courtesy Mystic Seaport.

176, top: **Naphtha launch at summer home on Harsens Island, near Detroit.** Published in Dixon, p. 47. Courtesy Library of Congress.

176, bottom: **Mr. and Mrs. H.B. Ogden by their 36-ft. naphtha cabin launch in Brooklyn.** Published in *Consolidated* catalog, 1899, p. 34. Courtesy Mystic Seaport.

177, top: **Interior view of 42-ft. naphtha cabin launch.** Published in *Consolidated* catalog, 1902, p. 14. From the Collections of The Henry Ford.

177, bottom: **Interior view of 50-ft. naphtha cabin yacht.** Ibid., p. 22.

178: **John Jacob Astor IV.** Courtesy Hart Nautical Collections, MIT Museum.

179: **Spacecraft *Callisto* en route to the planets.** Drawing by Dan Beard. Published in Astor, opposite p. 127.

180: **Grand Duke Alexander's electric launch.** Published in *Launches And Yachts: The 1902 Elco Catalog,* p. 78. Republished by Swanson Marine Enterprises. Courtesy Charles G. Houghton.

181: **John Jacob Astor's *Utopian.*** Drawing by Charles G. Davis, elevation. Published in *The Rudder,* Oct. 1896, p. 287. Courtesy Antique Boat Museum.

182: Ibid., sections, p. 288.

183: **S.C. Clayton's 60-ft. naphtha yacht, *Regina.*** Published in *Consolidated* catalog, 1902, p. 25. From the Collections of The Henry Ford.

184/185: **E.P. Hicks' twin-engine naphtha 59-ft. yacht, *Griffon.*** Photograph by Charles Edwin Bolles, July 14, 1895. (c) Mystic Seaport, Rosenfeld Collection.

186, top: **Frank L. Camp's twin-engine naphtha 67-ft. naphtha launch, *Victor Roy.*** Published in GEPC catalog, 1896, p. 39.

186, bottom: **Alfred Van Santvoord's twin-engine 76-ft. naphtha yacht.** Drawing by Charles G. Davis. Published in *The Rudder,* Feb. 1896, p. 58. Courtesy Mystic Seaport.

188, top: **J. Adolph Mollenhauer's twin-engine 76-ft. naphtha yacht, *Thelma.*** Drawing by J. Adolph Mollenhauer. Published in GEPC catalog, 1896, p. 40.

188, bottom: **William Banigan's twin-engine 76-ft. naphtha yacht, *Corinthia.*** Published in *Consolidated* catalog, 1899, p. 46. Courtesy Mystic Seaport.

191: **Wing's Marine Gas Engines,** advertisement. Published in *Manning's Yacht Register,* 1897. Courtesy Antique Boat Museum.

193: **Nathaniel G. Herreshoff and John Brown Herreshoff in naphtha launch, *Shearwater.*** (c) Mystic Seaport, Rosenfeld Collection.

196, top: ***Consolidated catalog, 1899,*** title page. Courtesy Mystic Seaport.

196, bottom: ***Consolidated's* works in Morris Heights.** Published in *The Rudder,* Dec. 1898, p. 409. Courtesy Antique Boat Museum.

197, top: **General Machine Shop.** Ibid., p. 411.

197, bottom: **Naphtha Engine Room.** Ibid., p. 410.

198: **Torpedo Boat Destroyer, *Bailey,* longitudinal section and plan.** Published in *Scientific American Supplement, Special Navy Edition,* Part IV. 1898.

199, top: **"High-class Yachts & Naphtha Launches,"** advertisement. Internet.

199, bottom: **Launching U.S. Torpedo Boat, *Wilkes,* in *Consolidated's* shipyard.** Published in *Consolidated* catalog, 1902, p. xii. From the Collections of The Henry Ford.

200: **Escher Wyss catalog, 1896,** cover. Courtesy Rodney Spurlock.

201: **Escher Wyss naphtha boat harbor in Zurich.** Published in Escher Wyss catalog, 1896, Ibid., opposite p. 1.

202: **Prince Wilhelm of Wied.** Internet: Pinterest.

203: **Prince of Wied's naphtha auxiliary, *Aluminia*.** Published in Escher Wyss catalog, 1896, opposite p. 24. Courtesy Rodney Spurlock.

204: **Emperor Wilhelm II of Germany.** Courtesy Hart Nautical Collections, MIT Museum.

205, top: **Emperor Wilhelm's Royal Yacht, *Hohenzollern*.** Retouched by Gayle Bonish. Photocrom Print Collection, Detroit Publishing Co. Courtesy Library of Congress.

205, bottom: ***Hohenzollern's* naphtha tender.** Published in Escher Wyss catalog, 1912, inside front cover. Courtesy Robert Kerr.

207, top: **Naphtha gunboat, *Wilhelmina, Koningin der Nederlanden,* disassembled.** Published in Escher Wyss catalog, 1896, opposite p. 18. Courtesy Rodney Spurlock.

207, bottom: ***Wilhelmina* afloat.** Published in Escher Wyss catalog, 1897, p. 24. Ibid.

208: **Russian naphtha troop carrier, *Wisla*,** plan and sections. Published in Escher Wyss catalog, 1896, p. 22. Ibid.

209: **Helicoidal turbine propeller system in *Wisla*,** p. 23. Ibid.

211: **F. W. Ofeldt & Sons shipyard in Brooklyn.** Courtesy Robert Francis Ofeldt.

212, top: **Sign: *F. W. Ofeldt & Sons, Vapor Launch Works*.** Ibid.

212, bottom: **Ofeldt catalog, 1903, cover.** Ibid.

213: Patent drawing, **"Vapor Engine"** (Compound Vapor engine) #538, 694, May 7, 1895, sheet 1. Courtesy Patent and Trademark Resource Center, New York State Library.

214, left: Ibid., sheet 4.

214, right: Ibid. sheet 3.

216, top left: **Production version, Compound Vapor engine.** Published in Ofeldt catalog, 1903, p. 7. Courtesy Robert Francis Ofeldt.

216, top right: **Compound Vapor boiler's copper coils,** p. 6. Ibid.

216, bottom: **Compound Vapor engine in boat,** p. 16. Ibid.

217: **Lillian Russell.** Original copyright: W.M. Morrison, Chicago, 1893. Courtesy Library of Congress.

218, top: **Garrett B. Linderman's *Nautilus*.** Published in Ofeldt catalog, 1903, p. 13. Courtesy Robert Francis Ofeldt.

218, bottom: **Ofeldt steam boiler,** p. 26. Ibid.

219: **William Gillette.** Published in *Vanity Fair supplement,* Feb. 27, 1907.

220, top: **William Gillette's houseboat, *Aunt Polly*.** Published in Ofeldt catalog, 1903, p. 18. Courtesy Robert Francis Ofeldt.

220, bottom: ***Aunt Polly,* interior.** Courtesy Gillette Castle State Park.

222, top: **Ernest and George Ofeldt in Ernest's steam car.** Courtesy Robert Francis Ofeldt.

222, bottom: **August Ofeldt and son, Frank, in August's steam car.** Published in *Old Timers News,* front cover, Feb. 1950. Ibid.

223, left: **Frank A. Ofeldt and family in his steam car.** Courtesy Robert Francis Ofeldt.

223, right: **Frank A.'s steam car.** Ibid.

224: Patent drawing, **"Multiple Cylinder Steam Engine"** (August Ofeldt's compound engine), #513, 650, Jan. 30, 1894. Patent and Trademark Resource Center, New York State Library.

225: **Minck Bros. steam delivery wagon.** Published in Ofeldt catalog, 1903, p. 27. Courtesy Robert Francis Ofeldt.

226: **Frank W. Ofeldt with sons and workmen.** Courtesy Ibid.

227: **Ofeldt works in Nyack.** Ibid.

228: **Ofeldt catalog, 1908,** pp. 1 & 2. Ibid.

229: **Ofeldt compound double-acting steam engine.** Published in Ofeldt catalog, 1908, p. 25. Ibid.

230, top: **Gillette Castle.** Photograph by author.

230, bottom: **Remains of *Aunt Polly*.** Ibid.

231: **Herman Frasch.** Courtesy Science Photo Library.

234: **Vapor stoves, a**dvertisement. Published in *Oil, Paint and Drug Reporter,* Jan. 15, 1890. Retouched by Gayle Bonish. Courtesy Library of Congress.

235: **E.C. Benedict,** cartoon. Published in Stone, p. 14.

236: **Americus Club dining room.** Published in Bassett, after p. 77.

237, top: **E.C. Benedict's villa.** Published in *Souvenir of Indian Harbor.* Courtesy Greenwich Historical Society.

237, bottom: **E.C. Benedict in alco-vapor tender, *Oneida II*.** Clipping from E.C. Benedict's scrapbook, published in unidentified newspaper. Courtesy Dr. Patricia Wood, and Whitney Moore.

238: **Marine Engine and Machine Company's works in Harrison, N.J.** Published in MEMC catalog, 1903, p. 12. Courtesy Dr. Jacques Valiquette, and Rodney Spurlock.

240, left: **Marine Engine and Machine Company catalog, 1903, original cover.** Courtesy Rutgers University Archibald S. Alexander Library.

240, right: **Ibid., revised cover.** Courtesy Dr. Jacques Valiquette, and Rodney Spurlock.

241: **Albert Bostwick.** Wikipedia: Mayhew, Augustus, *New York Social Diary,* "Oil Swells: The Standard Oil Crowd in Palm Beach."

242: **High-speed naphtha launch.** Published in *Consolidated* catalog, 1902, p. 2. From the Collections of The Henry Ford.

243: **Henry H. Rogers' steam yacht, *Kanawha*.** (c) Mystic Seaport, Rosenfeld Collection.

244: **William K. Vanderbilt's commuter, *Tarantula*, with naphtha tender in davits.** Photograph by James Burton, Sept. 5, 1904. (c) Mystic Seaport, Rosenfeld Collection.

245: **1885 naphtha launch and 1905 *Speedway* launch.** Published in *Consolidated* catalog, 1905, back cover. Retouched by Gayle Bonish. Courtesy Mystic Seaport.

247: **King Edward VII and the Royal Party aboard Alfred Yarrow's planing launch.** Drawing by Norman Wilkinson. Probably published in *The Illustrated London News,* 1906. Republished in Barnes, p. 179.

251: **Fiftieth anniversary of *Old Number One*, the prototype 3-cylinder naphtha launch.** Published in *The New York Times,* June 9, 1935, p. 6S.

252, top: **Naphtha launch, *Chiripa*.** Photograph by author.

252, bottom: **Rodney Spurlock and William C. Shaw examine *Chiripa*.** Ibid.

253, top: ***Chiripa's* condenser pipe.** Ibid.

253, bottom: **Holes through *Chiripa*'s hull.** Ibid.

254, top: **Naphtha launch, *Lillian Russell*, on Lake of Bays.** Photograph by Cameron Peck. Enhanced by Randy Foster. Courtesy John Peck.

254, bottom: ***Lillian Russell*'s naphtha engine.** Ibid.

255: **Naphtha launch *Frieda* in Minnesota Lakes Maritime Museum.** Photograph by Bruce Trudgen. Courtesy May Trudgen.

256, top left: **Horace J. Conley plaque in *Frieda*.** Ibid.

256, top right: **Gas Engine & Power Co. logo on *Frieda*'s engine.** Ibid.

256, bottom: **"Horace J. Conley, Western Builder of the ONLY NAPHTHA LAUNCH,"** advertisement. Published in *The Rudder,* Dec. 1900, p. xiv. Courtesy Antique Boat Museum.

257: **Richardsons' Naphtha launch, *Anita,* at 1977 Antique Boat Show, Clayton.** Courtesy William H. Richardson, Jr.

258, left: ***Anita*'s naphtha engine.** Photograph by author.

258, right: **Fireproof lining in *Anita*'s engine compartment.** Ibid.

259: **Richard McGinn's cabin launch *Papillon* – formerly naphtha, now electric – being restored at St. Lawrence Restoration, Clayton.** Ibid.

260: **Åke Bäcklund and Rolf Sjögren researching Frans Åfeldt's story in the Norrköping city archives, with inset of an Åfeldt entry.** Photographs by Per Wichmann. Courtesy Åke Båcklund.

261: **Interior of alco-vapor cabin launch, *Heather Belle*, 1902.** Published in MEMC catalog, 1903, p. 3. Courtesy Dr. Jacques Valiquette, and Rodney Spurlock.

262, top: ***Heather Belle* as she appeared in 1903, when she arrived on Lake Rosseau.** Composite photograph by Tim Du Vernet.

262, bottom: ***Heather Belle* with hotel guests at Thorel House on Lake Rosseau, when she was powered by an internal combustion engine.** Courtesy George R. (Geordie) Thorel.

263: **Graeme and Phyllis Ferguson's *Heather Belle* (now electric-powered) on the Lake of Bays.** Photograph by author.

264: ***Heather Belle* from above.** Ibid.

265: **The author's family and friends aboard *Heather Belle*.** Ibid.